The Challenge of K2

The Challenge
of K2

A History of the Savage Mountain

Richard Sale

Pen & Sword

First published in Great Britain in 2011 by
Pen & Sword Discovery
an imprint of
Pen & Sword Books Ltd
47 Church Street
Barnsley
South Yorkshire
S70 2AS

Copyright © Richard Sale 2011

ISBN 978-1-84884-213-7

The right of Richard Sale to be identified as Author of this Work has been asserted by him in accordance with the Copyright, Designs and Patents Act 1988.

A CIP catalogue record for this book is available from the British Library.

Typeset in 11pt Ehrhardt by
Mac Style, Beverley, E. Yorkshire

Printed and bound in India by Replika Press Pvt. Ltd.

Pen & Sword Books Ltd incorporates the imprints of Pen & Sword Aviation, Pen & Sword Maritime, Pen & Sword Military, Wharncliffe Local History, Pen & Sword Select, Pen & Sword Military Classics, Leo Cooper, Seaforth Publishing and Frontline Publishing.

For a complete list of Pen & Sword titles please contact
PEN & SWORD BOOKS LIMITED
47 Church Street, Barnsley, South Yorkshire, S70 2AS, England
E-mail: enquiries@pen-and-sword.co.uk
Website: www.pen-and-sword.co.uk

Contents

Acknowledgements vi

List of Illustrations vii

Introduction x

1. The Mountain, The Challenge 1

2. Early Explorations 13

3. The Americans Head for K2 47

4. The First Ascent: The Italians, 1954 76

5. The Next Thirty Years 97

6. 1986 131

7. The Next Twenty Years 150

8. 2008 162

9. The Next Step 175

Notes 180

Appendix 1: K2 Ascent Data 213

Appendix 2: Fatalities on K2 220

Index 222

Acknowledgements

The author is very grateful to the following for information and photographs: the American Alpine Club, Willi Bauer, the late Charles Houston, the late Lino Lacedelli, Mario Lacedelli, the late Bob Marshall, Lars Nessa, Wilco van Rooijen, Mike Searle, Pavel Shabalin, the US Library of Congress and Jim Wickwire. Thanks also to Reinhold Schmuck for assistance with translations, to Tadeusz Hudowski and Glyn Hughes at the UK Alpine Club Library, and to Eugene Rae at the RGS Library.

List of Illustrations

Note:
All reasonable efforts have been made by the author and publisher to trace the copyright holders of unattributed photographs. In the event that copyright holders come forward after publication of this edition, the author and publisher will endeavour to rectify the situation at the earliest opportunity.

Black and white plates:

Henry Godwin-Austen's sketch of K2 appearing above the northern Baltoro ridge from the flank of Masherbrum.

A drawing of the epic descent of the Muztagh Pass, from Younghusband's book, *The Heart of the Continent*.

Younghusband meeting Grombtchevsky during the final stages of the 'Great Game'.

The camp at Askole, from Conway, *Climbing in the Himalayas*.

One of the two McCormick drawings of K2 from Conway, *Climbing in the Himalayas*.

Roberto Lerco.

The Eckenstein–Crowley expedition of 1902.

Jacot-Guillarmod's photograph of K2, the first photo of the mountain to be published.

K2 from Windy Gap, photographed by the Duke of the Abruzzi.

Vittorio Sella's photograph of the west face of K2. (*American Alpine Club/Library of Congress*)

One of the series of photographs taken of the north side of K2 on the 1929 Spoleto expedition.

The 1938 American expedition.

The 1939 team camped among apricot trees. (*American Alpine Club*)

The Sherpas on the 1939 American expedition. (*American Alpine Club*)

A photo of the summit pyramid with Wiessner's 1939 route marked.

The 1953 American team preparing to board the flight for Pakistan. (*American Alpine Club*)

The famous drawing of the accident on the 1953 American expedition.
The successful 1954 Italian team.
Lino Lacedelli putting on his crampons at Camp IX.
Lino Lacedelli on the summit on 31 July 1954.
Achille Compagnoni on the summit on 31 July 1954
The shot of Compagnoni used in Desio's official expedition book.

Colour plates:
Celebrating the Italian success in 1954.
The North–West Ridge from the top of the first pinnacle. (*Jim Wickwire*)
During the second ascent in 1977 Japanese climbers had to wade through chest-deep snow during the last 200m to the summit.
Ashraf Aman, the first Pakistani to stand on K2's summit, during the Japanese expedition of 1977.
The knife–edge ridge between Camps III and IV, photographed on the 1978 American North-East Ridge expedition. (*Jim Wickwire*)
Lou Reichardt on the sickle-shaped ridge about 150m below the summit, during the 1978 American North-East Ridge expedition. (*Jim Wickwire*)
Lou Reichardt on the summit during the 1978 American North-East Ridge expedition. He was the first man to reach the summit without supplementary oxygen. (*Jim Wickwire*)
Broad Peak from Camp III on the West Ridge at 6600m during the 1981 Japanese West Ridge expedition.
Looking down on Angel Peak during the 1981 Japanese West Ridge expedition.
In 1982 the Japanese became the first team to attempt K2 from the north.
Climbers pushing the route out above Camp I during the 1982 Japanese North Ridge expedition.
High above the Chogori glacier on the 1982 Japanese North Ridge expedition.
Camp IV on the 1982 Italian North Ridge expedition.
Willi Bauer. (*Willi Bauer*)
Julie Tullis and Kurt Diemberger. (*Willi Bauer*)
Wanda Rutkiewicz and Dobroslawa Miodowicz–Wolf (Mrufka). (*Willi Bauer*)
House's Chimney. (*Willi Bauer*)
Imitzer and Mrufka at about 8300m. (*Willi Bauer*)
Al Rouse approaching the summit. (*Willi Bauer*)
Alfred Imitzer on the summit. (*Willi Bauer*)
Tadeusz Piotrowski photographed by Jerzy Kukuczka during their successful completion of the route on the south face originally attempted by Kukuczka and Kurtyka in 1982.
Christophe Profit on the summit in 1991.

Camp II at 6750m during the Russian 2007 expedition which established a new route on the West Face.

Vadim Popovich and Ilyas Tukhvatullin at about 7200m on steep ground during the Russian 2007 West Face climb.

Approaching the Bottleneck on the summit climb in 2008. Above it looms the ice wall, the collapse of which would precipitate disaster. (*Lars Nessa*)

The last few feet to the summit. (*Lars Nessa*)

Three photographs illustrating the unfolding disaster on the descent from the summit, 2 August 2008. (*Lars Nessa / Courtesy of Wilco van Rooijen*)

The memorial plaque to Irish climber Ger McDonnell at the Cronin's Yard car park at the base of Carrauntoohill, Ireland's highest mountain. (*Author*)

Introduction

In 1995 Jim Curran produced a fine biography of K2,[1] which took the story of the mountain up to that date (a paperback version of the book also included details of the 1996 season). The immediate question, then, is why produce another biography only fifteen or so years later? The answer is that there have been a number of significant events related to the mountain since 1996. In 2004, the 50th anniversary of the first ascent, Lino Lacedelli, one of the two Italians who made that historic climb, finally gave his account of the events of 30–31 July 1954. Importantly, Lacedelli confirmed Walter Bonatti's version of the events of the evening of 30 July, when he and the Hunza high-altitude porter Mahdi carried the oxygen cylinders necessary for the first ascent towards Camp IX, which had been established earlier in the day by Lacedelli and Achille Compagnoni. Lacedelli confirmed that Compagnoni had insisted on moving Camp IX from the agreed position so that Bonatti would not reach it, fearing that, if he did, Bonatti would have been in a stronger position to go for the summit. But though Lacedelli confirmed Bonatti's contention in that regard, he denied another of Bonatti's contentions – that the summit climbers' oxygen supply had lasted through to the summit rather than being exhausted some 200m below it. While Lacedelli did not confirm Compagnoni's account that the oxygen ran out at 8400m, he did maintain that it had run out before the summit was reached, though only just before.

Next, after the death of Ardito Desio, the leader of the Italian 1954 expedition, the Italian Alpine Club (CAI) finally decided to publish the results of its own investigation into the events of 1954. It concluded not only that Compagnoni had deliberately moved the position of Camp IX to prevent Bonatti reaching it – a decision that seriously endangered the lives of Bonatti and Mahdi, the latter suffering horrendous frostbite injuries as a result – but also that the oxygen supply had lasted right up to the summit. A further book has also been published, detailing the complex web of accusations, counter-accusations and law suits that had blighted what should have been a tale of national glory, and suggesting that an even more sordid, and distinctly machiavellian, twist lay behind the story.

Early in K2's climbing history, the book of the American expedition attempting to make the first ascent christened it the 'Savage Mountain'. The deaths in 1996, mentioned briefly in the update of Curran's book, the appalling loss of a Russian team of four just below the summit in 2006, and the tragic season of 2008, which rivalled the 1986 season in both death toll and suffering, cemented the mountain's reputation as difficult and dangerous. In terms of the ratio of deaths on the mountain to successful ascents, Annapurna is a more dangerous 8000m peak, its faces swept by avalanches, yet K2 retains its notoriety. Because it is both the second highest of Earth's mountains and the most technically difficult to climb – even by its easiest route, K2 is a mountaineering challenge, while the peak's position means it is subjected to a succession of storms which add a further negative dimension to any attempt – K2 will continue to attract the brave and the committed.

When the new information on the first ascent is added, together with data bringing ascents and attempts up to date, plus the addition of further information regarding early expeditions to the mountain, especially that of Roberto Lerco in 1890, and on several important early ascents, a new biography seems appropriate to bring the mountain into the twenty-first century. What follows celebrates a peak whose shape, a steep pyramid, epitomises mountains for many, and celebrates those who have risked – and sometimes lost – their lives in attempting to reach its top.

Chapter 1

The Mountain, The Challenge

'K2 … just the bare bones of a name, all rock and ice and storm and abyss.'

Fosco Maraini

The Mountain

In 1915 the German meteorologist and geophysicist Alfred Wegener[1] published a book entitled *Die Enstehung der Kontinente und Ozeane* ('*The Origin of Continents and Oceans*'), in which he set down his theory that the Earth's continents had once formed a single supercontinent, which he called Pangaea (from the Greek for 'all land'), surrounded by a single sea, Panthalassa ('all water'), and that the break-up of Pangaea and the drifting of its fragments over millions of years had formed the land masses we see today. Unfortunately Wegener's theory included an assessment of how long it had taken for Greenland to separate from Scotland, but his calculations were based on inaccurate data. That, combined with the fact that scientists could not envisage a method for the movement of land masses on a 'solid' Earth, meant the theory was dismissed for many years, despite offering an answer to why identical fossils were found in well-separated continents, and why the geology of some continental edges was surprisingly similar. Not until the 1960s did data accumulated by Harry Hess[2] finally establish the basis of continental drift, vindicating Wegener's theory. In general, continents move about 4cm/year, about the same rate at which fingernails grow.

Today it is known that the break-up of Pangaea resulted from the movement of seven major (and a few minor) 'plates', rigid sections of the Earth's crust (the continental land masses) floating on a fluid mantle. As Pangaea broke up, Eurasia rotated towards Gondwanaland (which comprised South America, Africa, India, Australia and Antarctica). Between them was the Tethys Ocean.[3] The tectonic plates beneath oceans are denser than those below continents and so sit lower in the Earth's fluid mantle. As the plates move, oceanic plates therefore slip below (or subduct) continental plates. The process of subduction crumples the surface of the upper, continental, plate, raising mountains. Perhaps the clearest example of this process is the Andean chain of mountains on the western edge of South America, still being formed as the tectonic plate beneath the Pacific Ocean subducts below the South American continental plate. As the Eurasian plate moved towards Gondwanaland, a process that began perhaps 250 million years ago and continued for around 200 million years, subduction of the Tethys plate created a similar chain of peaks, the first Karakoram. The rock from which K2 is built is, primarily, gneiss, a metamorphic rock, i.e. one created by the action of heat and pressure. The K2 gneiss is some 120 million years old,[4] the heat and pressure that transformed it from its granite parent rock deriving from the subduction of the Tethys plate in this first phase of the construction of one of the Earth's great mountain ranges.

About 150 million years ago India and Madagascar separated from Gondwanaland and began to move north. During the Early Cretaceous period the Indian plate rifted away, becoming an island and beginning a rapid northward drift, its speed of travel, at 15-20cm per year, probably setting the record for a tectonic plate. The pace of movement of the Indian plate meant that it closed the gap to the Eurasian plate, which was also moving north, and the Tethys Ocean disappeared as the distance between the continental plates narrowed. Approximately 50 million years ago India collided with the southern margin of the Asian landmass, which itself had been formed by an amalgamation of earlier plate accretions onto the stable Siberian craton (the stable interior of a continental tectonic plate). The India–Asia collision occurred at equatorial latitudes; following the collision and the closing of the Tethys Ocean that lay in between, India has continued its northward drift, ploughing into Asia and forming the Himalaya and the Tibetan plateau in the process.

The collision slowed the northward movement of the Indian plate, but it was (and is still) moving faster than the larger plate, resulting in an upthrust in the collision zone. One effect of the collision is that the area is seismically active: an earthquake close to K2 and Broad Peak in 1983 caused séracs to fall which then initiated avalanches on both peaks. But the seismicity of the area is much less than might be expected, despite the occurrence of the devastating earthquake of October 2005 which caused major destruction in Pakistan-controlled Kashmir to the north of Islamabad, killing an estimated 80,000 people.

The Karakoram is part of the Asian side of this great collision, and is geologically similar to the central part of the Tibetan plateau, but whereas Tibet is high and flat, the Karakoram is deeply incised by glaciers and rivers and contains many major peaks, several of them over 6000m and including four of the fourteen 8000m peaks (K2, Broad Peak, Gasherbrum I and Gasherbrum II). The other major 8000m peak in Pakistan, Nanga Parbat, is actually the western extension of the Indian plate Himalayan range.

The Karakoram stretches for some 450km west–east. To the west the range is often defined by the Karakoram Highway linking Islamabad with Kashgar, but geologists extend the range beyond the highway. Ardito Desio, the leader of the successful 1954 Italian expedition, extended the range to the Yasin valley, considering there was no sharp distinction between the Karakoram and the Hindu Kush, the two ranges merging. Today most geologists consider the junction between the Hindu Kush and the Karakoram is the Rushan Fault (south-east of Tirach Mir), the two ranges lying to either side.

To the east the range is usually defined by the Karakoram Pass (though there are those who argue for a boundary further east, in Ladakh). The pass, at 5540m, 5°30′48″N, 77°49′23″E, is on an ancient trading route between Leh, in Ladakh, and Shache (formerly Yarkand) in China's Xinjiang Autonomous Region. The pass may also be the point at which China, India and Pakistan meet, the hesitation resulting from the existence of a disputed zone between India and Pakistan which covers an area around the Siachen Glacier. The area from the glacier to the Karakoram Pass was controlled by Pakistan until 1984, when Indian troops took control. Since then there have been spasmodic firefights between soldiers of the two nations (one by-product of which has been the closure of the first ascent route on Gasherbrum I as it lies perilously close to the area of conflict). The maintenance of troops in such a climatically hostile area costs each country an alarming amount of money (some figures suggesting a total bill of up to $15 million daily, though a figure of $2 million or so seems more likely), but as the border dispute is seen in the context of the sovereignty of Kashmir, no clear end is currently in sight.

The pass is the likely source of the range's name, *karakoram* meaning 'black rocks' or 'black earth' in Turkic. However, this derivation is disputed by those who claim the name derives from the Mongolian *khara kherem* meaning 'black barrier', *kara/khara* being common for black in both Turkic and Mongolian. Even if it is not actually the true source of the range's name, 'black barrier' would be entirely appropriate, the area's combination of altitude and glaciation making it a barrier to travel and trade.

The height of any mountain range is a complex balance between the rate of uplift due to tectonic processes, the hardness of the rock and surface erosion effects. Though it has only four of the world's fourteen 8000m peaks, those four – and two other peaks above 7900m – form an arc only 25km in length to the north of the Baltoro Glacier; this arc, one of the great mountain features of the planet, also forms the border between China and Pakistan. The range also includes a further fifteen or so peaks above 7500m. Indeed, the Karakoram is the highest mountain range on the planet. The average altitude for such an incised landscape is hard to calculate accurately, but is considered to be comparable to that of the Tibetan plateau, where satellite GPS measurements indicate an average altitude of 5000m.

One consequence of this extreme altitude is that Karakoram winters are cold, viciously so, the cold and altitude resulting in a large number of glaciers, some of them vast. The longest glacier outside the polar regions is the Fedchenko in the

Pamirs, but the Karakoram has the next three longest, the Siachen, Biafo and Baltoro, the range also having more continental glaciers than any other locality outside the polar regions. The combination of altitude and glaciation which impeded ancient traders has also created one of the most spectacular mountain landscapes on Earth. But the nature of the landscape means that the traveller has to work hard in order to admire it. The Himalayan 8000m peaks and Nanga Parbat can be seen by the casual tourist with little or no great effort, and certainly without requiring glacier travel; in the Karakoram glacier travel is essential for any reasonable view of the highest mountains.

Geologically, the Karakoram is highly complex.[5] Prior to the India–Asia collision both the Karakoram and southern Tibet formed an Andean-type margin characterised by granite batholiths and extrusive volcanic rocks. During the collision the crust of the Asian plate was thickened by folding and thrusting processes. Crustal thickening increased pressures and temperatures, altering the sedimentary and volcanic rocks to crystalline metamorphic rocks. Most of the southern Karakoram consists of these metamorphic rocks, the Baltoro granite batholith intruding during the Miocene period approximately 23–13 million years ago. These spectacular granites now form most of the impressive towers and spires for which the Karakoram is noted: the Trango Towers, Uli Biaho Tower, Shipton Spire and Masherbrum are all formed of Baltoro granite. Glaciers have incised deep valleys through the granite, the resulting 1000–2000m cliff faces being a direct result of this glaciation.

To the north of the Baltoro granite Broad Peak and the Gasherbrum peaks are largely made up of sedimentary rocks of the Upper Palaeozoic and Mesozoic periods (Carboniferous to Jurassic, including Permian limestone and Carboniferous black shale). Dioritic intrusions also form part of Broad Peak and Gasherbrum IV, the junction between this dark quartzite rock and the paler limestone being clearly seen on the northern, left, side of Gasherbrum IV when viewed from Concordia. K2 is made up of a complex mixture of older pre-collision Andean-type granites that were strongly metamorphosed during the later collision and intruded by numerous leucogranite dykes. To the north of K2, and running along the Tashkurgan valley (Xinjiang) and Nubra valley (Ladakh), the Karakoram fault is a strike-slip fault that divides the rugged geomorphology of the Karakoram from the high-elevation low-relief geomorphology of the Tibetan plateau. There is good geological evidence that both the Karakoram and Tibet were high (possibly as high as the present-day Andes) before the Indian collision 50 million years ago, but have gained height and crustal thickness since that collision.

The Name
Knowing that to maintain dominance and control trade it was necessary to map an area, soon after they took Bengal in eastern India the British began to survey their

new holding. The early work was relatively crude, but in 1799 William Lambton[6] proposed a more precise survey which began in 1802.[7] One outcome of the survey was the discovery that the Himalayan peaks – which lay in Nepal, at that time closed to foreigners, though the peaks could be both seen and surveyed from India – were the highest on Earth. One in particular, a peak given various designations by different surveyors, was the actual highest.[8]

As British influence in India expanded, so did the survey work. When the British took control of the Punjab they befriended the ruler of Jammu (in part by giving him control over neighbouring Kashmir) and extended the survey to the mountainous region to the north. It was to prove a difficult job, the survey requiring the establishment of base stations at over 20,000ft (6,000m) where snow 11ft (3.5m) deep had to be excavated to reach the bedrock necessary to hold the instruments firmly. As a consequence, the survey took ten years. That it was completed at all is credit to the 25-year-old Royal Engineer captain who was put in charge, Thomas Montgomerie.[9]

The surveying station from which Montgomerie made his observation of the Karakoram was set up a few days earlier under the direction of another survey officer, William Henry Johnson, and it is likely that Johnson was the first European to see K2. Nevertheless, the honour of naming the peak fell to Montgomerie. Of his first view of the Karakoram Montgomerie wrote,

> During my three days residence on the snowy mountain Haramook,[10] at upwards of 16,000 feet above sea level, I had several fine views of the Karakoram Range to the north of the Indus. Amongst others, two very fine peaks were visible beyond the general outline of the Muztagh and Karakooram [*sic*] ranges. These two peaks promise to be high; they were faintly defined against the sky, being probably about 150 miles from me.[11]

Montgomerie made his observations on 10 and 11 September 1856 and made a sketch of the two peaks in his notebook:

He labelled the larger, double-summitted of the two peaks K1. The smaller, more pointed peak he labelled K2. K3, K4 and K5 stood to the right of the pointed peaks; these were later identified as summits of the Gasherbrum range. In these designations 'K' was for Karakoram. Montgomerie could make a bearing on the two peaks, but without a further bearing could not calculate their heights. The second bearing was obtained in 1857 when, during July and August, observations were made from close to Skardu. These allowed Montgomerie to make a preliminary estimate of the height of K2, which he gave as 28,400ft. Further observations in 1858 and 1859 allowed Montgomerie to refine his figure, dropping the height to 28,287ft. He was now able to write that the height 'will probably not alter much when all the refinements of computations have been applied. The peak may therefore be considered the second highest in the world.' As to the peak's name, Montgomerie noted that no 'reliable name for this gigantic peak' had been discovered but 'every endeavour will be made to find a local name it if has one'.

One month before K2 was surveyed, Henry Thuiller, Deputy Surveyor-General of the GTS, announced to a meeting of the Asiatic Society of Bengal that the world's highest mountain had been discovered. It was to be called Mont Everest, a name chosen by Thuiller's boss, Andrew Scott Waugh, in honour of the previous Surveyor-General, George Everest. In his letter to Thuiller announcing the discovery and the naming, Waugh had written:

> I was taught by my respected chief and predecessor, Colonel Geo. Everest, to assign to every geographical object its true local or national appellation ... I have always scrupulously adhered to this rule ... But here we have a mountain ... without any local name that we can discover, whose native appellation, if it has any, will not very likely be ascertained before we are allowed to penetrate Nepal ...[12]

There is good reason to believe that in suggesting that there was no known name Waugh was, to use the modern parlance, being economical with the truth. His idea that it would need access to Nepal to confirm a native name seems logical, but the mountain is visible from Tibet and the Tibetan name *Chomolungma* was already known. When Brian Hodgson, a former political officer resident in Kathmandu, suggested that the peak was actually called Devadhunga or Bhairathan, Waugh set up a committee to investigate these and other claims.[13] All were dismissed, but crucially no mention seems to have been made of Chomolungma. As a consequence, the name Everest was sanctioned; with occasional grumblings, it has become more or less accepted throughout the world, though the Chinese use a Sino-Tibetan form of Chomolungma.

In the aftermath of Montgomerie's designation, K1 was found to be called Masherbrum by the villagers of Kaphalu, from where it was visible. But K2 was not visible from any settlement. It is visible from near Paiju, close to the snout of the

Baltoro Glacier, but from there it is hardly imposing enough to have warranted a specific name. It is also visible from a small village near Shaksgam, to the north (see Chapter 2). In the apparent absence of a local name an attempt to name the peak after Henry Haversham Godwin-Austen mercifully failed, apparently because of strong Indian representation (Pakistan at the time being part of British India) over the application of the names of members of the ruling classes to prominent sub-continent features. That is also the likely reason why other suggestions – including Mount Waugh, Mount Albert (after Queen Victoria's consort) and Mount Montgomerie – were also rejected. As has been pointed out many times before, the oft-quoted name *chogori*, meaning 'great mountain', which has been suggested as a true alternative, is likely to derive from no more than the dutiful response of a local porter to the question 'what's the name of that peak', in much the same way that *dhaulagiri*, 'white mountain', was the frequent response to the same question in Nepal, before custom applied it to the true giant white mountain.

In the winter of 1936 the Karakoram Conference was held to decide upon nomenclature for the features of the range.[14] In the absence of a credible, established, local name, and with all other suggestions dismissed as inappropriate, the conference decided that K2 should be retained as the name of the peak because of its long usage. (The conference also decided that Gasherbrum I should be used in preference to Hidden Peak.) More importantly, the conference concluded that it was not appropriate for any personal (essentially European) names to be used for any glaciers or other features, and suggested that the Godwin-Austen Glacier, Savoia Saddle (or Savoia Pass), Savoia Glacier, De Filippi Glacier and Sella Pass should all be renamed. It is difficult to read the list without a feeling of xenophobia as almost all the names on it are Italian. In the event, despite the suggestion, long usage and the lack of alternative local names means that the majority of these names have been retained.

An attempt by Pakistan to rename the peak Lamba Pahar, Kashmiri for 'great mountain', failed, being considered too political, while a Chinese attempt to impose 'Mount Qogir' has not impressed. Chomolungma has gained considerable acceptance as a substitute for Everest largely because there are large numbers of aspirant climbers attempting the peak from the north (Tibetan) side. While attempts from the north side of K2 remain infrequent, there will be no such reason to accept Qogir.

As well as *chogori*, other native names have been suggested for the peak, though none appears to have any greater credibility. Consequently 'K2' has flourished. And it seems such an appropriate name – clipped and impersonal, well-suited to a peak which, in appearance, is pure mountain, a clean-cut pyramid, and which, as regards those wishing to climb it, remains singularly aloof and indifferent. In his book on the first ascent of Gasherbrum IV, a book that ranks high among the finest ever written on an expedition, Fosco Maraini, speaking of K2, notes its perfect shape by reference to the bulkier, less photogenic, Broad Peak. K2, he says, is architecture, while Broad Peak is simply geology.[15] In the same book, speaking of the possible alternative names that have been suggested, Maraini notes that K2's name

> may owe its origin to chance, but it is a name in itself, and one of striking originality. Sybilline, magical, and with a slight touch of fantasy. A short name, but one that is pure and peremptory, so charged with evocation that it threatens to break through its bleak syllabic bonds. And at the same time a name instinct with mystery and suggestion; a name that scraps race, religion, history and past. No country claims it, no latitudes and longitudes and geography, no dictionary words. No, just the bare bones of a name, all rock and ice and storm and abyss. It makes no attempt to sound human. It is atoms and stars. It has the nakedness of the world before the first man – or of the cindered planet after the last. And if the great mountain gleams with a light seen on no other, it is that letter and that number which shed it. What a disaster it would be to exchange them for some insipid bureaucratic choice! … What is more the name is well established by now: almost proof against the attacks still made by men of poor and arid spirit.[16]

The Height of K2

When Montgomerie reported the results of his survey he gave the height of K2 as 28,287ft (8624m). The survey carried out by the Abruzzi expedition of 1909 gave the height as 8610.7m, corresponding to 28,250ft, a difference of only 37ft. When it is considered how far Montgomerie was from the peak when he made his survey (about 150 miles), his value was astonishingly accurate and a tribute to the professionalism of the Survey of India men. Since 1909 there has been no change in the official height, though the metric figure has been rounded up to 8611m.

There have, however, been occasions when the height of K2 was re-evaluated with newsworthy results. In 1975 a survey suggested the peak was 28,741ft (8760m), though this was rapidly scaled back to the 1909 figure. Then in 1987 US newspapers reported that as a result of a series of incorrect calculations the whole topography of the Karakoram had been misjudged and that K2 was higher than originally claimed, new calculations suggesting it was higher than Everest by a margin which varied with the newspaper delivering the story, values of 11m to 150m being quoted. In fact, the error was in the reported work, not in the original surveys, with K2 being soon proved to be as high as the Italians of 1909 had claimed it was.

Maraini goes on to note a curious phenomenon: the local Baltis have absorbed the name into their own language, pronouncing it '*keitu*' and applying it indiscriminately to any mountain, so that when Gasherbrum IV was climbed the expedition's Balti porters asked the team if they 'finish your *keitu*?'

The numbering of the Himalayan peaks by the GTS counted from east to west, whereas Montgomerie's Karakoram nomenclature travelled in the opposite direction. Officialdom felt the need to regularise the situation when further peaks to the west of K1 (Masherbrum) were surveyed. On the new system K2 became K13. Having already had to grapple with the problems caused by the world's highest mountain being given differing codes on four separate surveys (and then called 'Everest', which did not appear on any survey list), those working in the field quietly shelved this idea. In view of the peak's reputation as a fierce, dangerous undertaking, and the enthusiasm for superstition and omen demonstrated by the public in general (and the press in particular), it is perhaps a blessing that the idea foundered.

Weather on K2

As is well-known, a major feature of the Asian climate is the monsoon,[17] which occurs during the northern hemisphere's summer. During the summer the Tibetan plateau warms, heating the air above it which then rises, resulting in air being drawn in from the south. This air, dragged in from above the Indian Ocean, has a high moisture content, the water falling as rain as the air rises over the mountains. One effect of the enhanced precipitation over the Himalaya is to make the high Tibetan plateau an arid place. Another is to cloak the lower slopes of the southern Himalaya with rich vegetation and to swell the rivers which irrigate India. But the precipitation falls as snow on the high peaks – deep, avalanche-prone snow – and the storms created by the monsoon winds mean that from June until September the Nepalese and Indian Himalayan peaks are essentially off-limits to climbers.

To the west, the northward curving arc of the collision mountain belt means that the monsoon does not directly affect the high hills, although in exceptional years monsoon rains falling on the peaks produce a massive run-off into the tributaries of the Indus. In the summer of 2010 the rising Indus waters flooded huge areas on both sides of the river, causing hundreds of deaths among people and their livestock, and the displacement of millions in the worst natural disaster to have affected Pakistan since its creation.

But the 2010 floods were an exception. Normally, the fact that the monsoon does not reach the high hills allows the climbing season to coincide with the higher temperatures of summer. But although the true monsoon does not reach the Karakoram, the weather of the Baltoro is affected by it, prolonged, fierce storms being a feature of most summer climbing seasons. To such storms, resulting from the proximity of the sub-continent monsoon, must be added the general preponderance of summer thunderstorms in mountain areas arising from an increase in barometric pressure. Ironically, the pressure increase not only aids the creation of thunderstorms but effectively reduces the height of the mountain relative to climbing in the spring and autumn seasons. This aids the climber ascending without the assistance of supplementary oxygen. The exact benefit depends, of course, on the local pressure on summit day, but some experts believe it may be worth as much as a few hundred metres in height.

K2's position at the head of a series of deep, narrow valleys which act as wind funnels, and with relatively flat, low-lying land to the north, also means it is exposed to severe winds, something which is commented on by most who visit. The predominant wind is west or south-west, but on occasions it may blow from the north and may also appear to circle the peak.

Almost without exception, accounts of climbing on K2 note that spells of bad weather are interspersed with periods when climbing is possible. The frequency of bad weather – and the suddenness of its arrival – offers yet another hazard for those intent on the summit. The intensity of the storms is also a frequent topic in expedition accounts, as is their prolonged nature: long periods of bad weather have been responsible for several tragedies on the peak, most notably the death of Art Gilkey in 1953, and the disaster that resulted in five deaths in 1986. Storms on K2 have also resulted in some memorable descriptions of nature at its most raw, none more so than that of Pierre Béghin during an early attempt of the North-West Ridge with Christophe Profit in 1991. The two French climbers were in a tent at 6900m (22,640ft) on the ridge:

Shortly before dawn, we're hit by the south-west wind. The violence is incredible; it smashes against the mountain, smothers it and runs in furious eddies along its flanks. Nowhere is safe. We're in our sleeping bags, fully clothed, boots, balaclava, gloves, all on, ready for a swift getaway. The gusts are so strong now that we're worried about our tent. Even though the outer poles are securely anchored to the slope, the tent is in danger of being torn apart at any moment. The gusts of wind follow one another, closer and closer together, each more violent than the last. The canvas swells then deflates with sharp cracks, almost explosions. In order to counteract the incredible pressure from outside and to avoid being crushed, slightly panicky, we sit with our backs pressed against the sides, muscles aching from staying huddled up. It's still dark outside. It seems like daylight will never come. I don't dare look to see what time it is in case I'm disappointed. In our enclosed shelter, the air is damp from our breathing. To warm ourselves up a bit, we light the stove. The flame is unsteady and the steam is thrown up in fits and starts by each fresh gust. Fearing suffocation, I open one of the air vents. The beam of my torch lights up the sleet which is flying past horizontally in a continuous stream. The snow piled up in front of the tent has considerably reduced our living space. At dawn we decide to wait another day.[18]

Dramatis Locus

The location of K2 and its sheer physical presence, allied to a reputation as a place where mere mortals are tested to their limits, have led to the mountain's association with the supernatural and investigations of the deeper meaning of humanity. Sacred mountains are not unusual throughout the world, but if one particular author is to be believed, K2 is the supreme peak in this regard. In a book entitled *K2: Quest of the Gods* (Edu Books, Cheshire, 2000), Ralph Ellis makes a claim for K2 being the repository of the 'Hall of Records', the chamber in which the architectural plans for the Pyramids of Egypt are stored. His conjecture is that the plan of the internal chambers, galleries and passageways of the Great Pyramid are a representation of the map of the world, the apex of the pyramid acting as the 'x' of a treasure map. Transferring this x to the world map places it at K2. Ellis further notes that two of the three Giza pyramids were only partially clad in white limestone, while the Great Pyramid was fully clad. The two smaller pyramids, clad at the top, but with exposed, rough-hewn darker rock at the base, would therefore have appeared, when constructed, as snow-topped mountains, while the Great Pyramid would have looked like a mountain entirely covered with snow, just as K2 does. K2 is also pyramidal, the length of its square base and the angles of its ridges being associated with those of the Great Pyramid and related to the value of π. There is much more, particularly on the true reasons for Alexander the Great's invasion of Egypt and later campaigns in the Hindu Kush. Skardu, Ellis notes, looks very similar to Skander, a local name for Alexander. Did the great man send scouts that way searching for the Hall of Records, knowledge of which he had discovered or been told in Egypt? Ellis concludes with the idea that just as the Great Pyramid once had a hinged stone door (rather like a giant cat flap) set high on one side and leading to a passageway, there should be a hinged stone door high on one of the faces of K2. Whoever is perceptive or lucky enough to find it will gain entrance to the Hall of Records and the secrets of the construction of the pyramids. Exactly who it was that went to such colossal lengths to construct such a hall, and the puzzle necessary to be solved to find it is not made clear, but it is to be hoped that they left rather more than architectural drawings for the pyramids.

    More down to earth or, at least, as much earth as can be found on a narrow ledge set at 27,000ft at the centre of a 600ft vertical cliff on K2 is the play written by Patrick Meyers, *K2* (Dramatists Play Service Inc., New York, 1980). Written before the event it most replicates, the cutting of Joe Simpson's rope by Simon Yates, after he had broken his leg during the descent of Siula Grande in the Peruvian Andes (as told in *Touching the Void*, the award-winning and best-selling book by Simpson), and before several incidents on Everest in which men climbed past sick or injured climbers without offering assistance (incidents that led to scathing newspaper articles), Meyers' play has two men trapped on a ledge, one with a broken leg, after an accident during a descent from K2's summit. The men fall out, make up, discuss physics, the American way of life and law, and the essence of life and death, as they fight to retrieve a second rope from above them which was lost in the accident but which will allow them to descend safely. Ultimately, an avalanche sweeps away the second rope and most of their equipment, further injuring the injured climber. They then discuss whether the uninjured man should abandon his friend in order to save himself. The man does not want to go, but he does not want to die needlessly. If he goes, he will spend his life regretting the decision, but he can tell the injured man's son, as yet too young to know his father, about him.

Meyers' play did not need to involve K2. Any mountain would have sufficed, the accident and the subsequent decision requiring only a remote location and a steep cliff. That K2 was chosen says much about the way that the mountain, even before the events of 1986 and 2008, had become recognised not only as the epitome of a mountain, but as a brooding presence, a dramatic set on which matters of life and death could be played out. The play was eventually used as the basis of an ordinary, somewhat cliché-ridden film (*K2*, first shown in 1991, starring Michael Biehn and Matt Craven), which traded the bleak but poignant ending of the play for the requisite Hollywood happy ending.

The Challenge
Climbers attempting Everest from its southern, Nepalese, side, can, and often do, abandon Base Camp for a day or two and seek out the Sherpa settlements where tea, coffee and meals can be bought, and grass can be walked on. But it is 100km from Askole, the last human settlement, to the base of K2 and almost throughout that entire journey the traveller is on ice or glacial moraine, the view dominated by snow and ice. Above Base Camp harsh, debilitating weather adds to the thin air to make any effort exhausting, while the geology ensures that continuous effort is required, much more so than on the 'normal' route of any other 8000m peak. In an article entitled 'A Margin of Luck',[19] Greg Child, who reached the summit in 1990, wrote that 'K2 is intolerant of human presence ... The atmosphere near the summit contains one-third the oxygen of sea level. Arctic cold and hurricane winds, vertiginous walls of rock and ice ring the mountain ... the fascination the mountain holds really has nothing to do with climbing. K2 represents an ordeal. To climb it is to confront your own mortal fears; K2 is the geologic personification of angst.'

It is the history of that challenge which follows.

Chapter 2

Early Explorations

We had just turned a corner which brought into view, on the left hand, a peak of appalling height.

Francis Younghusband, on first seeing K2 from the north

Man's knowledge of the existence of the Karakoram and Himalaya dates from pre-history, with the first settlement of the Tibetan plateau and the fertile regions of the northern Indian sub-continent, but news of the great peaks only reached the pages of recorded history with Alexander's invasion of India in 325 BC. Local legend in the Hindu Kush maintains that Greek warriors not only penetrated far into the area but also settled, various villages, river crossings and landmarks bearing Alexander's name or variations of it, though the authenticity of most of these is dubious, suggesting an enthusiasm for association with a legendary figure rather than solid evidence. Marco Polo's journey took him along the northern border of the Karakoram to Kashgar,[1] but it was another three centuries before Europeans began to penetrate the high hills.

The first travellers were Jesuit teachers invited to the Moghul Court of Akbar the Great at Lahore in 1579.[2] As well as attempting to convert the locals, the Jesuits were keen to explore north-east from the court, both to make contact with Nestorian Christians who had moved east in the fifth century when their religion was declared heretical, and to solve the mystery of whether Cathay and China were one and the same. In 1624 the Jesuit Antonio de Andrade and lay brother Manuel Marques crossed the Mana Pass and descended into Tibet, the first Europeans to reach that fabled land. Later travellers to Tibet included Johannes Grüber, who, on reaching Lhasa in October 1661, produced the only known drawing of the earliest Potala Palace, the present structure having been completed in 1694.

Though Tibet was still the main target for travellers, journeys were also made further west. In 1715 Ippolito Desideri, a young Italian Jesuit from Pistoia, together with an older Portuguese Jesuit, Emmanuel Freyre, left Srinigar and crossed the Zoli La to become the first Europeans to reach Leh, the chief town of Ladakh. Though Desideri – together with Freyre, the latter reluctantly – continued to Lhasa, he did describe a pass called Karakoram that linked Ladakh and Yarkand. The first known European crossing of the pass was by the German Schlagintweit brothers,[3] Hermann and Robert, who crossed it in 1856.[4] But before that crossing, other fine journeys of exploration in and around the Karakoram had been made, none better than that of G.T. Vigne,[5] who travelled in Kashmir, then reached Skardu, from a ridge above which he gazed at the Karakoram. From Skardu, Vigne travelled west and saw, but did not visit, Gilgit. He also went north up the Shigar and Basho valleys, and explored the possibility of crossing the Hispar and Muztagh Passes, but decided they were beyond him and his team. Vigne then failed to persuade the locals to allow him over the Karakoram Pass from Leh, and failed again to reach the pass when his attempt to detour around Leh was stopped by glacial ice. Vigne left Baltistan disappointed with his lack of success, but in fact he had achieved a great deal. Most particularly he had shown that north of Skardu there was a huge mountain range protected by glaciers, that could be easily crossed only by heading west towards Gilgit or north from Leh. The suggestion was greeted with amazement by the geographers of Europe, who were convinced that the Himalaya faded away at the western end, with a plateau (doubtless high and wild) existing in what is now northern Pakistan. Some continued to believe that was the case until Montgomerie's survey in 1856 proved beyond doubt that Vigne had been correct.

Subsequent to Montgomerie's survey a Piedmontese nobleman, Marquis Oswaldo Roero di Cortanze, who had bought land and developed tea plantations on the southern slopes of the north-western Himalaya, made a series of journeys towards Baltistan. The exact routes he took and how far he penetrated towards the Karakoram are not clear from his writings,[6] but it is likely that his explorations were less extensive than those of Vigne. But what the Marquis did establish was an Italian interest in the Karakoram that, together with the Abruzzi expedition of 1909, was to be the foundation of claims that K2 was an 'Italian' mountain.

Godwin-Austen, 1861
The next major step in the exploration of the Karakoram was taken in 1861 by Henry Haversham Godwin-Austen.[7] As well as being a member of the GTS, Godwin-Austen was a geologist and an excellent topographic artist. In India he worked under Thomas Montgomerie, though there appears to have been little friendship between the two. Keay (in *Where Men and Mountains Meet*) notes that a letter written by Godwin-Austen is very deprecating of his co-worker, suggesting honours gained out of proportion to effort put in. The suggestion seems unfounded, perhaps indicating the resentment of the men (such as Godwin-Austen) who filled in the triangles others (led by Montgomerie) created. The former required slow, painstaking, tedious work, a contrast to the glamorous work of the latter. In an article for the Royal Geographical Society, Godwin-Austen notes the problems the triangle surveyors had to endure:

The snowy range [of the Desoai Plains, viewed from an altitude of almost 17,000ft (5183m)] was only visible here and there amongst the clouds, which were gathering up fast, and I soon saw that a descent that day was out of the question. We made ourselves as comfortable as it was possible to be; the plane-table was set up, and as much as could be seen cut in at once. I got into a snug corner out of the wind, and then the day was spent in sundry rushes to the plane-table, whenever, on looking round, some peak would show out amongst the heavy clouds which hung about. Many such days as these – days of long dreary hours – have to be passed amongst the Himalayas.[8]

The work also involved occasionally uncomfortable encounters with local people: on one occasion Godwin-Austen was badly beaten by irate locals, probably after an inadvertent trespass on sacred ground, and needed evacuation to England to recover. The lack of empathy between Montgomerie and Godwin-Austen may have been the reason why the former sent the latter off to explore the Karakoram, seeing it as a good method of getting an irritating subordinate out of the way for a while. If that is the case, the decision benefited Godwin-Austen a great deal more than Montgomerie may have anticipated or desired.

In 1860 Godwin-Austen was given charge of a survey team exploring the Hushe valley. That trip was very successful and in 1861 he went to survey the remote valleys of northern Baltistan. Interested in the passes over the Karakoram which might lead to Yarkand, Godwin-Austen set out from Skardu with the intention of locating and crossing the Muztagh Pass, the existence of which had long been known, but which had yet to be seen, let alone crossed, by a Westerner (but see Note 11). Officially, the pass – or, rather both the passes: as we shall see later, there were Old and New passes – was out-of-bounds to the survey team, though Godwin-Austen had been asked to investigate the existence of possible passes through the Karakoram. The British were working on the assumption that the Karakoram watershed would be a convenient border between British India and whatever lay to the north (as it now is between Pakistan and China) and so surveys to the high passes were necessary, but Godwin-Austen had clearly intended to cross the pass and carry the survey on towards Yarkand.

With his team, which totalled 66 men including survey assistants, porters and guides, Godwin-Austen began by climbing the Borije La and the peak of Thyarlung (5135m/16,844ft) from the summit of which 'K2 … appeared of an airy-blue tint, surrounded by the yellower peak K1 (Masherbrum), K3, and others, all over 24,000ft. in height'. He next followed the Shigar valley, noting the changes in the landscape due to the flooding which occasionally occurred when local rivers rose. Godwin-Austen says that in 1841 there was an incident in the Nubra valley, close to Leh, when a dam of debris brought down by monsoon rains, accumulated in a narrow ravine over several years, collapsed, causing a catastrophic flood that killed hundreds of people and livestock, as water rushed towards the Indus. Later, he describes an evening when an unusual rumbling sound brought him out of his tent to see a black stream rushing out of a ravine carrying 'a mass of stones and thick mud, about 30 yards in breadth and about 15 feet deep ... No one, who has not seen a flood of this kind, can form any idea of the mighty power of transport which the accumulated masses of water and melting snow acquire at these times.' The two descriptions are a chilling reminder of the appalling loss of life in the summer of 2010 when monsoon rains caused the Indus to rise.

Godwin-Austen eventually reached the Panmah Glacier (he calls it the Punmah) and moved along its lateral moraine to a point below the New Muztagh Pass. Many years before, when ice had made impassable the approaches to the original pass (the Old Muztagh Pass), about 16km (10 miles) to the east, a new route had been forged over another low point on the ridge line north of the Baltoro. It was towards this new pass that Godwin-Austen was advancing. From a last camp, together with eight men, he went north along the glacier: 'For the first 3 miles the crevasses were broad and deep in places only, and we could avoid them by making detours. They soon became more numerous, and were ugly things to look into, much more so to cross.' As the sun rose, the softening snow reduced progress to a crawl. Finally, with still a mile of glacier to be crossed and 500ft to be ascended, the weather, fine until then, broke. It began to snow heavily and cloud descended, reducing visibility to a minimum. The team was forced to retreat in difficult conditions: 'the snow falling fast. The glacier was making most disagreeable noises – crunching, splitting, and groaning to an awful extent.'

The following day the team rested. Then Godwin-Austen decided not to try a second time and turned his attention to the older pass. Glacier movements in the high Karakoram frequently disrupted old trade routes, advancing glaciers cutting off once viable routes, while retreating ice might make them easier. Godwin-Austen had just been made very much aware of the power of ice to make routes difficult, if not impossible. Now he was intent on reaching the older Muztagh Pass, the one abandoned for the newer pass when glacial changes had made it unusable. And so, for the first time, a European was to see, and set off along, a glacier that has now been crossed by thousands of climbers and trekkers as they head towards the highest peaks of the Karakoram. That familiarity, at least in words and photographs, means that today's visitor or armchair visitor is familiar with the vast rock towers that overlook the huge, forbidding Baltoro Glacier. But for Godwin-Austen, the first European to be confronted by the sheer size of the glacier, the sight must have been overwhelming.

Godwin-Austen does not use the name Baltoro initially, instead calling the glacier the Biaho, after the Biaho river which emerges from it: 'the Biaho comes roaring from an immense cavern in the ice-cliff'. (He does, however, call the glacier the Baltoro later in his account of his journey.) Once on the glacier, Godwin-

Austen's main concern was not crossing the Old Mustagh Pass but discovering exactly where K2 stood in relation to the Karakoram watershed, and thus whether it was within, beyond, or on the border of British India and the lands to the north over which China had control. His team trekked up the Baltoro, seeing what would in time become known as Gasherbrum IV,[9] but with K2 hidden from view by the huge peaks of the Baltoro's northern flank. Of the glacier itself he notes: 'enormous blocks were to be seen on every side, some perched on knobs of ice. Some, lately fallen, lay by the sides of their old supports. The northern side of the ice was still a confused heap of debris, pile upon pile, with deep trenches and gullies ... The scenery along this glacier was magnificent.' But still K2 remained elusive.

Eventually, to spot the peak, Godwin-Austen was forced to climb over 2,000ft up the ridge towards the summit of Masherbrum. From there 'a distant bit of rock and snow could be seen just peering above the near snow-line. After another sharp push to a point where it was impossible to mount further, there no longer remained any doubt about it. There, with not a particle of cloud to hide it, stood the great Peak K2 on the watershed of Asia!' Godwin-Austen was the first man to see the mountain at close quarters, if a distance of 25km (16 miles) can be so termed. After assuring himself that K2 lay on the watershed, and therefore on the border of British India, Godwin-Austen forgot about the Old Muztagh Pass and reversed his route, doing further survey work near Askole and along the Basha valley before returning to his survey base station.

Younghusband, 1887 and 1889

After reading Godwin-Austen's report of his attempt on the Muztagh Pass, his British superiors decided that it might not be crossed at all, and even it could, it was certainly not a route that could be used with ease and safety. This view was contrary to that of Godwin-Austen himself, who was convinced that a packhorse track could be made up the Panmah's lateral moraine. But the official view prevailed and no further attempt was made on the pass for almost thirty years.

In 1887 a young British Army officer, Captain Francis Edward Younghusband,[10] set off from Peking (now Beijing) on a journey that would take him across the Gobi Desert to Kashgar and Yarkand, and on to Srinigar. It was an audacious journey, the more so as Younghusband was only 23 years old and was to be accompanied only by two Chinese, one a servant, the other a general factotum combining the roles of interpreter, cook and much more besides. At the time he set off, Younghusband was unsure exactly how he would make his way from Yarkand to Srinigar. It was probably just as well: had he dwelt too much on the finer details of any part of his journey, he might never have started at all.

After crossing the Gobi Desert and travelling west along the southern flanks of the Altai Mountains, Younghusband and his party went south, then west again along the Tien Shan Mountains, reaching Kashgar almost five months after setting out. Younghusband then headed south to Yarkand, where he found a letter addressed to him from his commanding officer, Colonel Mark Bell, telling him to try the Muztagh Pass as it was both the shortest route over the Karakoram and it needed exploration. Younghusband immediately engaged a Balti guide, some porters and packhorses, and headed south. They made their way through various villages, then crossed the Tapa Dawan and Chiraghsaldi Passes in the Kun Lun Mountains to reach the Yarkand river. They followed this downstream, then took a tributary back to the Aghil Pass, which they crossed to reach Shaksgam and the Oprang river. In the Oprang valley, Younghusband writes,

> we ascended [the Sarpo Laggo, a tributary of the Oprang] till we reached a patch of jungle called Suget Jangal. Just before arriving there I chanced to look up rather suddenly, and a sight met my eyes which fairly staggered me. We had just turned a corner which brought into view, on the left hand, a peak of appalling height, which could be none other than K.2 [sic], 28,278 feet in height, second only to Mount Everest. Viewed from this direction, it appeared to rise in an almost perfect cone, but to an inconceivable height. We were quite close under it – perhaps not a dozen miles from its summit – and here on the northern side, where it is literally clothed in glacier, there must have been from fourteen to sixteen thousand feet of solid ice. It was one of those sights which impress a man for ever, and produce a permanent effect upon the mind – a lasting sense of the greatness and grandeur of Nature's works – which he can never lose or forget. For some time I stood apart, absorbed in the contemplation of this wonderful sight …

In an article read to the Royal Geographical Society and included in the Proceedings of the Society magazine (see Note 10), Younghusband elaborated a little on that first view:

> We could see it through a break in the mountains, rising up straight, bold, and solitary, covered from foot to summit with perpetual snow. The upper part, for perhaps 5,000 feet, was a perfect cone, and seems to be composed almost entirely of ice and snow, the accumulation of ages. The lower part was more precipitous, but steep enough to throw off snow altogether, while at the base was a great glacier formed by masses of snow which fell from its sides. It was a magnificent sight, and I could scarcely tear myself away from it.

Younghusband is the first European known to have seen K2 from the north, but was there a precedent? If the story of an earlier crossing of the Muztagh Pass is correct, then it is very likely that there was.[11]

As Younghusband and his party climbed the valley of the Sarpo Laggo they eventually found it blocked by a series of 'enormous heaps of stones and fragments of rocks ... between two and three hundred feet in height'. When he approached one, Younghusband was amazed to discover that it was actually a massive block of ice covered with debris: the heaps were the terminal moraine of a massive glacier: 'Here and there, breaking through the mounds of stone, I had seen cliffs of what I thought was black rock, but on coming close up to these I found them to be of solid dark green ice.' The party struggled to get their supply ponies through the heaps, the animals' hooves scratching away the thin debris covering, so they slipped and cut themselves on the ice in a way, Younghusband writes, 'which distressed me much'. An easier path along the lateral moraine was found, but that offered only temporary respite, the terrain forcing the party back on to the glacier again, where a line of medial moraine allowed further progress. But eventually the ponies were brought to a halt. Younghusband himself could now barely walk, his last pair of boots completely worn out. He sent men forward to reconnoitre the route, but they returned with discouraging news. Younghusband had already decided to try the New Muztagh Pass, the one Godwin-Austen had failed on, but the men reported that there was no chance of the ponies crossing it and that there was little likelihood of men crossing it either. Younghusband now faced a dilemma. If he turned around and went back, then headed east to the Karakoram Pass, his supplies would run out before he got to Ladakh, even if the men killed and ate the ponies as they marched. So he decided to turn back most of the party, and the ponies, taking a few men over the Old Pass and down to Askole where they would pay the locals to carry extra supplies back over the pass to the main party.

His chosen party set off, carrying 'a roll of bedding for myself, a sheepskin coat for each man, some native biscuits, tea and a large tea-kettle, and a bottle of brandy'. The ascent to the pass was hard work (the pass is at over 5422m/17,784ft, though Younghusband says that it was over 19,000ft) but reasonable straightforward. But the descent was a very different proposition. Younghusband wrote a letter to his father soon after completing his journey, a letter he reproduced in his book. It has an immediacy that his book account, which was perhaps written several years later, lacks. In the letter he says: 'On reaching the summit we looked about for a way down, but there was nothing but a sheer precipice, and blocks of ice broken and tumbled about in such a way as to be quite impracticable. I freely confess that I myself could never have attempted the descent, and that I – an Englishman – was afraid to go first. Luckily my guides were better plucked than myself ...' The book continues by noting that Younghusband's silence on staring down from the pass was a master stroke, though more, one gathers, by his being dumbstruck than by design. His men, 'looking at me, and imagining that an Englishman never went back from an enterprise he had once started on, took it as a matter of course that, as I gave no order to go back, I meant to go on'.

But they had no ice axes or other climbing equipment and, as Younghusband admits, he had no experience of Alpine climbing. But they did have a pickaxe and a length of rope. The latter was tied around the waist of the hired guide Wali, who was a native of Askole, and he was sent ahead to carve steps in the steep ice with the pickaxe. The others followed, each holding the rope in case Wali should slip. On their feet they had only soft leather boots, little more than leather stockings, which offered no grip on the hard ice and around which the men tied handkerchiefs and other scraps of cloth to offer some sort of purchase. Halfway across the slope Younghusband's Ladakhi servant became so frightened he had to turn back, returning to the main party and the ponies. The rest reached the safety of a rock tower, but below that was a near-perpendicular cliff. As they climbed down,

> all we generally found was a little ledge, upon which we could grip with the tips of the fingers or side of the foot. The men were most good to me, whenever possible guiding my foot into some secure hold, and supporting it there with their hands; but at times it was all I could do to summon sufficient courage to let myself down on to the veriest little crevices which had to support me. There was a constant dread, too, that fragments of these ledges might give way with the weight upon them, for the rock was very crumbly ...

At one point a huge falling rock almost wiped out the party, but eventually the bottom of the cliff was reached. Next came a long ice slope down to the head of the glacier at the base of the pass. Along its length were three projecting rock towers. To overcome the ice between these towers, all the rope the party could muster was tied together with the mens' unravelled turbans and waist-clothes. One man was then lowered down the ice, hacking steps as he went. The 'rope' was then anchored at the top and each man used it and the steps to reach the next rock tower. One man slipped, tearing the skin from his hand as he clutched the rope to stop his fall. Finally, the last man had to untie the 'rope' and climb down the steps, the others taking in the line to hold any fall. The job was given to 'the man who had especially troubled me by knocking pieces of ice over the precipice when we were at the head of the pass'. The process was then repeated to the next rock tower, then to the last, then to the glacier, where 'those moments when I stood at the foot of the pass are long to be remembered by me – moments of intense relief, and of deep gratitude for the success that had been granted'.

But crossing the pass was not the end of the journey and neither was it entirely successful, Younghusband discovering that the bottle of brandy had not survived the descent. The men turned west along the Baltoro Glacier, Younghusband marvelling at the mountain and rock architecture on each side – 'a region unsurpassed for sublimity and grandeur by any in the world' – but longing to get to Askole, both for himself and to resupply his main party. In the village ('a dirty little village') Wali and another Askole man kept close to their leader, fearful that the villagers would attack them for showing a foreigner the way over the pass. Men were dispatched with supplies for the main party – three were badly injured in crossing the pass – while Younghusband went to see if Godwin-Austen had been correct about the New Muztagh Pass. He concluded he had been, and continued to Srinigar to complete his journey.

The crossing of the Muztagh Pass had been an epic, a journey of immense, near suicidal, risk, but one which was to make Younghusband a hero to the British. He was made the youngest-ever Fellow of the Royal Geographical Society and given its Gold Medal. While in each case the honour was given for the journey as a whole rather than the crossing of the pass, there is little doubt that it was the pass that had captured the public imagination.

Younghusband returned to the field two years later when he explored the approaches to the Saltoro Pass, to the east of the Gasherbrum peaks, and the Shimshal Pass, north-west of the Baltoro, each from the north. He did not cross either pass: that was not the object of his mission, which was to judge how easy it might be for an invader to use the Karakoram as a route to British India. The Great Game might be in its final phase, but Younghusband was still playing. The game was a hard one: on the approach to the Saltoro in a heavy snowstorm, Younghusband's party was almost annihilated by an avalanche which they heard above them. 'We heard a report like thunder, and then a rushing sound. We knew at once it was an avalanche; it was coming from straight above us, and I felt in that moment greater fear than I ever yet have done, for we could see nothing, but only hear this tremendous rushing sound coming straight down upon us.' The avalanche sped past them, close enough for a cloud of snow dust to envelop them. Later, as they retreated, another avalanche wiped out the trail they had made on the ascent, the descent being made with the constant fear of another avalanche heading their way.

Younghusband's look at the Shimshal and Saltoro Passes, together with his knowledge of the Muztagh Pass, convinced him that the high Karakoram did not offer a possible invasion route for the Russians into India. But then news came that Bronislav Grombtchevsky was also in the field. Polish born, but now an officer in the Tsar's army, Grombtchevsky can be seen as the Russian counterpart of Younghusband, each man probing the border between their nations for weaknesses, and seeking alliances with local tribes. This time, in fact, Grombtchevsky was heading a scientific expedition (with, almost certainly, a little intrigue on the side), but Younghusband did not know that, and he altered his course to shadow the Russian. But before any cat-and-mouse manoeuvring could start, Younghusband received a letter from Grombtchevsky suggesting a meeting. And so one of the most intriguing, yet bizarre episodes of the Great Game took place close to the junction of the Ilisu and Yarkand rivers. The two men obviously found each other to be very good company and spent the day talking and inspecting each other's troops (Grombtchevsky's Cossacks and the Gurkhas accompanying Younghusband). In his book, Younghusband notes that a Gurkha non-commissioned officer became convinced that Grombtchevsky had commented on their height – they were shorter than the Cossacks and overtopped by Grombtchevsky, who was over 6 feet tall and also powerfully built – and asked Younghusband to tell the Russian that most Gurkhas were over 6 feet tall, but 'I could not commit myself to quite so flagrant an "exaggeration", but I told Captain Grombtchevsky how the Gurkha had wanted to impose upon him, and he was immensely tickled'. But there seems to have been a corollary to the tale. Grombtchevsky had a photograph taken of the meeting and sent Younghusband a copy: it was only ever reproduced twice, then lost for ever. In it Younghusband and Grombtchevsky stand together and are head to head. But Younghusband was only 5 foot 6 inches tall. His feet are obscured by what appears to be an unlit bonfire, suggesting that the Gurkhas had made sure their leader at least was not overtopped by the Russian captain, by standing him on something which they then covered with brushwood.

When the two men finally parted, Younghusband noted that,

> Captain Grombtchevsky [said] to me that he hoped we might meet again, either in peace at St Petersburg or in war on the Indian frontier; in either case I might be sure of a warm welcome. I thoroughly enjoyed that meeting with a Russian officer. We and the Russians *are* rivals, but I am sure that individual Russian and English officers like each other a great deal better than they do the individuals of nations with which they are not in rivalry. We are both playing at a big game, and we should not be one jot better off for trying to conceal the fact.

Roberto Lerco, 1890

The year after Younghusband's second journey, a mysterious traveller arrived on the Baltoro. Many writers mention the 1890 journey of Roberto Lerco, but give few details. That is not surprising as all references ultimately tie back to a delightful book produced to coincide with an exhibition organised by the Museo Nazionale della Montagna 'Duca degli Abruzzi', Turin, which was shown at several locations in 1991/92.[12] Lerco was a native of Gressoney-La-Trinité in the Aosta valley of north-west Italy, but spent much of his adult life in Vienna. An accomplished climber, during an 1887 expedition to the Caucasus he made the second ascent of Elbrus and the third of Kasbek; he was also an explorer of note, heading for the high Karakoram at a time when it was not only unexplored and unmapped, but a daunting mountain wilderness. Lerco did not write a book about his climbs or travels, but he did correspond with a friend, the German ethnographer/photographer Hermann Burchardt, who had also travelled in the Middle East; indeed, the books Burchardt produced about his own travels are an excellent memorial of that area in the last years of the nineteenth century. It is from these letters[13] that we can piece together Lerco's Baltoro journey. The first letter was written from Simla on 1 May 1890. By 20 May Lerco had reached Srinigar, from where he travelled to Leh, though he did not arrive there until mid-August. The next letter is dated 2 November 1890 and was written from Quetta. Subsequent letters were written during a long homeward journey, the final one being posted from Smyrna in March 1891. The letters are fascinating, but reveal very little of what Lerco actually did between mid-August and late October, other than suggesting that he penetrated the Karakoram. The true extent of his explorations did not become apparent until 1909, when the Abruzzi expedition was heading towards K2 with the intention of climbing the mountain. During several conversations[14] Lerco revealed that he had attempted the peak along what is now known as the Abruzzi Spur, but that the climb was not possible because of a steep cliff which prevented further progress. The clear implication from Lerco's comments is that he had climbed the Abruzzi until stopped by the cliff split by House's Chimney. In the absence of documentary proof this is, of course, supposition, but if true, it is a marvellous story, though it is worth noting that if Lerco had been able to force the Chimney, he would likely have continued on what may well have been his last climb, given the limited knowledge of high-altitude physiology of the time.

Conway, 1892

Though there seems little doubt that Lerco did indeed travel along the Baltoro Glacier, even if what exactly he did when he reached K2 is speculative, the first traverse for which published details exist was in 1892 when William Martin Conway[15] took a small expedition along the glacier to the foot of K2. Though often considered the first attempt on the peak (in his own book on the trip Oscar Eckenstein[16] states that one objective of the expedition was the ascent of K2), in reality the expedition was primarily exploratory, as Conway himself notes in the Preface to his book. Interestingly, the Preface also includes Conway's comment that he had wanted to call K2 'Watchtower' (and he was to give several other peaks English names on his trip, most notably Broad Peak), but 'as any alternative designation seemed to give offence, where none was intended, I have confined myself to the letter and number of the Indian Atlas'. The Preface of Eckenstein's book includes a note that he was aware of Conway's book on the trip, but had chosen not to read it before writing his own. As relations between the two men seem to have broken down, with Eckenstein leaving the expedition, this may have been a generous gesture aimed at not using his own book to settle scores. Eckenstein also notes that one aim of the expedition was the study of the 'as yet quite unsettled questions as to the physiological effect of reduced pressure of the atmosphere on the human system'. But it seems that was Eckenstein's own view.

In addition to Eckenstein and Conway, the team that left London included A.D. McCormick, [17] Matthias Zurbriggen, [18] Parbir Thapa, a Gurkha sepoy, who was to be in charge of the porters, and an American, J.D. Roudebush, who was travelling only to reach a suitable spot where he could do some hunting. (Eckenstein suggests in his book that Roudebush did not join the party until Srinigar was reached.)

The two books on the expedition are very different. Conway's is much more factual, almost scientific, though he does have the occasional fine lyrical touch: in describing the sea voyage he notes at one stage that 'the bright sky and breeze, just crisping the water and scattering diamonds above the waves, made laughter over the sea'. Later, when the sea was more belligerent, he described it as 'hateful', suggesting that he was not a great sailor. In contrast, the sense of enjoyment in Eckenstein's book is palpable, with the occasional hilarious passage.

The expedition travelled by train at first and at Srinigar was joined by Lieutenant Colonel Lloyd-Dickin, a collector of birds (who, along with Roudebush, left the expedition near Gilgit), and Lieutenant C.G. Bruce. [19] During the journey through Kashmir both Conway and Eckenstein noted the difficulties of dealing with the locals, though again their examples reveal differences, Conway being exasperated, Eckenstein being, on the whole, amused. Conway notes that dealings were 'unhampered by prejudice in favour of veracity', detailing a conversation in which a local offered as many sheep, chickens and eggs as the expedition needed, but was eventually forced to admit, after questioning at length, that there actually no sheep, chickens or eggs. Later, trying to find out how far away the house of a British officer was, Conway asked if it was a mile away. Yes, was the response. Was it two miles? Yes. Then exactly how many miles – 'as many as the sahib pleases'. Eckenstein describes haggling over the purchase of a piece of embroidery, the price of which started at 75 rupees. When it had reached 40–50 rupees the vendor suggested a coin be tossed to decide whether 40 or 50. The piece was eventually bought for 10 rupees. Eckenstein seems to have been somewhat amused by the idea of a coin toss to decide the final price, but on his return journey noted a couple of incidents when the method was repeated, with him losing out.

Eckenstein is also excellent at describing the mode of transport used early in the journey. This, the *ekka*, 'is emphatically an invention of the devil. It is a two-wheeled contrivance devoid of any kind of or apology for springs ... the worst means of progression that I have ever attempted.' They were, however, necessary, though hiring them required 'much profanity and a little violence'. One crashed, an incident that Zurbriggen luckily escaped more or less unharmed, after which the badly damaged, barely serviceable, ekka was taken over by Eckenstein, who 'made the driver's life a misery for him'. Eventually, the party had to walk, Eckenstein noting they followed what were known locally as roads, but were actually paths, 'occasionally bad and sometimes invisible'. Eckenstein seems to have survived a series of trying events by swearing a lot, either at the local people or at the conditions, noting that on one occasion 'my stock of bad language was not equal to doing justice to the circumstances; anybody having a surplus stock of the article on hand in England is requested to send it along here where the article is in strong demand'.

The party travelled to Gilgit, Conway noting on the way that Bruce's carrying capacity 'is about equal to that of a goods train' – an early indication of the strength for which Bruce was to become renowned. Eckenstein described Nanga Parbat, commenting that as it was viewed from 4,000ft, some 22,000ft of the peak rose before him. At Gilgit most of the team fell ill with diarrhoea. Bruce also suffered recurrences of what Eckenstein called Burmese Fever (probably malaria). During their recovery, Conway notes that several team members gathered and pressed local flowers, while others set about slaughtering the local wildlife, bears being especially highly prized. Conway also notes that at Nagyr he raided the local cemetery, removing skulls (apparently at night) and sending them back to Britain; two of these skulls finished up in a museum at Cambridge. The theft is distinctly unpleasant, particularly for what it says about the Imperial attitude of the British. There are several episodes in Eckenstein's book which show the ruling class in a poor light in terms of their dealings with the native population: he notes, for example, that when a sheep was killed the Europeans ate the best bits, the rest being given to the Gurkhas and servants; and that when rope bridges needed to be crossed, a loaded native was sent across first to test the strength before the Europeans attempted it, as it was known that no maintenance was carried out on such bridges – they were used until they collapsed, invariably resulting in the deaths of those on it, then replaced.

Beyond Gilgit, Conway split the team, sending Bruce and Eckenstein over the Nushik La to Skardu, while he, McCormick and Zurbriggen crossed the Hispar Pass. Eckenstein clearly enjoyed the journey, particularly a meeting with the headman of a village along the way. When asked if he knew the way to Askole, the man claimed there was no such place, or if there was he had never heard of it. Of a way to it, there was no such route, or if there was it had been in use long ago, but no longer, or if there still was it was long and difficult. As Eckenstein notes, given enough time and presents the man would not only have admitted to knowing Askole and the route to it, but would have supplied guides and porters. The Hispar party were treated to a sunset which Conway's lyrical writing was equal to:

Our long shadows marched before us as though they would hasten towards the wondrous east which served as a canvas for the sun's bold painting. All the mountains and the clouds, that curled around them like a long breaking wave, were coloured with the richest gold. Shortly after the sun actually set, the foot of the valley was bathed in purple, and the snowy mountain at the end, barred with light stripes of cloud, was grey against a band of bluest heaven. The blue melted into red, which faded upwards to a violet zenith.

The tragedy was that there was no time for McCormick to stop and paint the scene, and he was 'almost mad with rage' as a result.

At Skardu Conway writes that 'Eckenstein had never been well since reaching Gilgit. It was evidently useless for him to come further with us, so I decided that he had better return to England.' Those two sentences are all he says of the matter, but it is clear from Eckenstein's own account that they do not tell the complete story.

On the ascent to the Nushik La, Eckenstein writes that he decided to test the effect of altitude on his performance. Previous tests had shown him that between sea level and 8,000ft he could climb at a rate of 2,700–2,800ft/hr. He therefore timed his ascent and found that he had achieved 2,815ft in an hour to a height of 11,000ft. This figure hardly suggests a sick man, rather one who was clearly well-acclimatised (as well as fit). Eckenstein's writing makes it clear that the primary problem between himself and Conway arose from a difference of opinion about the expedition's aims. At one point he notes that Conway's decision to waste time moving a camp meant another opportunity missed, and it was an issue that had clearly been rankling for a while:

> We could have ascended two or three decent peaks in the last fortnight or so, instead of doing practically nothing. I had frequently been of a similar opinion before, and having regard to the position in which Professor Conway asked me to join the expedition, I think it fair to record my personal view of the subject.

Clearly there had been an exchange of views, Eckenstein going on to note that, 'It is, however, right to point out that Conway disagreed with me on the point.' Eckenstein was not happy with the frequent changes of plan. On another occasion he notes that the two of them, having reached a pass, 'had a rather animated, not to say heated, discussion' as to the advisability of trying to ascend either of the peaks situated on the two sides of the pass.

Though Eckenstein was clearly exasperated by Conway's frequent changes of plan, he was obviously happy when the party was split and he and Bruce crossed the Nushik La. Of his departure Eckenstein writes:

> On Wednesday (27-7-92) we had a sort of general meeting, at which it was arranged that I should leave the expedition. There had been a good deal of friction from time to time, and, as we had now been some two and half months in the mountains without making a single ascent of importance, having only crossed two previously known passes, I was not anxious to go on, and accordingly we agreed to separate.

While differences in aims between the climber (Eckenstein) and the explorer (Conway) may have been at the heart of the disagreement between the two, it is also true that the radical socialist (Eckenstein) and the establishment man (Conway) were never likely to have become personal friends.

Eckenstein's writing became increasingly downbeat as the expedition moved into the mountains, almost certainly reflecting his growing frustration. Liberated from Conway's influence, it improved, the humour and joy returning. In Skardu, after the others had departed, he agreed a price for a beautifully decorated dress being worn by a pretty girl; it was to be delivered the following day. Only when the girl arrived did he realise that the transaction had been seen differently from the other side, 'and it appeared that what I had purchased was not the dress, but the contents. I explained that I had no use for them, and they then gave vent to what I am quite sure was something very superior in the way of heathen profanity.' Later, Eckenstein was bitten by an insect he did not see but which 'to judge by its biting power, seems descended from a crocodile'.

And so Eckenstein leaves the K2 story, but one more passage from his book has to be mentioned as it relates to the question that all of us who climb have met at some stage. In one village the headman requested that he be allowed to ask this visiting European a number of questions. In the main they were what one might expect: do you work for a living? do you have money?, and so on. But then the man asked Eckenstein why he had come to the area when he could easily have stopped in Kashmir, 'where everything could be obtained that man might desire'. Eckenstein answered that he 'prefers mountains'. The man was clearly puzzled: 'but mountains were rough and difficult to travel on', and hard work. Eckenstein responded that he liked such work. But how could he like such work, the man asks, 'how could a sensible man prefer to make himself uncomfortable?' 'Well,' writes Eckenstein, 'that was rather too much of a poser for me.' And for many more climbers since.

With Eckenstein gone, the others headed north from Askole, Conway noting that the Biafo Glacier had retreated significantly since Godwin-Austen's visit thirty-one years before. Eventually they reached the Baltoro, of which Conway writes:

> Undoubtedly this glacier far surpasses in discomfort, and in the size of its mounds, both the Hispar and the Biafo. They are a Piccadilly promenade to it. There can scarcely be in the world anything more loathsome and fatiguing to travel over. And what made matters worse was that, when we climbed to the top of an exceptionally high mound, and could see from it about two days' journey up the glacier, there was still nothing but stones in sight, so that the hope of better things deserted us, though even then we did not know the worst.

For two days they trudged along the glacier in rain, with Conway noting that the route was continually 'inhospitable'. Then the weather improved, as did the view as they arrived at a point where the Baltoro, Conway thought, was formed by the confluence of three separate glaciers. He writes:

The great Baltoro glacier is formed by the union, at the west foot of Gusherbrum [*sic*], of three chief affluents. I named them Godwin-Austen glacier, Throne glacier, and Vigne glacier. The Godwin-Austen glacier descends from K.2. The Vigne glacier comes in from the south, and is fed by the snows of the Chogolisa peaks. The Throne glacier divides, about eight miles above the great crossing, or *Place de la Concorde* (as a similar place at the head of the Aletsch glacier is called), into two branches, and between them rises a rounded mountain mass.

Today Throne Glacier is considered to be the 'true' Baltoro, Conway's name being discarded. What has not been discarded is his *Place de la Concorde*, though this is now known by its German form, Concordia. Conway also named several local peaks: Golden Throne (now known as Baltoro Kangri), Bride Peak (even though he also refers to Chogolisa, though as a range rather than a specific top), Mitre Peak, Pioneer Peak, Crystal Peak and, perhaps most famously, Broad Peak and Hidden Peak.[20]

Conway's team climbed Crystal Peak (5913m/19,315ft) and Pioneer Peak (6550m/21,484ft). The latter was climbed by Conway, Bruce and Zurbriggen, together with the Gurkhas Harkbir and Parbir, McCormick having been unable to accompany them as he was suffering from headaches and toothache. Conway had stopped smoking above 20,000ft because of problems a few days earlier, but at the summit, despite the fact that all the party 'felt weak and ill, like men just lifted from beds of sickness', Zurbriggen lit a celebratory cigar. In his book (see Note 23) Aleister Crowley claims that the porters on Conway's expedition told him in 1895 that the Pioneer Peak ascent claim was false, the climbers turning back after reaching the ice-fall at the foot of the peak. Given the climbing ability of the team that seems very unlikely – perhaps it was another case of porters telling sahibs what they wanted to hear.

Conway optimistically claimed that Pioneer Peak was over 23,000ft high, a claim in keeping with his curious view that Golden Throne, of which Pioneer is a satellite peak, was the most impressive of the local mountains. Of K2 he was dismissive. Climbing to a saddle on the north side of the Baltoro in the hope of seeing K2 from base to summit, Conway and McCormick were disappointed to find their view partially blocked by a snow ridge above which

there rose into the air an ugly mass of rock, without nobility of form or grandeur of mass, broken up into a number of small masses of snow. McCormick, with his bag of blocks and colours, cried out in disgust, 'What have I brought these here for?' and down we both sat in comfortless positions on angular rocks, and lit our pipes for solace.

When climbing Pioneer Peak, Conway notes that 'Gusherbrum, the Broad Peak and K.2 showed their clouded heads over the north ridge of the Throne, and were by no means striking objects'. The classic view of the peak from the south is dismissed in one sentence: 'K.2 showed himself from time to time, but not in a picturesque fashion', though Conway's book is illustrated by beautiful drawings of it by McCormick. And finally, 'In fact, under almost any circumstance of light and weather, Gusherbrum [sic: Conway is actually referring to Gasherbrum IV] is a finer mountain from this side than his loftier neighbour. The north face of K.2 appears to be its best front.' As Curran has pointed out,[21] Conway must have based the final sentence on information from Younghusband as the North Face is not visible from the Baltoro. Curran also wonders at the curiosity of Conway's insistence on Golden Throne over K2 as the dominant peak at Concordia and concludes that it can only be explained by sour grapes. That does indeed seem the only logical explanation: having decided, ironically, given the friction between himself and Eckenstein over the aims of the expedition, to climb something, Conway had to choose a target. But the big peaks – K2, Gasherbrum, Masherbrum – were just too difficult to contemplate. It was therefore preferable to have a go at the lower, more amenable Golden Throne. And having agreed that necessity, it was even more preferable to suggest that the reason for the choice was that it is actually more aesthetically pleasing, a 'better' peak.

But that is a minor grouse. Conway's had been a major journey of exploration, even if the actual climbing accomplished was minimal. In the absence of anything written by Roberto Lerco, and with Conway having been scrupulous in terms of surveying the area, as far as he was able, the expedition had laid down an excellent framework for the future.

Eckenstein and Crowley, 1902
During the period from 1899 to 1912 further explorations were made in the area around the Hispar and Biafo glaciers by Fanny Bullock-Workman and her much put-upon husband William Hunter Workman,[22] though it was to take later journeys to prove some of the pair's geographical claims to be false. The couple's enthusiasm for the Karakoram apparently derived from a snap decision to visit Ladakh during a bicycle tour of the sub-continent. In all they made seven journeys to the area, an astonishing achievement given that they had no mountaineering experience prior to their first trip. Their journeys filled in some geographical gaps, but they did not approach K2 or make any claim to be attempting an ascent. That was most definitely not the case with an expedition which made its way along the Baltoro in 1902, that trip having set out with the intention of climbing the world's second highest mountain.

The expedition's leader was Oscar Eckenstein, and his deputy was Aleister Crowley.[23] The friendship between Eckenstein and Crowley, seventeen years his junior, seems so unlikely that it is worth considering its origins. Crowley commented of Eckenstein after his death that provided the older man 'could get three fingers on something that could be described by a man far advanced in hashish as a ledge, would be smoking his pipe on that ledge a few seconds later, and none of us could tell how he had done it'. Tom Longstaff (see Note 33), a young man who was to become a leading British climber of his day (in 1907 he was to reach the summit of Trisul, 7120m/23,354ft, with Alexis and Henri Brocherel, who were later to be on the Italian 1909 K2 expedition; at that time Trisul was the highest summit to have been definitely reached), was once in Montenvers with Eckenstein and Crowley. The former gave him a sensational exhibition of the value of crampons by sitting Longstaff on his back while perched on a steep ice slope. But Longstaff also notes that Crowley had made the first climb up the true right side of the Mer de Glace, a dangerous and difficult route, solo. Longstaff and Crowley had decided to go over the Col de Géant, but Crowley had been feeling unfit and so started out an hour early. Halfway up his route he was yelled at by Longstaff's guide for taking the wrong route, and when the party met up was told that what he had done was impossible. Crowley offered 150 francs to anyone who would repeat his climb: there were no takers.

It seems that Eckenstein and Crowley had much in common: both were considered outsiders by the British establishment, and both took their climbing seriously. Crowley was impressed by the older man's technical ability and innovative ideas, Eckenstein by the younger man's willingness to take risks. That Eckenstein's friendship was not in the least based on any sympathy with Crowley's wild ideas is clear, the latter writing that 'he openly jeered at me for wasting my time on such rubbish'. On one occasion Eckenstein told Crowley to 'Give up your Magick, with all its romantic fascinations and deceitful delights. Promise to do this for a time and I will teach you to master your mind.' Rather than reject the notion and dismiss its proposer, as might have been expected, Crowley took Eckenstein up on the idea, listened and learned, though ultimately he went back to his old ways.

The two men had been together in the Alps and in 1901 made a climbing trip to Mexico (where Crowley practised the art of becoming invisible and persuaded himself that his image in a mirror had become faint and flickering: it would be fascinating to hear what Eckenstein's scientific mind thought of it). The Himalaya therefore seemed the logical next step. Before departure they drew up an agreement between them which was imposed on the other members. It gave Eckenstein leadership of the expedition, though Crowley could also be leader if the two agreed. No other member of the expedition was allowed to be leader. Two interesting clauses of the agreement were:

4. The Leader's orders shall be otherwise without appeal, and shall be obeyed cheerfully and to the best of ability: except that no member of the party is to be obliged anywhere to risk his life, his own judgement to be the arbiter as to

whether such and such an order involves danger, whether from men, starvation, animals or other causes.

5. All members pledge themselves to have nothing whatever to do with women in any way that is possibly avoidable: not to purchase any article without O.E.'s knowledge and consent; not to interfere in any way whatever with native prejudices and beliefs.

The other members of the team were Guy Knowles, Heinrich Pfannl, Victor Wesseley and Jules Jacot-Guillarmod.[24] Crowley was to complain that the Austrians could not comprehend the scale of what was intended, noting that Pfannl 'proposed to rush Chogo Ri [the name Crowley consistently used in his writings] from Askole. He thought he could get there and back in three days.' Of Jacot-Guillarmod, Crowley writes:

he knew as little of mountains as he did of medicine, and proved a great source of weakness, though his delightful geniality helped both with the psychology of the party and our relations with the natives. He was our comic relief and did much to make things more tolerable for all of us. For all that, I think we should have done better to take none of the foreigners.

This faint praise is in sharp contrast to another opinion set down in the same book in which Crowley stated that taking Jacot-Guillarmod to K2 was 'the one great mistake of my climbing career ... utterly ignorant, vain and untrustworthy'. Yet he subsequently took the doctor on his expedition to Kangchenjunga in 1905 – perhaps Jacot-Guillarmod's ability to boost team morale outweighed his faults.

As in 1892 the journey started in *ekkas*, Crowley noting that the device is impossible for one European to use in comfort while 'a second constitutes outrageous overcrowding. A party of eight or ten natives, on the other hand, finds itself at ease.' But the expedition had not travelled far when a telegram arrived, followed by the deputy commissioner of Rawalpindi in person, to say that Eckenstein was not being allowed into Kashmir. The exact reason for this decision has never been identified. Crowley thought Conway was behind it, keeping Eckenstein out of the Karakoram being a continuation of the 1892 feud, but there is no evidence to support that. He also suggested that there were fears about Eckenstein being a Prussian spy. Given his German surname and the continued heightened suspicions over Russian aims in central Asia (within 12 months Younghusband would be marching on Tibet to counter a perceived Russian threat), this is not an altogether ludicrous idea, despite Eckenstein having been in the area previously. Indeed Crowley notes that as the remaining team members travelled to Srinigar, 'there were all sorts of excitement at the frontier, and telegrams and spies were bustling about. It reminded me of the turmoil in an ant-heap which had been disturbed.' Another idea has been put forward by Louis Baume,[25] who contends that an erroneous press report suggesting Eckenstein's real plan was an attempt on Everest had reached the ears of Lord Curzon, Viceroy of India. As Curzon was quietly negotiating with the Nepalese for a British expedition to be allowed into that country to reconnoitre Everest from the south, an illicit attempt from Tibet would have created political waves, so Curzon vetoed the trip. This seems credible, but it begs the question of why only Eckenstein was stopped, though as he was the expedition leader and the only man with prior knowledge of the area he might have been regarded as the main threat. Of course, no one contemplating an attempt on Everest from the north would start from Rawalpindi, but the official mind moves mysteriously. In the event, Eckenstein gained an audience with Curzon and, whatever the problem was, it was smoothed away, Eckenstein rejoining his team after three weeks had been lost.

The onward march to the Baltoro went reasonably smoothly, Crowley describing his impressions in unusually lyrical terms: 'The scenery is exhilaratingly grand and beautiful, and the climate perfect. The whole thing may be described as an exaggeration of all that is best and loveliest in the Alps, plus the enchantment of Asiatic atmosphere.' But later he remarks on the 'utter monotony and ugliness of the landscape. The mountains are huge heaps of shapeless drab', suggesting that, as with all travellers, Crowley's opinion on the view was dependent on tiredness, state of health, etc.

As the days passed, cracks began to appear in the team. The Austrians 'had become rather a nuisance ... We encouraged them to go off all day and make heroic ascents.' It was at this time that Pfannl and Wesseley suggested a three-day ascent of K2, Crowley noting how astonishing it was that 'so many days of travel had taught them nothing about the scale of the mountains'. But despite his ire, Crowley had not learned either. Later he objected to Eckenstein when refused permission to cross the bergschrund to the base of K2's 'south-eastern slopes' because had he crossed it 'I could have gone on without any difficulty up those slopes to the well-marked shoulder immediately beneath the final pyramid, and had I done so, I have no doubt whatever that we could have made a successful dash for the summit.' The camp at the bergschrund was Camp 10, reached after the team had arrived at the junction of three major and several minor glaciers which reminded Crowley 'of the Concordia Platz in the Oberland', which he had therefore named as such 'in affectionate remembrance.' Given that Conway had named it for exactly the same reason ten years earlier, this is a marvellous piece of completely shameless effrontery.

From the Godwin-Austen Glacier Crowley had an uninterrupted view of K2 and could see that there 'should be no difficulty in walking up the snow slopes on the east-south-east to the snowy shoulder below the final rock pyramid'. Crowley's description has previously been discussed by Curran,[26] who, while acknowledging that he had correctly identified the line of weakness on the southern side of the mountain that would eventually be exploited, had completely failed to identify any of the obvious difficulties climbers on that route would need to overcome.

Camp 10 was established by Crowley at 5711m (18,733ft) below the point from which he intended to launch his final assault. Eckenstein criticised the position as lacking shelter, which Crowley thought unreasonable as his explorations in the area had convinced him there was no more suitable site and that no weather 'would make Camp 10 other than a desirable country residence for a gentleman in failing health'. Camp 10 was not moved and the whole team gathered there towards the end of June. A period of bad weather kept them at the camp until early July, when a reconnaissance by Pfannl and Wesseley suggested the North-East Ridge offered an easier ascent than Crowley's. They were very wrong: this ridge was not climbed until 1978, when a strong American team spent many weeks following it. But in 1902, with the decision made, Camp 11 was placed close to the ridge's base, at about 6100m (20,000ft). From here Crowley climbed to a height that he claimed was at least 6555m (21,500ft), perhaps 6710m (22,000ft), but then fell ill, apparently with a recurrence of malaria. He was high enough, he says, to see clearly over Windy Gap, at 6150m (20,172ft). Assuming the height Crowley claims is correct, and he was not a man given to self-doubt, he suggested it was a world-record height for a malaria sufferer. He also noted, with what one might call characteristic modesty, that 'I have always been very amused at Shelley's boast that he had "trodden the glaciers of the Alps" – the Mer de Glace and Glacier des Boissons! But I was actually writing poetry in these camps. *Better* poetry.'

However, the accounts of the expedition of Pfannl and Jacot-Guillarmod make no mention of Crowley's climb. The day after Crowley said he made his solo climb, Wesseley and Jacot-Guillarmod climbed from the camp, Jacot-Guillarmod writing: 'Departure was set for 5am, but we waited half-an-hour for the sun to warm the air as the temperature last night was -12.5°C.' The snow was also cold, freezing the two men's feet. The climbing was easy at first, but then the angle steepened:

Wessely [*sic*] breaks trail, but is forced to rest every fifty steps: it is easier for me as I only have to follow his tracks ... I check the aneroid: at 6.05am we are at 20,350ft, at 7am, 20,500ft and at 7.40am, 20,700ft ... the angle eases again, but at the edge of the ridge we are following there are cornices which make the going dangerous, probably too dangerous for the coolies, particularly if they are working in a metre of powder snow ... Around 11am we reach 21,600ft where there is a shelf suitable for a camp site if we levelled it a little. But then the slope steepens to 52° and snow, half-a-metre deep at every step, looks likely to avalanche ... Around noon we are at 21,800ft, but the angle steepens again. We want to make a summit on the ridge ahead where it seems there will be a suitable camp site. It is at exactly 22,000ft. I had hoped to go higher, beating the record set by Zurbriggen on Aconcagua, but Wessely says he can go no further today.

It may be that when he heard of Jacot-Guillarmod's claim of 22,000ft, Crowley's egotism got the better of him and he felt the need to make a similar claim. Whatever the truth, when the Italians surveyed the North-East Ridge in 1909 they estimated, based on the height of the obvious feature Jacot-Guillarmod mentioned, that the two had actually reached 21,400ft (6524m).

At this point Crowley stated that the two Austrians had become intolerable and were persuaded to go off together to establish Camp 12. The other accounts suggest that the two had realised that K2 would not be climbed and had suggested instead an attempt from Windy Gap on Staircase Peak (named for the appearance of its East Ridge: the peak is now called Skyang Kangri). The two Austrians established the camp at about 6400m (21,000ft). From it Wesseley climbed to Windy Gap (the name given by Jacot-Guillarmod), but the attempt on Skyang Kangri had to be abandoned when Pfannl became ill. Jacot-Guillarmod climbed up to help, and it became clear that the Austrian was actually very ill indeed, and had to be brought down, the diagnosis being oedema of both lungs. Crowley also notes that Pfannl's 'mind was gone'. It is not clear who made the oedema diagnosis – it is mentioned by both Crowley and Jacot-Guillarmod in their books – but given the relatively poor understanding of high-altitude physiology at the time, it was a remarkable one. Perhaps Jacot-Guillarmod was a rather better doctor than Crowley gives him credit for.[27] Knowles also mentions oedema but puts it down to Pfannl's enthusiasm for keeping fit: 'Pfannl's breakdown, though he is a very hard and muscular man, does not surprise me so very much. It is, in my opinion, due absolutely to over-training. Ever since he got on the ship at Suez he has never ceased taking exercise at every opportunity.'

In his own accounts, Pfannl is dismissive of the illness: though admitting he was ill, he insisted that his move to a lower camp was because it was his lungs that were the problem and that 'respiratory organs need close attention'. Prior to this statement he noted that he and Wesseley had once spent time around the Finsteraarhorn when he (Pfannl) was convalescing from a bronchial problem, suggesting that he may have had a history of respiratory illness. Jacot-Guillarmod also notes in his book that Pfannl had had two bouts of oedema in Europe, each at altitude. This seems unlikely, though, of course, Jacot-Guillarmod had not been present either time and so was making a judgement based on symptoms only. Pfannl also implied that his descent was as much to do with bad weather as ill-health, though Crowley said that the need to get Pfannl down prevented him from making use of the last of the good weather, as he was 'obliged to superintend the caravan of invalids'.

Pfannl's illness brought the expedition to an end, though the return to civilisation brought its own traumas. On the way down the Baltoro, Jacot-Guillarmod appeared at a camp alone. When asked the whereabouts of his porter he said 'he had left that specimen of the Creator's handiwork in a crevasse'.

Eckenstein and Crowley immediately went back and rescued the man. Next Wesseley was found to have stolen all the emergency rations. It was decided to expel him from the expedition, the recovered Pfannl going with him. Pfannl makes no mention of an early departure in his accounts, or of any team problems, while Jacot-Guillarmod merely states that the two Austrians left for '*raisons particulières*', giving no further details.

For Crowley the departure of the Austrians was probably a blessing as Wesseley's eating habits had revolted him:

> None of us had ever seen such a perfect pig. He was very greedy and very myopic. In order to eat, he would bend his head over his plate and, using his knife and fork like the blades of a paddle wheel, would churn the food into his mouth with a rapid rotatory motion. There was always some going up, and always some going down, until he deposited his well-sucked instruments of nutrition on a perfectly clean plate and asked for more. It was the most disgusting sight that I have ever seen. Explorers are not squeamish; but we had to turn our heads away when Wessely [*sic*] started to eat. I admit and deplore my human weakness. All forms of genius should be admired and studied and Wesseley was a world's champion.

The expedition was over, and not for the last time a trip to the high hills had ended in personal disappointment and bitterness, and collective disorder.

The Duke of the Abruzzi, 1909

It is difficult to consider the Eckenstein/Crowley expedition as a real (or, rather, realistic) attempt on K2, given the limited number of climbers and the inadequacy of both equipment and understanding of the magnitude of the task. The same could also be said of the Italian expedition of 1909, though it is generally better regarded because it was much more successful in terms of both exploring potential routes on the mountain and in making ascents in the area. The expedition was led and organised by the Duke of the Abruzzi,[28] and included Vittorio Sella,[29] one of the finest of all mountain photographers. In addition to Sella, the expedition included Filippo De Filippi,[30] a scientist who had been with the Duke on the Mount St Elias and Rwenzori trips, Federico Negrotto Cambiaso, a surveyor, and seven mountain guides. Filippi was interested in the physiology of man at high altitude, and also collected geological and botanical samples: his book includes appendices on both, as well as meteorological and survey data. The guides were Joseph and Laurent Petigax (father and son), the brothers Alexis and Henri Brocherel (who had been with Longstaff on Trisul), Emil Brocherel, Albert Savoia and Ernest Bareux.

Filippi and his fellow travellers were no more impressed with ekkas than their predecessors had been, but all survived the experience. Filippi seems to have spent much of the early part of the journey worrying about the geography of the area, his book including long discourses on the opinions expressed by Conway on the reasons for the desolate nature of the Indus valley. But he also shows a greater, and more compassionate, interest in the local Baltis than did the English travellers who had preceded him: Filippi notes, for instance, that in one village in each of three cemeteries most graves are those of children, a clear indication of his understanding of the tribulations of these mountain people, with high rates of infant mortality being an inevitable consequence of poverty and the unavoidable lack of hygiene. When reading this passage, it is difficult not to recall Conway's midnight raid on a cemetery and his acquisition of specimen skulls. Filippi also notes the reaction of the Askole men when they saw the equipment which was to be handed out to them – 'the mere sight of all this wealth filled the coolies[31] with joy' – and the way in which they made chapattis for daily consumption, wrapping flat cakes of dough around red-hot pebbles and rolling them across a hot stone slab. The daily ration given to the porters was one *seer* (about 900g) of coarse meal. This was hardly generous, and indeed Filippi notes that he knew of 'no other race capable of an equal amount of work in such a severe climate, upon nourishment so poor in quality and meagre in quantity'. Perhaps to compensate, or to assuage their collective conscience, the Italians occasionally gave as 'a special reward a little tea, sugar or tobacco'.

For whatever reason – better food, better health at the start of the expedition, better mountain conditioning – the Italians were in superior condition to the 1902 team when they reached the Baltoro. Guillarmod writes (see Note 24) that he and the other team members noted the first signs of altitude sickness as they approached the glacier, despite having spent eight days at Askole, whereas Filippi writes that the Italian team had no such experience and arrived in good health and spirits. On the Baltoro, Filippi was entranced by the views of the surrounding peaks, noting when 'marvellous and symmetric' Gasherbrum IV came into view, the 'marvellous Masherbrum ... its gigantic northern wall deeply furrowed and loaded with glaciers breaking into icefalls down the sides of a tremendous central rib of rock', the Mustagh Tower standing up 'alone and menacing. It has not even yet revealed the full splendour of its outlines.' And, finally, K2,

the indisputable sovereign of the region, gigantic and solitary, hidden from human sight by innumerable ranges, jealously defended by a vast throng of vassal peaks, protected from invasion by miles and miles of glaciers. Even to get within sight of it demands so much contrivance, so much marching, such a sum of labours. It fills the whole end of the valley, with nothing to draw attention from it. All the lines of the landscape seem to meet and converge in it. The mountains group themselves about it, yet without any intrusion upon it or interference with its extraordinary upward effort. Its lines are ideally proportioned and perfectly balanced, its architectural design is powerful, adequate to the majesty of the peak without being heavy; the steepness of its sides, its ridges and its glaciers is appalling; its rocky wall is 12,000 feet high. For a whole hour we stood absorbed.

As a description, it could hardly be improved. And to think that Conway was disappointed with K2 in comparison to the view of Golden Throne.

But for the Italian climbers, their first view of K2 also filled them with dismay:

We gazed, we minutely inspected, we examined with our glasses the incredible rock wall. All the time our minds were assailed with increasing doubt, culminating almost in certainty, that this side of the mountain was not accessible, and did not offer even a reasonable point of attack. Meantime the atmosphere grew gradually thicker, the veil of whitish vapour heavier, stretching and expanding and melting together, until even the last spectral image disappeared and a uniform grey curtain of mist filled the end of the valley. The vision was gone.

K2, it seemed, had observed these men who had the temerity to challenge it, had given them a glimpse of its strengths, enough to appal them and douse the fire of their enthusiasm, and then quietly withdrawn.

But within a few days the Italians had recovered from the shock of that first sight of the mountain and had decided to move closer and explore for weaknesses. The Duke took a team along the Godwin-Austen (K2) Glacier and found

a small stretch of marginal moraine, shut in between the valley wall and the side of the Godwin Austen, below a depression in the south-western spur of K2 [Negrotto Pass]. Here there was a refuge from falling stones and ice, protected on three sides from the wind, and getting the sun from early morning till four in the afternoon. Upon this spot the Duke fixed his camp.

It was the spot that all subsequent expeditions would also use (though it is only fair to point out that Eckenstein and Crowley had camped in much the same spot seven years earlier). From this camp two parties set out. One, comprising four of the guides, went further up the Godwin-Austen to probe the eastern side of the mountain. They returned with discouraging news: 'the long north-eastern ridge was out of the question, as well as the whole eastern side of the mountain, which was extremely steep, covered in ice and exposed to avalanches and séracs.' But the ridge running from the glacier to the 'edge of the great snowy shoulder of the mountain' seemed to offer more chance. Meanwhile, the Duke explored the glacier that ran along the western side of the peak (the Savoia, which links with the Praqpa before joining the Godwin-Austen). From there he could see the Savoia Saddle (marked as 6666m in the Appendix map of Filippi's book, but now mapped at 6250m). This seemed to offer the chance of an ascent because descending to it was the 'north-western ridge of the mountain, which is less steep than the southern ridge. If one could, with the help of the coolies, once set up a camp on this saddle, there would remain only about 6,500 feet to conquer between it and the peak.' The Italians had clearly regained their optimism.

Having returned from the Savoia Glacier, the Duke considered the two identified options and decided that the southern ridge offered the best chance of success. Scanning his chosen route, the Duke noticed a prominent red-yellow rock on the well-defined spur that appeared to offer good chances of success. His plan was to establish a camp at the base of the spur, then to climb to the rock, where another camp would be set up. From there, he believed, the snowy shoulder could be easily reached. He reasoned that although the route above might prove impossible, reaching the Shoulder itself would be a major achievement. Together with several of the guides he therefore set out for the base of what is now termed the Abruzzi Spur.

Leaving the Duke at the camp, the guides climbed the Spur. At first things went well and they returned to report that they thought there would be 'no very grave obstacles to encounter'. But when they continued up the next day things began to look much less rosy. Rather than a well-defined and comfortably negotiable ridge, 'they found themselves on a slender crest of rocks quite broken and crumbling, so as to give no security to the foot nor safe hold for the hands'. The climbing was also exposed. But worst of all, the men were discovering the true scale of the challenge, the 'incredible optical illusions they suffered, all due to the deceptiveness of these mountains. Slabs of rock which at a few yards distant looked like gentle and easy inclines, turned out to be little less than perpendicular.' To add to the perspective problems, there was the problem of distance – 'climbing always toward the reddish rock … and never reaching it, though it always seemed constantly within a few steps of them'. Ultimately the guides gave up, not because the climbing was too difficult, but because it had become clear that the undertaking was too much – they could never, they believed, make the route safe for the porters, and the idea of a quick, essentially lightweight, ascent was just not tenable. Reluctantly they retreated, bringing the bad news back to the Duke, who immediately called off any further attempt.

It can be argued that the Italians had fared no better than Eckenstein and Crowley, making little more progress and making the same mistakes as regards what was involved. But that would be unfair: the Duke had explored the climbing options in a much more systematic way, and when the main prize proved elusive, was intent on pushing the boundaries of man at altitude as far as possible.

But before attempting a lower peak the Duke decided to complete his exploration of K2. He therefore first went back along the Savoia Glacier and climbed to the

Savoia Saddle. From there he could see little of the north side of the mountain, but enough of the west flank to 'utterly annihilate the hopes with which he had begun the ascent', those hopes being the possibility of an easier route. It would be seventy years before K2 was climbed from the west, proving the Duke's judgement correct. Of the climb to the saddle, Filippi notes that the Duke and his three guides arrived back at a camp established on the glacier after a 16-hour day spent between 18,000ft and 20,000ft (about 5500m–6100m), and involving some steep ice climbing, showing no signs of exhaustion – a remarkable testament to their fitness.

The Duke now turned his attention to the eastern side of K2 and a team climbed to Windy Gap (6234m/20,449ft), where, to emphasise the name, 'a villainous wind was blowing'. From the pass the view of K2's East Face was impressive: 'it looked like another mountain entirely; and of all the manifold aspects of the colossus this is certainly the most imposing, the richest and boldest in design. Alas, it is also such as to annihilate the last remnant of hope that might linger in the mind of the mountaineer.' But the Duke decided that there was a chance to climb Skyang Kangri ('Staircase Peak', 7357m/24,131ft). Setting off with the three guides, but obliged to send back the ailing Henri Brocherel, the Duke reached about 6600m (21,650ft) before abandoning the attempt in the face of difficult ground. During the trip to the Gap he found articles left by the Eckenstein/Crowley expedition at the 1902 Camp 10, allowing a calculation of the rate of flow of the Godwin-Austen Glacier. It was 214m/year which equated to a speed of about 0.6m/day (just under 2ft/day).

The exploration of K2 was over, and the Duke could make a final judgement on it. He had seen it from west, south, east and north-east, and on each side it was 'equally fortified with the most formidable defences against the attack of the mountain climber'. After weeks of examination, after hours of contemplation and search for the secret of the mountain, the Duke was finally obliged to yield to the conviction that K2 was not to be climbed: 'Its height is not a factor in the case. It is the obstacles peculiar to mountain climbing and familiar to the mountaineer that closes the paths of ascent to K2.' Having noted that statements of inaccessibility require exhaustive evidence (and have invariably been proved wrong over the years of climbing history), Filippi goes on to suggest that if the peak were in the Alps a siege of several years would end in success unless, and here he contradicts himself, height proved a 'physiological obstacle not to be overcome'. But the Karakoram is not the Alps, he notes, and camping near the peak's base for more than a few weeks is impossible, and the climate often unfavourable. He concludes the paragraph with a further thought on an Alpine K2, noting that 'step by step a way would be gained up one of the ridges' of such a peak, and then adds a final sentence: 'The giant would probably claim its victims, but in the end would yield perhaps to repeated assaults.' So it was to prove. And so it continues to prove.

The Duke bade farewell to K2, but he had not yet done with the Karakoram, still having plans to make a significant ascent. He turned his attention to Chogolisa

(Bride Peak) and after following the Baltoro eastwards attacked the eastern side of the mountain, which was 'quite clothed in glaciers falling from a height of some 5,500 feet, great foaming white cataracts like frozen Niagaras'. Despite this far from optimistic prospect, the Duke set up a series of camps on the eastern side, following a rising line around to the eastern ridge. Chogolisa Saddle was reached and a camp established there at 6335m (20,780ft). But the conditions then deteriorated, with waist-deep, soft snow which meant that the Duke, Joe Petigax, Henri Brocherel and Emil Brocherel were forced to camp again at 6607m (21,673ft). The next day they reached 7151m (23,458ft) before bad weather forced them to retreat back down to the Saddle. The men were then marooned by bad weather for four days. Their health seems remarkably good during this period and subsequently, with no reports of headaches or breathing difficulties, and with pulse rates that were as for sea-level (the Duke's resting pulse was 60 beats/min at the Saddle camp – 6335m – while those of the three guides were abut 70). The only indication of high-altitude living seems to have been a reduction in appetite.

When good weather returned, the Duke's team started up again, this time camping at 6854m (22,483ft). Next day, in poor weather, they made one last effort, reaching a height they calculated, by barometer, as 7498m (24,593ft).[32] At that point poor visibility put an end to further progress. The men waited for 2 hours, but it became clear that the weather was not going to improve quickly enough for them to continue and still return safely to camp by nightfall. Though the men were still fit, the weather, which had offered only one fine day in the previous 14, seemed to have become resolutely bad, and the Duke called time on his expedition.

Overall the Italian expedition had been a major success. K2 had been explored and a likely route to the summit identified. The Baltoro had been further surveyed so that future expeditions would be working from excellent maps. On Chogolisa it seems reasonable to assume that the Duke would have summitted if the weather had been other than dreadful, and he and his team had achieved a height record, one which would stand for thirteen years until bettered by the British on Everest.

The Duke of Spoleto, 1929

In the same year that the Duke of the Abruzzi was considering potential routes on K2, the British climber Tom Longstaff[33] was exploring in the eastern Karakoram with two other Britons. The team crossed the Saltoro Pass and made important discoveries on the positions of the huge eastern glaciers. They also discovered the Teram Kangri range of mountains, which had not been previously surveyed, causing a great deal of excitement when data from triangulation of the main peak using a short baseline of estimated length yielded a height of over 30,000ft when analysed by the Indian Survey at Dehra Dun. When an improved survey was carried out in 1911, the main peak was actually just below 24,500ft.

As a result of Longstaff's explorations in the east, and further explorations in the Shaksgam valley area.[34] the mapping of the Karakoram had been improved, many gaps having been filled in. But there was still work to be done and in 1929 another Italian expedition arrived in the Karakoram with a very ambitious programme. In the event, the Italians were highly successful, but the expedition's inception had been far from auspicious.

In the aftermath of the First World War the Paris Peace Conference gave Italy much less than it had been promised in terms of new lands and colonies, despite it having been on the winning side. Almost bankrupted by the foreign loans needed to support the war effort, and having lost over half a million men in the fighting, there was both simmering resentment and widespread poverty among the population, a mix which the political left sought to exploit. Fear that the unrest caused by unemployment and the plight of the rural poor might spark revolution – only a few years before, in 1917, the Bolshevik Revolution had overthrown the established order in Russia – the property- and business-owning classes threw their weight behind a new movement, the Fascists, headed by Benito Mussolini. Having started out with a vaguely left-wing agenda, Mussolini altered his outlook to accommodate his powerful new friends, taking an increasingly anti-Communist stance and embracing capitalist economics. In addition he established a strong foreign policy, one which reflected the national mood. Unified only fifty years before, and shabbily treated at Paris, Italy needed to restore its national pride and establish its rightful place among nations.

In 1928 the city of Milan, then as now the capital of northern Italy and powerhouse of the Italian economy, decided to both celebrate the tenth anniversary of the ending of the war and place Italy at the forefront of world exploration by underwriting two expeditions, one to reach the North Pole and the other to climb a high Himalayan peak; the latter would be led by Giotto Dainelli,[35] who had been a member of a 1913–14 expedition to the Karakoram led by Filippo De Filippi (who had been with the Duke of the Abruzzi in 1909). Though this expedition had not gone to the Baltoro, it had carried out important scientific and surveying work and had resulted in Filippi receiving the Royal Geographical Society's Gold Medal and an honorary knighthood (KCIE – Knight Commander of the Indian Empire). Perhaps because of his Karakoram experience, coupled with the exploration and mapping of 1909, Dainelli suggested K2 as the Himalayan mountain of choice, with Broad Peak as reserve, but declined leadership of the expedition. Details of the North Pole expedition are scant, but would almost certainly have involved Umberto Nobile, who had designed the airship *Norge* which had successfully overflown the North Pole in 1926.[36] But in May 1928 Nobile was involved in a disastrous Arctic journey. Having begun to believe his own propaganda that he was a brilliant polar explorer and airship pilot, Nobile took a new craft, *Italia*, and a largely Italian crew back to Svalbard to repeat the North Pole flight. On the return from the pole low cloud caused heavy icing of the airship fabric, causing the craft to sink rapidly. It hit the ice and the gondola was ripped off. The airship, and six men still within the balloon structure, immediately headed upwards and were never seen again. On the ice, one man was dead, Nobile had a broken arm and leg, and others had severe injuries. The damaged radio was eventually restored to working order and an SOS was picked up in Arkhangelsk. A plane flown to the site of the crash had room for just one survivor and Nobile was duly taken to safety, together with his dog. On the next trip the plane crashed, the pilot surviving to become another member of the survivor team. One man of a trio that tried to walk to safety died, and another died from frostbite injuries soon after rescue. There were rumours that the third man had survived by resorting to cannibalism. The survivors on the ice were eventually rescued by a Soviet ship. Worst of all, Roald Amundsen had borrowed an aircraft to help in the search for the lost men: he and five others were killed when it disappeared on the way to Spitsbergen. The press had a field day at Nobile's expense – Italian general saves himself and his dog before his companions – and a furious Mussolini demoted him.[37]

The *Italia* disaster, coupled with Dainelli's refusal to act as leader, dampened Milan's enthusiasm for a Karakoram climbing expedition – one blow to Italian pride was already one too many. It would also have reverberations twenty-five years later when the nation returned to K2. But in 1928 work was already in hand for the scientific programme that was to have been carried out in parallel with the mountaineering expedition, and it was decided that this programme should continue. After Dainelli's refusal the leadership was given to the Duke of the Abruzzi's nephew, the Duke of Spoleto,[38] whose appointment seems largely due to his aristocratic connections as Spoleto himself appears to have had little of his uncle's enthusiasm for mountaineering and exploration. The Duke's team included the respected geologist Ardito Desio, who was later, of course, to lead the expedition which made the first successful ascent of K2. From various accounts of the expedition it seems Desio supplied much of the enthusiasm on the trip and did most of the work.

The expedition comprised twelve members, the sciences of anthropology, botany, geography and zoology being included, as well as geology. Survey work was also carried out. Five of the team were climbers, but these were included solely to aid the scientists in travelling through mountain country or to reach specific study areas. After reaching the Baltoro, Desio and three climbers followed the Muztagh Glacier and crossed the Old Muztagh Pass, the aim being to circumnavigate K2, finding a pass to the east in order to regain the Baltoro. Having crossed the pass, Desio took the first photograph of K2 from the north. In the Shaksgam valley the team split into two, Desio continuing east with three climbers and a group of porters. They saw Windy Gap from the north, then crossed the North Gasherbrum Glacier to the Urdok Glacier. With supplies running short, Desio sent two of the climbers back to the Shaksgam, continuing with only Umberto Balestreri and a group of porters. Desio had hoped to reach the Conway Saddle (in the Baltoro Kangri (Golden Throne) group) but that proved impossible. He therefore went east to the Staghar Glacier, hoping that might give easier access. Spoleto calls the glacier *Stagar,* meaning 'many coloured', and says it was so-named by the Balti porters because it comprised 'alternating strips of ice and moraine'. Progress was eventually stopped by the Singhie Glacier (Spoleto calls the glacier *Singye* – 'difficult' – and says it was named by Desio's porters, for obvious reasons) and the two Italians were forced to retrace their steps, recrossing the Old Muztagh Pass to regain the Baltoro.

On the Baltoro the remaining members of the expedition had set up a camp on the Conway Saddle, making a complete survey of the upper Baltoro, around Baltoro Kangri, as they awaited Desio's return. Subsequently Desio completed further glaciological studies on the Trango Glacier and several glaciers further west – the Panmah, Choktoi, Nobande Sobande and Chiring, among others. As we shall see, in the prelude to the 1954 K2 expedition, as well as during and after it, Desio's behaviour was questionable. But the importance of his geological work in the Karakoram cannot be denied. Equally clear when reading the accounts of the 1929 expedition is the man's boundless energy and continuing enthusiasm for his work. He had his 32nd birthday on the expedition and was six months in the field, a tribute to his fitness and persistence.

The 1929 expedition is a tribute not only to Desio but to the entire team, not least because when the Italians left the Baltoro, bad weather and flooded rivers made the outward trek an epic feat of endurance, but their perseverance in the face of miserable conditions meant that all of the collected scientific results and specimens were successfully brought out.

After their return to Europe, Spoleto and Desio visited the RGS and Spoleto read his paper, 'The Italian Expedition to the Karakorum in 1929'. It was very well-received, Younghusband himself congratulating the Italians. He noted that the photographs reminded him of his own journey and were the best ever taken, though having spoken with Desio he was sorry the best vantage point of the mountain, from Suget Jangal, had been missed due to bad weather. What an extraordinary meeting this must have been: the first man to have seen K2 from the north conversing with the man who would lead the first ascent almost seventy years after that first sighting. To complete the evening, General Bruce, leader of the 1922 Everest expedition, and Tom Longstaff also thanked the Italians for their presentation.

Shipton, 1937

In the 1920s and up to 1935 the Dutch husband and wife team of geographer Phillips Christian Visser and ethnographer Jenneatte Visser-Hooft, with various coworkers, made a series of expeditions to the Karakoram.[39] Giotto Dainelli, who had declined leadership of the Italian 1929 expedition, also explored the southern Karakoram in 1930. These trips filled in many of the gaps in the map of the area, but left some areas still unexplored, particularly the northern side of K2 and the country to the north-east (around the Aghil Pass) and north-west (around the Skamil – or Crevasse – and Braldu Glaciers). It was to this area that a small team of Britons went in 1937. The nominal leader was Eric Shipton,[40] nominal because Shipton's mountain ethos eschewed such things as defined and dictatorial leadership. Shipton was at his best with a small group of like-minded people intent on travelling, the actual objective being rather more loosely defined. The 1937 expedition was typical of the type Shipton loved. With him were Bill Tilman,[41] who shared his passion both for the hills and for small teams, and two surveyors, Michael Spender, who had been with Shipton and Tilman on the Everest reconnaissance of 1935, and John Auden of the Geological Survey of India. In reading his account of the trip, it is difficult to shake off the view that Shipton and Tilman were there to explore the countryside, while Spender and Auden were there to do the work necessary to secure funding from the Royal Geographical Society and the Survey of India.

Shipton's attitude to mountaineering lost him the leadership of the 1953 Everest expedition, but it won him many devotees over the years. In one sense that is curious, as the Britain of Shipton and Tilman was, by modern standards, an inhibited place. Throughout his account of the ascent of Kamet, author Frank Smythe refers to all the team members by surname only,[42] while Tilman's account of reaching the summit of Nanda Devi with Noel Odell (the last man to see Mallory and Irvine alive on Everest in 1924) notes, 'I believe we so far forgot ourselves as to shake hands on it.'[43] But behind these stiff social conventions were men whose attitudes to the hills still resonate today. Early in his book on the 1937 Karakoram expedition Shipton sets down views which underline his mountain philosophy: 'With a wistfulness, perhaps a little tinged with sentimentality, I think of the leisurely days of a few hundred years ago, before life was so mad a rush, before the countryside was spoiled by droves of people, and beauty itself exploited as a commercial proposition.' He continues by noting that the man who has money can take a luxury liner to Africa, hire a big game hunter for his knowledge of the bush and the prey and return home with

> a number of tall stories and several crates of trophies. But he has not lived the real life of a hunter; nor has he made the experience a part of his own life. He has taken an easy short cut to vicarious adventure. The mountaineer who goes to the Alps for a season's climbing, with a desire to climb more peaks than other men, and by more difficult routes, misses the real value of the experience – the love of mountains for their own sake. The real purpose of climbing, and of any other

sport, should be to transmute it into a way of living, however temporary, in an environment which appeals to the individual. Often when I have been climbing in the Alps I have thought how enthralling it must have been to see the Alps as De Saussure saw them, before they had been civilized out of their wild unspoiled beauty and tamed into a social asset.

There are things to discuss here, but many will concur with the essence of Shipton's view.

To complete his party, Shipton added not local porters, but seven Sherpas, including Ang Tharkay (Shipton calls him Antarkay), the best-known Sherpa of the time. The expense of bringing them from Darjeeling was justified by their performance, Shipton actually wishing he had been able to afford double the number. The trip was obviously a delight for Shipton, his pleasure shining through his prose: there is Tilman gloating over the opportunity of waking the team very early in the morning by 'clumping about self-righteously. There was no hope of sulkily defying his onslaught', and then there is Shipton gleefully getting his own back when he carried the single glacier lantern the team possessed, so that when local porters were added to the eleven team members, Tilman was 38th in the queue and 'did not derive much benefit from its faint light'. The expedition was perhaps the closest to Shipton's ideal, and the book, reflecting that, the best he wrote. But though there is much to admire and recall, it is the section dealing with K2 from the north which is of chief interest here.

The team had intended to cross the Muztagh Pass but, alerted by Ardito Desio to the possibility of crossing at the head of the Trango Glacier, they went that way, crossing the Sarpo Laggo Pass at the head of the tributary Kruksum West Glacier and descending the Sarpo Laggo Glacier to Suget Jangal, the village which Younghusband had referred to as a jungle. From there Auden, Shipton, Tilman and two Sherpas headed south along the Chogori Glacier.[44] Leaving the Sherpas behind at one point, the three Britons climbed towards a peak of 20,700ft (6311m). Auden fell ill, but Shipton and Tilman reached a sharp summit from where the view 'was astonishing … To the south were the colossal northern faces of K2, and other peaks of the main watershed, a breath-taking panorama of sweeping ridges, lofty summits and hanging glacier terraces, dazzling in the midday sun.' Later Shipton was disappointed not to have a clear view of the North Face:

Heavy mists hung in the upper glacier basin. Above them the summit of K2 appeared, floating at an incredible height above our heads … But though we waited a long time this shifting drapery of cloud still clung to the mountain, and we had to leave the ridge without a clear view of the stupendous north face.

But later, as he sat alone,

The afternoon was fine, and nothing interrupted my view of the great amphitheatre about me. The cliffs and ridges of K2 rose out of the glacier in one stupendous sweep to the summit of the mountain, 12,000 feet above. The sight was beyond my comprehension, and I sat gazing at it, with a kind of timid fascination, watching wreaths of mist creep in and out of corries utterly remote. I saw ice avalanches, weighing perhaps hundreds of tons, break off from a hanging glacier, nearly two miles above my head; the ice was ground to fine powder and drifted away in the breeze long before it reached the foot of the precipice, nor did any sound reach my ears. To the right of K2 lay the famous Savoya [*sic*] saddle which had been reached twenty-eight years before by the Duke of Abruzzi from the Baltoro glacier. It presented a formidable appearance from this side. To the left of K2 was a bewildering mass of peaks and alone gazing at the cirque forming the head of the K2 glacier was an experience I shall not forget; no mountain scene has impressed me more deeply.

Chapter 3

The Americans Head for K2

'We therefore had to go down.'

Fritz Wiessner in 1939

Bob Bates was just climbing into bed late at night when the telephone rang ...

'Yes?'

'Hello, Bob, this is Charlie. Sorry to wake you up, but I want to ask you something.'

'What is it?'

'Can you go to the Himalaya this summer?'

'What's that? What do you mean?'

'Well, the club has just received permission to send a small party to K2 and they've asked me if I could get a group together.'

'I'll be darned!'

So opens the book which relates the first genuine attempt on the world's second highest mountain.[1] The telephone call between New York and Philadelphia allowed Charles Houston, in the former city, to ask Robert Bates, in the latter, if he would be willing to join an expedition on which the two would become leader and deputy. But why were Americans thinking of K2? – or, rather, why was the established climbing world, which meant the Alpine countries of Europe and the British, *not* thinking of it?

In the period between the two world wars Nepal's borders were firmly closed to foreigners. Of the world's highest mountains that left three available in Tibet (Everest, Cho Oyu and Shisha Pangma), one in British India (Kangchenjunga) and the five in the Karakoram, of which only one, Nanga Parbat, was easily accessible. In Tibet only the British had ready access, and they were solely interested in Everest, making five attempts and sending reconnaissance parties in the inter-war years. In 1924 Edward Norton and Howard Somervell reached a height of 8570m (28,115ft), only 41m lower than the summit of K2, a record which would stand until the Swiss Everest expedition of 1952. On Kangchenjunga Aleister Crowley (with a party that included Dr Jacot-Guillarmod) made a half-hearted attempt in 1905. A real attempt had to wait until 1929, when a German expedition reached 7400m. An international team (Austrian, British, German and Swiss) did not get as high in 1930, while a second German expedition reached 7700m in 1931.

On Nanga Parbat a small team led by British climber Alfred Mummery made a genuine attempt in 1895, though with very limited success (Mummery dying on the trip), and it was not until 1932 that a German team with two American members made a more realistic attempt, reaching 7000m. The team's Germans included Fritz Wiessner (later to lead the American 1939 K2 expedition), though the financial backing for the expedition was mainly American, acquired, in part, from Wiessner's US contacts. Although there were no deaths on the expedition, in retrospect the peak's lethal reputation was seen as having begun when, during a stopover in Cairo on the return, one of the Americans, Rand Herron, slipped and fell to his death while descending a pyramid at Giza. In 1934 the Germans tried again, reaching 7480m but losing ten men, nine of them in one of the most long-drawn-out tragedies, occasioned by bad weather, in Himalayan history. The tenth man died of what was diagnosed as pneumonia, but may well have been oedema. The Germans returned in 1937. This time the entire expedition (seven climbers and nine Sherpas) was wiped out by an avalanche at Camp IV, only the team doctor and cartographer, who had been lower on the hill, surviving. This remains the worst Himalayan death toll in a single event (though rumours of a major Russian accident on the north side of Everest in 1952 are still occasionally brushed off and given a new airing). German expeditions to Nanga Parbat in 1938 and 1939 failed to break new ground, and the latter was anyway curtailed when some members (notably Heinrich Harrer) were interred on news of the outbreak of war.

In the Baltoro expeditions were scant by comparison. In 1934 Günther Dyhrenfurth led an international (German and Swiss) team to Gasherbrum I. Though technically an attempt on the peak, the trip was largely a reconnaissance of the Gasherbrum group. A height of just 6250m was reached on Gasherbrum I, but the team did manage to climb Conway's Golden Throne. Two years later a more concerted effort was made on Gasherbrum I by a French team which reached 7069m.

Reading this list of attempts it is easy to see that in the inter-war years attempts on the 8000m peaks were defined more by accessibility than by any other consideration. Excluding Dyrhenfurth's trip as being primarily exploratory, it leaves us with just one attempt. Getting to the peaks at the end of the Baltoro was logistically difficult and time-consuming. In Europe, and in continental Europe especially, there were climbers who would certainly have joined expeditions to the mountain, but the costs and timescale of the approach would have frightened off potential organisers. Add in the known difficulties of K2, with the Duke of the Abruzzi declaring it impossible, and the problems of high altitude experienced by the British on Everest, and it is not such a surprise that K2 saw no attempts for almost thirty years.

The fact that the accessible peaks had been attempted might explain why the Americans were keen to try K2, but it was still an ambitious, audacious even, idea for a nation still young in terms of climbing on the world stage. Americans had climbed in Alaska, reaching the top of Mount McKinley (6194m/20,320ft; this peak is now often called Denali, as is the National Park in which it stands) as early as 1913 (if Frederick Cook's claimed ascent in 1906 is discounted). Given the position of the mountain, close to the Arctic Circle in what was, at the time, largely unexplored country with minimal infrastructure, that was a considerable achievement. Other Alaskan peaks and some in the Rockies had also been climbed, and while the technical standard of climbing in the USA was not as high as it was in continental Europe, many ascents involved longer treks to the mountain base and weather conditions every bit as harsh. There had also been American expeditions to the Himalaya: in 1932 four Americans had climbed the second-highest summit to have been reached at that time, the 7558m (24,790ft) Minya Konka (now called Gongga) in China's Sichuan province,[2] and some Americans had been on the 1936 Nanda Devi expedition. The history of the latter climb is illuminating. It had begun as the idea of a group of Harvard students (one of whom was Charles Houston; another was Arthur Emmons, who had been on Minya Konka and lost toes to frostbite there); with their passion for climbing and their experience in Alaska and the European Alps, they decided to make the next step – to the Himalaya. They invited the leading British climbers of the day, including Bill Tilman and Noel Odell, to join them in an attempt on Kangchenjunga. The British agreed to a joint expedition, but suggested Nanda Devi might be a more reasonable target for the team, given its size and relative inexperience. The four Harvard students (Houston, Emmons, Farnie Loomis and Adams Carter) joined Tilman, Odell, T. Graham Brown and Peter Lloyd in India. The expedition was a great success, Houston only missing out on the summit climb because of a serious attack of food poisoning.

The success of the Americans on Nanda Devi (with a hint, perhaps, of American enthusiasm for showing those Old World colonialists what the New World could do) meant that when the American Alpine Club (AAC), which had been negotiating over access to the Karakoram for several years, finally received permission in 1937, they decided to attempt K2, the 1938 expedition being viewed primarily as a reconnaissance for a concerted attempt in 1939. The AAC wanted the man recognised as the foremost American climber of the time, the German-born Fritz Wiessner, to lead their trip but when he declined they asked Charles Houston[3] to take the role. He was 25 years old. Houston and many others, both at the time and since, believe that Wiessner's decision not to accept the leadership had less to do with the business commitments which were the ostensible reason and more to do with the idea that the reconnaissance party would fail to summit, but would return with the information needed for success in 1939.

Houston, 1938

Houston's team comprised Bob Bates, Dick Burdsall (who had summitted Minya Konka), Bill House and Paul Petzoldt, a small team considering that Houston was hoping that the summit rather than a reconnaissance was the main objective. The Americans were joined by British officer Norman Streatfeild to help with transport, and six Sherpas, chosen by Bill Tilman. The *sirdar* ('foreman' is perhaps the best translation) of these was the highly experienced Pasang Kikuli. Pintso and Pasang Kitar were two of the other five.

Houston says that foods were agreed after blind testing of various kinds, while the choice of biscuits was made by dropping samples out of high windows and leaving them out in the rain overnight, then selecting those brands which passed this rigorous testing. The resulting food stocks consisted of a combination of dietary necessities, bulk foods and luxuries, the latter including two tins of caviar. Clothing and some equipment was based on lessons learned by the British on Everest.

The trek to the Baltoro seems to have been a delight, with the Americans enjoying both the scenery and their interaction with the locals. In a section he authored, Bates notes a fascinating encounter between western and eastern medicine. One local, a ponyman, came to the camp indicating a headache, chiefly caused, it seemed, by a cord tied tightly around his head as a cure for headaches. The band was loosened and the man was given a fruit drop to suck, the 'cure' working immediately. The alternative cure would have been, Bates says, 'branding his foot with a red-hot wire. The ponyman would have completely forgotten he had a head after that.' The effect of placebo care of the ailments that the locals presented to Houston is mentioned several more times, but there were also cases too difficult to diagnose or treat, although Houston gave as much genuine care as he could with his limited supply of drugs. Eventually the team doctor was presented with a real problem when Petzoldt fell ill, his temperature rising and falling alarmingly. Eventually Petzoldt and Houston were forced to abandon the trek, the former too ill to continue, the latter too concerned to leave him. The rest of the team wondered whether they would ever see the pair again. When they did, Houston's best guess was that Petzoldt had not eaten enough, which is so unlikely a diagnosis of transient fever that it must have been a mask for the doctor's continuing concern. After the expedition Houston admitted he had actually had no idea what was wrong with Petzoldt, other US doctors suggesting an insect-carried fever of some form.

During the walk-in to the Baltoro the team passed a scratched graffito on a rock – 'H.H.G.-A. 1861-2-3'. Bob Bates was entranced by this message across 75 years of Karakoram history, which was clearly left by Godwin-Austen. (It raises, however, obvious questions about when casual vandalism becomes history – does it depend on who the offender was, or how remote it is, or how long it has remained?) The Americans were also told by the locals that they occasionally built artificial glaciers to feed streams for crop irrigation. None had been built for thirty-five years or so, but the construction method was still understood: ice blocks would be taken from an existing glacier and placed in a high valley where they would be

> covered with charcoal and thorn bushes, which in turn are hidden by numerous goat-skins of water. The water keeps things cool before the thorns prick the skins and let the water drip through the charcoal to the ice. This water, freezing in the cool autumn nights, helps the glacier to survive, while in winter snow packing in around the ice helps it to expand. Baltis carry snow to the glacier for the next 20 years to help it along, till finally the ice river is firmly established.

Bob Bates, who wrote this section of the book, was clearly sceptical, wondering if he was being told a tall story. But the principle is scientifically sound, the passage being brought to mind when it was reported that an artificial glacier was constructed in Ladakh in late 2009.[4]

The Americans admired the impressive peaks that confine the Baltoro, but were eager to get to Concordia, from where they could see along the Godwin-Austen Glacier.

> Before us the valley was dark with sullen clouds, but directly ahead of us a rift in the vapor suddenly disclosed, not ten miles away, though high in the air, the glittering apex of a ghostly summit. It was like something from another world, something ethereal seen in dream. For a few stunned moments we stared at the peak we had come so far to see; then it was gone.

Again, it was almost as though the mountain had stared down at these mere mortals who had dared to challenge it.

In the expedition book Bill House takes up the story after Base Camp had been established, suggesting that his first impression was that the Savoia Saddle and the North-West or West Ridges offered the best hope of a route as the rock strata there sloped upwards, suggesting good holds for climbers and good ledges for camps. The alternatives were the North-East and South-East Ridges, the latter being that attempted by the Italians in 1909 (and now known as the Abruzzi Spur). House did not favour these as the strata sloped downwards, acting against the climber. The faces between the various ridges appeared avalanche-prone, which ruled them out.

The team tried the Savoia Saddle first, but it proved impossible to reach a pass which the Duke of the Abruzzi had reached comfortably, conditions having obviously changed in the intervening thirty years. On the glacier the Americans were faced with soft snow, which made route-finding difficult and hazardous, but on the steep face to the pass there was hard, green ice, rather than the snow which the Duke had climbed. In ten-point crampons, and therefore having to cut steps, the ascent would be long and difficult to make safe for load-carriers. To make matters worse Petzoldt was again suffering from transient fever; worse still, back at base the Savoia team found that Bates and Streatfeild had studied the mountain from near Concordia, concluding that the South Face was definitely too dangerous, while the Abruzzi Spur looked continuously steep.

On that discouraging note, the team headed up the Godwin-Austen Glacier to reconnoitre K2's eastern side. Bill House described the glacier:

> a broad highway between the two mountains [K2 and Broad Peak], its narrowness and the masses of ice poised thousands of feet above it making us apprehensive of avalanches which might sweep entirely across … good walking came to an end in a maze of crevasses, some covered, others open chasms. It was a labyrinth of troughs and pinnacles through which we swarmed single file.

From a camp Petzoldt and Houston reconnoitred the Abruzzi Spur and came back with encouraging news. The next day Houston, Bates and Burdsall reconnoitred the North-East Ridge, coming to the conclusion that it was both difficult and dangerous, while House and Petzoldt had another look at the Abruzzi, which was

> more of a shoulder than a true ridge, being composed of a number of small rock ribs interspersed with ice *couloirs* converging on a snow and ice plateau at 25,000 feet. From the upper edge of this rises the summit cone – a pyramid of rock 2200 feet high. Halfway up this cone is a great hanging glacier which sweeps the upper part of the north-east ridge as well as one corner of the Abruzzi ridge. Care would be needed in crossing the plateau from this last ridge, but it looked as though it could be done safely.

In that one brief description House had identified the route that most ascents of the mountain still take and identified the feature that would, many years later, precipitate one of the peak's worst disasters.

That night it was decided that one team would try once more to reach the Savoia Saddle, while another (Houston and Petzoldt) would investigate the Abruzzi. But Petzoldt's fever returned and it was House who accompanied Houston. Some 1000ft above the Godwin-Austen they discovered evidence of the Abruzzi expedition at the only place suitable for a campsite. Above this, at first following a couloir used by the Abruzzi team, the two men met steep, occasionally difficult, ground, a route being feasible, but crucially they passed no sites suitable for a camp.

Henry Godwin-Austen's sketch of K2 appearing above the northern Baltoro ridge from the flank of Masherbrum. To the right, the image of Gasherbrum IV has faded with time.

A drawing of the epic descent of the Muztagh Pass, from Younghusband's book, *The Heart of the Continent*.

Younghusband (*centre*) meets Grombtchevsky (*to the right, in uniform*) during the final stages of the 'Great Game'. The original of this famous photograph has now been lost. As noted in the text, Younghusband's feet are obscured and it seems likely he was standing on something so as not to be overshadowed by the Russian, who was almost a foot taller.

The camp at Askole, from Conway, *Climbing in the Himalayas*. The personnel are not identified, but from other images it is likely that from left to right they are McCormick, Zurbriggen, Eckenstein and Conway.

One of the two McCormick drawings of K2 from Conway, *Climbing in the Himalayas*.

Roberto Lerco.

The Eckenstein–Crowley expedition of 1902. Standing are Wesseley (*left*) and Pfannl. Seated in the middle are Eckenstein (*left*) and Crowley. At the front are Jacot-Guillarmod and Knowles.

Jacot-Guillarmod's photograph of K2, the first photo of the mountain to be published, in his book *Six Mois dans l'Himalaya*.

K2 from Windy Gap. This photograph was taken by the Duke of the Abruzzi and was reproduced in Filippi's book on the 1909 expedition. In the foreground is the North–Western Ridge, which the American 1978 expedition followed to reach the right-hand skyline ridge, which was followed before a traverse beneath the summit pyramid reached the Abruzzi Spur route at the clearly visible Shoulder.

Vittorio Sella's photograph of the west face of K2. (*American Alpine Club / Library of Congress*)

One of the series of photographs taken of the north side of K2 on the 1929 Spoleto expedition.

The 1938 American expedition. From left to right, back row: Ghaffar Sheikh (in charge of porters), House, Houston, Streatfeild, Petzoldt, Bates, Burdsall and Ahdoo (Ghaffar's lieutenant); sitting: Pemba, Pintso, Pasang Kikuli, Pasang Kitar, Tse Tendrup and Sonam.

The 1939 team camped among apricot trees. In the foreground Dudley Wolfe is washing his feet. (*American Alpine Club*)

The Sherpas on the 1939 American expedition. Pasang Kitar is fourth from the left. Beside him (*fifth from the left*) is Pasang Kikuli. Next to him is Pasang Dawa Lama. Pintso is second from the right. (*American Alpine Club*)

A photo of the summit pyramid with Wiessner's 1939 route marked. 1 is Camp IX; 2 is where Wiessner chose not to follow the Bottleneck in favour of taking the headwall to the left; 3 is the high point reached in the Bottleneck on the second summit attempt; 4 is the high point reached on the first summit attempt. So-Schulter is the southern edge of the Shoulder. The image is taken from Wiessner's German book on the 1939 expedition.

The 1953 American team preparing to board the flight for Pakistan. From left to right, on the tarmac: Mr White (the expedition agent), Art Gilkey and Bob Craig; on the steps: George Bell, Pete Schoening, Dee Molenaar and Charles Houston. Bob Bates and Tony Streather were already in Pakistan. (*American Alpine Club*)

(*right*) The famous drawing of the accident on the 1953 American expedition.

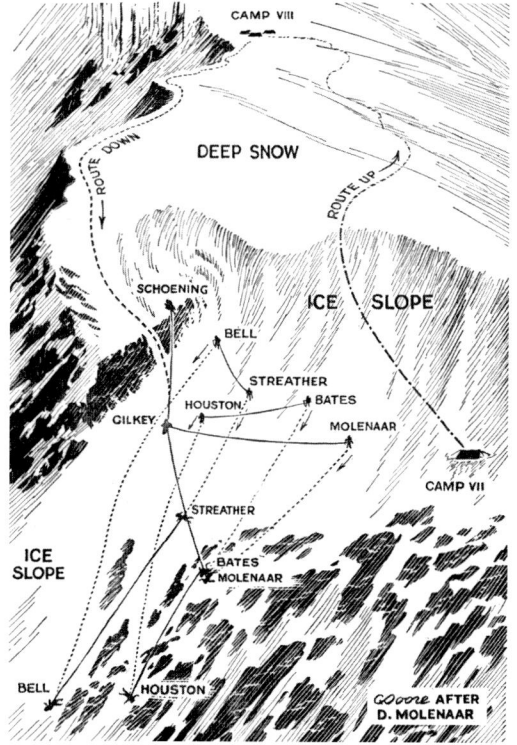

(*below*) The successful 1954 Italian team. Ardito Desio stands at the centre. Standing at the back, from the left, are Achille Compagnoni, Ugo Angelino, Ubaldo Rey, Pino Gallotti, Bruno Zanettin (scientist) and Mario Fantin (photographer). Standing to the left are Mario Puchoz, Cirillo Floreanini and Sergio Viotto. In front, from the left, are Gino Soldá, Lino Lacedelli, Guido Pagani, Erich Abram and Walter Bonatti.

Lino Lacedelli putting on his crampons at Camp IX. This photograph, clearly taken in full daylight, showed that Compagnoni's insistence that the summit pair started very early in the morning of 31 July was not correct.

Lino Lacedelli on the summit on 31 July 1954. The complete oxygen set is at his feet.

Achille Compagnoni on the summit on 31 July 1954. He is clearly still wearing his oxygen mask: the straps beneath his woollen cap and the tube connecting it to the set (which he has removed) are visible.

The shot of Compagnoni used in Desio's official expedition book. He has now removed his oxygen mask.

Discouraged, they retreated to the glacier camp, finding the descent even more trying than the ascent. Once back at the camp the news they brought seemed so bad that it was decided to have another look not only at the Savoia Saddle, but also at the North-East Ridge.

The Savoia Saddle team again failed to reach the pass, thwarted by ice and bad weather. The weather made life difficult for the North-East Ridge team as well, avalanches falling off both K2 and Broad Peak threatening their route on the glacier. At one stage the Sherpas claimed to have heard voices from high on K2: when they later found an avalanche had crossed the tracks made earlier they were convinced that the mountain's gods were looking after them. When the two teams rejoined, the Americans were thoroughly dispirited: all three of the routes they had tried seemed hopeless. In discussion, Houston and Burdsall favoured another try on the North-East Ridge, Petzoldt and House another on the Abruzzi, while Bates and Streatfeild were undecided. After a further, long discussion it was decided to give the Abruzzi one more try, transferring to the North-East Ridge if, again, no reasonable route could be found.

On the Abruzzi Petzoldt and House tried a different line and found a perfect camp site. The route to it was steep, but feasible: at last there was a glimmer of hope and to make things even better an easier route was found during the descent. Agreeing now that the Abruzzi offered the best chance of success, the Americans established Camp II (about 5884m/19,300ft) at the spot found by Petzoldt and House (Camp I being at the base of the Spur). From the camp the two climbed mixed ground, steep but feasible for porters if protected by fixed ropes. House took a short fall at one point when the snow step he was standing on collapsed, but overall the men were encouraged, especially when a rocky outcrop appeared to offer the chance of a campsite if loose rock was levelled. They had climbed 1000ft above the camp, and were higher than anyone else had ever been on the mountain. Next day, Petzoldt and House fixed rope to the intended camp site, returning to find Camp II resupplied from below and a note congratulating them on their efforts – a nice touch which was much appreciated.

The weather now turned bad, and Petzoldt again succumbed to fever, but when morning came he was well enough to continue and the weather relented enough for climbing to be possible. On one steep slope, as House struggled to enlarge some steps in the snow while balancing precariously from a finger wedged in a piton, Petzoldt chose that moment 'to deliver an enlightening and thoroughly sound discourse on step-cutting, with particular respect to how I might improve my technique', not realising 'I was hanging on by my eyelashes.' The response, Petzoldt claimed, was a 'blasphemous torrent ... [that] melted all the ice on the rope between us and that for the rest of the day it had been much easier to handle.'

After Camp III (6311m/20,700ft) had been established, Houston and Petzoldt pushed the route out across slabs covered in loose rock, all of which fell into the camp below, damaging the tents and endangering those carrying loads. Bad weather added to the hazards of the route, but the Americans took great care to supply the camps as it was clear that severe weather would maroon climbers, retreat down the steep route they had pioneered being too difficult. Camp IV was placed at 6555m (21,500ft) and from it House and Bates climbed to the foot of a cliff split by a diagonal, chimney-like gash. Bates belayed and House followed a crack to its base. He banged in a piton and started up the chimney:

> With my feet and hands gripping both sides, I climbed up 20 feet to where the walls flared outward and became so smooth that I had to put my back against one and feet against the other to hitch myself up a few inches at a time. It was at this point I discovered that I had neglected to leave my crampons with Bates, for they were in my rucksack, pressing into my back and catching on the rock. This carelessness cost me dear, but after a while I was able to use feet and hands on both sides of the chimney. A little ledge 40 feet up gave me a timely rest, for any progress under such conditions is exhausting.

House tried to get a piton in, but it crumpled uselessly. He continued:

> I felt I was pretty close to my margin of safety, but there were no piton cracks and I thought anything would be better than climbing down without some protection from above. Bates ... shouted up that maybe I had better come down. It was a suggestion I certainly would have liked to follow ... Another struggle of 15 feet took me beyond where the chimney narrowed to a foot and a half, its back a wall of ice, and placed me on some holds wide enough for my boots. Still another rest and I scrambled over the easier upper part, emerging on a tiny ridge 80 feet above Bates.

House says that the climb from Camp IV had taken 2½ hours, of which about an hour had been spent reaching the base of the cliff. He had therefore taken almost 2 hours to climb the 80ft chimney. It had been a *tour de force*, future years showing that 'House's Chimney' was the major obstacle on the lower Abruzzi, later parties using a variety of ladders to aid its ascent. At the time it was almost certainly the hardest pitch to have been attempted at a comparable height anywhere in the Himalaya. Above the chimney House and Bates climbed a further 350ft to reach a likely site for Camp V beneath an imposing 'great black pyramid' of rock.

With Camp V established, Houston and Petzoldt attacked the Black Pyramid. They went right at first, but failed to make much progress and returned to camp to eat. They then tried to the left where the route seemed more reasonable. Next day, poor weather stopped further progress, but the following day was fine and the two continued, carrying loads to establish Camp VI. The site (at 7104m/23,300ft) was reached before noon, Bates, House and three Sherpas setting up the camp while Houston and Petzoldt continued, pushing the route out another 500ft or so. Another good day allowed the two to continue the route towards the top of the Black Pyramid. The climbing was exposed, Houston noting that one slip would have landed the pair in Camp I, but the top of the Pyramid, at 7470m (24,500ft) was reached by midday. Above, only 500ft of snowfield led to the Shoulder. 'After a restful cigarette' (another reminder that tobacco played an important role in the early exploration of the Karakoram), Houston and Petzoldt pushed the route up steep ice, then through a small icefall to the edge of the Shoulder.

At Camp VI a decision was now needed. The lower camps were reasonably well stocked but it seemed likely that two more camps would be required before an attempt on the summit could be made. Allowing for poor weather, that might take two weeks, and the margin of safety would become slimmer by the day. Was it wise to continue or had they done enough? A compromise was reached: two men would be placed in a high camp with supplies for three days and would go as far up as possible in one day, then return. Houston and Petzoldt were the chosen pair.

Bates, House and Pasang Kikuli therefore carried loads as high as they could and Houston and Petzoldt continued with these to establish Camp VII at 7531m (24,700ft). There the two were horrified to find they had brought no matches to light their stove: a potential disaster. A hurried search discovered nine in Houston's pocket: three were needed before the stove was lit. (Next day three more were needed to make breakfast, leaving just three, all of which were needed to light the stove on the last evening, ensuring a cold breakfast before the last descent: even without the decision that just one day was to be allowed for further climbing, the lack of matches would have forced a retreat.) On another perfect day the two crossed easier ground, though with occasional deep powder snow. They quickly crossed an avalanche zone below the final summit pyramid. At the base of the pyramid, at about 7927m (26,000ft), Houston stopped and sat in the snow:

Mingled with a deep and heartfelt regret at abandoning the attack, when success seemed within our grasp, was a sense of relief that at last the hard struggle was over … There were other emotions too deep to be expressed. I felt all my previous life had reached a climax in these last hours of intense struggle against nature, and yet nature had been very indulgent. She had scarcely bothered to turn against us the full force of her elements. Indeed, she had favored us with perfect weather and not too difficult conditions, preferring to let our puny bodies exhaust themselves in the rarefied atmosphere. How small indeed we were to struggle so desperately to reach one point on the earth's surface, a point which had been so real a goal for us for so many months! I believe in those minutes at 26,000 feet on K2, I reached depths of feeling which I can never reach again.

Above Houston, Petzoldt continued upwards, probably reaching, or getting close to, 8000m, and returning with news that he had found a great camp site. The pair descended to Camp VII. Five days later the entire party was at Base Camp: apart from the trek home the adventure was over.

Five Miles High is one of the great expedition books, suggesting a trip which was entirely idyllic, with barely a cross word between a group of friends. But in her biography of Houston (see Note 3), Bernadette McDonald notes that there were tensions in the party, with the leader claiming that Petzoldt (a guide from the Tetons) was a 'blue collar guide', and Petzoldt, the only westerner in a group of east coasters, saying that Houston and Bates were 'two Eastern nabobs'. McDonald also notes that in a letter home Houston complained about Bill House, who constantly niggled about the lack of food, whose route-finding was poor and who was often depressed and bad company. After the trip Petzoldt stayed on in an ashram in India, but was forced to flee back to the US with a charge of manslaughter hanging over him when the ashram leader died in disputed circumstances after a fight over a loaded shotgun. Back in the US Petzoldt several times suggested the decision to retreat had been wrong, once implying that rather than fears over the weather and a lack of matches, it had been made because Houston felt unwell – a charge that both hurt and angered Houston. The relationship between the two, only ever, it seems, based on mutual respect for climbing ability, never recovered.

Wiessner, 1939
But regardless of the tensions below the surface that the expedition book chose to hide, the 1938 trip had been a remarkable success. It had achieved its main purpose of identifying a route to the summit and it had returned with the entire party intact. While it was the case that the last 600m of the route seemed difficult and that the objective dangers of it were high, it seemed that there was every chance that the 1939 American expedition would be successful. But it was not to be. Tragedy rather than triumph was the outcome, and with tragedy came mystery – why had an expedition which achieved so much end in such appalling circumstances?

The essential story of the expedition is well known, set down in the leader's report to the American Alpine Club and in a book which he wrote. But these accounts left unanswered important questions, the answers to which fuelled an unpleasant trial by insinuation which followed the return of the surviving members of the team to the USA. In 1992 new material allowed a more definitive account of the expedition and the sequence of events which led to tragedy to be written, though even that still left some mysteries unresolved. In the story set down here, all these sources[5] have been used to prepare an account of the climb. Given the nature of this book, that account is necessarily brief, but hopefully covers the salient points and identifies the critical unanswered questions.

Having been, or made himself, unavailable in 1938, in 1939 Wiessner[6] was able to lead the expedition. His team was to have included several capable mountaineers, but these dropped out one by one, some because they could not afford it, one because he broke a leg skiing. One who dropped out was Bill House, the only one of Houston's 1938 team Wiessner approached, which seems odd. Nor did Wiessner consult Houston on any details of his climb. Given that the 1938 trip was supposed to have been a reconnaissance for the real attempt in 1939, that is very curious. Wiessner may have seen the expedition book, and perhaps attended the lectures given after the 1938 team's return, but neither contained the depth of detail that the leader of an expedition would find invaluable.

As a result of team members dropping out, Wiessner's intended team of ten shrank to five. Of these Chappell Cranmer and George Sheldon were inexperienced though technically able, while Eaton (Tony) Cromwell was very experienced but not at a high level. Bestor Robinson was an excellent rock climber who had begun to open up Yosemite's walls. The fifth man was Dudley Wolfe.[7] When there had been ten in the team, the four men other than Robinson had been included largely because they were rich and were prepared to help finance the expedition in order to take part in the adventure. Now they made up the bulk of the team. Another man was hastily drafted in. Jack Durrance was a medical student (though he had yet to start his studies) and a fine climber with a list of excellent routes to his name. Kauffman and Putnam claim that Wiessner had never met Durrance, the latter being chosen by AAC officials, but Jordan claims that the two had spent the weekend climbing together (with Cranmer and Sheldon) and Durrance had impressed the expedition leader sufficiently to offer him a place on the team. This, taken with other differences between the two apparently authoritative accounts, suggests that the definitive account of the 1939 expedition has yet to be written.

Bestor Robinson then dropped out (Jordan says he broke a leg skiing, but that seems to have been another possible candidate, who would have been the team's doctor). With Wiessner and Wolfe already on their way to Europe, this meant that Wiessner was unaware of Robinson's defection until he met Durrance, not Robinson, in Genoa harbour on the ship that was to take the expedition to India. To add to Wiessner's dismay, he discovered that Durrance was already talking to Vittorio Sella, the great photographer, who had agreed to meet Wiessner on the ship. Kauffman/Putnam say that Wiessner was aggrieved by not having been first to shake Sella's hand, to such an extent that Durrance, taken aback by the team leader's reaction, considered abandoning the expedition. He did not, but only because he did not have enough money for a return fare. In India the team was joined by a British liaison officer, Lieutenant George Trench, and by nine Sherpas. The sirdar was Pasang Kikuli. He and four others had been on K2 the previous year. Of the others, one was Pasang Dawa Lama, who was in later years to become famous as part of the summit team with Austrians Herbert Tichy and Sepp Jöchler on the first ascent of Cho Oyu, the world's sixth highest mountain. Pasang was also in the summit team which made the second ascent of the same mountain. An Indian interpreter and a cook also joined Wiessner's team.

The team enjoyed the walk-in and one another's company, Durrance tending to the various ailments presented by the locals despite his rudimentary medical knowledge. Everyone seemed to be both impressed and awed by the mountain scenery. One night Wiessner heard the distant cry of a snow leopard. There was the usual porter strike, and an incident occurred which appeared minor, but which was to have consequences later. A porter dropped a tarpaulin into a crevasse and Cranmer spent a long time on a rope within the icy gash retrieving it, eventually being hauled out soaking wet, cold and exhausted. He seemed to recover well, and the team moved on to the foot of the mountain.

Wiessner went off to look at the Abruzzi Spur, but back at the camp Cranmer began to feel unwell and went to rest in his tent. Within a short time he was seriously ill and medical novice Durrance was faced with an emergency. At first, Durrance writes, Cranmer 'expectorated quantities of flegm and slime', his temperature rose and his pulse raced. Later his condition deteriorated rapidly. He called to Durrance, who found himself having to administer artificial respiration to keep his patient alive. Then things got worse. In an interview Durrance gave to Kauffman/Putnam when he was 75 years old, dropping, in part, professional language for the vernacular, he said that Cranmer

coughed up a huge quantity of clear, frothy fluid, or mush, from his lungs ... Horrible, bubbly stuff. Poor fellow, he was completely out of it, delirious, unconscious, babbling nonsense from time to time about a baseball game he dreamed he was playing ... I fought a losing battle to keep him and the immediate vicinity clean ... everything smelled to high heavens. Then the worst happened: Chappell developed diarrhoea and simultaneously lost control of his body functions. Well, I reached outside the tent, grabbed a piece of plywood, cardboard, or whatever, and shoved it under Chappell's butt. But the damage was done. I could only keep the filth from growing worse. It was hours before I managed to clean things up – even then everything stank of vomit, mucus, urine and, above all, plain shit. I never knew anyone could be so sick and stay alive.

Durrance added that in thirty-five years of pulmonary medicine since the Cranmer incident he had never had a sicker patient.

Durrance believed Cranmer had pneumonia. With the benefit of decades of study of high-altitude illnesses, Kauffman/Putnam consider it probable that Cranmer had high-altitude pulmonary oedema (HAPE), the understanding of which, at the time, was limited. However, Jordan maintains that the likely explanation was celiac sprue, a genetic disorder in which gluten consumption invokes an anti-immune response. Today's best opinion[8] favours HAPE, but whatever the cause, that Cranmer survived the crisis is remarkable, though Durrance's care (however limited by circumstance) undoubtedly helped, particularly in terms of nursing his patient back to health once the critical phase had passed. But although he did recover – and without being evacuated – Cranmer was unable to take any realistic part in the expedition, though he did go to Camp II. Wiessner had lost one of his strongest team members. He also effectively lost another, as the high-altitude boots ordered by Durrance had not yet caught up with the expedition; with his patient care duties and inadequate footwear (an old pair of boots that leaked) Durrance was not able to go high.

Now even more reliant on his deputy Tony Cromwell, Wiessner headed up the mountain to set up camp sites, leaving those left at Base Camp to sort themselves out. The lower camps were soon stocked, the Americans and Sherpas carrying loads, though Durrance was increasingly hampered by his inadequate footwear. Little things, such as tent hygiene, were also beginning to strain the previous harmony in the team, while Wolfe's clumsiness and his lack of useful camp skills (he could not light the cooking stoves, for instance, and even after being taught often used an entire box of matches getting one alight) were making him something of a liability on the hill. The clear nervousness of the others upset Wolfe, who increasingly attached himself to Wiessner, who, whether through genuine friendship or because Wolfe was the trip's major sponsor, welcomed his company. To support the latter contention, in a diary entry later in the expedition, Wiessner wrote 'It is unfair to take a man along and use valuable time hauling him about just because he was able to finance the undertaking – and also dangerous if conditions hit him just right when he is dependent on his own resources.'[9]

Wiessner then left Cromwell in charge of pushing the route out to House's Chimney while he descended to supervise events at Base Camp. When he got back to Camp II he found that nothing had been done. He faced a dilemma. Wiessner was clearly the most able climber, but if he was out in front, how could he also direct the necessary operations below? Now on the mountain, Wiessner's natural inclinations as a climber took over. From 21 June to 23 July he spent all but three days at or above Camp IV (at 6553m/21,500ft, below House's Chimney). This period was not only physically debilitating but it left him only partially in control of events lower on the hill. And, as a consequence of their relationship, whatever its basis, when Wiessner went up to Camp IV on 21 June, Wolfe went with him. Wolfe was never again to go below 6553m.

At Camp IV a violent storm struck. It lasted eight days. It was, said Wiessner, worse than anything he had endured on Nanga Parbat, and was a daunting experience for the rest of the team, further stressing their already low morale. The only other person at Camp IV, George Sheldon, was so alarmed by the storm, and by the incipient frostbite in his feet, that for him the expedition was over. Only

Wiessner and, surprisingly, Wolfe appeared to have remained entirely resolved to complete the climb at the end of the battering. Wolfe's enthusiasm for the venture seems at odds with his playboy background, which seemed to imply to a casual observer that once the going got really tough he would decide he had had enough and retire to more genteel surroundings. But Jordan's biographical notes on Wolfe, particularly of his war record, indicate a far tougher individual than might be expected. Certainly any man who could carry out the ambulance work he had done in the war, and sailed the Atlantic in relatively small sailing craft, was made of very much sterner stuff than has often been implied.

With his team now unenthused at best, or utterly unable to help at worst, and with no competent deputy, if Wiessner was pushing out the route he would have no way of knowing if the necessary work to support his attempt was being done. But despite this, on the first day after the storm, he set out for House's Chimney, climbed it and established Camp V. An exchange of notes between Durrance, the only technically competent and still willing team member, and Wiessner now effectively ruined the relationship between them. Durrance's, sent up to Camp V, noted that his expedition boots had arrived, and that men were ready to carry loads to Camp IV, but needed assurance that movements above would not threaten them with stonefall as had happened in 1938. The response was a note expressing disappointment that so little assistance was being offered.

At Camp V Wolfe, having been hauled up House's Chimney, waited as Wiessner, with two Sherpas, established Camp VI and pushed on to the site of Camp VII. The men then returned to Camp V to discover that no supplies had arrived from below. Wolfe told Wiessner he had gone to the top of House's Chimney each day and called down, but there was no answer from Camp IV. To find out why not, Wiessner descended to Camp II, leaving Wolfe and the two Sherpas at Camp V. His arrival, and the cheering news that he had reached the top of the Spur, seemed to revitalise the others and several carries were made up to Camp IV.

Durrance now went up to Camp V – he was the only American apart from Wiessner and Wolfe to get that high – where he became concerned that Wolfe's feet were showing signs of frostbite. But despite that fear, on 12 July Wiessner, Durrance, Wolfe and seven Sherpas headed up to Camp VI. Durrance was horrified by Wolfe's lack of climbing ability and his apparent exhaustion at Camp VI. Sharing a tent with him, Durrance was even more horrified to discover Wolfe intended to continue up, and attempted to persuade him to go down. Wolfe interpreted this as jealousy, an attempt to usurp his position at the front of the expedition, and talked to Wiessner, who took the same view. In reality, Durrance's diary notes that he was not pleased when he discovered that he himself figured in Wiessner's summit plans.

After Durrance's remarks to Wolfe had been argued over, the team all headed up again, but Durrance soon had to stop, with a headache and faintness. Wiessner sent him down to recuperate. The plan was that, if he recovered, he and some of the

Sherpas could make another load-carry the following day. Wiessner, Wolfe and the Sherpas established Camp VII and next day moved up to Camp VIII, at 7711m (25,300ft). But Durrance did not recover. Feeling increasingly ill (and probably suffering from either HAPE or HACE), after a bad night at Camp VI he descended to Camp IV, taking the Sherpas with him. Still feeling ill, he left them at Camp IV with instructions to carry supplies up to Camps VI and VII, then descended to Camp II. There were now no Americans between Camps II and VIII, and those Sherpas that were in the intermediate camps were consequently unsupervised. And soon there would be limited supplies in the intervening camps as well, as deputy leader Cromwell sent up a message from Base Camp to the still unwell Durrance telling him to strip the higher camps. The reason was that the porters hired to carry the expedition out were expected to arrive soon. With adequate supplies in the upper camps, bringing surplus equipment down to Base would at least allow the withdrawal to start. This message got through to the Sherpas high on the hill; knowing that some equipment was more valuable, they started to strip that preferentially from Camp VI downwards. Added to this, those Sherpas charged with moving supplies upwards, to Camp VIII, had not been able to reach it because they feared the final slope to the camp would avalanche. They also saw the tracks of earlier avalanches and wondered about the fate of Wiessner and the others, especially when they shouted and there was no reply. With no supplies delivered, and the lower camps stripped, the scene was now set for tragedy.

Another storm had prevented movement in the top camp for two days, then on 17 July Wiessner, Wolfe and a single Sherpa, Pasang Dawa Lama, started up from Camp VIII. Wiessner, in the lead, found the going hard: 'Below the bergschrund the snow is bottomless. It takes me a long time to plow through this.' Wolfe could no longer follow, even along the track Wiessner and Pasang made, and returned to Camp VIII to await either Wiessner's return or help from below. The two out in front pitched a temporary camp, then moved up again on 18 July to pitch Camp IX at 7940m (26,050ft). From it Wiessner scanned the route ahead. Easy ground led to a point from where there were two options. One offered an apparently straightforward rising leftward traverse on snow to the summit cone, but was threatened by an ice wall. The other was safer, but ascended steep, probably icy, rocks. Wiessner, the rock climber, chose the latter, and at 9am on 19 July he and Pasang started up. It was a very late start, one which Wiessner never explained, and the hours lost may well have cost them the summit. But the pair made good time and by 11am they had covered 240m and were only 430m (1414ft) below the summit.

Wiessner now went left towards the rocks rather than right to gain the snow traverse, heading for a black couloir: 'The black verglaced couloir soon became very steep and terminated in an overhang. With piton-protection I was able to overcome this obstacle by traversing to the left under the overhang; the rock was very difficult and covered with verglas in places, but the weather was so warm that I could climb without gloves.' More difficult climbing followed, then Wiessner was stopped by an unclimbable steep slab and was forced left, climbing up 'with great difficulty for about 8 metres, putting in two pitons for protection'. In his book (and the *Appalachia* article which translates it) Wiessner says that only another 8m wall, one that was clearly climbable, now separated the two men from easy ground, though in his account to the AAC he says a 60ft (18m) traverse was needed. The heights he gives for the point reached also differ: 8390m (27,520ft) in the book, 8369m (27,450ft) in his AAC account. The difference is small (though 20m at 8400m is, by most accounts, non-trivial), and each means that the two men were only about 230m (750ft) from the summit. Wiessner was anxious to continue, believing that with the last obstacle overcome, climbing straightforward snow to the summit would be feasible at night, but now Pasang Dawa Lama would no longer follow him. Wiessner does not specify a time in his book, but in his account to the AAC says it was 6pm. The AAC account does not give a reason for the Sherpa's reluctance, but in the book Wiessner speculates (implying he either did not ask for a reason or did not receive a satisfactory explanation) that, with night approaching, Pasang was afraid of the evil spirits that spent the night on mountain summits.

For the time Wiessner's idea of climbing through the night was utterly revolutionary, but his logic for continuing seems impeccable – going up an easy-angled snow slope in the dark would be easier than going down difficult rock and would allow that tricky descent to be made in daylight. The night also turned out to be surprisingly warm (about -3°C to -5°C, Wiessner estimates) and so would have been bearable. But despite his best efforts at persuasion, Pasang was adamant. Wiessner had to accept defeat and the two started the difficult descent. Night arrived 'while we were roping down over the overhang into the black couloir. While Pasang was hanging in the air during this rope-down the rope became tangled in our crampons, which he was carrying on his back. He succeeded with difficulty in freeing it, but in the process the crampons fell off down the mountain.' Camp IX was not reached until 2.30am next day. If Wiessner's time of 6pm for the turn-round is correct, the descent had taken only 30 minutes less time than the ascent.

Next day the sun shone and it was warm. Wiessner had thought of moving the tent higher, ready for another summit attempt on 21 July, but instead the two spent a day resting in sun so warm that Wiessner could lie naked on his sleeping bag. Wiessner notes that by the afternoon he and Pasang felt fresh again and so he decided to make another summit attempt the following day.

In 1939 the effect of prolonged stays at altitude on the human body was poorly understood. Scientists were becoming aware of the deleterious effects, but climbers still in general believed that as humans went higher they acclimatised to reduced oxygen levels. True, it seemed that at great heights the degree of acclimatisation appeared to reduce, but some benefit was still considered to derive from prolonged stays. Today we know that at altitudes much in excess of about 5300m, most people deteriorate, both mentally and physically, over a period which varies with the individual but is usually measured in weeks even if they are supplied with adequate levels of food, drink and warmth. As the altitude increases, the time for significant deterioration to set in decreases. Above 8000m, it decreases to the point where a human being will die in a relative short time, even if bodily needs are catered for. These great heights are now termed the 'Death Zone': the name is not merely a press concoction, but a true description of the effect of a sustained stay. There will still be a spread of survival times, but the outcome is certain.

By now Wiessner had spent six days at and above 7700m, and the second summit attempt would be his third day above 7940m. In terms of his ability to survive the rigours of height, Wiessner was a remarkable man, but his 'rest day' at Camp 9 actually offered no rest at all and it is surprising he was able to function at all on 21 July and, subsequently, to cope so well with the fraught descent to Base Camp which followed.

In fact, on 21 July the two men reached the point where the possible summit routes diverged at 8am, two hours after an early start. That is the same ascent time as on 19 July, an amazing feat. In his account to the AAC Wiessner writes that he and Pasang 'traversed to the East to the top of a snow couloir which ends about 90 feet below the western end of the ice wall. The 400 feet snow gully between the ice wall and the ridge was hard and icy.' Wiessner was describing what is now called the Bottleneck Couloir. Without the crampons lost during the descent on 19 July, step cutting would be required the whole way up it: that would take too long and so the two men returned to the base of the route taken on the 19th. But it was now 11.30am and Wiessner knew there was no time to follow his original line before nightfall. He writes, 'We therefore had to go down'. That seems an astonishingly laconic, restrained statement considering the degree of disappointment which he must have felt. On the 19th only darkness had stopped him achieving the crowning glory of his climbing career. On the 21st only the loss of their crampons had prevented the two from reaching the summit (assuming, of course, that their bodies had survived the onslaught of thin air).

Back at Camp IX Wiessner decided to descend the next day unless fresh supplies arrived from below. A new partner would also be needed as Pasang 'asked me whether he could be relieved in Camp VIII by another Sherpa for the next attempt on the summit; this I naturally promised him. Since the day before he had no longer been his old self; he had been living in great fear of the evil spirits, constantly murmuring prayers, and had lost his appetite.'

No one arrived from below so on 22 July the two men descended to Camp VIII, Pasang slipping on the way, his fall being held by Wiessner. At Camp VIII 'Wolfe was standing there and called to us. He was greatly pleased to see us again, but considerably put out that no one had come up from below. Two days before his matches had given out, so that for drinking he had had only water from melted snow which he had caught in a fold of the tent.' The fact that Wolfe had chosen to stay put despite the circumstances is another curiosity. Was he so in thrall to Wiessner that he was willing to wait even when conditions had become life-threatening, or was he so lacking in confidence in his own abilities that he dared not move, either up or down the mountain, for fear of killing himself?

Wiessner decided that there were insufficient resources at the camp to sustain another summit attempt, and with Pasang reluctant to try again Wiessner also needed to find a rope mate; although he does not say so, Wolfe was hardly a suitable candidate. The three therefore decided to descend to Camp VII, where there should have been lots of supplies. As they neared the camp

> we slipped off as we were traversing a slope of hard snow. I had scratched a step with the ice-axe and was just in the act of taking a step forward when suddenly a sharp jerk by the rope from behind pulled me off balance. I slipped off, and Wolfe could not hold me when the rope tightened. As it came to light later, he had inadvertently stepped on the rope, which had then become wound about his foot. My fall brought him off and Pasang, who had not been sufficiently on guard, was likewise pulled off. We all three plunged down the steep slope, where the snow became harder and harder. Using my axe, and with my boots scratching against the slope, I obtained a hold and holding the rope with the strength of desperation was able to check the fall of my companions. Luckily for me, at this point the snow was somewhat softer; a few metres below, where Wolfe and Pasang were hanging on the rope, it was again so hard that both of them required help from the rope to climb up to me. Only about 60 metres below us were the great ice cliffs of the summit snowfield and beneath these the east wall plunged down over 2000 metres to the Godwin-Austen Glacier. During the fall we had all three of us given up hope of being saved.

In his diary Wiessner also says that Wolfe's lack of technique had caused the team to descend slowly, which meant they were all cold. At the time of the fall he was making steps for Wolfe to use: presumably as he stepped down to make another, the rope on which Wolfe had stood pulled him off.

The fall delayed them and night was already falling when they reached the camp, and 'there awaited us the disappointment of our lives. Not a human being was in the camp.' One tent was open, half collapsed and had holes in it, the other was snow-filled. The food was in the open and frozen solid. There were no sleeping bags. Pasang and Wolfe had brought theirs, but Wiessner's was still at Camp IX, so sure was he of going back. And in the fall Wolfe's had been lost. The men repitched the snow-filled tent. Fuel was found so food could be thawed and cooked, but a meal could only make the night to come marginally less unbearable. At night air mattresses were needed to ward off the gnawing cold that seeps up from the ground. In Wiessner's book he says they had none, but his diary states they had one each. What is definite is that there was only one sleeping bag, Pasang's. Thrown over them, but barely covering more than their midriffs, it was a long cold night.

Next morning descent was imperative, at least as far as Camp VI, where Wiessner hoped he would be able to find sleeping bags he could bring up to VII. Wolfe apparently asked to stay at VII to rest so as to be ready to carry a load up to Camp VIII. The sheer optimism of Wiessner and Wolfe is now either admirable or laughable, depending on the chosen point of view. But Wiessner's decision to leave Wolfe has been the subject of debate for years. Given the conditions found at Camp VII, Wiessner must have been nervous of what he might find lower down, but set against that, the descent to Camp VI was more difficult than that to Camp VII and Wolfe had shown how ill-prepared he was for that. Without crampons, it is possible that Wiessner actually thought the best chance of getting Wolfe off the mountain safely was to leave him at VII, to descend with Pasang, re-equip and climb back up to him.

So, leaving Wolfe alone, Wiessner and Pasang descended, but Camp VI was also 'broken up. Only a cache of folded-up tents, gasoline and food was still there.' There were no sleeping bags or air mattresses. A return to Camp VII was now out of the question, so the two men were forced to continue the descent. Camp V had only ever been a support camp, and was never fully equipped so they continued to IV. That too was empty, both of people and essential equipment. The two men therefore had no choice but to continue down. 'Almost exhausted, mentally and physically, we reached Camp II at nightfall.' There were tents, but no supplies or air mattresses: the two had to make do with dropping one tent and using it as a rough cover in the other. 'The cold tentcloth, however, gave no warmth and we shivered miserably; our toes and fingers frostbitten in the preceding night, became much worse.' Next day they stumbled down again towards Base Camp. Just before they reached it, 'Cromwell with several Sherpas caught up with us. They had been searching the glacier higher up, under the precipices of the Abruzzi Rib, for our bodies! It now came to light that we had long been given up for lost by a fall.' Both men were in very poor shape, and only managed to reach the camp with frequent pauses.

Once he had recovered his strength Wiessner wanted to climb up again, but it is clear that he was intent not on a rescue but on another summit attempt, collecting Dudley Wolfe along the way. Durrance and three Sherpas therefore set off on 25 July, planning to reach Camp VII as soon as possible with the aim of taking supplies from it to Camp VIII ready for Wiessner's return. That, at least, was Wiessner's idea, though the less optimistic Durrance thought he was likely to be on a mission solely to rescue Wolfe.

But Durrance could go no higher than IV and he and one unwell Sherpa returned. The other two, Pintso and Pasang Kitar, continued, reaching Camp VI on 27 July. At Base Camp, with Durrance and all the other Americans low on the mountain now unavailable for the summit, Wiessner finally realised the climb was over. Pasang Kikuli and Tsering were therefore dispatched to join the two at Camp VI and to bring Wolfe down. They reached Camp VI on 28 July after a climb of over 2000m in a single day – an astonishing achievement. The following day three Sherpas went up to Camp VII, leaving Tsering at VI.

By 29 July Dudley Wolfe had spent thirty-nine days at or above 6550m, and sixteen days at or above 7530m. In all the time he had been on the hill Wolfe had descended only twice, each time going down only one camp and for only one night. He had now also spent six days on his own as the highest man on the mountain. During part of that time he was the only man on the mountain (though he did not, of course, know that). When the Sherpas reached him he was, by their account – and it is impossible not to believe it – in a terrible, pitiful state. He had used up his matches and so could not make warm food or drinks. His only drinking water, again, was from meltwater on the tent. Unable, or perhaps too afraid, to leave the tent and the warmth of Pasang's sleeping bag, he had used the tent as a latrine, body wastes staining the tent floor and sleeping bag. And as Wolfe had been sleeping on the food supplies, presumably for extra insulation, the food was contaminated with his waste – rendering it inedible even if he had been able to cook. The Sherpas urged him to descend, but he refused to do so, saying he would rest and go down the next day. Without sleeping bags the three Sherpas were forced to descend. At Camp VI they decided to try once more, and to ask Wolfe to sign a paper clearing them of responsibility if he still refused to leave and they were unable to carry him down. But 30 July was stormy and they could not leave Camp VI. On 31 July Pasang Kikuli, Pasang Kitar and Pintso again left Camp VI and started up towards VII. They did not return. On 2 August Tsering climbed down with the bad news. A rescue attempt was started, but Wiessner was too exhausted to get further than Camp I. A storm then prevented further movement until 7 August. By then, even the ever-optimistic Wiessner realised the futility of further effort. The rescue was called off and the mountain abandoned.

Nothing was found in 1953 which gave any indication of the fate of Wolfe or the Sherpas, but in 2002 the remains of Dudley Wolfe were discovered near K2's Base Camp, together with tent fabric and poles, and a cooking pot. There were no signs of any remains of the Sherpas. A few years earlier the remains of one body had been found, still with a climbing rope attached to the waist – it was assumed to have been one of the Sherpas, identified by 1939 Emperor George V rupees carried in a small wallet. The clear implication of the two finds is that either the three Sherpas did not reach Wolfe on their final attempt, presumably falling to their deaths on their way to him, or they died on the descent, having failed to reach him due to bad weather or conditions. Dudley Wolfe must have died alone in, or close to, his tent, his body brought to the base of the mountain by avalanches and deposited on the glacier that eventually brought it to Base Camp.

The aftermath of the climb was as unpleasant as some aspects of it. Cromwell accused Wiessner of murdering Wolfe and the three Sherpas, and Trench also considered that all responsibility for the deaths lay with Wiessner. Then, as the expedition reached Srinigar, Britain declared war on Germany: Wiessner was German-born and now sitting in British India, while the Americans were faced with the problem of how to get home. (In the event, they were able to take an Italian ship through the Suez Canal and then to cross the Atlantic.) Durrance tried to prevent Cromwell's suggestion of murder from becoming known in the US, but Cromwell wrote to the AAC and then repeated the accusation as soon as his ship docked in the US. When the press talked to Wiessner on his arrival, he merely said that on mountains, as in war, casualties were to be expected.[10] Given his heavy German accent, German birth and the war in Europe, it was hardly a sensible analogy. In the furore which followed, Wiessner resigned from the AAC (he was subsequently made an honorary member in 1966, not as a result of his achievements on the K2 expedition, but for his climbs within the US). But by 1941 Americans had other, more important, matters to concern them, and the issue faded away. Ironically, in later life Wiessner transferred his enmity from Cromwell to Durrance, who, he claimed, was responsible for stripping the camps and thus causing Wolfe's death. Surprisingly, Durrance did not defend himself against this accusation, despite his innocence of the charge, only years later saying he had remained silent because he did not think anyone would believe his word against Wiessner's. But while it is clear that the lack of sleeping bags in and below Camp VI meant Wiessner and Pasang were forced to descend to Base Camp, rather than attempt to climb back up to Wolfe, other decisions also had an impact on the outcome.

Wiessner's decision to take Wolfe high on the mountain has to be questioned, as does his decision to absent himself as leader from low on the mountain, despite knowing that there was no effective leadership in his absence. Once high, there was a nine-day silence during which the rest of the team, at or towards the base of the peak, not only malfunctioned, but – on the basis of Sherpa evidence that proved false – assumed the worst and acted accordingly. When Wolfe demanded to stay at Camp VII, Wiessner should have insisted he descend. Leaving such an incompetent mountaineer at a high camp while he went off towards the summit was one thing. Leaving him alone as the highest man on the mountain was very different, and Wiessner already had enough information to know that something had gone radically wrong with his expedition. Wiessner had taken a poorly balanced team to the mountain: Dudley Wolfe and three brave Sherpas had paid a high penalty for his errors.

And yet, with better Base Camp management and a little more luck, Wiessner could have climbed K2, collected Wolfe on the descent and returned in triumph. As it was, a magnificent individual achievement, albeit from a man who allowed personal ambition to get in the way of the requirements of leadership, would be for ever tainted by the first deaths to have occurred on K2.

Houston, 1953

War stole men and their aspirations away for a decade. When peace returned, the Americans thought again of K2. Negotiations began, but soon stalled. In the wake of British India being granted independence, two nations, India and Pakistan, were created in August 1947, the disputed border between them cutting through the Karakoram and making it a no-go area. The situation seemed hopeless, but Charles Houston was determined to make another attempt on K2 and used his friendship with the US ambassador to Pakistan to obtain permission for an expedition. So in 1953, with war-hero Dwight D. Eisenhower newly installed in the White House, a team flew from New York to London, landing there on 25 May at a time when preparations were under way for the coronation of Queen Elizabeth II.

The team Houston was leading included only Bob Bates from the 1939 expedition.[11] Bill House had been asked, but declined because of business commitments. Dick Burdsall had been killed on Aconcagua just a few months earlier, while, as we have seen, the relationship between Houston and Paul Petzoldt had broken down. Petzoldt did apply for membership, but was turned down. In addition to Houston and Bates, there were George Bell, Bob Craig, Art Gilkey, Dee Molenaar and Pete Schoening.[12] The transport officer was Lieutenant Tony Streather, who had reached the summit of Tirich Mir (7701m/25260ft) in 1951. Streather would prove a valuable addition to the climbing team. The Pakistani liaison officer was Colonel Ata Ullah.

The Americans' equipment was state of the art,[13] including down jackets, but the decision was made not to take supplementary oxygen, apart from a couple of cylinders for medicinal purposes. The choice was not dictated by ethical issues, but because oxygen sets were expensive, cumbersome (and so required a lot of porters to move) and regarded as unreliable, the latter creating a major problem as failure would leave an unacclimatised climber extremely vulnerable to high-altitude sickness. The team also had radios, the need for good communications being one lesson of the 1939 tragedy. Sherpas were not allowed into Pakistan, so the team was supported by six Hunzas, though they were used only low on the mountain as Houston was concerned about how they would perform on the difficult sections of the route, and he was reluctant to have men strung out over the mountain because of the risks of stone fall. He therefore did not take the equipment necessary to allow the Hunzas to go high, something he rather regretted later when the men proved far better than he had anticipated.

Having flown from the US to Pakistan (where the news was heard that Hillary and Tenzing had climbed Everest), the team then flew to Skardu, dramatically cutting the time it had taken to reach the town in 1939. As in 1938, the team seemed to have had a great time on the walk-in to K2, marvelling at the peaks on each side of the Baltoro, and having fun at each other's expense – Molenaar offered his services as a barber, claiming to have had experience in the trade 'which his sample demonstration did nothing to confirm'. Base Camp and the lower camps on the Abruzzi were established, though not without some problems in locating the route pioneered in 1938. The site of Camp III was moved to avoid the problems of stone fall from climbers operating above, which had damaged tents and threatened injuries in 1938. At Camp IV the remnants of the 1939 expedition were still strewn about: some food that was still edible after fourteen years in the deep freeze, and three sleeping bags that were usable once thawed and dried. Houston led up House's Chimney – something he had wanted to do, but feared might be beyond his capabilities – and Camp V was established. A haulage system was then set up to move supplies up the face split by the chimney, saving the need for loaded climbers to negotiate it.

The expedition book[14] details the build-up of camps and supplies on the mountain, together with descriptions of Houston's feelings on reaching the debris of the previous attempts, particularly at the site of the 1939 Camp VI. He found the wreckage very moving, the sleeping bags, stove, and 'a small bundle of tea wrapped in a handkerchief' being evocative of its last inhabitants, the Sherpas who had come to rescue Dudley Wolfe, and who had died trying. But in addition the book also contains lyrical passages that reveal a deep love for the mountain environment:

> Dawn on June 25 was unforgettably beautiful. Tags and tatters of clouds shredded by the high wind lay scattered in the valleys below. Infinite myriads of tiny ice crystals sparkled in the air about us. The sky was deepest blue. Across the valley below us range after range of unknown peaks faded to the horizon. The rising sun colored all.

The passage is a delight, but the next sentence adds a touch of stark reality to the scene: 'But it was cold, terribly cold.'

Of the 1939 Camp VII Houston makes no comment, but apparently no sign of it or the 1938 camp was found: Houston was later to say that the entire area looked very different than it had in 1938, consistent with the view that avalanches had not only wiped the mountain clean but changed the topography significantly. The team's site for Camp VII was found by luck when Craig, idly chipping at the ice during a rest in the seemingly futile search for a suitable site, found an ice cave which, when the surrounding ice was excavated, allowed space for a tent in which Schoening and Gilkey could spend the night. But the site was on a slope which seemed avalanche-prone and the next day was spent searching for a better position. None was found, but a good site was found for Camp VIII and the decision made that the team would climb directly from VI to VIII if conditions allowed, to avoid the dangers of VII. Houston describes that long climb (about 600m/2000ft), which he undertook with a 35lb (16kg) rucksack ferrying supplies; the climbing began early in the morning, taking five hours to reach the site of Camp VII, and the day finished at 6pm with him completely exhausted.

When the last of the supplies had been brought up from Camp VI the entire team, seven Americans and Streather, were gathered at Camp VIII (7774m/25,500ft). There was no one on the mountain between them and Base Camp, where Ata Ullah was radioing weather reports to the high camp, and the six Hunza porters waited. After the expedition Houston was criticised for his decision to gather everyone high on the mountain with no back-up lower down, but the team supported the decision, reasoning that having sufficient load carriers at height allowed the best chance of success as Camp IX still had to be established. At Camp VIII a summit strategy was worked out. All eight men would climb upwards, carrying enough supplies to last two men three days. Those two men would be established in Camp IX (at about 8232m/27,000ft, it was hoped) with the other six descending to Camp VIII. The next day the two men at IX would attempt the summit, while two others moved up again from VIII to IX, to assist the first summitteers down if successful, to attempt the peak if they were not. The two teams were selected by secret ballot, each man choosing those he thought were strongest. Bell and Craig would be the first team, Gilkey and Schoening the second (though the official newsletter of the expedition reversed this order). Houston did not tell Ata Ullah these names: indeed, the plan was to tell no one – this democratic team, though with Houston always holding a casting vote as leader, would merely announce to the world that K2 had been climbed, two men reaching the summit. It was a wonderful idea, though history suggests it was doomed to failure in the longer term.[15]

The plan needed three days of fine weather. Up to that point the weather had been mixed, with frequent, usually short-lived storms, and the news from Ata Ullah was not optimistic that things would improve soon. They did not, Camp VIII being storm-bound from 3 August. The tent Houston and Bell shared was wrecked, forcing two two-man tents to accommodate three. And still the storm raged. On the fourth day the men discussed retreat. Several had incipient frostbite and a couple were feeling unwell. They decided to stay. But next day (the fifth day of the storm), with the weather improved enough for the men to leave their tents, Art Gilkey collapsed unconscious in the snow. On examination, Houston knew that this was different from the odd sick feelings, aches and pains of other team members, which indicated only a growing fatigue. This was serious: Gilkey had thrombophlebitis in his left leg. The condition, caused by blood clots forming in veins, can lead to clots breaking off and migrating. If they lodge in such a way that vital functions are stopped or impaired, such embolisms can be very serious or fatal. Houston knew that such a thing might happen at sea level, but his patient was over 7000m up on a storm-bound mountain where descent, even in good weather, was non-trivial. Add dehydration, cold and anxiety, and Houston was already convinced that Gilkey was very unlikely to reach Base Camp alive.

Gilkey's condition vetoed any summit bid, but Houston was of the view that there was almost no hope that they could evacuate their stricken companion: the descent was just too difficult. But there was no alternative. Not for one moment was the possibility of leaving Gilkey at Camp VIII considered. The team would attempt to get him down, a decision that, if the storm continued to rage, might doom them all. Given the lull in the storm, an immediate attempt was made to descend, Gilkey being wrapped in a sleeping bag and attached to ropes. As they were preparing to depart, Houston started to clear the camp site, throwing food down the slope and preparing to do the same to the tents. He was told to leave it: time did not permit, and the weather would take care of the mess. It was extremely fortunate that he took notice: the slope up which the team had climbed was now heaped in fresh snow and ready to avalanche, and after a short while it was clearly too dangerous to continue and the men moved back to the camp. Had Houston persisted with his housekeeping the men would not have survived the night. Now, though safe in the tents, the whole team seemed trapped.

Taking advantage of the continuing relative calm, Schoening and Craig went out again, searching for the less dangerous route to the west. They found one, but it was too late to try it that day. On 8 August, with Gilkey's condition having improved a little, Houston decided that they would wait one more day in the hope of an improvement in the weather. If it did not improve, most of the team would descend in the hope of being able to recover their strength before returning to aid a rescue. Houston and Streather would stay with Gilkey. As the day was now free, Schoening and Craig climbed up in a desperate and futile attempt at the summit. The managed about 130m (400ft) before being defeated by the conditions. On the following day (9 August) the storm worsened, and so did Gilkey's condition. There was now no doubt that he had pulmonary embolism, confirming Houston's opinion that he would not survive the descent. But if he was to have any chance at all, time was now critical.

And so on 10 August, despite the continuing storm, the descent began, with Gilkey in his sleeping bag attached to several climbing ropes, on which two men pulled when needed and two men braked when required. Out in front Schoening and Molenaar prospected a safe route. In the expedition book Bates notes 'we all knew that some of us might never get down the mountain alive'. When lowering the casualty, visibility was so poor that it needed a man at the makeshift stretcher, signalling to another standing above who passed the signal back to those holding the ropes – yet the ropes were only 36m (120ft) long. The work was exhausting, and it was also freezing cold, all the rescuers losing sensation in fingers and toes in the intense cold, but the men were now almost level with Camp VII, where a single tent still stood on the dangerous ledge which had been cut into the slope. Then an avalanche swept away the stretcher, but it was held by those at the top. When the avalanche had passed, Schoening and Molenaar climbed up to Gilkey and took over the task of lowering him. He was lowered over a cliff, firmly belayed by Schoening, who was standing behind a large boulder. This allowed Craig, who had been frozen and exhausted by the effort of holding Gilkey during the avalanche, to climb across to Camp VII to try to warm himself. Molenaar tied himself on to the rope Craig had vacated, attaching himself to the sick man, and then moved towards Camp VII. Slightly above Molenaar were Bell and Streather on one rope, Houston and Bates on another. Bell then slipped.

In the expedition book Bates writes:

I never saw Bell fall, but to my horror I saw Streather being dragged off the slope and making desperate efforts to jam the pick of his ax into the ice and stop. Streather had been standing above the rope from Houston to me. In almost the same instance I saw Houston swept off, and though I turned and lunged at the hard ice with the point of my ax, a terrible jerk ripped me from my hold and threw me backward headfirst down the slope. *This is it!* I thought as I landed heavily on my pack. There was nothing I could do now. We had done our best, but our best wasn't good enough. This was the end. Since nobody was on the rope with Houston and me, there was no one else to hold us, and I knew that nothing could stop us now. On the slope below, no rock jutted out on which the rope between us could catch. Only thousands of feet of empty space separated us from the glacier below.

But Bates did stop, his arms tangled in a rope so taut he could not free them. Only later would the men realise the exact sequence of events and how that sequence had prevented four of them from falling to their deaths. As Bell and Streather fell, they became entangled in the rope linking Houston and Bates. That pulled the latter two off, but as the four continued downhill, Streather then hit and tangled with the rope from Molenaar to Gilkey. Molenaar was swept off his feet, but remained attached to the sick man. Above Gilkey, Schoening was now the only man attached to the mountain. He described what happened:

Well, I was lucky. My ice ax was driven into the snow and braced against the upper side of that big boulder frozen into the ice. The rope passed around the ax to where I stood in front of the boulder, and went around my body, so that the force was widely distributed. Of course I was belaying Art anyway, and when I saw George slip and then Tony and the others pulled off, I swung weight onto the head of the ax and held on as the rope slid a bit. The force on me was not too great, but at the ice ax that seven-sixteenth-inch nylon rope stretched until it looked like a quarter-inch line, and I was scared stiff the boulder would be pulled loose. If that happened, the ax, which was braced against it, would go, too, and we would be lost.

The rope held, as did the boulder, but Schoening's account downplays his own part in saving the lives of his team mates. Those who fell had slipped as much as 90m (300ft), and with Gilkey on his rope as well, Schoening had held six men.

The condition of those who had fallen varied. Bates and Streather were shaken but unhurt. Molenaar had a cut on his left thigh and chest pain which pointed to bad bruising or a cracked rib. Bell had lost his gloves and his hands were freezing: they were saved only because Bates climbed down to him and gave him a spare pair. Houston was concussed. Bates next climbed down to him. Houston was capable of standing and moving, but was very confused, not knowing where he was or why. Bates got him to move by telling him, 'Charlie, if you want to see Dorcas and Penny again [his wife and daughter], climb up there *right now*!'

Craig, alerted by Schoening, climbed across to Gilkey. With Streather's help, he secured the injured man to the slope with two ice axes. That released Schoening, who could make his way across to Camp VII, where he tried to get some warmth back into his hands, frozen by holding on to the rope that had held the fall. He was joined there by the rest of the party, Gilkey having been assured they would be back for him soon. The situation of the team was precarious: some were injured, some equipment had been lost, and at Camp VII there was only one tent, and that capable of holding only two men. Another ledge was carved and a bivouac tent that had been carried down by Schoening was erected. During the work shouts were exchanged with Gilkey, though because of the wind no one at the camp could make out what the sick man was saying. Then, with the worst of the wounded – Bell and Houston – settled, and Schoening still warming his hands, Bates and Streather went back to Gilkey. Both were slightly snow blind, snow was blowing off the slope and 'we seemed to be moving in a dream. Fortunately, the wind had dropped as we reached the rock rib and looked into the gully where Art had been left suspended. What we saw there I shall never forget. The whole slope was bare of life. Art Gilkey had gone!' Everything, including the two axes that had secured him had gone, a groove suggesting an avalanche had swept the slope clean.[16]

Back at the camp the men spent a miserable night. In the larger tent four men sat on a single air mattress. They had one double sleeping bag, three men sharing the outer, Houston being wrapped in the inner. Houston was still confused, spending the night constantly asking how the others were, then asking again a few minutes later. The men had to sit with their backs to the slope, taking care not to push too hard on the tent fabric opposite as the tent overhung the ledge. The situation in the other tent was no better. Next day, after brewing some tea and eating a little cereal, with the storm still raging, a desperate retreat began. The men were exhausted, Bell's hands were frostbitten and he had lost his glasses, without which he was almost blind, and Houston was still confused, so that almost any slip would have resulted in a pair, or more, falling to their deaths. Houston started off well, but 'after going 20 feet he sat down in the middle of a steep snow patch, put his chin in his hand, and looked around as it to say "What are we doing here?" Schoening looked perplexed. After a few minutes he shook the rope and called down "Come on Charlie. Let's go!" And Charlie, still looking bewildered, got up and continued to climb down.'

Mountaincraft built up over years allowed the men to descend safely, despite their exhaustion and injuries. One obstacle after another was overcome, and Camp VI was reached. The tents had to be freed of snow, but soon a degree of comfort had been established. By chance Bell also found his spare glasses, and they were intact. Houston's condition seemed to improve, but he kept Bates awake much of the night by crawling around the tent they shared and announcing 'I'm terribly sorry to bother you. If I can just get out of this warehouse, everything will be all right.'

Next day (12 August) the storm abated a little and Streather and Schoening descended to Camp V, but then the storm blew harder again and the rest were forced to stay in Camp VI. On the 13th everyone reached Camp IV, the descent of House's Chimney being especially trying. Houston had now recovered and insisted on belaying the others down. He had been the first man up the Chimney: now he was the last man down, arriving at the camp in darkness. On the 14th Bell had to make slits in his boots to enable them to accommodate his frostbitten, swollen feet, but Camp II was eventually reached, the Americans meeting three Hunzas who had climbed up to offer support. Next day the men reached Base Camp. The Hunzas erected a cairn in memory of Gilkey, on which the Americans placed his ice axe, flowers and a box holding the flags they had intended to take to the summit, a message and a poem. Now there was only the journey home.[17]

The climbers all recovered from their injuries, though Bell lost one toe and part of another. Schoening and Streather went on to make significant Himalayan ascents (Schoening the first ascent of Gasherbrum I, Streather being in the second team to reach the summit of Kangchenjunga, the world's third highest mountain, the day after the first ascent, in 1955). In many ways Charles Houston appears to have been the main victim of the climb. In her biography of him Bernadette McDonald says that while Houston later claimed to have given up climbing after the expedition because he thought he had failed his team and because he could no longer put his family at risk of losing him, the reality was much darker. Houston had actually applied, and received permission, for a K2 expedition in 1955, but the 1954 Italian success made it pointless. Worse still, the first ascent 'seemed a violation of [my] mountain'. The day after he heard of the Italian success Houston entered a hospital 65km (40 miles) from his home with no idea of who he was and why he was there. The police were called and inquiries revealed his identity. He was released into the care of his wife and a friend as he was not suicidal, the episode being put down to amnesia. Houston also claimed to have had a vision of blood splashes on a road, Gilkey's blood. For years afterwards Houston would be tense and depressed during the first ten days of August, and in an afterword to the third printing of *Savage Mountain*, he wrote,

Those first ten days in August 1953 inexorably changed my life. After 1954 I quit climbing. I had lost interest in attempting the great mountains perhaps because the guilt I felt had soured them for me. As the prime mover for the expedition and the doctor I had failed: we did not reach the summit, and I had been unable to save our friend's life. That our peers praise us for actions we saw implicit in the mountain spirit is irrelevant. I turned to teaching and practising medicine, and to research and writing about high altitude. To me, K2, though a failure, was a glorious epiphany.

Chapter 4

The First Ascent: The Italians, 1954

'The burden of K2.'

Lino Lacedelli

Following the 1929 Spoleto expedition to K2, the co-leader, Ardito Desio,[1] attempted to raise enthusiasm for another attempt on K2, a seemingly strange ambition, for although he was obviously at home in the mountain environment, he was no climber and seemed to take little interest in climbing: in his book of the 1954 K2 expedition, for instance, he refers to the ascent of Annapurna, the first 8000m peak to be climbed, as being in 1951, not 1950, a mistake no true mountaineer would make. The debacle of the *Italia* expedition was unlikely to have made Mussolini's government any more receptive than it had been when the 1929 expedition set out, and the Italian Alpine Club (Club Alpino Italiano, or CAI) seems to have been equally lukewarm for several years. But in 1939 Desio finally persuaded the Club to take the matter seriously, only for war to bring an abrupt halt to any thoughts of mountaineering expeditions. The conflict left Italy destitute, both economically and psychologically, ordinary Italians paying a heavy price for the disastrous fascist adventure, with its ill-advised imperialism, catastrophic alliance with Hitler's Germany, the near-civil war following the collapse of government after invasion, the destruction wrought as the Germans retreated and the Allies advanced, and occupation.

But by 1948 the tenacious Desio was once again trying to persuade officialdom of the merits of an attempt. Desio envisaged using aircraft to drop supplies by parachute to Base Camp to avoid the time and expense of the Baltoro trek, and even considered helicopters as a better alternative until discovering that their short range and low ceiling ruled them out. Desio's enthusiasm for aircraft derived from their use during an expedition to Iran in 1933. That trip, which used military aircraft, and others which he led, or was engaged in, to Libya in search of oil and to Ethiopia and Albania in search of mineral mining opportunities have led to suggestions that Desio was closely linked – for some rather too closely linked – to Italian fascism. Given the patrician attitude he showed on K2 in 1954, his undoubted (if, arguably, well-founded) intellectual arrogance, and, especially, his very pronounced love of his country, it would be very strange if Desio did not see fascism, at least in its early stages, as a force for good, particularly as it also financed trips which he was academically interested in pursuing. But that, of course, is very different from saying Desio was himself a fascist.

Not until 1951 was Desio able to persuade anyone to take his venture seriously. In that year the Italian Olympic Committee put up the money to send Desio to Pakistan. But the funds were not made available until the following year and by the time Desio arrived in Karachi the Pakistan government had already given the Americans permission for 1953. Desio therefore had to settle for 1954.

Back in Italy Desio began preparations for an expedition that would have a dual purpose, both mountaineering and science, and he decided to make a reconnaissance in 1953. On this Desio was accompanied by Riccardo Cassin.[2] Of the decision for the two men to go, Desio states, 'To accompany me ... I had chosen Riccardo Cassin, a climber, to whose travelling expenses the Italian Alpine Club had generously contributed.' The idea that Cassin was merely 'a climber' seems to indicate damnation by faint praise, or, and more likely, Desio's view that mountaineers were considerably lower on the social pecking order than were scientists, especially important scientists such as himself. In Cassin's book he confirms that something along the latter lines was clearly at work. Cassin lived in Lecco and travelled to Milan, where Desio lived, by train. He then continued to Rome by train, while Desio flew down. Although both men flew from Rome to Karachi, only Desio flew on to Rawalpindi while 'I again followed by train. It was a tedious journey of more than 1,300 kilometres. It took 36 hours ...'. At Rawalpindi there was news that the Americans had failed in their attempt on the peak. 'On the evening of 30 August, there was a reception given in Colonel Ata Ullah's house [Ata Ullah had been with the Americans on K2 as liaison officer and would go with the Italians in 1954], with members of the American expedition. Professor Desio went alone. The Americans, I was told, showed photographs of their route and campsites.' Cassin, it seems, was being shown his place in the scheme of things, though the following day he met the Americans at the airport and talked at length with them.

At Skardu Desio was asked his professional opinion of an advancing glacier which was threatening a valley and so detoured to view it. He was able to report that the glacier presented no real danger. At Rawalpindi the Italians had heard that other groups had also applied for permission to attempt K2 in 1954: Desio was keen to stress at every opportunity that his investigation of the glacier and his reassurance were the main reasons the Pakistanis found in the Italians' favour, but it is more likely that the substantial aid Italy was giving Pakistan at the time was more influential. Following the detour Desio and Cassin then trekked to the base of K2, examined the route and returned to Italy. There they learned that permission for 1954 had been granted.

Desio's official account of the expedition notes Cassin's participation in the 1953 reconnaissance, but makes no comment on why he was not a member of the expedition, Cassin's name not being mentioned again after the reconnaissance was over. This is strange considering that not only was Cassin on the reconnaissance, but in November 1953, when the CAI formally announced the expedition, it stated that the expedition leader was Desio, but the climbing leader was Cassin. But while Desio thought Cassin's absence from the team not worthy of mention, Cassin's book, in a chapter headed 'An Unfair, Bitter Exclusion', is much more forthcoming. Cassin notes that all those proposed for membership by the CAI, himself included, were given medicals, and that he, and others, were declared unfit. A disbelieving Cassin went for a further, more demanding medical, at which he was told he was fit. Details of this test were then posted to the CAI. Cassin was delighted: 'I went straight to Milan to tell Professor Desio, convinced that the results would please him too. But I could see from his reaction that he was not at all pleased.' Cassin goes on to say that Desio then persuaded him to resign from the expedition, telling him that only one person was necessary to organise it and that he should not waste time away from work and home. And so Cassin resigned.

Why exactly he was foolish enough – he says naïve – to agree is beyond understanding and he offers no real clue in his book. Later, Cassin was to realise that the problems he had noticed his presence on the reconnaissance had caused were the real reason behind Desio's attitude:

> Then came the growing doubt (since confirmed by fact) that it happened [i.e. his exclusion] because the head of the expedition, Professor Desio, was afraid that his reputation might be obscured by mine: in fact, when we were on the way from the Baltoro, the journalists, reporters and mountaineers preferred to talk to me, a climber, rather than to a geologist. Desio, apparently irked by this, had even asked me not to talk to reporters, warning me that this could cause my exclusion from the expedition. He told me to tell the reporters that if they wanted news they should talk to him.

In Desio's writing there is an underlying inference that climbing the mountain was the secondary purpose of the expedition. But the activities of the reporters had alerted him, in unwelcome fashion, to the idea that the general public would actually be more interested in the mountain than in his science. As the public just could not be trusted to get the emphasis right, and given Cassin's reputation in that field, that might mean the spotlight would be upon him, something which Desio could neither risk nor tolerate. So Cassin had to go.

But getting Cassin to resign was not enough. Soon after, the results of the second set of medical tests were published; they were said to have confirmed the results of the first – Cassin was unfit to participate. Of this, Cassin writes that 'even if the committee [the expedition's overall organisational committee, primarily involved in financing the trip] did not want to publicize the real reason for my exclusion, they should not have based it on the fabrication of "physical unfitness" – a very serious accusation and one that was a real shock to me and which affected me for a long time'. The passage begs the question of what the 'real reason' for his resignation was, and whether the committee knew that 'real reason'. Not content to be rid of Cassin from his expedition, Desio, by declaring the, albeit false, medical reasons, ensured there would be no opportunity for an embittered man to make trouble by offering an alternative take on events. The medical reasons themselves were not formally mentioned, though there were leaks about heart and other problems. In his book *K2: The Price of Conquest*, Lino Lacedelli says varicose veins were also mentioned.

Desio's plan for the expedition is set out in his book. First is the science, a programme with six parts covering geology, geography and anthropography. Then comes the mountaineering. He writes: 'The expedition will of necessity be organized along military lines ... The need for rigid discipline will become apparent to every man once he has grasped the essential fact that everything must be subordinated to the attainment of the final goal, which is the conquest of K2.' But it would be wrong to read too much into this clarion call. Desio had talked with John Hunt and had learned well from the militaristic approach Hunt had employed in 1953. The dovetailing of science and climbing, Desio admits, caused 'bewilderment in mountaineering circles, where it was felt that so much scientific activity might seriously interfere with the work of the climbing party'. But Desio was not interested in such criticism and refused to compromise. He would have his science, arguing that the two strands meant an overall economy for each and 'should the mountaineering venture fail, the expedition would at any rate be able to point to the results of its scientific researches'. Desio would have his results, and the mountaineering might even provide a bonus.

Desio's book next considers the finances of the trip, setting down the professional qualifications of the CAI committee set up to deal with them – two barristers, two engineers, four doctors, a solicitor and a chartered accountant – and noting that small contributions were also received from 'all manner of humble and obscure folk'. The sort of folk, one imagines, who could not be trusted to enthuse for the right reasons.

After the medical tests, the possible candidates for the expedition were taken on a winter training camp after which a team of eleven climbers was chosen from eighteen hopefuls. The team was Enrico Abram, Ugo Angelino, Walter Bonatti,[3] Achille Compagnoni,[4] Cirillo Floreanini, Pino Gallotti, Lino Lacedelli,[5] Mario Puchoz, Ubaldo Rey, Gino Soldà and Sergio Viotto. The choice of Bonatti and Lacedelli, two of the youngest team members (Bonatti was the youngest at 23, Lacedelli was 29), might have caused tension because of events on the East Face of the Grand Capucin.⁶ Lacedelli claims that was not the case, but it is not clear if Bonatti was of the same opinion: certainly in one of his later books he makes the point that Laccdclli's claim was disputed, though, of course, by then Bonatti had many more reasons to be aggravated by Lacedelli's behaviour.

In his book Lacedelli says that during the training camp it was already clear that Desio and Compagnoni were close, each flattering the other: the leader's enthusiasm for Compagnoni is mentioned in his book (see below) but only later in the expedition, the impression given being that it was Compagnoni's performance on the trip which singled him out as a valued team member, rather than their closeness having developed much earlier.

Desio's account of the trek to Base Camp is as staid as might be expected, even when he recounts the inevitable porters' strike, which seems to have been sorted out by the Italians leaving the job of negotiating to Ata Ullah. Desio does, though, have moments when the sheer beauty of the Baltoro cannot be tucked away behind a mask of objectivity: 'Concordia Amphitheatre is perhaps the most beautiful sight that a climber could wish to see. It would indeed be difficult to find a ring of mountains architecturally so beautiful and at the same time so diversified as those which surround the undulating, icy plain of Concordia.'

Base Camp was reached late because of a problem getting enough flour to feed the porters, and with more bad than good weather the climb took longer to establish than had been anticipated. Then, to add to the woes of the Italians, Mario Puchoz suddenly died at Camp II; the diagnosis was pneumonia. The news stunned the team and after the body was brought down for burial near the memorial to Art Gilkey, there was conflict between Desio and the climbers, the leader wanting the climb to resume the following day, the men wanting a day of rest to recover from the shock of Puchoz's death. The latter got their way.

But this was one of very few occasions when Desio was over-ruled; he controlled the climbing team in an authoritarian manner (referring to the climbers as 'my little boys') which allowed no debate and certainly accepted no criticism. Each day, Lacedelli says, Desio wrote down orders which Compagnoni pinned to a tent. The orders were to be followed without discussion. To ensure this was the case, Lacedelli writes, one day a specific instruction was set down: 'If anyone doesn't obey my orders they will be punished with the most powerful weapon in the world, the press!'

Despite the lack of empathy between team and leader, progress on the mountain was maintained (in part, Lacedelli says, by the lead and support climbers occasionally doing what was required rather than what was ordered) and four camps were placed below House's Chimney, which Compagnoni and Rey then climbed to establish Camp V. Learning from the experience of the Americans, a windlass had been brought to aid the hauling of supplies up the steep chimney. But poor weather, with a succession of storms, made life difficult for the climbers strung out along the Abruzzi Spur, though rather less so for the expedition leader, who commanded from Base Camp, keeping in touch with the men on the hill via regular radio transmissions and written notes exhorting greater effort. Desio's book is short of actual details on the way the route was established, in part no doubt because he directed everything from Base Camp, but also, according to Lacedelli, because after the expedition he demanded the diaries of all the climbers. Fearing, probably correctly, that they would never see them again and would never be able to dispute what was published, all but Compagnoni refused.

But Base Camp living had its moments. One day five Hunzas arrived from the mountain, having arbitrarily decided to abandon their work. Desio sacked several to encourage the others, but this precipitated a walk-out by the rest of the Hunzas. Again Ata Ullah negotiated a settlement, one which saw three men sacked and the remainder heading back up the Spur. To make sure these men worked properly, Desio decided to accompany them to the high camps 'but my companions pressed me to abandon the idea in view of the fact that the tents were already filled to capacity'. It is difficult to read that passage without a smile and the thought that his companions were keener on Desio staying put in Base Camp for more fundamental reasons. (Desio did later go to Camp II to deliver in person the exhortation to greater effort detailed below.)

But the weather, already disrupting the effort of climbing the mountain, now became much worse, and Radio Pakistan predicted no change in the near future. Desio re-analysed the weather data from previous expeditions, which he used to define his timetable, and sent another message up to his team. It noted that

> the bad weather which has persisted this summer almost without a break, upsetting our plans for the assault on K2 and, moreover, imposing a severe strain on our physical and moral resources, cannot and must not weaken our will to succeed in an enterprise which has attracted the attention and fired the imagination of people throughout the world ... We can afford, if need be, to spend a further two months here waiting for a favourable opportunity. If we were to return home before we had exhausted all the possibilities that remain to us of reaching the summit of K2, or without at any rate making a serious attempt on the peak, we should be breaking faith with the Nation.

Reading this communiqué it is difficult to decide between admiration at Desio's tenacity and unbridled optimism, and astonishment that men who were marooned, fatigued and apprehensive after a succession of storm-lashed days, not to mention debilitated by high-altitude living, did not immediately mutiny when subjected to another example of Desio's autocratic rule.

In the same section of Desio's book in which he sets down this need for even greater efforts by his team, he notes: 'I had a long conversation that day with

Compagnoni, and at the end of it I was left with the unshakeable conviction that he was a man of iron will who would allow nothing to deflect him from his main purpose.' That description was to turn out to be very accurate, and, as we shall see, reaching the summit was Compagnoni's main purpose, and nothing, not even the use of tactics that were, at best, dubious, would be allowed to interfere. Desio goes on: 'There is no denying, in fact, that in Compagnoni I had a most valuable ally.' That, too, would prove to be very much the case, and Desio would do whatever was required to protect that ally. After noting the valued assistance of Compagnoni, Desio states that when the weather improved a little he sent another message, one which 'entrusted Compagnoni, who had revealed a staying-power and a determination that were altogether remarkable', with 'the duty and responsibility of directing the attack on the summit'. After that delegation Desio continued by noting the interest the outside world was taking in the climb and adding:

> Remember that if you succeed in scaling the peak – as I am confident you will – the entire world will hail you as champions of your race and your fame will endure throughout your lives and long after you are dead. Thus, even if you never achieve anything else of note you will be able to say that you have not lived in vain.

The message ends by noting the 'enormous moral responsibility' that each climber bore for success.

Up on the hill, when the weather improved Bonatti and Lacedelli used the ropeway to hoist loads up House's Chimney and then transported them to Camp VI, from where Compagnoni and Rey were pushing the route out over the Black Pyramid. Then, in cold, windy conditions, the four men extended the route towards the intended site of Camp VII. Bad weather now returned, pinning the team down, and not until 25 July, eight weeks after Camp I had been established, did the Italians finally establish Camp VII. It was occupied by Abram, Bonatti, Compagnoni, Gallotti, Lacedelli and Rey on the 26th, but a storm then stopped them moving until the 28th. When they did start up again, Bonatti was not with them, having succumbed to food poisoning. Rey turned back, but the others continued up, establishing Camp VIII. The height of the camp is disputed, the climbers saying it was at about 7745m (25,400ft), Desio maintaining 7843m (25,725ft), while Bonatti believes it was about 7625m (25,000ft). Compagnoni and Lacedelli stayed at the camp: it would be these two that would try for the summit. But to make the attempt they needed the equipment that was still lower on the mountain, including the oxygen sets. On 29 July the two started out towards the summit intent on exploring the route to Camp IX and leaving loads as high as they could. Below them Abram, a recovered Bonatti, Gallotti and Rey carried supplies up towards Camp VIII. Only Bonatti and Gallotti made it, the other two leaving their loads about halfway between the camps. On 30 July Compagnoni and Lacedelli set out for Camp IX while Bonatti and Gallotti went down to collect the loads left by Abram and Rey. These they brought back to Camp VIII, where they were joined by Abram and the Hunzas Mahdi and Isakhan. The equipment now at Camp VIII included what Desio calls 'oxygen masks[7] and other equipment.' Realising that the summit attempt would likely fail unless the oxygen equipment was taken to Camp IX, at 3.30pm Abram, Bonatti and Mahdi set out in the tracks of Compagnoni and Lacedelli. Abram was eventually unable to continue and went back to Camp VIII, reaching it at 7pm. Bonatti and Mahdi continued.

Of Bonatti and Mahdi, Desio states:

The sun was now low in the sky, but Camp IX still lay far ahead. Slowly, painfully, the two men plodded on through the twilight. As darkness descended they began to shout in an effort to attract the attention of Compagnoni and Lacedelli, but for some time the north wind rendered their voices inaudible. At last they heard their companions shouting to them to go down as quickly as they could: there were some very steep, ice-coated slabs of rock immediately below Camp IX which it would have been dangerous to attempt to negotiate in the dark. The two men, realizing they could only descend at risk of their lives, dug a hole in the snow and prepared to spend the night in it – a night which at such an altitude was bound to be terrible beyond words.

Beyond words is almost correct, for in the last pages of the book Desio offers very few on Bonatti and Mahdi's night in the open, and those he does seem indifferent to the 'terrible' ordeal and its consequences. Having noted that Compagnoni and Lacedelli had suffered frostbitten hands, Desio states that 'Mahdi's toes had also been affected during that terrible night which the three men had spent in the open below Camp IX'. (Note: 'three' men is an error by the translator of the English version, the Italian original not mentioning the number of men.) Later the Hunzas decided to postpone 'their departure from Camp V until they had administered first aid to Mahdi' and again 'we were joined by Mahdi and the other Hunzas who had lingered in the camps on the Abruzzi Ridge'. On the trek out 'Mahdi was apparently no longer in a fit state to walk and would have to be carried on a stretcher'. The difficulties of carrying Mahdi's stretcher are mentioned briefly again later. Of Bonatti there are merely two short mentions: that he was excited and sleepless at Camp IX after the summit party returned, and that he and Gallotti arrived in Base Camp on 3 August, a day after Compagnoni and Lacedelli. That the leader of the expedition was only 'apparently' aware that Mahdi was not fit to walk seems almost beyond comprehension. In the event Mahdi had fingers and toes amputated because of his frostbite injuries.

The Summit Climb: Official Version

The section of Desio's book on the summit climb is credited to Compagnoni and Lacedelli, but was, according to Lacedelli, constructed from conversations between the former and Desio. On 30 July the two men climbed up from Camp VIII, eventually setting up a small tent at 8102m (26,575ft), where 'it had been agreed that Abram, Bonatti and one of the Hunza would join us before evening (bringing) the oxygen cylinders'. Above them was the 'sinister wall of rock' which Weissner had tackled in 1939. The two men were concerned about the lack of oxygen, but decided to attempt the summit even if the sets did not arrive. But then they saw three men slowly climbing up towards them. As darkness fell the two men could make out Bonatti's voice but not what he was saying as 'the high wind made conversation extremely difficult' (Bonatti claims it was perfectly still and conversation was easy across a basically horizontal distance of about 100m[8]) and eventually called down that the men should leave the oxygen equipment and go back to Camp VIII. Assuming they had done that, the two settled down to an uncomfortable night. Unable to eat or to do more than doze, they endured a bitterly cold, interminable night. Next morning they were astonished to see a man below them heading down towards Camp VIII.

> We were simply flabbergasted. What in the world could have happened? ... Try as we might, we could find no solution to the mystery. We thought of all the possible explanations except the right one. How could we suspect the truth – namely that two men had survived the rigours of a whole night spent in the open at an altitude of more than 26,000 feet?'

Early in the account Compagnoni states that when it appeared the oxygen sets might not reach Camp IX, he and Lacedelli considered an attempt without supplementary oxygen, and that 'success was now absolutely certain'. However, in his own book on the climb, Compagnoni describes what happened the following morning as the two crossed to retrieve the oxygen sets: 'After twenty or so steps, we realized that without oxygen we would not be able to go on: our lungs heaved uselessly like the gills of a fish out of water; our heads buzzed, our legs buckled ...'. As the two had already climbed to Camp IX without supplementary oxygen the previous day, this presumably mirrored their progress on that climb and suggests that the idea of a bottled gas-free ascent was not the certain success Compagnoni suggests. In his book Lacedelli says he is not sure the two would even have tried for the summit without the oxygen, given that received opinion at the time was that such climbs were not possible, though he does say that with the benefit of hindsight (i.e. later ascents which showed that K2 could be climbed without bottled oxygen), perhaps they might have succeeded.

The official account continues by stating that the two men climbed across to where the oxygen sets, three cylinders each, had been left, reaching them at about

5am, and that the summit climb began at 6.15am. Before describing the climb Compagnoni notes: 'If we triumphed, the credit would go to all without distinction. And it was only right and proper that it should.' It was an impressive and worthy sentiment, but one that would not survive the return to Italy.

Compagnoni and Lacedelli made their way towards the rock wall Wiessner had attempted. The conditions were difficult, with waist-deep snow and the men's balance severely affected by the 19kg (42lb) weight of the oxygen sets on their backs. They soon realised that following Wiessner's route was not feasible, the first couloir being unclimbable due to the condition of the snow. They therefore tried other options, wasting, they say about two hours, and with Compagnoni taking a short fall, before Lacedelli was able to make progress after removing his gloves and crampons. By now they had arrived below the ice wall that threatens the upper section of the route and, at about 9am or 10am, the first of the three oxygen cylinders the men were carrying was exhausted. They next traversed left below 'a row of precarious-looking pinnacles of ice which seemed as if they must come crashing down on our heads at any moment', reaching a 16m (50ft) snow slope which Compagnoni took an hour to climb. The second oxygen bottle was now exhausted. The two men continued until 'suddenly, at intervals of a few seconds, we both experienced a horrible sensation. We found ourselves gasping for breath, an oppressively hot feeling surged through our heads and feet, our legs grew weak, we could no longer stand.' The third oxygen bottle was empty. For a moment the two were 'absolutely terrified', but after removing their masks and breathing deeply, they relaxed. Looking about they could see that the weather had improved and they were above the summit of Broad Peak (8047m/26,401ft). As they felt reasonably good, despite the loss of the supplementary oxygen, they therefore decided to continue. But they did not remove the dead weight of their oxygen sets, they say, because

> Firstly, in order to discard the crates we should have had to throw ourselves flat on the snow, which was very deep and unstable. The operation would accordingly have been both difficult and dangerous, particularly as the slope at this point was exceedingly steep. Secondly, we were convinced that it would require very little further effort to reach the summit, Thirdly, the sun was already sinking and every minute was precious. Fourthly, we were by no means hostile to the idea of leaving something bulky and solid on the summit as evidence of our achievement.

But the summit was not as close as they had thought. Slowly the two plodded up a slope which became less steep: 'The angle of the slope continued to diminish, by this time the ground was almost flat – now it *was* flat!' It was 6pm.

Compagnoni took off his gloves to film the summit but his hands soon showed signs of frostbite. One glove blew away, but fortunately Lacedelli had a spare. On the climb they had neither eaten nor drunk anything. After 30 minutes, just before starting the descent, each took a *sympamine* (amphetamine) tablet. Then, after one last look at the summit, 'that windswept solitude where it would probably be true to say that we had both just experienced the greatest moment of our lives', they started to descend.

The sun had now set, making the descent a formidable challenge, the only light being that shed by the stars of a clear night and a small torch. Instead of reversing their upward route, they eventually decided to plunge straight down the gully which they had avoided on the ascent[9] and found themselves at the point where they had collected the oxygen sets. From there on they continued almost by instinct, finally arriving close to Camp VIII. But then Compagnoni slipped over a cliff, pulling Lacedelli off. Compagnoni somersaulted downhill, landing relatively unharmed in soft snow, but fearful that Lacedelli, crampons and all, would land on him. But Lacedelli stopped higher up, equally unharmed. Their time of arrival is not mentioned in Desio's book, but Bonatti says it was about 11pm.

Bonatti's Story

Walter Bonatti has written several accounts of his climb towards Camp IX on 30 July (see Note 3) but the story is the essentially the same in each. It starts with the attack of food poisoning which forced him to stay in Camp VII while five others ascended to Camp VIII. First Rey returned, then, later, Abram and Gallotti, 'so Compagnoni and Lacedelli were to be the lucky ones who would make the final assault'.

At Camp VIII Bonatti says there was 'a long argument' (but the Italian original allows the translation to read 'long discussion') about what best to do. Supplies would not last the two days necessary for fetching the oxygen left halfway between Camps VII and VIII, and so it was agreed that Bonatti and Gallotti would fetch it and carry it up to Camp IX, which, it was agreed, would not be placed where originally planned, but 90m (300ft) lower to enhance the chances of the two men reaching it after their exhausting climb down, then up. The four men would then spend the night together at Camp IX, huddled into a single two-man tent. Bonatti says Compagnoni was exhausted and that he felt the best option might have been for him to replace the older man. But he wondered if Compagnoni would have the strength to fetch the oxygen and reach Camp IX if he suggested it. Bonatti was therefore relieved when Compagnoni said, 'If you are still in good shape tomorrow up there at Camp IX, it might well be that you have to change places with one of us.'

The next day, after the oxygen sets had been retrieved, only Bonatti was initially fit enough to start up for Camp IX. Bonatti then writes that he made an offer which was later to become one aspect of the subsequent controversy. 'It would have to be Mahdi who would go with me to Camp IX with the oxygen packs, but how was I to induce him to make such an effort without letting him believe that he too might have a chance of reaching the summit? That was the lever which would serve to enlist the services of the proud and stout-hearted Mahdi.' The men ate and 'then, beginning with the promise of a reward in rupees when victory was ours, we put the proposal to Mahdi, giving him the impression that he might be able to go to the summit with me, Lacedelli and Compagnoni. It was a necessary deception which had, however, a grain of truth in it.' It is worth pointing out here, before discussing the unpleasant aftermath of the climb, that Mahdi spoke no Italian and only a little English, while the Italians had limited English. Bonatti also says 'we', not 'I', implying that all the Italians were involved in the persuasion, and it is the case that Mahdi was kitted out in clothes taken from Abram and Gallotti. Apart, that is, from their boots, which did not fit. As a consequence Mahdi climbed up in ordinary mountain boots, not the high-altitude boots the Italians were wearing.

At 3.30pm Bonatti and Mahdi, accompanied by Abram who had recovered a little, started out. Bonatti called to Compagnoni and Lacedelli and they answered, but he could not see the tent. He called again and the answer was 'follow the tracks'. Assuming the tent was hidden behind a spur of rock, the men continued. But it soon became apparent it was not there. Bonatti was now getting desperate. He wondered if the two had continued to the altitude originally planned rather than stopping lower, as agreed. But he dismissed that idea as the tracks did not lead that way. The sun went behind the mountain and it grew very cold. At 6.30pm Abram decided he could go no further and returned to Camp VIII. The slope now steepened and there was no answer to Bonatti's shouts. Convinced that the tent must be behind a rock barrier ahead, Bonatti continued upwards, the now fearful Mahdi beginning to shout incomprehensibly. Bonatti reached the rock and looked behind it. There was no tent. It was now dark and Bonatti knew he would have to go back to Camp VIII, but what was he to do with the oxygen sets? He decided to make one last effort to reach the tent and went up again, with Mahdi continuing to shout.

By now Bonatti feared he had come too far to make a safe return to Camp VIII feasible. He had to find the tent: 'Suddenly I surprised myself by shouting, "No, I don't want to die! I must not die! Lino! Achille! Can't you hear us? Help us, curse you!" and breaking into violent threats.' Bonatti began to carve out a platform from the ice, and at that point a light appeared above and Bonatti could plainly hear Lacedelli. He asked if Bonatti had the oxygen, and when he replied that he had he was told to leave it and go down.[10] Seeing the light, Mahdi started off towards it, but the ground was so dangerous that Bonatti had to shout to him to come back. Then the light went out. Mahdi shouted, 'No good, Lacedelli Sahib! No good, Compagnoni Sahib!', but the light did not go on again.

Mahdi now tried to return to Camp VIII, but Bonatti knew that such a descent was suicidal. The two men might not survive the night, but they would definitely not survive the descent. They were therefore forced to bivouac. The height of their bivouac is disputed. In his book Lacedelli claims it was at 7950m. In an official map of the Italian Military Geographic Institute (IGM) it is given as 7990m, with Camp IX at 8060m. Bonatti, on the basis of the topography of the mountain, believes that both the camp and the bivouac were at 8100m, separated by about 100m or so of steep slabs. At the bivouac, despite the dangers of the situation, Bonatti had time to admire the sheer beauty of his surroundings:

> the sky was studded with a myriad of stars so bright as to cast strange reflections on the snow … There was no moon, yet all the summits around us could be distinguished clearly. In the valleys an immense sea of cloud grew more and more dense … All the high summits of the Karakoram seemed to be born magically as dark skerries rising out of a milky sea.

But this intensely beautiful vision did not survive the arrival of the night time cold and, later, a blizzard that blew up, so fierce that snow threatened to fill the men's eyes and noses and suffocate them.

The storm ceased as dawn approached. Bonatti was almost frozen into position, but Mahdi, desperate to reach safety, moved down as soon as he could see. Bonatti watched as Mahdi made it down the steep slope and disappeared towards the camp, but he himself did not move until the sun had risen and warmed him. It was 6am when he was ready to descend. He looked up for a sign of the tent, but could see nothing. Down at Camp VIII, Gallotti recorded in his diary that Mahdi arrived just before 7am.

The Summit Climb: Lacedelli's Version
Lacedelli is explicit in his version that after the agreed site for Camp IX had been reached, Compagnoni refused to set up the tent, saying the site was too dangerous, and that instead the pair should continue up and left. The chosen site, Lacedelli says, was sloping and precarious. Only later, Lacedelli says, did he understand the reason for the change:

> While we were at Camp VIII we had decided that whoever was least tired, whoever was fittest, would go up. Compagnoni had earache and wasn't feeling well … If Bonatti had arrived with the Hunza [Mahdi] it would have been impossible to bivouac with four in the tent [and there were also only two oxygen sets]. This was the point. Bonatti was certainly fit, more so than the two of us.

At this point in the story, Lacedelli's co-author Cenacchi poses a question: 'So you maintain that Compagnoni wanted to move Camp IX from the agreed position so that Bonatti wouldn't reach it. He was concerned at having to spend the night with four people in the tent and, worse, that he would be replaced by Bonatti who was in better physical condition?' To which Lacedelli replied, 'Yes, but I understood this only much later.'

Although Bonatti disagrees with the specifics of the conversation between them high on the mountain, Lacedelli's version does not differ significantly. However, Lacedelli does say that when he saw a figure descending the following morning, contrary to the official story, he knew immediately what must have occurred. He also says that he suggested to Compagnoni that they call off the summit attempt in order to go back to Camp VIII, though does not give reasons for why he then decided to continue towards the summit. He notes that if the tent had been set at the agreed site, then Mahdi would probably have descended, and so the three of them would have had to decide who would go for the top. Lacedelli says that reaching the top was more important than who got there, though he does add that had he been replaced, he might have tried for the summit later, suggesting – and who would doubt it? – that he was keen on getting to the top. As to the time of starting, Lacedelli thinks that by the time the two men had fetched the oxygen from Bonatti's bivouac and set off, it must have been about 7.30am. However, he also says that he had, from Camp IX, seen Bonatti descending at 6-6.30am and that it took 90 minutes to reach the oxygen sets, so the start time he quotes, about 7.30am, must be an earliest possible time. Bonatti claims it was more likely to have been closer to 8.30am.

Lacedelli's account of the ascent is very similar to the official story, though he believes the oxygen ran out at 8500m–8550m. He says that at the summit Compagnoni removed his gloves to take cine film; fearful of losing fingers to frostbite, he was intent on bivouacing on the summit so as to climb down in daylight. (After the climb, Lacedelli lost the top of a thumb and Compagnoni the tops of two fingers as a result of frostbite.) Compagnoni's suggestion appalled Lacedelli and he ordered the older man to descend. Lacedelli's description of the descent also corresponds closely to the official version. At Camp VIII, he says, he was angry with Compagnoni, having worked out during the ascent why Camp IX had been moved. He says he apologised to Bonatti at Camp VIII, saying that it was Compagnoni's decision to move the tent and 'Bonatti said to me, "Don't worry, I'm not upset with you but with him".' Bonatti, however, is adamant that Lacedelli did not apologise and says that he did not make the comment about being upset only with Compagnoni. Lacedelli also notes that after the two summit climbers had reached Camp VIII, it was Bonatti who massaged his fingers.

The Aftermath

When the expedition arrived back in Italy, some forty thousand people lined the docks at Genoa as the ship sailed in. The footprints left by two men on the summit of the world's second highest mountain had, at a single stroke, restored national pride. There were stamps (in Pakistan as well as in Italy), and K2-branded cigarettes and chocolate. A K2 hotel was built at Igea Marina. Companies used the name K2 or associated themselves with the expedition to boost sales of articles as diverse as batteries, baby food and *spumante*. The film of the expedition played to packed houses. A comic book was produced for children.[11] Desio, Compagnoni and Lacedelli became heroes, their names as well known in Italy as Hillary and Tenzing were to the British public. The success brought honours and a degree of financial security. Across the world the ascent was heralded, K2's reputation as a difficult mountain to climb and the fact that at that time it was only the fourth of the fourteen 8000m peaks to have been climbed meaning the ascent was seen as a brilliant exhibition of skill and courage. In the USA, which naturally took a special interest because of the history of American involvement with the peak, a photograph of Lacedelli climbing between Camp VII and Camp VIII graced the cover of *Life* magazine.[12] But buried beneath the triumphalism was a major issue that would, in time, push the expedition into the law courts.

When the expedition gathered for its return to civilisation, Ata Ullah expressed to Desio his concerns over Mahdi's terrible frostbite injuries. Then, as the expedition neared Karachi, news of Mahdi's injuries, and the sharp contrast they represented compared to the relatively unscathed Italians, was picked up by the Pakistani press, which published a damning report claiming that Compagnoni had forced Mahdi to stop climbing just below the summit, cheating him of a share of the glory of the climb, and, because his equipment was inferior to that of the Italians, causing his appalling injuries. For Desio, Ata Ullah's concerns and these more public accusations threatened to disgrace the expedition and to tarnish his own reputation. For the Italian ambassador to Pakistan the accusations threatened to cause a full-scale diplomatic incident and the complete loss of the international prestige the success on K2 had brought. The ambassador therefore held an immediate inquiry, interviewing Bonatti, Compagnoni and Lacedelli, as well as Ata Ullah and the expedition doctor Guido Pagani. The inquiry issued a statement which set down the basic facts of the situation.[13] This refuted the suggestion that Mahdi had been left below the summit, and accounted for his injuries, and so put an end to the more hysterical press campaign. But there was still the issue that while Mahdi had been severely injured, the Italians, Bonatti in particular, had not. In his book Marshall suggests that to account for this Desio deliberately concocted a story in which the blame for the bivouac was placed squarely on Bonatti's shoulders. To do this, Bonatti would need to be accused of trying to usurp the position of the pair at Camp IX. Bonatti had the oxygen sets and was known to have offered Mahdi the chance of going to the summit. What better idea than that the ambitious young climber had therefore decided to make his own bid for the summit, taking the innocent Hunza along. Then, as night fell, Bonatti, still intent on reaching Camp IX to carry out his plan, climbed up rather than attempting to get Mahdi back to safety. By the time darkness prevented Camp IX from being reached, it was too late too retreat and the bivouac was forced on the reluctant Mahdi. With his inadequate clothing, frostbite was inevitable – though not for the better-clad Bonatti.

Marshall's suggestion seems appalling, but it explains all the details of the aftermath of the expedition, and also accords with Desio's known characteristics. A martinet with a clear disdain for the climbers, here was a man who was not going to allow some young man whose only ability was to shin up steep rock faces stand in the way of a scientist of proven worth from receiving the just rewards for his efforts. If a sacrifice were required so that Desio's reputation could flourish unhindered, Bonatti was as good as anyone. Brand him as treacherous and irresponsible, neither of which was a crime, so it could all be hushed up and glossed over in the service of the greater, political good, and Desio could be content. When Lacedelli's co-author, Giovanni Cenacchi, put the theory to Lacedelli during the production of his book, Lacedelli responded: 'I would say it went something like, but I can't be completely sure. I haven't known about this for very long, and I certainly have no proof, but articles like that of Marshall have made me think. But whatever the case, the accusations made against Bonatti were absolutely false.' Later Cenacchi asks: 'You say that Bonatti was the victim of an injustice. Was that more because of the events at Camp IX, or because of what happened afterwards in Italy with the press?', to which Lacedelli replied: 'I would say afterwards. The final part of the ascent we did together. We spoke about it afterwards and I think we reached an understanding. What happened to Walter was unpleasant, but it could have happened to anyone.' The last sentence is particularly interesting, suggesting that Lacedelli knew very well that Desio was both willing and capable of demolishing anyone who stood in his path.

Compagnoni, it must be assumed, was complicit in the decision to blame Bonatti for the bivouac and Mahdi's injuries. It was certainly to his advantage, since he had deliberately moved Camp IX to avoid the younger, fitter man from reaching it. The rest of the team seem to have been fed the official line, though quietly and subtly, and over time Bonatti became estranged from them all. But when Desio's book came out, with its scant reference to the bivouac and the fact that the Bonatti/Mahdi carry towards Camp IX had been pivotal in the final success, and even more so when the film of the climb made no reference to the bivouac and the carry, Bonatti went on the offensive. His particular line of attack was the timeline of the summit climb. To understand why, it is necessary to briefly consider the use of supplementary oxygen at high altitude (see Box).

With the state of knowledge at the time, Compagnoni's and Lacedelli's climb of K2, continuing to the top when their bottled gas had run out, was extraordinary. The *Life* magazine article was titled 'Italians conquer the "Unclimbable Peak"', and quoted Charles Houston as saying K2 was 'the most challenging mountain in

Oxygen and Altitude

The percentage of oxygen in the atmosphere does not vary with altitude, but the decrease in pressure of the atmosphere with altitude means that there is less of the gas available for a climber to use. Although the British expeditions to Everest in the 1920s had shown that a climber could reach altitudes comparable with the summit of K2 without bottled gas and survive, the evidence indicated that at such altitudes the ability to function for any period of time was limited and that almost any difficult situation encountered by a climber would likely mean that his reserve strength in the thin atmosphere would be insufficient to cope. The science of human physiology was also poorly understood until the early 1950s, so that the lessons learned by the British regarding, for instance, the need for hydration, which allowed a successful ascent of Everest in 1953, were not understood throughout the climbing world. From their accounts of Camp IX it is clear that neither Compagnoni nor Lacedelli ate before their climb, that they were cold, and that each was extremely dehydrated, Compagnoni commenting: 'We were chilled to the bone. Our parched throats were beginning to fester. We both had an insatiable thirst ... neither of us was hungry.' Although both Annapurna and Nanga Parbat had been climbed without supplementary oxygen, they were much lower than K2 and Everest. Adding the perceived difficulties of K2 to its great height suggested that, as 1953 had proved on Everest, bottled gas was necessary, probably essential, to the climbing of those two peaks at least. It would take more than twenty years and associated improvements in equipment to prove that suggestion wrong.

the world'. Given those descriptions of the mountain, the article's conclusion is not surprising:

> One of the wonders of the K2 conquest remains that Compagnoni and Lacedelli were able to make it after their oxygen had given out. A leading Italian physiologist who plans to study the two men in this regard says: 'So far we can only say it was something on the order of superhuman.' Maurice Herzog, heroic conqueror of Annapurna, gives another explanation – one that has held before when man pushed back supposedly invulnerable frontiers. 'They must,' said he, 'have been men of very, very great courage.'

Herzog's assessment is, of course, true; the two men did indeed show great courage and fortitude, but was their story credible? Was it really credible that they had humped useless 19kg loads to the summit simply because they could not remove them easily and to add a transitory memento of their passage to the peak? Bonatti was not convinced.

The oxygen system the Italians were using differed from that used by the British on Everest in 1953. With the latter, there was a demand valve which allowed gas to be inhaled from the cylinders on the climber's back at the same time as air was inhaled. Thus the more often the climber inhaled, the more gas was consumed. But in the Italian system, using German Dräger cylinders, the oxygen flowed freely once the system was turned on. The rate of flow of oxygen was therefore independent of the rate of inhalation, the climber taking a mix of bottled gas and air, the quantity of the former reaching the lungs being dependent on how often he inhaled – breathe slowly and it was a reasonable quantity, breathe frequently and each breath received less. In the accounts of the climb, both Compagnoni and Lacedelli agree that their three oxygen cylinders became exhausted at exactly the same time (within a very few minutes), which is exactly what would be expected with a free-flow system, but would be an astonishing coincidence with a system in which bottled oxygen usage was dependent on the individual climber's inhalation rate. In his book Lacedelli states that Bonatti's view on how long the bottled gas should have lasted was incorrect because 'it's possible that we might have used more oxygen than we thought because of the altitude and the effort. Also the mixture wasn't necessarily very precise.' The final sentence can be dismissed (assuming Lacedelli means the filling pressure, i.e. the oxygen content of the bottle: there was no 'mixture' as such, the cylinders holding pure oxygen): as the cylinders ran out almost simultaneously each time, the filling had clearly been very precise. But the first sentence can also be dismissed – as the oxygen was free flow, effort – i.e. rate of breathing – was irrelevant to consumption.[14]

Compagnoni's account had the two men starting out at 6.15am. The oxygen ran out at about 8400m. The system had a life of 10 hours, so 8400m must have been reached at about 4pm. So Compagnoni was saying that he and Lacedelli had taken 10 hours to climb from 8000m (or 8100m if Bonatti is correct about the position of Camp IX) to 8400m, an ascent rate of 40m/hour (or 30m/hr if Bonatti is correct) while using oxygen. Even allowing for the 2 hours wasted in choosing the wrong route early in the climb, the ascent rate only increases to 37–50m/hr. Once they had stopped breathing supplementary oxygen, the two men climbed 200m to the summit in 2 hours, an ascent rate at least double, perhaps triple, that of the lower section of the climb. Admittedly the climbing was easier, but they were still carrying the 19kg spent oxygen systems which must have slowed their progress.

Next Bonatti consulted an almanac and discovered that sunrise on K2 on 31 July 1954 was just before 5am, an hour *after* Compagnoni and Lacedelli claimed to have prepared to climb.[15] As there is a photograph of Lacedelli fixing his crampons outside the tent at Camp IX, which was clearly taken in full daylight, and as Bonatti did not leave the bivouac site until around 6.30am, he was clearly correct in pointing out that the two had not turned on their oxygen until much later than the 6.15am they claimed. But how much later? Lacedelli says 7.30am, Bonatti says 8.30am. Lacedelli claims that the oxygen did indeed run out before the summit was reached, but only just before, perhaps at 8550m, some 60m (200ft) below the top, which would be consistent with his start time. If Bonatti is correct, then the oxygen was still flowing at the summit.

In July 1964, the 10th anniversary of the climb, the journalist Nino Giglio published two articles on K2[16] in which he accused Bonatti of attempting to beat Compagnoni and Lacedelli to the summit and persuading Mahdi to accompany him; he also claimed Compagnoni and Lacedelli had asked Bonatti from Camp IX if he needed help and been rebuffed, that Bonatti had used the oxygen system to aid his survival during the bivouac and then had abandoned Mahdi at the bivouac site, going down ahead of him. The latter claim was clearly nonsense as both Abram and Gallotti confirmed that Mahdi had arrived first at Camp VIII, but the other claims were much more contentious. The appalled Bonatti sued for libel. The case was heard in 1966 and Bonatti won.[17] Most specifically, the charge that he had used the oxygen during the night was refuted. It could hardly have been otherwise for, as Lacedelli admits in his book, although Bonatti had the oxygen cylinders, the masks and connecting tubes were up at Camp IX, so Bonatti had no means of using the gas. But who had given the information to Giglio which allowed him to write the articles? Robert Marshall concludes that it could only have been Compagnoni. With Bonatti's timeline of the summit day suggesting that the oxygen lasted to the summit because the claimed 12-hour climb had been reduced to something closer to 10 hours, it seems Compagnoni needed to lose an hour or so of oxygen so that exhaustion at 4pm (8400m) could be sustained.

In support of Bonatti's contention, shots came to light of Compagnoni wearing his oxygen mask at the summit, and one of Lacedelli with rime around his mouth, looking very much as though he had just removed an oxygen mask. Though published in *The Mountain World*[18] in 1955, the Compagnoni photograph was not used in Desio's book, which included a photograph of him after he had removed his mask. The shot of Lacedelli was used in Desio's book. The obvious question regarding Compagnoni was why he was wearing the mask at the summit, still apparently connected to the oxygen system by the breathing tube. Lacedelli says Compagnoni put the mask on at the summit in order to 'humidify and warm up the air', the cold summit air inflaming the climbers' throats. But the straps are beneath Compagnoni's woollen cap. Why, given the cold, did he remove the cap in order to fit the mask rather than simply fit the mask with the cap in place?

But there was yet more evidence to come. Only many years after the expedition did Enrico Abram, who was responsible for the gas systems, point out that the oxygen cylinders set aside for the summit bid were at a higher pressure and had a

12-hour capacity. So, even allowing for Lacedelli's revised start time of 7.30am, the oxygen would still have been flowing at the summit – it seems Compagnoni had been correct all along, and the oxygen had indeed run out at 8400m. But on the way down, not on the way up.

And Finally …

Ardito Desio died on 12 December 2001, aged 104 years, 8 months. While he was alive, all branches of the Italian establishment who had felt constrained to avoid embarrassing a great national figure were released from such shackles. Some suggested that as the climbing world had by now realised the truth, there was no need for Bonatti to continue the fight. But Bonatti knew better, as did Compagnoni. When *Le Monde* telephoned Compagnoni for a comment for their article,[19] he told them that the reason Bonatti had to bivouac was because he spent too much time resting at Camp VIII. When the caller tried to point out inconsistencies in his story, Compagnoni cut him short, saying 'I don't care if you say it's unbelievable, that's what's written!' It was an echo of what Bonatti had said all along: that only the official history, Desio's book, would matter when all the expedition members were dead. And it was the official history that Bonatti wanted to see changed.

At the 40th anniversary of the climb the CAI had declared that it was to investigate the circumstances of Bonatti's bivouac and the summit climb. Bonatti was elated, but nothing happened and it seemed it never would. It finally did in early 2004, when *i tre saggi* ('the three wise men') were charged with the task of preparing an official version of the summit climb in time for the 50th anniversary. The three were Fosco Maraini, a high-flying academic who had led the successful expedition to Gasherbrum IV, Alberto Monticone, a professor of modern history, and Luigi Zanzi, a professor specialising in the history of science, but with a particular interest in the history of alpinism. Not long after the *tre saggi* were appointed, Lino Lacedelli's book was published.[20]

Compagnoni's reaction to the appointment and the book was swift and furious. The idea of reviewing the official story was a disgrace, he said, and Lacedelli's book an attempt at humiliation. He denied Lacedelli's claim that the supplementary oxygen lasted to the summit (Lacedelli does not actually say this, though he does say it lasted almost to the summit), insisting that the gas had definitely run out and that the two men had not taken off the backpacks as each was trying to kid the other that gas remained and so give him encouragement. That added a new, fifth explanation to the four Compagnoni had already set down in Desio's book. As for Bonatti, Compagnoni noted that on the expedition everyone gave what he could – 'Bonatti did a great deal. I did even more.'

The *tre saggi* investigation was duly completed, but the CAI sat on it for a further three years. Finally, in 2007, they published a new official version of the K2 summit climb, including the report.[21] The report came to several conclusions, the main ones being that the official reason for moving Camp IX from the agreed position to a higher position (to place it as high as possible) was not correct; that Bonatti and Mahdi had not used any of the bottled oxygen during their bivouac; that Compagnoni and Lacedelli had started their summit climb between 8am and 8.30am; and that the supplementary oxygen lasted to the summit.

Compagnoni's reaction was even more furious than it had been in 2004. He noted that he had climbed up and down more than any other member of the team, had set up seven of the nine camps on the mountain, had directed the summit climb, committed himself each day, never sparing himself. Unlike 'some others' he had 'never even considered the need to acclimatise myself and so preserve my energies for a possible final assault'. He stated, 'This was my K2' and 'I conquered K2'. It is worth recalling Compagnoni's words in Desio's book: 'If we triumphed, the credit would go to all without distinction. And it was only right and proper that it should.' But when he wrote the 2004 paean to himself, Compagnoni was 93 years old. It is difficult not to feel a little sympathy for the man, but the overwhelming sympathy must be for Walter Bonatti, whose life had been utterly transformed by the lies told about events on the mountain for over half a century.

Bonatti's view of the events on K2 hardened over the years. In an interview he gave to the UK's *Guardian* newspaper in July 2010,[22] in response to a question about why the summit pair had moved Camp IX from the agreed position, Bonatti replied simply, 'To kill us. It may sound far-fetched, but they were terrified we were in such good shape that we would be able to accompany them to the summit without using oxygen.' Bonatti may be overstating Compagnoni's position, though there is no doubt that the latter's decision to move Camp IX put Bonatti and Mahdi's lives at risk.

In conversation with Robert Marshall,[23] Bonatti admitted that he had retired from climbing because of the continuing unpleasant aftermath of K2 and, even more disturbingly, he had chosen not to have children because of the stigma which might attach to their name if the truth about K2 did not come out. In his book, Lacedelli has a chapter entitled 'The Burden of K2'. Lacedelli's burden was chosen by himself. Bonatti's was chosen by others.

Chapter 5

The Next Thirty Years

'Please measure your strength against the difficulties of the climb to the summit as if you miscalculate, you will, of course, die.'

Masatsugu Konishi

Walter Bonatti returned from K2 upset that a bout of food poisoning had denied him a position in the summit team which he believed his fitness and ability had warranted. Although the worst of the machiavellian intrigue which was to trouble him for decades had yet to become truly apparent, he was already aware that politics would deny him recognition for his part in the final success. Sure that he could survive the rigours of high altitude without supplementary oxygen and that the climbing on K2 was within his capabilities, he therefore decided to return to the mountain and climb it alone. In the face of national euphoria over the ascent of K2, and a good deal of understandable scepticism, the prevailing view being that the climber was looking for an expensive way to commit suicide, Bonatti's plan failed to attract any backers and he was forced to abandon the idea.

Another man with unfinished business with K2 was Charles Houston, who had applied for permission to attempt the peak in 1955 but abandoned the idea after the Italian success; he applied again for 1958, but was unable to raise a team and was again forced to abandon his plan.[1]

The ascent of K2 was part of what might be termed a 'Golden Age' of mountaineering on the world's highest peaks. Between 1950, when the French climbed Annapurna, and 1960, when Dhaulagiri was climbed, thirteen of the fourteen 8000m peaks were climbed. The exception was Shisha Pangma, a mountain wholly within Tibet, which the Chinese had closed to foreigners following its invasion and annexation in 1950. Few doubt that had Shisha Pangma been accessible to the world's mountaineers in the 1950s it would have been climbed earlier; it was eventually climbed by a Chinese expedition in 1964.[2] The ascents were, in the main, made by large nationally financed teams using siege tactics, American, Austrian, British, French, German, Italian, Japanese and Swiss teams all being involved. Over the next ten years there were attempts to climb several of the high peaks again, Everest especially receiving the attention the world's highest mountain might have been expected to attract. On K2 an American-German expedition led by William D. Hackett attempted to repeat the Italian climb along the Abruzzi Ridge in 1960. The team established six camps, the last at 7064m (23,175ft). The expedition seemed to be progressing well until 11 July, when a period of bad weather, with violent winds and heavy snow, effectively put an end to further climbing for almost three weeks. During one brief period of respite two climbers reached 7285m (23,900ft), but the continuing storms eventually forced Hackett to abandon the attempt.[3]

The Pakistani government then closed access to the Karakoram for fourteen years as a consequence of the continuing tensions in Kashmir and border negotiations with China. In the early 1960s the Pakistani government signed a series of agreements with China in which it ceded areas of Kashmir and Ladakh (which Pakistan claimed but which were actually under the control of India), in exchange for China giving up any claim to land on the southern side of K2. The agreements represented a threat to India's claimed sovereignty and raised tensions in Kashmir still further. India has never recognised the legitimacy of the Sino-Pakistan agreements.

Americans on the North-West Ridge, 1975
Not until 1974 was the Baltoro opened again, and by then the climbing world had moved on. In the Alps the 'Golden Age' when peaks were first climbed, and repeat ascents made along the line established by the pioneers, was followed by climbers seeking more challenging routes to the summits. That trend was repeated in the Himalaya with a new generation of climbers heading for steeper, more difficult, lines. In 1970 a British team climbed the formidable South Face of Annapurna, while a German team climbed the equally daunting Rupal Face of Nanga Parbat. The trend was continued on K2 in 1975 when an American team attempted the North-West Ridge.[4]

It had been intended that the leader would be Pete Schoening, veteran of the 1953 expedition, but he had no interest in visiting the Baltoro again, and when permission from the Chinese for a north side attempt was not forthcoming, leadership passed to Jim Whittaker, the first American to summit Everest,[5] though one of his conditions for accepting the job was that his wife, Dianne Roberts, should be a team member. Dianne was not a climber but a photographer, both factors that would cause problems later on. Other team members were Lou Whittaker, Jim's twin brother, Jim Wickwire, Leif Patterson, Fred Dunham, Fred Stanley, Robert Schaller (team doctor) and Galen Rowell,[6] as well as Steve Marts, who was making a film of the climb. Early on in the organisation of the expedition it became known that, despite her lack of climbing experience, Roberts was being fitted for an oxygen mask, which implied she was hoping to go high, a fact that alarmed the other team members. It was not to be the only cause of unease and tension.

Matters began to deteriorate when the team was held up in Rawalpindi for eleven days as the weather was too poor for an onward flight to Skardu, which was time enough for opinions on other members, most of them uncomplimentary, to be formed. Rowell records all the problems and misgivings in his book, quoting from the diaries of the various team members, which indicates a remarkable willingness to have their inner thoughts exposed to public gaze. The Whittakers, Wickwire and Roberts formed what came to be seen as an inner circle group, which threatened team cohesion and led Fred Stanley to record that he would

> like to enjoy the company of the Big Four … but they seem very content to exclude the rest of us … I'm getting pretty tired of their ego thrusts, of trying to fend them off while searching for something significant in the conversation … When with the Big Four I've the impression that everything is all elbows, each man for himself.

Rowell is even willing to include unflattering comments about himself, noting that Lou Whittaker wrote: 'I've just finished tea and juice with Galen. I've never heard a guy talk so much about everything and nothing … He is even worse than Dianne … I hope Galen is a good climber and not just a lot of talk.'

The notion of Dianne Roberts being included as a member of the climbing team also continued to rankle, and Lou Whittaker and Jim Wickwire eventually approached Jim Whittaker with their concerns. Jim listened and then told his wife, who, not surprisingly, was none too pleased, seeing her efforts to get the expedition organised as being rewarded only with suspicion and bruised male egos. In a filmed interview before leaving the US Roberts had said:

> At the beginning I felt a little bit like I was peripherally involved in it. I was on the team because I was married to Jim and that was the only reason. But now I don't feel that way at all because I feel I've contributed as much as anyone else to the planning and I can do as much on the mountain as anyone else. I feel I've earned my place on the team. I've paid my dues.

It doesn't require any hint of misogyny to note that Roberts actually was on the expedition only because she was Jim Whittaker's wife, that helping with planning doesn't make you a climber, and neither does the few days' training she had received on Mount Rainier before the trip, even if you prove you can carry a big pack and keep up with the rest. Irrespective of what commercial climbs on Everest have proven about the potential ability of amateurs to go high, the climbers on the 1975 team seem altogether justified in their concerns that a novice mountaineer had high-altitude ideas on a new route on a difficult peak. There was also some personal antagonism between Rowell and Roberts, in large part because they were both professional photographers. Roberts considered Rowell a hopeless chauvinist, while Rowell thought Roberts a rabid feminist. A misunderstanding on the eventual flight to Skardu did not help. Having chartered their own flight, the Americans turned it into a sight-seeing flight of the mountain. Many of the team were on the flight deck, Rowell avoiding taking a window space as he was waiting for K2. When it appeared he moved into position, only to be told by Jim Whittaker, who had just arrived on the flight deck and assumed Rowell had been at the window the whole time, to move back to allow someone else a turn. Roberts stayed in position and took some wonderful photos, while Rowell 'felt as if someone had robbed me of a priceless possession'.

At Skardu there was further delay, and three members of the team – Patterson, Rowell and Schaller – took the opportunity to go for an extended walk, returning to find that the others had decided to pack loads that afternoon (after initially deciding that no work would be done). The three were bawled out, Rowell especially. Later the three and Marts were 'advised' to sleep in the expedition cook tent, which, though he does not say so directly, Rowell obviously believed was the equivalent of being made to sit on the naughty step. He also appears to have believed that the incident might have ruined his summit chances as he suggests that on the Baltoro there was an unstated competition in terms of speed and load-carrying capacity, and that the Whittakers and Wickwire were winning it, confirming their positions in the team hierarchy. Rowell was anxious not to overstrain an ankle healing from a sprain and also wished to be at the front of the party to photograph the route before the crowd of porters arrived. He therefore carried a comparatively light rucksack, claiming it weighed 45lb against the 70lb or so carried by the other three. When they caught up with him at lunch stops 'my pack was frequently hefted by Jim, Wick, or Lou. One would say "Wow, that's light. Not over thirty-five pounds." Another would lift it and say, knowingly, "More like thirty".'

On the trek the expedition had a succession of porter problems. As Rowell notes, the days of single expeditions were over, so expedition members no longer had the whip-hand in negotiating with striking porters (never an unusual occurrence); they could no longer simply say, carry the load or go home without pay. Now, when there might be a dozen or more expeditions in the field, the balance of power had shifted. In particular, porters could get the same money for carrying another expedition to the Baltoro as they could for the colder, more exhausting carry along the glacier, so there was a tendency to demand more money and, if it was not forthcoming, to leave and go back to seek easier work. The strikes caused delay, overran the expedition budget and brought out the worst in terms of American attitudes to the Baltis. Dianne Roberts seems to have been almost alone in considering that the expedition had its priorities wrong:

Team members talking about how we're getting ripped off. What shit! They sit (some of them) huddled in tent city, unwilling to share any of themselves with the people here. So we're paying them high wages. So what? We'll still leave this country with far more than we've given the people here. Does it occur to anyone that perhaps, just perhaps, some of the people here are just simple, friendly, honest mountain people? ... We invade their land, their culture, and expect everything to run the way it does in America. Christ, we need some humility – both towards the people and the mountain. What arrogant, cold bastards we can be.

It is difficult not to sympathise with Roberts' view, though, of course, if it is your money and ambition being held to ransom, it is likely to make you rather less sympathetic.

Eventually there was one strike too many and the Americans chose to make a stand. The porters were told that unless they did what they were being paid to do, the Americans would burn everything they had right there, and go home. The porters would therefore get nothing, not only no money, but also none of the equipment they had been expecting. To make the point, Jim Wickwire took out a 10-rupee note and held it while Lou Whittaker set light to it. As it burned, the Americans walked away. The demonstration worked, but it upset Manzoor, the team's liaison officer, who felt the burning of the note had been disrespectful to Pakistan. In his book, Wickwire notes the incident, but is not specific about his own involvement. He says that half the porters had decided to go home and 'in an effort to keep the rest from leaving, we threatened not to pay them. To underscore our threat we burned some Pakistani currency – much to Manzoor's horror.'

Finally the team reached Concordia and saw K2. It was somewhat anti-climactic, Rowell noting that 'we had all expected that coming suddenly face to face with K2 ... would be a soul-stirring experience. To the contrary – the mountain was everything we expected it to be, and nothing more. No pulses quickened, no tears flowed. Ecstasy, if anyone felt it, was well contained.' Rowell considered the long days of battling with the porters had sapped the team's emotional energy, but the Italian ascent of the peak had also taken away K2's aura of invincibility. It also seems possible that the relationship problems among the team dulled any personal joy. The competitiveness still persisted: Rowell, suffering bronchitis and using skis with inferior skins fell behind Wickwire and Lou Whittaker, the former noting that 'Lou and I smoked out in front of everyone ... it was a joy to run Galen into the ground.' Lou Whittaker also started to take down a tent while Fred Dunham was still in it and when Dunham complained threatened to 'deck' him (knock him down), causing Dunham, who was almost a foot shorter, to note that 'there is only way to handle a guy like Lou who shoves his weight and size around. That is to say what you think to anyone and if he resorts to physical strength he should end up with an ice axe in the back of his head or a bullet between the eyes. There is no other way for a smaller person to get vengeance or justice.'

Once at the base of the mountain, the Americans used a spell of good weather to climb fairly rapidly to the Savoia Pass (the Savoia Saddle of the Duke of the Abruzzi's expedition), where a camp was established 15ft (4m) on the Chinese side of the border with Pakistan. But they were shocked to find that the pass was at only 20,400ft (6218m; the presently agreed height is 6250m) rather than the 6666m (21,870ft) calculated by the Abruzzi team. That increased the height to the summit by well over 1000ft, throwing their logistics into disarray. To compound the problem, as they were leaving the US they had heard that a recalculation of the height of K2 had raised the summit to 28,741ft (8760m), which had already caused a rethink in their plans. They were now, they thought, climbing a ridge that was almost 1500ft (457m) taller, meaning an extra camp would be required. At the same time Fred Dunham and Fred Stanley had finally had enough of what they felt was the second-class treatment they were receiving. They declared that they were convinced there had been a secret plan hatched in the US to ensure that the Whittakers and Wickwire were to reach the summit,[7] all other team members being merely high-altitude porters. A number of conversations followed, which, judging by the diaries of those involved, reproduced in full in Rowell's book, were such that 'acrimonious' hardly serves as an adjective. Fred Stanley suggested that Jim Wickwire was sitting on the fence; he hoped it was 'a picket fence and he gets one up the ass' (to his credit, Wickwire also notes the comment in his own book). Stanley also suggested to the Whittakers and Wickwire that they should 'quit treating the rest of us as piles of shit into which they could pick their crampons to get a little higher on K2'. The response was to suggest that Stanley was 'bordering on insanity'.

It is surprising that the expedition managed to continue at all in such a poisonous atmosphere, but at Camp II on the Savoia Pass those still fit and eager were keen to push the route out. But there were more problems. No route had been found around a series of steep, icy gendarmes on the ridge immediately above the camp, and now Rowell, one of the diminishing number of the fit and willing, was becoming ill, his bronchitis deepening to pneumonia. Too sick to carry loads upwards, he was told by Lou Whittaker:

> I have the same symptoms and I'm going to climb this mountain. If you wanted to climb K2 as much as we do, you wouldn't stay back for every little thing. I thought you were shaping up, but now I see you're no better than the Freds [i.e. Dunham and Stanley]. I think you're just scared of the mountain.

Rowell was forced to descend (indeed, his life was probably saved by the decision to do so). On the pass, another attempt to push the route out came to a stop at about

22,000ft (6100m) when the lead climbers realised that the route was just too difficult given the resources and time available. The Americans retreated to Base Camp, where another crisis loomed, the best of the high-altitude porters vomiting up a collection of twenty-five roundworms, each about 10in (25cm) long. They had caused an intestinal blockage, creating a perforation and peritonitis. The man's survival was miraculous, particularly as an asked-for helicopter to evacuate him did not arrive. The incident was the last straw, and the expedition withdrew from the mountain. On the trek out from the mountain the team met Reinhold Messner and Peter Habeler on their way to Gasherbrum I, where their ascent by a new route in three days would represent a step-change in climbing on the world's highest peaks. As the expedition ended some harmony was restored to team relationships, not least, back in the US, when rumours spread that the prime reason for the trip had been CIA backing for the setting up of a listening post aimed at China from the Savoia Pass. Faced with such a ludicrous suggestion the team members were forced to stand together.

Poles on the North-East Ridge, 1976
The year after the Americans had attempted a new route on the mountain, a very strong Polish team arrived at the mountain's base with the same ambition. Led by Janusz Kurczab, the team of nineteen included several climbers who would later be involved in significant ascents on the high hills.[8] The Poles had porter problems similar to those which had plagued the Americans the year before, causing Janusz Onyszkiewicz, who was in charge of the logistics of the trek-in, to write that when he 'saw the pile of loads at the foot of the Negrotto Peak and the backs of the departing porters, I felt an enormous relief'. Having put back their attempt from 1974 because of lack of time to organise an expedition, the Poles had had plenty of time to consider alternatives. In what was to become a familiar approach to the high hills, they were not interested in following the crampon marks of others and so decided on exploring a new route. They were torn between the West Spur and the North-East Ridge. The former was steep and looked difficult all the way, but the steepness reduced the risk of avalanches and, with logic as faultless as it was surprising, made it shorter. The North-East Ridge was much longer, probably as difficult, and also much more dangerous. It had also been dismissed by some as unfeasible. The Poles now applied a simple, ruthless logic. The Spur involved hard climbing at altitude and was therefore likely to require a lot of supplementary oxygen. The Ridge would need much less oxygen, but was risky. As they could afford the risk but not the oxygen, they would go for the Ridge.

The risks were apparent early, the route from Base Camp to Camp I being regularly swept by avalanches. Four men were caught in one and were lucky to escape uninjured, but each time a carry was made it was, Onyszkiewicz says, 'a sort of Russian roulette'. But at least the Poles were risking only themselves: having too little money for either a great deal of oxygen or high-altitude porters, they were doing all the load-carrying. The route followed a rib at the northern end of the peak's vast Eastern Face, joining the North-West Ridge at a pinnacle at 6845m (22,457ft), following the route first reconnoitred by Jacot-Guillarmod and Wesseley in 1902. The lower part of the rib was mainly steep snow fields, any exposed rocks being loose. The Poles put Camp II on the rib. From it to the junction pinnacle the route went up a steep, icy wall, then descended and traversed 400m of near horizontal ridge before climbing another steep wall defended by menacing séracs. From the junction with the North-West Ridge the Poles were faced with about 800m of sharp ridge, topped by a number of equally sharp pinnacles. Huge cornices overhung both sides of the ridge.

Camp III was placed at about 6750m (22,150ft), close to the junction pinnacle. From there teams of four climbers took it in turns to fix ropes along the ridge. The climbing was easier than had been feared (though all things are, of course, relative), the climbers revelling in the joys of front-pointing because, Onyszkiewicz says, the altitude was 'low enough' – only about 23,000ft (7000m). The only problem, he goes on to say, was 'traversing under the giant cornices [which] caused twinges of unease'. The end of the ridge was reached on 17 July, Camp IV being established there and the route pushed out to 7375m (24,200ft). Most unusually, the Poles had experienced four weeks of good weather but now it turned against them. At first the teams sat out the storms, but that merely consumed supplies in the high camps which had taken great effort to carry up. They were all therefore forced to return to Base Camp. The retreat was a nightmare, the slopes which had been such a pleasure to climb avalanching under any imposed weight. Only the fixed ropes allowed a safe descent from Camp IV to Camp III, the journey, which normally took no more than two or three hours, taking ten.

The bad weather lasted two weeks, by the end of which there was a metre of fresh snow at Base Camp and the Poles had almost run out of fuel for cooking, porters tasked with bringing in fresh supplies having failed to get through. Eventually cooking was only possible over open fires fed by cardboard and wooden boxes. Yet despite these difficulties the Poles were determined to make an attempt on the summit. A secret ballot was held to choose two summit teams. The first would be Leszek Cichy and Janek Holnicki, the second Eugeniusz Chrobak and Wojciech Wróż. To support these teams, leader Kurczab asked all fit climbers to carry loads to Camp VI, while all those who were sick or unfit need only carry to Camp V.

In better, but still uncertain, weather the fit climbers started out. The following day the *Krank-Kommando* (sick team) followed, their rucksacks weighing no more than 50lb (22.5kg). The first group had a hard job, the established camps being snow-filled. Camp IV was only found at all because one climber suddenly realised he was standing on top of it, so completely had it been buried. When dug out, the tents were found to be completely shattered and unusable. As they were carrying the tents for the higher camps, the first group could use those, but the 'sick team' had no such option, and were forced to dig out and mend the tents at the lower camps, repairs being effected with plasters from the medical supplies. Bad weather now held the teams in the lower camps for another few days, making supplies at all points critical. It might have been sensible to retreat, but when good weather returned the Poles started up again. Camp V was established on 12 August at a height of about 7500m (24,600ft), at the base of the summit pyramid. To the left a snow field led across to the Shoulder of the Abruzzi Spur, while above steep ice walls separated by an equally steep rock rib led directly to the summit.

At Camp IV, Onyszkiewicz and Laukajtys had run out of fuel, but as they needed to make one last carry to Camp V in support of the summit attempt, they made a fire out of a book they found in the tent and the flammable material from a medical kit they rifled. The weather was fine but windy, so the fire was inside the tent, cooking being a compromise between having enough heat to warm the meal and too much flame which threatened the tent. Above the bonfire watchers, the first summit team was returning to Camp VI (established at the base of the rock rib, at 8000m/26,246ft) after a disappointing day. They had made progress but were eventually stopped by difficulties they felt would take too long to overcome.

Undaunted, Chrobak and Wróż set out the next day at 5am – later than they had planned after a poor night – carrying oxygen sets and climbing equipment which totalled over 25kg (60lb). To maximise the oxygen they had agreed to use it only above 8150m, so the first three hours of climbing was hard work. It was also dangerous, Chrobak writing that 'above us towers a roof of yellow rock already lit by the sun. Tiny single pebbles and pieces of ice spin and leap past us. Suddenly I'm terrified that something will roar down on us from above.' He tried to speed up, but could not: 'I have reached the limit of my lung capacity.' Switching on his oxygen, Chrobak found his first bottle was only half full. Despite this, the pair decided to continue, Wróż leading on an enhanced oxygen flow, Chrobak following in his tracks. The first summit team had been stopped by a barrier of vertical rock and hard ice: Wróż climbed through this, reaching a steep (70°) ice slope.

Chrobak now took over the lead, using a new bottle of oxygen with the flow set at the high rate of 4l/min. It was hard going:

[The ice] is so steep that I am afraid [while using his axe] that I may damage the rubber balloon of my breathing set, which hangs on my chest. 1 move under a rock overhang. Jamming my helmet against it to hold myself in balance, I hammer in a peg. It doesn't go in far. Now there's an awkward traverse to the left. Wojtek is far beneath me ... The rock is sound and vertical. I remove my gloves and search for tiny rugosities. I must get a peg in. My foot, contacting the rock only through one crampon spike, starts to shake. There is a crack. The peg goes in well.

Wróż then joined Chrobak on the exposed stance and led on up a steep couloir, running out almost 60m (about 180ft) of rope. They exchanged leads again and kept climbing. It was now 5pm and both men were exhausted and in need of food and drink, but there was no comfortable place to stop. They continued, traversing right towards what they hoped would be the final snowfield below the summit. But then it started to snow. They had reached 8400m (27,560ft), but it was 7pm and they calculated it would take a further 3 hours to climb the final 210m (700ft). Their supplementary oxygen was also almost exhausted. They decided to retreat.

They abseiled down to the top of a rope they had fixed on the difficult barrier, reaching it as darkness fell. Wróż abseiled down the rope. When Chrobak followed, he abseiled with the rope under his armpits as a classic abseil would not work over the oxygen set – the Poles clearly did not have abseil devices.

> Suddenly my crampons are sliding on rock. I see them sparking in the darkness. Then I am hanging free; the rope is breaking my arms and I am suffocating. Down quickly! I try to grab the rock. I throw myself to the left – and again. My lungs are bursting. I would tear off my mask, but I can't let go of the rope … Wojtek quickly turns my oxygen flow to five litres. I am getting my breath back when I hear the hiss from the valve dying away. No more oxygen!

At 11.30pm the pair rested above the first barrier above Camp VI. They were both freezing cold and the wind had sprung up, cooling them further. But they survived, reaching their tent in the early hours of the morning, almost 24 hours after setting out. There was no time for rest and at 6am they set off in deteriorating weather towards Camp V, staggering into it in a white-out at 10am. The Poles still at Camp V included the expedition doctor, Piotr Kintopf, and Kazimierz Glazek. Glazek had become paralysed a few days earlier and looked as though he would need immediate evacuation. But that would have left the summit teams without support, so the doctor gave him injections and oxygen and that, fortunately, led to a partial recovery. Now the doctor had to inject Wróż to save him from frostbite. Glazek could move, but could not recognise anyone and was still sick, and there was a clear need for everyone to descend, but a storm now prevented movement. With their fuel having run out, the situation looked desperate, particularly as there was no fuel at Camp IV either. Next day, despite the continuing storm, the stark choice was descend or die. Camp IV was reached, and the descent continued. The men did not eat for two days until they reached a rescue team heading up from Base Camp.

Yet despite it all the Poles were intent on another try for the summit, but the attempt foundered in waist-deep snow as yet another storm enveloped the mountain. This time supplies ran out before the weather improved and forced a final retreat.

The Japanese on the Abruzzi Spur, 1977
The Polish expedition of 1976, though it was very large by the later standards of the nation's Himalayan endeavours, and used supplementary oxygen high on the hill, was, it can be argued, modern in outlook, with climbers setting up their own camps and carrying their own loads. The following year saw what could be termed an expedition from the older tradition. In 1976 a team of six Japanese climbers led by Takeyoshi Takatsuka made a reconnaissance of the Abruzzi Spur, reaching a height of about 7160m during a four-week period, which included eleven consecutive days of good weather, before bad weather put an end to further prospecting. The trip was a prelude to a full-scale expedition in 1977. That year forty-six Japanese climbers under the leadership of 73-year-old Ichiro Yoshizawa and five Pakistani climbers, assisted to Base Camp by over nine hundred porters, made the second ascent of the mountain. The trek to Base Camp was completed in poor weather, but apparently without any major problem from the vast throng of porters.

Camps were established up the Spur during June and early July, but then bad weather set in. As a result, it was late July before Camp V was established at 7925m (26,000ft). The Japanese then lifted over 700kg of equipment to that camp. In early August the top camp (Camp VI) was established at 8130m/26,675ft, only 205m above Camp V. From it, a first summit attempt by three Japanese and two Pakistanis on 4 August managed to climb only 150m before being driven back by a violent storm. A second attempt was made on 8 August, Shoji Nakamura, Tsuneo Shigehiro and Takeyoshi Takatsuka (leader of the previous year's reconnaissance) reaching the summit at 6.50pm. The climb had taken almost 14 hours and was not without incident, Nakamura falling 20m into a crevasse when a snow bridge collapsed under him. It took 2 hours for his companions to extricate him. The three men descended safely, reaching Camp VI just before midnight and continuing down to Camp V. They did not stay at Camp VI because it was occupied by Mitsuo Hiroshima, Masahide Onodera, Hideo Yamamoto and the Pakistani Ashraf Aman, who reached the summit on 9 August without incident, making better time as they used ropes fixed by the first summit team. A further summit attempt on 10 August was cancelled because of the bad weather and the mountain was cleared.[9]

The British on the West Ridge, 1978
After the success of the large expedition he had led to Everest's South-West Face in 1975, British climber Chris Bonington[10] was keen to take a team to K2. But he wished to try with a smaller group. He also wanted to attempt a new route and, after listening to persuasive arguments from other team members, he chose the West Ridge. The team was the nucleus of the 1975 Everest group: Doug Scott, Nick Estcourt, Paul 'Tut' Braithwaite and Pete Boardman, with the addition of Joe Tasker, who had been Boardman's partner on an impressive first ascent of

Changabang's West Face. Jim Duff was the team doctor, with Tony Riley as film maker. Both Scott and Boardman had reached the summit of Everest on Bonington's 1975 expedition.

Boardman and Estcourt climbed to the Savoia Pass (Saddle) and confirmed that the ridge from there was steep and icy, so the British then decided on a more southerly approach. From a Base Camp on the Savoia Glacier they established a route directly up towards Pt6590, a pinnacle at the lower end of the ridge. Camp I was set at about 6000m (about 19,700ft) and the route was then pushed out below Pt6590. Bonington, leading out the route with Tasker, writes 'Joe murmured about Doug [Scott] thinking that we should follow the gully to the crest of the ridge, but this seemed a long way round. I urged for the basin and Joe agreed without further demur, climbing down into it. The angle was so easy we didn't even bother to rope up. We just plodded steadily across.' The basin led to a suitable spot for Camp II at about 6400m (21,000ft).

The next day, in superb weather, loads were carried to Camp II. Boardman and Tasker stayed in order to push the route out the following day. But the weather then changed, a storm keeping the climbers in their tents for two days. In Camp II fresh snow almost buried the tent, an air hole having to be excavated to allow the two men to breathe. On the second morning, Tasker writes, 'we were all but suffocated again by the depth of snow over the tent. Only a corner poked clear. Pete spent a long time braving the furious wind to dig free the tent. Most of the time we did not need to stir outside.' When the weather improved, Boardman and Tasker pushed the route out from Camp II. According to Tasker,

> It was wonderful to be out in front ... I stood gazing at countless mountains that had come into view now that we were so high. The day was completely calm, I was content to be there. There was something unreal about the situation, something of the atmosphere of a bank holiday in sunny weather, a day quite different from an ordinary work day.

While Boardman and Tasker were climbing above Camp II, Estcourt and Scott carried further loads up. Watching from Camp I after Jim Duff had arrived with porters, Bonington

> felt relaxed, happy to be ensconced on this high perch surrounded by some of the most magnificent peaks in the world when suddenly, with little more than a muffled rumble, a huge avalanche billowed down the icefall between us and the main mass of K2. Instinctively I dived for my camera and started taking pictures. Jim shouted: 'For God's sake, stop. The lads could be in that.' 'They can't. I'm sure they can't ... They'll be above it.'

Up above, Tasker

> heard vaguely the roar of an avalanche. There were so many in this cirque of mountains that one hardly glanced up any more ... I heard Pete shout and caught the note of awe in his voice as if this avalanche was particularly spectacular. I glanced round and looked at the distant peaks. Seeing nothing, I turned to move upwards again. 'No, look!' It was urgency, not awe, and below me I saw the slope beyond our tent sliding away in a billowing cloud. Where I had last seen two figures there was now only one.

Scott writes:

> I was leading across the slopes to Camp 2 when there were two shudders through the snow, followed by a cracking noise. I was plucked off as the rope came tight and I hurtled down, totally out of control. There was no fear. I registered only curiosity at being in my first avalanche and contemplated the prospect of dying. Time was in suspension during those few seconds until I suddenly stopped – my heavy sack anchoring me firmly in the snow sufficient to snap the rope. I stood up and watched, horrified, as the avalanche, with Nick in the middle of it, poured down the cliffs to the glacier below.

Scott had been paying out a security rope across the snow basin. Estcourt had been clipped into the rope, which ran back to the high-altitude porter Quamajan on the far side of the basin with a karabiner. Scott had almost reached the basin's far side when the avalanche struck: Estcourt had been in the middle. Quamajan's hands had rope burns from holding the line until it had snapped.

The remaining team members returned to Base Camp, Scott checking the avalanche debris for any sign of Estcourt's body, but without success.[11] At Base Camp, Bonington, Boardman and Riley wanted to continue the climb, but the rest were adamant that the expedition was over, and with only three climbers, continuing was not feasible.

Americans on the North-East Ridge, 1978
As the British, trekking back from the western side of K2, reached Skardu, an American expedition arrived there ahead of their trek-in to the eastern side with the aim of completing the line the Poles had followed in 1976. As in 1975, Jim Whittaker was team leader. Dianne Roberts was there again, as were Schaller and Wickwire. They were joined by Craig Anderson, Terry Bech and his wife Cherie, Chris Chandler, Skip Edmonds, Lou Reichardt, Rick Ridgeway,[12] John Roskelley and Bill Sumner. Chandler had summitted Everest in 1976, while Reichardt and Roskelley had made the third ascent of Dhaulagiri in 1973, reaching the summit

with the Sherpa Nawang Samden. On the hill the Americans also used four Hunzas as high-altitude porters.

The expedition started badly, most of the team leaving Skardu in a jeep which created clouds of dust that enveloped a party of town officials who were gathered for a formal farewell ceremony during which postcards would be signed by the team. Saleem Khan, the team's liaison officer, was appalled and threatened to pull out immediately, which would have meant the end of the trip. Jim Whittaker was left to smooth things over – and then to bawl out his team at Shigar.

As a result of the efforts of Saleem Khan, the expedition had almost no trouble from the porters and reached their Base Camp in just two weeks, an amazingly short time. In his book Ridgeway spends several pages exploring Whittaker's decision on pairings for the early stages of the climb, and it is clear that there was already some jockeying for position that would later cause disharmony. There were also lifestyle differences, Ridgeway noting that some of the climbers smoked cannabis, while others did not and evidently disapproved (if silently).

Early in the climb Cherie Bech fell into a crevasse and had trouble with her jumars and needed to be hauled out. Chris Chandler offered to teach her jumaring, but others were unimpressed, thinking K2 was no place to learn basic climbing techniques. There was also concern that Bech was carrying loads that were too heavy in order to prove she was up to the job of climbing the peak, as she seemed determined to be the first woman to reach the summit. John Roskelley was not impressed:

> I'm afraid it might be a repeat of what I've seen on other trips. Every time I go on one of these big climbs with women it's the same story. Every single time – I swear to God, this is the last time I'm climbing with any of them. I've seen them kill themselves trying to prove they are as strong as men … People always criticise me for being down on women on expeditions, but I've never yet been on a mountain with one that's worth a damn.

Though misogynistic, the words have to be seen in the context of Roskelley's experience. He was on an international climb in the Pamirs when eight women had died in a storm below the summit of Pik Lenin, having continued beyond the point where they should have turned back, and then on Nanda Devi Willi Unsoeld's daughter had died after staying high when Roskelley, among others, had said she should descend.

The Americans had the usual mix of good and bad weather as they set camps along the line explored by the Poles. There were problems of clashing egos, but one relationship was causing more concern. On the trek-in Chris Chandler and Cherie Bech had become very friendly. Now, it seemed, the friendship was becoming deeper: if it caused a serious rift with Terry Bech, the team would lose 25 per cent of its manpower. An attempt was made to discuss the issue with both Chandler and Cherie, the latter taking an extremely hostile position: 'I'm tired of hearing all this stuff about Terry being upset, everyone whispering behind our backs. You're all bastards. Bastards, bastards, bastards.'

For a few days high on the mountain the lead climbers continued, oblivious to the gathering storm below, Ridgeway being entranced by the sight of a butterfly perched on the rope as he belayed Roskelley at over 6700m (22,000ft) on the way to establishing Camp IV. But when they were heading down, to be replaced by climbers lower on the hill, Ridgeway met Terry Bech, who told him that attempts to undermine his relationship with his wife were based on bad information. Ridgeway apologised for his part in the rumour-mongering and things seemed to have been patched up. Bad weather now caused problems with establishing Camp V and carrying loads towards it. The climbers with the job of pushing out the route – Chandler, Cherie Bech, Edmonds and Anderson – were also considered by the stronger climbers to be making insufficient effort.

The situation became much worse when Whittaker announced that the first summit team of four would be Reichardt, Ridgeway, Roskelley and Wickwire, with only a vague suggestion that there might be a second team built around Chandler and Cherie Bech. He also suggested that the first team might try without supplementary oxygen (word having come through that Messner and Habeler had climbed Everest without using bottled gas). The decision on summit teams caused rancour, with Terry Bech soon referring to the two summit teams as A and B. When asked what the letters stood for, he replied that B was for Best, while A was for Assholes. Sharp words were exchanged several times after Whittaker's decision was announced, particularly at Camp III, where climbers arriving from below discovered that Chandler and Cherie Bech had not moved up as intended. Roskelley announced, in their hearing, that the two were 'on extended honeymoon. Nice place here, Camp Three, warm, plenty of food. No reason to go anywhere else.' Not surprisingly, the awkward atmosphere created by the remark led to further exchanges with Cherie, who was incensed that she and Chandler were seen as the weak link in the team when the reality was that they were being used as scapegoats, her particularly as she was considered a weak woman when she could carry loads as well as any one of them. Stunned by her comments, Whittaker told her she should be more polite, to which she replied: 'Oh, look who's talking now! Mr Universe. Big Jim. It all makes me sick. All you bloody machos.' Whittaker replied that he wished she was a man 'because then I could punch you on the frigging nose'. Later, on the climb to establish Camp V, Roskelley and Chandler had an argument over the latter's relationship with Cherie Bech, particularly over the blame Roskelley thought had been unfairly placed on him for starting the rumours when everyone could see what was going on. The argument continued when Reichardt, who was leading the rope of three men, fell into a crevasse, despite the fact that it was Chandler who held him. As Reichardt pulled himself out, the argument continued to rage, with as much breath as Roskelley and Chandler could muster at 25,000ft.

Another storm forced most of the team back down to Camp I, where Terry Bech confronted Whittaker with a revised summit plan, one which involved setting up two Camp VIs, one below the Polish direct finish, the other on a traverse towards the Shoulder on the Abruzzi Spur. If the first route turned out to be too hard, the traverse would allow a surer summit option. If the first route was climbed, the second Camp VI would allow the summit climbers to retreat down an easier, safer line. It seemed to offer the best chance of success given that it was now nearing the end of August and the Karakoram winter was approaching: of the last thirty-three days, only seven had been clear, and the team had to be off the mountain by 10 September.

The suggestion was agreed in principle, and in order to try to gain a day some climbers went from Camp I to Camp IV in a day, a vicious wind between Camps III and IV meaning they arrived after dark, exhausted. The party included Dianne Roberts, recording a (short-lived) record high for a North American woman (Roberts is Canadian by birth, American by marriage). Those following, mostly B team members, were appalled on arriving at Camp III to find it empty, believing that a deliberate plot to keep them from the summit had been hatched. Next day a radio conversation, with an exchange of insults every bit as vicious as the previous day's wind, resulted in Chris Chandler deciding that rather than risk a fist-fight with John Roskelley high on the hill, he would descend and leave the expedition. The others at Camp III felt betrayed, but agreed to carry on higher in the hope that someone would summit. But bad weather forced the climbers in Camp V to return to Camp IV, while those in Camp IV retreated to Camp III. With limited supplies to last out a prolonged storm, it looked as though the expedition was over.

But in improved weather the four nominated summit climbers decided on one more try. Moving up into Camp V, Ridgeway and Roskelley then climbed on to establish Camp VI on the Polish route, while Reichardt and Wickwire, supported by Terry Bech, set off towards the Abruzzi hoping to establish the second Camp VI. The direct route pair succeeded, but the Abruzzi trio failed, the deep snow taking so much time to wade through that they were forced to return to Camp V, where Wickwire wrote: 'We are so close, yet so far. Deep snow, cold, lack of support from below. Tonight depressed about our chances, we are out on a limb.' The following day the pair at Camp VI tried to follow the Polish route, but were defeated by deep, dangerous snow. Down at Camp V the idea of climbing up to join Ridgeway and Roskelley was abandoned when the three climbers saw a huge avalanche sweep the projected route. Instead they decided to try to reach the Abruzzi again. With Reichardt and Wickwire making trail but carrying light loads, and Bech carrying a massive pack, the three followed the route made the previous day, then continued.

After all the conflict, some of it centred on his wife, Bech's contribution to the final outcome was both crucial and impressive, and it is sad that history records only the names of summit climbers.

As darkness approached the Americans were forced to make camp at about 7850m (25,750ft), about 200m (650ft) lower than the top camps used by both the Italians and the Japanese on their Abruzzi climbs. Summit day would be a long one. Wickwire, in control of the cooker, spilled water on the half sleeping bag he was using. He had hoped to take it towards the summit in case a bivouac was needed. When cooking at 1.30am next morning he did the same again, this time soaking his gloves. Now he would have to climb in an inferior pair, perhaps trading fingers for the summit. Then he dropped his water bottle down the mountain. Things were going badly. At 4.30am, helped by Bech, Reichardt and Wickwire were ready to climb. With limited oxygen, the pair decided to climb initially without turning their sets on, but Wickwire had to at about 8080m (26,500ft) as he was having trouble finding a rhythm. Then at 8300m (27,250ft), having finally turned on his oxygen set, Reichardt discarded it, having found the chest bladder was punctured and useless. He also discarded all his emergency equipment to conserve energy, asking Wickwire to watch if he showed any sign of 'fuzzy talking': if he did he would descend. The two also now left behind their rope, continuing solo. They followed the now-standard route through the Bottleneck and then traversing left. Despite climbing with supplementary oxygen, Wickwire found he could not catch Reichardt until they were only 500ft or so from the top. Then, out in front, Wickwire stopped to await his companion. He writes, 'At five-fifteen I told him, "We've come this far, let's go the rest of the way together". Lou Reichardt and I walked arm in arm the last few steps up the tilted snow ramp to the summit. There, on top of the world, we watched the setting sun bathe the surrounding mountains in a soft, orange light.'

After forty years the Americans had finally climbed K2, and Lou Reichardt had made the first ascent of the peak without supplementary oxygen.

The oxygen-starved Reichardt wanted to descend immediately and set off, leaving Wickwire still taking photographs. His camera iced up and stopped working, so he spent time looking on a scene 'I would never see again. So, for a few minutes, I scanned the horizon. In one direction K2's shadow stretched over the Karakoram for what seemed like a hundred miles; in the other, a sea of mountains turned orange, then purple in the setting sun.'

Reichardt made it down to Camp VI Abruzzi at 8pm and was met by Ridgeway and Roskelley, who had abandoned their attempt on the Polish route and were keen to attempt the summit. After initially overshooting the camp, Reichardt was guided in by a light they shone for him; his appearance appalled the other two: 'his face was frozen, looking like a spectre raised from a frozen underworld. Large clumps of ice were frozen in his beard – not just snow, or spindrift, but heavy pieces of blue ice. There was a large icicle hanging from his nose. His lips were puffed, red and split from the ordeal.'

Above, Jim Wickwire had stopped descending when the light disappeared. There was no moon, and the risk of continuing was higher than the risk of a bivouac. His gas soon ran out, so having had little to drink (or eat) since starting out, dehydration was an issue. He knew that he was about to make the highest solo bivouac ever, at 8300m (27,230ft). Cutting a step in the ice, he climbed into his bivouac sack. In his book he writes:

> The cold became unbearable. Shivering so much I could barely control my limbs, I forced myself to flex my hands and feet, fingers and toes, hoping to forestall frostbite and hypothermia. Writhing from the cold, I slowly slipped over the edge of the platform, down the slope. Still in the bivouac sack, I instinctively dug in my boot heels and stopped.

He did that several times more before getting out of the sack to sort out the platform. Horrified, he found himself on the edge of a steep slope – one more slide and he would have disappeared down the South Face. As the night wore on, he concentrated on moving and thought of previous bivouacs, knowing that the sun would eventually rise.

When it did, Wickwire had to talk aloud to encourage himself to carry out the necessary activities to get ready. He giggled when one crampon was loose, a sure sign of hypoxia. But actually moving was a problem. Finally he told himself to think of his family: 'You cannot die. You must survive for them. You must return to them.' And eventually he began to descend. As he did, he saw Ridgeway and Roskelley coming towards him. Unsure whether they were going for the summit, beginning a rescue or looking for a body, they had started out early. Now, above them, a scarecrow-like figure was standing upright but not moving. They wondered if Jim Wickwire had frozen to death standing up, but when they reached him, Wickwire assured them he could make it to Camp VI and continued down.

Just like the previous pair, Ridgeway and Roskelley had decided to climb at first without bottled oxygen, but when the time came to turn on the taps, Roskelley decided to ditch his system, reasoning that oxygen at a low flow rate would not compensate for the extra weight. Ridgeway was not so sure, but when his mask failed to fit tight he also jettisoned the system. The two men were therefore climbing without bottled oxygen; they were also unroped, soloing the route from their top camp. The two reached the summit at 3pm: Roskelley was back at Camp VI Abruzzi around 5pm, Ridgeway an hour later. That night there was a further episode when a gas canister exploded while being changed, setting fire to Ridgeway's sleeping bag and burning the tent down. The four men squeezed into a tent made for two and with three sleeping bags between them spent an uncomfortable night, Ridgeway having difficulty breathing and coughing up blood.

The descent and trek-out were an ordeal for the summitters; Wickwire in particular was very sick with pneumonia and pleurisy, and eventually needed a helicopter evacuation. Back in the US he lost parts of two toes to frostbite, but in medical terms, the loss was minor in comparison to the surgery required to remove fluid and tissue from his left lung.

After the expedition Cherie Bech left her husband, reverting to her maiden name Cherie Bremer-Kamp, and got together with Chris Chandler. In 1985 they attempted to climb Kangchenjunga in winter with one Sherpa. Close to the summit Chandler developed oedema and died. Cherie and the Sherpa suffered horrific frostbite injuries, but survived. Despite her disabilities, Cherie returned to her nursing career.

The Magic Line, Messner and the French, 1979

By 1979 Reinhold Messner[13] had already established himself as the world's leading high-altitude mountaineer. In 1970 he had climbed Nanga Parbat and two years later Manaslu. Then in 1975 he had pushed forwards the boundaries of the possible with an audacious alpine-style ascent of Gasherbrum I with Peter Habeler. Another barrier fell in 1978 when, again with Habeler, he climbed Everest without supplementary oxygen. It was logical therefore that he should look next towards K2, and also that he should consider a new line. He called his chosen route the Magic Line, and it follows the South-South-West Ridge from the Negrotto Pass, between K2 and Angel Peak, and was clearly going to offer very difficult climbing. Messner therefore chose a team of first-class climbers, the Italians Alessandro Gogna and Renato Casarotto, the South Tyrolean Friedl Mutschlechner, the German Michl Dacher and the Austrian Robert Schauer. The journalist Jochn Hoelzgen also joined the team, and later became part of the climbing party. Robert Schauer would later climb Gasherbrum IV's West Face in 1985 with Wojciech Kurtyka, as well as Everest and several other 8000m peaks. Casarotto would die on K2, Mutschlechner in a lightning storm on Manaslu after climbing other 8000m peaks.

To approach the Negrotto Pass, Messner wanted to have a Base Camp on the Savoia Glacier as the British and Americans had done, but on the carry to the site there was an accident, Casarotto writing:

> Reinhold discovers an exposed, but easy, way through the snow-covered band of rocks and fixes a rope on it. Fearfully the first porters attempt it, the others shake their heads. The traverse ends on a terrace where the glacier no longer poses any threat. Some specially courageous porters swing back and forth, carrying loads for the weaker ones, who then follow. They attach themselves to the fixed ropes,

trembling and praying. Michl and I also help shift loads. Suddenly I am startled by shrieks. Further up, on easier terrain, one of the porters has fallen into a crevasse. Not heeding the warnings of Terry [Mohammed Tahir, the team's liaison officer] and Reinhold, the man had left the safe spot on the glacier and suddenly broken through into a hidden hollow. Reinhold, Terry and I immediately lower Friedl down into the crevasse on a rope, but he finds the man dead.

The other porters then refused to carry to the proposed Base Camp, and Messner, believing the ascent to the Pass from the southern side to be too dangerous, decided to abandon his Magic Line. He and Mutschlechner made a reconnaissance of the South Face, but Messner then decided to make a fast ascent of the Abruzzi Spur. The decision did not go down well. Casarotto in particular was not keen, saying that he had no interest in the Abruzzi, while Gogna questioned whether 'the summit of K2 is more important than the aesthetic perfection of the line', and decided that 'in my opinion the summit is not important, not even on K2'. But the others wanted to make the summit and so, with some reluctant, the whole team headed for the Abruzzi. On the Spur they established three camps, at 6100m (20,000ft), 6700m (22,000ft) and 7350m (24,100ft) with fixed ropes between them to aid retreat in the event of a storm. From the last, Messner and Dacher climbed to 7910m (25,950ft), where they erected a small tent. Next day they headed upwards at 7am, late because of a night of wind and snow. As he approached the Bottleneck Couloir, Messner writes: 'I thrust my axe into the snow. And stop, stricken, it is like accumulated quicksand. That's that then – hopeless! I gasp for breath, everything is whirling and my body feels like lead. I don't know why I don't turn back at once.' The snow was waist deep, but despite Messner's initial thought he moved forward, ploughing a trail through it. The deep snow was continuous, requiring both effort and time and Messner wondered

> why do I keep climbing if I know we shall never reach the summit? The sun is on its way down and it is already cold. We do still have some time left, although to me it seems we are much too late for the summit. This continual feeling of helplessness every time I take a rest and then look up to see how far we still have to go.

But the two men continued and finally reached the summit, from where Dacher contacted Base Camp to order flowers for his wife. That night a storm blew up preventing any further summit attempts.

In the aftermath of the climb Messner was ungenerous towards his team mates, writing 'I felt let down by Robert on a personal level, by Renato as a climber.' After Casarotto's death he wrote 'on our expedition he proved so slow as to be something of a liability: that was one of the reasons why I gave up the idea of climbing the South Pillar [the Magic Line].' Given Casarotto's lack of enthusiasm for the Abruzzi, the criticism seems harsh. And given the fact that prior to the decision to abandon the Magic Line there had only been the Baltoro trek, the idea that Casarotto's slowness was a factor seems unlikely. Messner's claims for his K2 ascent also raised hackles. He claimed the first ascent by a small party, and while that was true his team had the same number as Houston's in 1953, which would likely have succeeded but for the storm (though, it must be added, Houston had Sherpas). He also claimed the first alpine-style ascent of the upper mountain and, while it is true that he and Dacher carried all of their equipment to their last camp, much the same could be said of the Americans in 1978. His claim of a fast ascent was also true, measured from Base Camp to summit, but it was not quite as fast as the claim, which missed out the timeline of establishing the Spur camps. There have been other instances of Messner polishing up his climbs to a higher gloss: given his achievements it is sad that he feels the need.

While Messner's team was moving down the Abruzzi, a large French team was only just starting another attempt on the Magic Line. The French expedition was massive: 30 tons of equipment and a team of twenty led by Bernard Mellet. The team was very strong, and included Maurice Barrard, Pierre Béghin, Ivan Ghirardini and Yannick Seigneur. Perhaps because the book of the expedition[14] was not translated into English, the French attempt on the Magic Line has not received the credit it was due, though the large number of climbers and the siege tactics they employed already seemed outdated by 1979, particularly after the massive Japanese expedition of 1977. Having gained the Negrotto Pass from the east (De Filippi Glacier) side, the French established a series of five camps along the line. The expedition was marred by the death of the Hunza sirdar Lasker Khan from a heart attack while climbing with Ivan Ghirardini, the latter recording that 'suddenly he [Lasker Khan] let out a cry and fell backwards ... I quickly reached him, but when I did he died in my arms ... It was horrible, unfair. It was a nightmare.' After consulting with the expedition's Pakistani liaison officer, it was decided to bury Lasker Khan where he lay, as bringing the body to the base of the mountain would be too risky.

The death, and a period of bad weather, delayed the French until early September. When the climb began again, Jean-Marc Boivin established a world record when he flew a delta glider (a specially modified fixed-wing hang-glider) from Camp IV at 7500m (24,600ft). Bernard Mellet was enthusiastic about the attempt, but had refused Boivin permission to attempt it before the summit was reached. However, on 6 September Boivin, at Camp IV, was diagnosed with a retinal haemorrhage and needed to descend quickly. Mellet therefore gave permission for him to fly as he would probably not recover in time to climb back up if he downclimbed. Preparations for the flight took 3 hours, but by the time

Boivin was ready there was no wind and he was concerned whether taking off was too dangerous. But finally, as Mellet writes, 'He raises the wing, takes two steps forward and jumps! He falls sharply, the wing vibrates, shaves a boulder and then there it is, gliding away majestically, almost horizontally.' Just 13 minutes later Boivin landed safely at Base Camp.

Time was now getting very short, the approaching winter threatening to end the expedition before a summit attempt was made. Ghirardini suffered frostbite pushing the route out and had to be brought down by Seigneur and Jean-Claude Mosca, and tempers among the other potential summit climbers became frayed as bad weather again stopped them. Pierre Béghin attempted a solo ascent, but was forced back by bad conditions, leaving only Thierry Leroy and Daniel Monaci capable of making one last attempt. On 9 September they set out from Camp V (7900m/25,900ft) hoping to establish a higher camp, from which they could make a summit bid. Leroy writes (in Mellet's book) that they climbed 200m of slope at 50° through snow which was always knee-deep, often thigh-deep. They followed ropes fixed earlier by Ghirardini and Seigneur, then, in worsening weather, continued over unexplored ground. At about 8300m (27,230ft), having found nowhere flat enough to pitch a tent, the two men dug a snowhole. They had intended to share a single sleeping bag, but the hole was too narrow for that, so Monaci had the bag while Leroy got inside a bivouac sack. The temperature that night was, says Leroy, 'bearable', which sounds a masterly understatement. It snowed all night, but by morning the weather had cleared. In bright sunshine, but extreme cold, the two climbed upwards.

The climbing was very difficult and took many hours, the pair fixing ropes as they went to secure the descent. Finally, at about 8400m (27,750ft), just 200m (about 650ft) from the top, but with all their rope fixed, Monaci said he wanted to go down. Leroy was anxious to continue, and wanted to climb down to retrieve 20m of rope to secure what appeared to be the last difficulties. When Monaci declined, Leroy climbed on alone, but at about 8460m (27,750ft), with difficult climbing still ahead, he was forced to accept that he would not reach the summit and retreated.

The British on the West Ridge and Abruzzi Spur, 1980
In 1979 Pete Boardman, Joe Tasker and Doug Scott, veterans of Bonington's 1978 expedition, made the third ascent of Kangchenjunga by a new route on the North-West Face/North Ridge. The following year they decided to apply the same lightweight idea to completing K2's West Ridge route attempted in 1982. Aware that the route on K2 would be more demanding, they brought in a fourth climber, Dick Renshaw, who had been Tasker's partner on an alpine-style ascent of Dunagiri (7066m/23,182ft) in 1975. The attempt used the ridge above the basin from which an avalanche had swept Nick Estcourt in 1978, but the use of fixed ropes in order to make stocking high camps easier took more time than anticipated and led to

problems between the team members. Scott wanted to make an alpine attempt from the established high point (about 7000m/23,000ft) but Renshaw, who had narrowly escaped the amputation of frostbitten fingers after the Dunagiri climb, did not. There were also other problems. Scott writes (in *Himalayan Climber*) that Boardman and Tasker were competitive towards each other and Tasker resented Scott's position as an older, more experienced climber. Ultimately Scott decided to leave. In his book (*Savage Arena*) Tasker diplomatically states that Scott had limited time and other engagements. The result was the abandonment of the West Ridge, Boardman, Renshaw and Tasker deciding on a fast, alpine-style ascent of the Abruzzi Spur. Before the climbing, Tasker reports, there were arguments at Base Camp when the Italian-born French climber Ivan Ghirardini (accompanied by his wife) demanded permission to attempt K2 from the British liaison officer, something which, of course, he could not give. Ghirardini later claimed to have made a solo attempt on the peak, reaching 8300m.

The British found the Abruzzi much harder than they had imagined, their respect for the early pioneers of the route growing with each foot ascended. The idea of a five- or six-day climb was defeated, both by the difficulties of the route and by the weather, which at one point kept the trio marooned for four days, and reduced the climbing rate much of the time. Tasker notes that the difference between the weather information they were given by their liaison officer at Base Camp and what they were actually experiencing was astonishing, particularly when they were being battered by ferocious storms that were apparently not felt at Base. The trio fixed a retreat rope on the Black Pyramid, which Tasker describes with awe:

We knew of the Black Pyramid by descriptions from the earlier ascents but nothing prepared us for its sustained and improbable passages ... The rock was compact, with few foot-holds or cracks for pitons. This was one area where we took care to secure in place a life-line of rope for our descent.

At a camp at 7742m (25,400ft) the team was trapped for a day by a snowstorm, but the forecast from Base Camp was encouraging, suggesting the next day would be cloudy, the one after fine. So next day they continued, making camp below a boulder at the base of the Bottleneck Couloir at 8100m (26,575ft). They were only 500m or so from the summit now, and success seemed assured. But the camp site was far from ideal:

the ledge was barely wide enough for the tent and when all three of us tried to lie down inside, Dick, who was on the side of the tent nearest the edge, had to pad out the floor of the tent beneath him with the rucksacks. Half of his place in the tent was poised over nothing, but the alloy stays in the rucksacks formed a platform over the drop.

Tasker was closest to the boulder, which, they hoped, would provide protection from the avalanches that seemed to scour the couloir above them. Eventually, despite the precariousness of the position and the fact that it was snowing, the three slept.

Tasker describes what happened next:

> I awoke in an instant awareness of a sordid death. All was black, the tent collapsed on top of us. A heavy avalanche of snow was pouring over the tent. I was lying face down, cloaked by the fabric of the tent, my body and limbs moulded and held in place by the weight of snow, solid as concrete.

Held rigid, unable to move, he shouted, but there was no reply. He assumed the others were unconscious or dead, and

> knew I would not be long in dying too. The blows on my head from the avalanche went on and on, at any moment I expected the tent to be torn free and sent tumbling and cartwheeling for 10,000 feet with us inside ... before the impacts and collisions of the fall brought oblivion. I felt no fear, only regret that our death should be so paltry and that we were to be extinguished without trace, because no one would ever know what had happened and there would forever be questions and guesses about our disappearance ...

Tasker blacked out. When he came round he could move a little, and with a penknife was able to cut a small hole in the tent as the air in the minimal air space he had was becoming foul. Unsure whether he would ever be able to extricate himself from his coffin of tent and snow, Tasker was hugely relieved to hear voices.

When the avalanche struck, Renshaw had been tipped off the ledge: only the tent fabric held him above the huge drop. Boardman had less snow above him and was able to struggle out of the tent. He pulled Renshaw free and the two of them dug away the snow on the tent so Tasker could breathe freely. Then a second avalanche arrived. Still outside the tent, Boardman, who was clipped into pitons above the tent, had to grab and hold Renshaw, who was not. They then had to dig Tasker free again. When dawn came, all thoughts of the summit were gone and the three climbed down, Tasker taking a direct line down the couloir, risking starting an avalanche rather than attempting to downclimb ice-encrusted rocks. It took 6 hours to descend 275m (900ft) to a safe camp site where the battered tent was erected. With much equipment lost to the avalanche, there was only one cooker and gas stove. They heated water, but there was little to eat. The descent over the following days was a nightmare of route-finding in poor weather and bad conditions, but Base Camp was safely reached. Then, after a few days' rest, the three men all contracted dysentery. When they had recovered from the illness, they decided, probably to the astonishment of the casual reader, to go back for one more try despite the unsettled weather. After eight days, with their food having more or less run out, they had almost regained their high point, camping a little below it in a safer spot. They were up at 2am but the weather was poor and, as the forecast from Base did not look promising, they abandoned the climb. By 9pm they were back at the base of the mountain.

French on the South Face, Japanese on the West Ridge, 1981
In 1981 an expedition to the still unclimbed West Ridge was mounted by the Alpine Club of Japan's Waseda University, Tokyo. The leader was Teruo Matsuura.[15] The alpine clubs of Japan's universities are a leading source of mountaineers, who retain their university club membership after graduation, so that the clubs are capable of calling upon numerous high-class mountaineers to mount their own expeditions. In 1979 a team from the Waseda Club made the first ascent of the North Ridge of Rakaposhi (7788m/25,552ft), that success, and the view of K2 from the summit, providing the incentive to attempt the higher peak. From the start the Japanese decided to attempt a new route. Aware that the West Ridge was unexplored above about 7000m, that was the chosen line.

Matsuura's summary of the climb says it was a six-man team, but, as indicated by the photographs of team members and his article in AAJ, there were actually thirteen Japanese, one being the team doctor, plus the Pakistani Nazir Ahmad Sabir, as well as the standard Pakistani liaison officer. Sabir, a Hunza, had been a high-altitude porter with the Japanese 1977 expedition and had made a rapid transition to fully fledged climber, good enough to be invited to be a member of the climbing team. The Japanese attempt was forced to climb late in the season as early permission had been granted to a team of four led by the Frenchman Yannick Seigneur; the others were the French climber Jean Afanassieff and the Germans Reinhard Karl and Hans Martin Goetz. This team, using no porters on the mountain, attempted to climb a new route on the mountain's South-East Face. Following a rib on the true left side of the De Filippi Glacier, the team intended to cross the huge face diagonally to reach the Abruzzi Spur near the base of the Shoulder. Beset by bad weather, however, the four men eventually retreated from a height of about 7400m (24,300ft).

The Japanese now had the mountain to themselves. They were also aided by their liaison officer being able to persuade three hundred porters to carry all the way to their proposed Base Camp, when they had originally thought they might only be able to get a very much smaller number to shuttle loads from the Abruzzi Base Camp. On the mountain the Japanese followed the British line, placing two camps, the second at 6600m (21,650ft). Above this, easy climbing led to the first major difficulty, a 40m (130ft) cliff where a loop of rope indicated they were on the line of the British 1980 attempt. The cliff had been described by Joe Tasker as 'extremely difficult and steep', and required, Matsuura says, the Japanese climbers to rope up before Eiho Otani 'muscled his way up'. Above the cliff, Camp III was established at 7100m (23,300ft), at the high point of the British attempt.

Bad weather had delayed the establishment of Camp III for six days, but now the weather relented and Hideki Megumi pushed a route up two snowfields separated by a band of slabby rocks. Camp IV was placed at the top of the second snowfield, at 7650m (25,100ft). The most dangerous part of the route had now been reached. High above Camp IV was a Y-shaped couloir prone to avalanches, and on 19 July, as Harashige Yabuta and Matsui Yamashita were setting out to establish Camp V, a huge avalanche swept down the couloir, the two Japanese being lucky to escape death: the blast from the avalanche hit Base Camp several thousand metres below. However, the avalanche swept the face clean of unstable snow, allowing the two climbers to make safer progress to the foot of the couloir. They climbed steep rocks to the side of the lower couloir, then took the easier, right-hand, branch at the junction of the Y. Over a four-day period ropes were then fixed all the way along the right-hand branch to Camp V at 8050m (26,400ft). In fact, to aid load carrying, and also to make the route safer because of the constant threat of avalanches, the Japanese fixed ropes virtually all the way from Base Camp to Camp V, running out some 5.5km of rope.

Eleven successive days of bad weather after Camp IV had been established also obliged Matsuura to change his plan. He had intended to establish a Camp VI at about 8250m (27,050ft), but now time was running out and he had lost two climbers to ill-health. He therefore decided to dispense with a top camp, launching a summit bid from Camp V. Megumi and Osamu Iwata fixed ropes above the camp, sleeping with supplementary oxygen that night. Then Otani, Sabir and Yamashita, using bottled oxygen, continued the route to 8300m (27,230ft), before returning to Camp V where they were joined by Yabuta and Takao Yonemoto.

At 5am on 6 August the summit team of Otani, Sabir and Yamashita, all using supplementary oxygen, started for the summit. They were accompanied by Yabuta and Yonemoto carrying spare oxygen bottles that were to be deposited as high as possible for use by the returning summit party. At 10am the summit team reached the South-South-West Ridge (Magic Line). According to Matsuura, the three men were convinced they would be unable to climb the ridge carrying the heavy oxygen sets and so they unloaded them. Sabir says that his decision was based on the fact that he was 'sick of carrying the weight and dumped it [the oxygen set]'. The three moved to the right of the ridge on to what turned out to be an equally difficult face of mixed snow and rock. At 6pm, at about 8400m (27,550ft), they decided to bivouac rather than climb on into the approaching night. (Sabir says the bivouac was at 8500m, which seems too high in view of the events of the following day: he also says that Matsuura advised them to descend rather than bivouac, which seems consistent with the radio conversation next day.) The men took 3 hours to dig a snow cave. Inside, like 'three chickens in a cage', they had neither fuel, food, water or oxygen, and the candle they used to try to warm themselves – Sabir says it seemed 'like the last source of heat and light on earth' – was hardly likely to offer more than a boost to morale. Then, in the middle of the night, Sabir, while massaging his feet, knocked against the cave wall, collapsing it. The three were then left more or less open to the elements and, according to Sabir, 'not very sure of surviving the night'.

But they did survive, the weather both during the night and on the following day being good. By 6am they were climbing again. But progress had now slowed dramatically and by 10am they had managed no more than 100m, with Yamashita trailing behind the leading pair. At this stage there was a bizarre conversation with Matsuura at Base Camp. Matsuura says he 'ordered them by walkie-talkie to return immediately, in view of the difficulty of the descent, and even though a similar failure just short of the summit on Lhotse Shar 16 years previously had been nagging at me all through the years. My first responsibility was to bring the team back alive.' Sabir says that 'for the next forty-five minutes there was a dramatic war of emotions, of confusions within confusions, between the higher heavens of K2 and base camp'. From the recollections of Otani and Sabir, the conversation took place when they were no more than 50m below the summit, though, as the trailing Yamashita believes he reached 8460m, perhaps 150m might be more realistic. (The given heights of Camp V, the bivouac and various other points along the way do not add up to a consistent picture, so constructing a timeline for the summit climb is not easy: if Otani and Sabir's view is correct, and Matsuura agrees with them, then Yamashita reached 8560m, just 150ft below the summit). Sabir realised he was likely to fall victim to cultural differences that conflicted with his own ambition:

> I said 'Forget about what the leader said. I'm not going down because I missed K2 from so near last time.' [Sabir had been with the 1977 Japanese expedition on which Ashraf Aman had been chosen as the first Pakistani to summit.] I said that in Pakistan we don't listen to a leader sitting far below. But the Japanese think of a leader as a god. I talked to the liaison officer three times on the radio – he abused me and wanted to throw all responsibility on to me if someone should die. I said I don't care. I just wanted to go on. Finally, the leader agreed to let us continue.

Matsuura's version is that Yamashita told him that he would remain where he was if the others were allowed to continue, a compromise as extraordinary as the conversation itself.

Leaving Yamashita behind, Otani and Sabir climbed on, reaching the summit at 11.30am after what Sabir says was 'an easy walk'. If the conversation started at 10am and lasted 45 minutes, then Yamashita was just 45 minutes from the top, which makes 50m more realistic than 150m, given the rate of progress up until then. Sabir's view is that the 'easy walk' took an hour.

As they neared the top Otani tried to persuade Sabir to go first as it was a Pakistani mountain, but he declined and the two went on arm-in-arm. At noon they left the summit, reaching Yamashita at 12.30pm. Sabir says that when he and Otani reached Yamashita, 'he was praying. I couldn't stop my tears when I saw him, as he should have been with us.' As night fell they reached Yabuta and Yonemoto, who had climbed up towards them with hot drinks. All five men were in Camp V by 8pm. By now the summit team had not eaten or drunk anything for 36 hours and Sabir's lips were bleeding from dehydration. It took a further three days to reach Base Camp. Then the weather window which had allowed the successful climb closed shut, seven days of continuous snow forcing Matsuura to end the expedition.

Japanese and Poles on the North Side, 1982
On 10 August 1981 the Chinese Mountaineering Association announced that access would be granted to the northern side of Mount Qogir, as well as the other three 8000m peaks of the Baltoro area, the border between Pakistan and China running through the summits of each. Although the Chinese had been active on Everest and Shisha Pangma during the time the borders of the country had been closed to foreign mountaineers, there seems to have been no attempt to climb K2 and so the 1981 decision allowed climbers the opportunity not only to explore an area not seen by Westerners since Shipton's visit, but to tackle a ridge that had dominated their thoughts and dreams for years. During the American ascent of the North-East Ridge, Rick Ridgeway was able to look out across China as John Roskelley led out the next fixed rope (*The Last Step*, p.121):

> We could see the lower section of K2's north ridge. Entirely on the Chinese side of the mountain, this ridge is one of the most outstanding features of mountain architecture on earth. It rises at a continuous angle of forty-five to fifty degrees, uninterrupted by any major steps or irregularities in its crest, from the head of the north glacier to the summit, a vertical rise of nearly fifteen thousand feet. It is the longest uninterrupted mountain ridge on earth ... It is, without doubt, one of the most awesome challenges remaining for tomorrow's mountaineers.

Over the years that 'awesome challenge' had taken on a mythical quality. It was no surprise, therefore, that immediately the announcement was made Kenjiro Imaida, President of the Japanese Alpine Club, travelled to Beijing (still called Peking at the time) and signed an agreement that would allow a reconnaissance team into the area in September 1981 with a full-scale expedition in May 1982. The agreement was formally announced on 2 September 1981.

The Japanese team was enormous, with nine 'summit' climbers and a total of thirty-six support climbers, doctors and Base Camp personnel. The overall leader of the expedition was Isaoh Shinkai, with Masatsugu Konishi being 'climbing leader'. Even allowing for the need to transport equipment to the peak's base, the army of men on the expedition seems a throwback to the era of national teams and siege tactics, in sharp contrast to what was now happening on the southern side of the mountain, but the number needs to be seen in context. There are no locals to act as porters, and pack animals can get no closer than Suget Jangal, which is 16km (10 miles) from the base of the mountain. Everything therefore had to be packed in by the team, necessitating enough broad shoulders and strong legs to sustain a potentially lengthy campaign. The approach to the Suget Jangal is also a different world from the long trek along the Baltoro, camels being used once vehicles can no longer cope with the terrain, the rivers forded along the way rising with the summer's meltwater and effectively marooning those who have crossed.

The Japanese arrived in early May but it was early June before they had moved the expedition to the foot of the peak. Most of the support climbers then departed, a handful staying on to act as porters on the mountain. The obvious target was the long North Ridge,[16] along which four camps were established and fixed ropes installed to a height of 8000m. The weather on the north side of the peak was, unsurprisingly, no better than on the south, with periods of bad weather preventing any climbing and avalanches destroying the fixed ropes so that good days were frequently lost to the necessity of repairing the route.

When a weather window finally opened for the Japanese, Konishi's decision for the summit teams was a dramatic mix of understanding of high-altitude climbing and a restatement of ancient Japanese values:

Please measure your strength against the difficulties of the climb to the summit, as if you miscalculate, you will, of course, die. The responsibility for your final decision rests with yourselves. You are experienced climbers and responsibility for your welfare rests with yourselves. In my case, if I become exhausted at 8500m, I do not expect you to help me as it is my decision to have climbed so high and my failure not to have descended from a lower point. No one can help others at such altitudes. Our summit bids are, I believe, covered by the code of the ancient Samurai. In an ancient duel, anyone who was inferior, even if only slightly inferior, to an opponent should fall on his sword.

With these words of encouragement, the dozen climbers – the original nine summit climbers and three support climbers – set out for the high camp and the end of the fixed ropes.

On 14 August Naoé Sakashita, Hioshi Yoshino, Takashi Ozaki and Yukihiro Yanagisawa set out for the summit. Each was climbing solo and nominally following his own preferred line, though at first they climbed as two pairs. The first two named started first to expose the last of the fixed ropes. They then traversed left into a snow basin. Ozaki followed a different line, continuing straight up, but was forced to retreat by a line of séracs, and returned to the top camp. Yanagisawa followed the first pair. These three reached the summit, Sakashita first, Yoshino last about an hour later. Subsequently they were forced to bivouac on the descent some 200-300m below the summit. Yanagisawa spent a cold, miserable night as he did not have a down jacket, but Sakashita hugged him all night in an effort to keep him warm. The following day Sakashita descended while Yanagisawa and Yoshino waited for the next team of four summit climbers who brought hot tea and a rope, in a gesture of humanity that contradicted Konishi's Samurai ethic. The second summit group of four (Hironobu Kamuro, Haruichi Kawamura, Tatsuji Shigeno and Kazushige Takami) reached the summit but were also forced to bivouac on the descent. Yanagisawa and Yoshino descended roped to the top of the fixed ropes, then unroped. Yoshino successfully reached the top camp, but Yanagisawa disappeared. It is assumed he fell down the North Face. A third summit party did not attempt the summit. As the expedition was clearing the mountain Dr Toshitaka Sakano, the team doctor, died of exposure after injuring himself in a fall on a minor peak near Advanced Base Camp while taking photographs.

In an interesting evaluation of the expedition, Konishi claimed a 30 per cent success rate. He had intended to get all twelve climbers to the summit without using supplementary oxygen. Seven men made it, but only six got down alive, so he reckoned a 50 per cent success rate, but reduced that by 10 per cent because of Yanagisawa's death and by another 10 per cent because both Yoshino and Kamuro had digits amputated because of frostbite.

While the Japanese were climbing the North Ridge, there was another team working on the western edge of the North Face, but these climbers had arrived from the southern side and without permission to travel into China. A team of a dozen Poles and six Mexicans led by Janusz Kurczab[17] had set out with the intention of attempting the North-West Ridge which had defeated the Americans in 1975, though they had arrived on the ridge not by climbing to the Savoia Saddle but by making a route from the Savoia Glacier up a cwm formed by a spur of the North-West Ridge and the West Ridge. The Poles climbed the headwall of this cwm, reaching the North-West Ridge at about 6700m (22,000ft). During the climb up the headwall one climber was carried 200m by an avalanche and was lucky to escape with only a broken arm.

Once reached, the ridge proved to be much less of a crest than it had appeared from below, being a wide area of mixed rock and ice. The general trend of such features as existed was northward and the Poles discovered that, as they followed the obvious lines of weakness this strata formed, they were heading across K2's northern face towards the North Ridge. By early August the Poles had fixed ropes (some 3.5km of rope in total) across the face on an upward traverse which reached the ridge and the Japanese fixed ropes. The Polish line now apparently crossed the Japanese route, the two lines of fixed ropes also crossing, leading the Japanese to inform their Chinese hosts, who made a formal protest to the Pakistani government about the trespass on to Chinese territory. However, it was not the ensuing diplomatic furore but bad weather that caused the Poles to abandon their route and retreat. When the weather turned good again on 11 August, the Japanese used the short weather window to go for the summit, but the Poles did not, making no further progress before the weather broke again. By the time it had cleared up almost two weeks later, the Poles discovered that their Camps III and IV had been destroyed. As a consequence, it was early September before they had established a final camp, Camp V at 8050m (26,400ft), on the Japanese line. From it, on 6 September, Leszek Cichy and Wojciech Wróż[18] climbed upwards. A storm broke and they were forced to retreat from about 8200m (26,00ft), suffering minor frostbite injuries. A series of storms then set in and the Poles abandoned their climb.

As well as the Poles on the northern side of the peak, there were also two other Polish teams on the south side. On the Abruzzi Spur Wanda Rutkiewicz[19] was leading a female expedition. The Poles had near-perfect weather and quickly established Camp II at 6700m, where Halina Krüger-Syrokomska and Anna Okopinska took up residence. The two women had climbed Gasherbrum II together in 1975 and were in high spirits. When speaking to Krüger-Syrokomska from Base Camp, Rutkiewicz asked how the weather looked for the following day. Krüger-Syrokomska answered 'I'll just have to ask God what he's got in mind.' Soon after, as the two Poles talked over tea, Krüger-Syrokomska fell unconscious. Despite mouth-to-mouth resuscitation and heart massage by Okopinska and members of an Austrian team, she died within an hour. The exact cause of her death remains a mystery, with cerebral bleeding, heart attack and oedema all being suggested. After they had brought her body down to Base Camp, the Poles considered their options. They decided to continue the climb, but bad weather forced them to abandon the route at 7100m (23,300ft).

The Austrians who helped in the attempt to revive Halina Krüger-Syrokomska were members of a four-man team led by Georg Bachler, also attempting the Abruzzi. They had reached 7500m (24,600ft), but time lost in aiding the carry of the Polish woman's body down the mountain and the bad weather which followed forced them to abandon a further attempt.

The other south-side Polish team comprised Jerzy Kukuczka and Wojciech Kurtyka.[20] The pair had been added to Wanda Rutkiewicz's permit on the grounds that they were offering protection to the women in a Muslim country and taking photographs, but had no intention of climbing with them. The permit allowed expedition members to acclimatise in the neighbourhood of K2, which the two Poles interpreted as allowing them to climb Broad Peak, which they did, alpine-style. That the Pakistani authorities would certainly not have viewed such an ascent as 'acclimatisation' was perfectly clear to both of them, so they stayed very quiet about the climb. They then tried to make a new route up the centre of K2's South-East Face, having given up on their original plan of an East Face route in the face of dangers from séracs hanging above the route. The South-East Face route also turned out to be threatened by a sérac in an area which the two Poles called the 'twenty minutes of fear' when they had to cross it. At a height of about 7200m (23,625ft) bad weather put an end to their attempt. Back in Islamabad, Wanda Rutkiewicz was questioned about the two men's ascent of Broad Peak; she insisted she knew nothing about it and as far as she was concerned they had only been taking photographs. Considering the Pakistani attitude to illegal ascents, particularly of significant peaks (which, by definition, includes 8000m peaks), Kukuczka and Kurtyka were lucky not to receive lengthy bans, especially after Messner published a book in which he stated that he had met the pair returning from the summit after his own ascent of Broad Peak.

The Italians on the North Ridge, and an International Team on the South Face, 1983

In 1983 an Italian team made the second ascent of the North Ridge route pioneered by the Japanese the previous year. Led by Francesco Santon,[21] the team of twenty comprised a doctor and nineteen climbers, the latter including Fausto De Stefani and Sergio Martini,[22] Mario Lacedelli, nephew of Lino Lacedelli, and the Czech Josef Rakoncaj. Travelling with the team to make a film of a north-side expedition were Kurt Diemberger and Julie Tullis.[23] On 31 July Agostino Da Polenza and Rakoncaj reached the summit, but were forced to bivouac, without equipment or food and having drunk almost nothing for two days, at 8500m (27,900ft) on the descent. They survived without frostbite. Four days later De Stefani and Martini summitted. Also intending to reach the summit, Tullis and Diemberger climbed to Camp IV, at 8000m (26,246ft), hoping to be able to make an attempt on the summit the following day. Two other team members, Giuliano De Marchi and Alberto Soncini, were attempting the summit that day. These four – the two Italians somewhere close to the summit, the Briton and Austrian at Camp IV – were now the only people on the mountain, everyone else having descended to Base Camp after the second successful summit bid. During the night a storm blew up. Tullis writes:

> That night we got no sleep. Wind whistled and howled around us, funnelling up from the steep ten-thousand-foot drop on one side of the ridge and catching us in its full blast as it reached the top. It tugged and tore at the thin Goretex

material of our tunnel-shaped tent, and we wondered how long it would be before the guy lines broke or the fabric ripped.

It was still raging the following morning, and 'not until noon … did the storm calm down sufficiently to allow us outside'. Tullis and Diemberger decided to abandon their summit attempt, but were anxious about the two Italians still high on the mountain. Then they saw them moving slowly towards the camp. De Marchi and Soncini were able to make it back to camp after having survived a torrid bivouac. Soncini was showing signs of mountain sickness and needed help to descend, the four taking two days to reach the base of the mountain. All four escaped without frostbite injuries. During her climb Julie Tullis had established a female height record for K2, one that was to stand for three years.

In the same year a Spanish expedition failed in an attempt to climb the West Ridge on the southern side of the mountain, and a small team attempted a new line on the South Face. This team, Britons Doug Scott,[24] Andy Parkin and Roger Baxter-Jones, together with Frenchman Jean Afanassieff, took the South-South-East Spur to the left (south) of the Abruzzi, a line that had been explored to 6000m by Parkin, Alan Rouse and American Steve Sustad, who were on the same expedition. As noted in Chapter 1, this exploration had been cut short by the earthquake which set off avalanches on both K2 and Broad Peak: the three were not in the direct line of any avalanche, but were concerned that shockwaves created by them might blow them off the Spur.

The four-man team bivouaced four times, the last being at about 7500m (24,600ft) about 200m below the Shoulder, Scott noting that as they climbed they watched a Spanish team installing fixed ropes on the Abruzzi which they thought might come in handy for an easy descent after a summit bid. But it was not to be. After an hour's climbing from the last bivouac site, with only about 100m to go before the Abruzzi route was joined at the Shoulder,

> Jean suddenly announced 'I'm going blind.' He felt a pain around his kidneys, he said his face felt numb and so were his arms and fingers. 'Go down, must go down,' he said. It took some moments for this to register but such was his insistence that I had no hesitation in shouting to Andy [who was leading] that he had better come down.

Afanassieff was deteriorating and he was mumbling about who he would leave things to, clearly thinking death was imminent. With fresh snow making all movement hazardous, the team descended. As they did, Afanassieff's condition improved, though he was still 'stumbling around like a drunken man' if he attempted to move quickly. Base Camp was safely reached: Afanassieff was safe and made a full recovery. Scott and Parkin now wanted to go home, but Baxter-Jones made another attempt on the mountain with Mari Abrego, of the Navarre team, which had abandoned an attempt on the Abruzzi at the Shoulder. Baxter-Jones and Abrego reached 8300m (27,250ft) before bad weather forced a retreat.

1984/1985

There were no successful ascents of the mountain in 1984, the only expedition being a very strong international team which included Peter Habeler and Wanda Rutkiewicz. Another member was Dobrosława Miodowicz-Wolf who would return, with tragic consequences, two years later. The team reached 7500m (24,600ft) on the Abruzzi Spur before continuous bad weather finally put an end to hopes of a summit bid.

In 1985 four expeditions put a total of eleven men on the summit during the five weeks from 19 June until 24 July, all by way of the Abruzzi. One of the successful summitters was Erhard Loretan, on his way to becoming the third person to complete the set of fourteen 8000m peaks, but another of the eleven, Frenchman Daniel Lacroix, disappeared during the descent.

By the end of 1985 thirty-nine men had stood on the summit of K2. Twelve men had died on the mountain, including two – Yanagisawa and Lacroix – on their way down from the top. The deaths had occurred over a period of forty-six years from the first four – Wolfe, Pasang Kikuli, Pasang Kitar and Pintso – in 1939. K2 was a difficult mountain to climb, all the routes attempted involving hard climbing and the weather of the Karakoram summer bringing storms that could be relentless. But in comparison to the appalling death toll on the early expeditions to Nanga Parbat, K2 did not seem to be such a deadly mountain. In 1986 that view was to change dramatically.

Chapter 6

1986

'The rock … was murderously hard at this altitude. I fought for every step.'

Jerzy Kukuczka

By 1986 Pakistan had changed its policy of allowing one team on the mountain at any one time and had begun issuing multiple permits. That year there were nine separate groups on the south side of the mountain, and a single group on the north side. By alphabetical order of team leader these were:

- Frenchman Maurice **Barrard**[1] led a team of four, his wife Liliane Michel, the Pole Wanda Rutkiewicz[2] and Frenchman Michel Parmentier; they were attempting the Abruzzi Spur.
- Italian Renato **Casarotto**, accompanied by his wife Goretta and two Basque climbers; Casarotto was attempting a solo ascent of the South-South-West Ridge (Magic Line), while the Basques were heading for the Abruzzi Spur.
- Italian Agostino **Da Polenza**, who had already summitted from the north side in 1983, led the 'Quota 8000' team which was attempting to climb the Magic Line. His team included Josef Rakoncaj, Julie Tullis and Kurt Diemberger[3] from the 1983 expedition, as well as Frenchman Benoît Chamoux.[4]
- German Karl-Maria **Herrligkoffer**[5] was leading a large (sixteen climbers) team attempting both a new route on the South Face and a repeat of the Abruzzi Spur. The team included Pole Jerzy Kukuczka.[6] Some of the climbers on the trip had paid to secure their places and so a good case can be made for Herrligkoffer leading the first commercial K2 expedition. The team also included Norman Dyhrenfurth,[7] who was making a film of the expedition for German TV.
- Austrian Alfred **Imitzer** led a seven-climber team on the Abruzzi Spur.
- South Korean **Kim** Byung-Joon was leading the largest team on the mountain (nineteen climbers) on the Abruzzi Spur.
- The Pole Janusz **Majer** was leading a team of five men and three women who were attempting the Magic Line.
- Briton Alan **Rouse** was leading a team attempting the North-West Ridge. Early on, Rouse had handed the leadership to John Barry, but then took it back. Rouse

had applied for permission to attempt the South-South-East Spur, which he had reconnoitred in 1983 and which he wished to climb alpine-style. When permission was granted, however, it was for the North-West Ridge. That route had been explored in 1975 by the Americans, who had been defeated by the towers above the Savoia Saddle. It had also been explored in 1982 by the Poles, who avoided the towers and then avoided the top part of the ridge by straying over the border into China and continuing up the North Face. The British had originally intended an alpine-style ascent but the full ridge was unlikely to provide suitable ground for one.

- American John **Smolich**'s team was also attempting the Magic Line.
- On the north side of the mountain American Lance **Owens** led a team which reached 8100m (26,575ft) on the North Ridge.

Exactly why the Pakistanis issued so many permits is a matter of debate. The main reason put forward by outsiders was financial, since there was a fee for each permit, and as well as the K2 permits others were granted for the remaining Baltoro 8000m peaks. But even that suggestion cannot entirely explain why so many permits were granted for the Abruzzi when there were other routes that eager expeditions might have snapped up, or why permission was given to Renato Casarotto to attempt to solo a line for which two other expeditions had permits: officialdom had obviously failed to understand the concept of a solo climber.

Whatever the reason, the fact that so many climbers were to be on the hill, over eighty in total, many of them on the Abruzzi route, seemed to some a recipe for disaster as in some places there was just a single route along the Spur. What all those eighty climbers wanted was to stand on the summit, and so it was inevitable that some whose permits did not allow them to climb the Abruzzi would gravitate towards that route when it was festooned with fixed ropes and represented the best hope of success. Pakistani liaison officers were supposed to prevent climbers making illegal ascents, but it was difficult for them to keep a determined mountaineer off the peak. Sanctions could be applied later to those who did climb illegally, but by then the offender had achieved a life's ambition and so neither the likely fine, nor the probable ban, which might extend for a few years, was much of a disincentive.

Summit Climbers on the Abruzzi

On the mountain the season got off to a far from auspicious start when the Americans John Smolich and Alan Pennington were killed by an avalanche on the approach to the Negrotto Col. Above the Americans' Camp 2 a huge boulder they were using to belay their fixed ropes, apparently loosened by the rising sun, fell into the couloir below the Col causing a massive avalanche that engulfed the two men. Pennington attempted to outrun it and almost succeeded, his body being recovered from close to the edge of the avalanche debris. He was buried near the Gilkey memorial. Smolich's body was not found.[8] The remainder of the team abandoned the climb and returned home.

The deaths occurred on 21 June. Two days later the first successful summit climb of the season was recorded by the Barrards, Rutkiewicz and Parmentier. Maurice Barrard had not wanted to spend either the time or the effort needed to establish 'permanent' camps and so had devised a scheme which involved using small tents as temporary camps from which supplies could be cached at points up the mountain. This allowed the team to reach their highest bivouac carrying minimum loads as they picked up the supplies during their final ascent. Wanda Rutkiewicz was very happy climbing with the Barrards:

> The Barrards were an important influence on me, and I felt that they had the perfect marriage, equally happy in the mountains as in their daily groundling life. I have always found marriage a brake on my life, and I would never climb with a husband. The bonds of marriage are not the same as the bonds between members of an expedition, and I need independence in the mountains. Within the community of an expedition, a couple is liable to constitute a sub-group who may provoke tensions. But the Barrards proved that this needn't always be the case.

However, her contentment with the Barrards did not extend to Michel Parmentier. For some unexplained reason the two did not get on, and Rutkiewicz carried her own tent to avoid sharing one with him. On the Abruzzi, Rutkiewicz says, the four occasionally used old fixed ropes, and tended to climb ice rather than rock, in part because the latter was often unstable, but below 7000m found nothing harder than Grade IV and did not rope up until they were at 7800m (about 26,000ft).

Wanda's lack of enthusiasm for Parmentier was not helped when, on the final climb, he punched a hole in a snow bridge he had used to cross a crevasse, exposing a drop which unnerved Liliane Barrard. She wanted a rope, but that was with Parmentier, who declined to return with it, insisting the bridge was no problem. The other three disagreed and spent time searching for an alternative crossing, and were then forced to climb steep ice unroped. The atmosphere as the four of them huddled into a single tent for their last bivouac was not great, and was not improved by the fact that their 'minimum supplies' approach meant they were all hungry and cold. Next day the four again climbed without ropes. There were no fixed ropes in the Bottleneck Couloir so great caution was needed as 'the rock slabs were completely coated in a thin layer of ice, compacted and clear as glass, with absolutely no hand-holds or foot-holds'. Above the Bottleneck, the snow on the long leftward traverse was chest deep, slowing progress so much that the four were forced to bivouac at 8300m (27,230ft). Next morning they climbed on.

Below the summit the Barrards and Parmentier stopped to cook soup. Rutkiewicz continued alone:

Climbing on alone was really exciting, and I was thrilled to be so near the summit, etched ahead like a crown with three points. It was a beautiful day. My dream of reaching the second highest peak in the world – so much more beautiful than Everest – was coming true and the weather was perfect for the occasion. When I stood alone on the very top it was 10.15. Around me lay a stupendous ring of slightly lower mountains. Clouds hung in the valley below, and above was nothing but the infinite expanse of the sky.

Wanda was the first Pole and the first female to reach the summit. She was descending when she met the Barrards and Parmentier, and returned with them briefly to enjoy a summit gathering. Then she descended, meeting Mari Abrego and Josema Casimiro, the two Basques in Casarotto's team, as they approached the summit. They had made an impressive five-day alpine-style ascent of the Abruzzi, their last bivouac being at 8100m (26,575ft) near the foot of the Bottleneck.

Rutkiewicz reached the bivouac at 8300m first and decided to move on after a short rest. But when Maurice Barrard arrived he persuaded her to spend the night there as they were all tired, despite her reluctance to spend another night in the Death Zone. Later Rutkiewicz was to note that it was 'a big mistake':

When you climb without oxygen, success depends on your speed and how long you spend in the Death Zone. It was a terrible night. With no sleeping bags, we sat miserably uncomfortable, shaking with cold and racked with anxiety. Sleep was impossible. In my physical and mental distress my intolerance of Michel and of his body touching mine became unbearable. And of course all these feelings were heightened by the altitude. I thought I might escape my pain and shorten the night by taking sleeping tablets, and took all of two-and-a-half Mogadon – with dreadful consequences. I felt sick and unpleasantly sleepy, but couldn't sleep. My limbs felt distant and leaden while my mind stayed all too active.

Parmentier left at first light, the others packing up the tent before descending. Rutkiewicz, feeling dizzy from the effect of the Mogadon, left before the Barrards. Below her Parmentier fell, tumbling head over heels down the Bottleneck Couloir to land close to the Basque tent. Rutkiewicz was sure he was dead or badly injured, but he got up and continued to descend. The weather was deteriorating and she had problems crossing the featureless plateau of the Shoulder. Before descending the Black Pyramid she looked back and caught sight of the Barrards at the Bottleneck. She was surprised they were going so slowly, but saw nothing to alarm her. At some point the two Basque climbers passed her as she descended to the tents the four had left at 7700m. Parmentier was already there. The two of them, in separate tents, waited for the Barrards, but they did not arrive. Exhausted, and with visibility almost at zero, the two could not climb up to search for them; they also dissuaded a group of Italians and Benoît Chamoux who had arrived from below to attempt a search in such conditions.

Next day Parmentier decided to wait for the Barrards, but Rutkiewicz and the Basques descended. They spent another night on the mountain, reaching the bottom as a rescue team was setting out in the futile hope of finding the Barrards. A little later Parmentier arrived. In a white-out his descent had been a nightmare, and the fact that he got down at all owed an enormous amount to a radio call to Benoît Chamoux at Base Camp; Chamoux's memory of the route was almost picture-perfect, and he had given Parmentier instructions on how to reach the top of the fixed ropes. (Chamoux's description of the radio conversations with Parmentier in his book *Le Vertige de L'Infini* is riveting.) When the two had finished talking, Chamoux announced to those listening that he felt Parmentier had no better than a 50 per cent chance of finding the ropes and, therefore, of surviving. But he did survive. Both the Basques and Rutkiewicz were slightly frostbitten, but otherwise the four survivors were uninjured. Days later Liliane Barrard's body was found at the base of the mountain. Wanda Rutkiewicz believes the Barrards were good enough climbers not to have made a mistake and speculates that they were the victims of an avalanche or of losing the route in poor visibility. But all four of the Barrard team had spent too long above 8000m and it is equally likely that, weakened by the prolonged stay and, perhaps, concerned for each other, one of them did make a mistake which resulted in both tumbling off the peak.

The Italians who had retreated with the first summitters when the weather broke now returned to the Abruzzi, four of them – Gianni Calcagno, Soro Dorotei, Martino Moretti and Tullio Vidoni – summitting on 5 July together with Josef Rakoncaj and Benoît Chamoux. The Italians had been given permission for both the Magic Line and the Abruzzi, though at the time many climbers believed they were climbing the latter illegally, changing their plans to the standard route when the deaths of the two Americans suggested that the approach to the Magic Line was too dangerous. The ascents of two of the team aroused particular interest. For Czech climber Rakoncaj it was his second ascent – becoming the first man to climb K2 twice – as he had already reached the top as part of the Italian North Ridge expedition in 1983, while Benoît Chamoux had reached the summit from Base Camp in under 24 hours – an astonishing feat.

Chamoux and the Italians had reached their Base Camp on 4 June, and had set up two camps on the Magic Line, the second at 6300m (20,670ft), within a very short time. The Italians were actually climbing both Broad Peak and K2, and on 19 June Chamoux left K2 and bivouaced below Broad Peak at an altitude of about 4900m (16,100ft). At midnight, using a head-torch, he began to climb Broad Peak.

In 1¾ hours he was at Camp I (5700m/18,700ft); another 1¾ hours saw him at Camp II (6350m/20,830ft), where he stopped for 30 minutes. As the sun rose he climbed up to Camp III (7100m/23,290ft), reaching it at 7am. He left at 8am, reaching the col between the Forepeak and Central Peak (7800m/25,590ft) at 1pm. He was on the summit (8047m/26,401ft) at 4pm and back in his bivouac at the base of the peak at 11pm, having ascended and descended over 3100m (about 10,200ft) in under 24 hours.[9] Chamoux then moved back to K2 Base Camp, where he heard about the deaths of Pennington and Smolich. Having decided to abandon the Magic Line in favour of the Abruzzi, Chamoux and two others started a fast ascent of the Spur, reaching the camp of Rutkiewicz and Parmentier as the storm in which the Barrards were lost was breaking. It was they who suggested searching for the missing French couple. After returning to Base Camp, Chamoux set out alone at 6.15pm on 4 July, reaching the Italian Camp I (6200m/20,340ft) at 8pm, where he enjoyed a dish of rice. He started climbing again by the light of his head torch. He reached Camp II (6700m/21,980ft) at 10.30pm, where he rested for an hour and prepared a drink bottle for the remaining ascent. He completed the hardest part of the climb before dawn, reaching the base of the Shoulder at 7am, where he rested for an hour. During this period he made himself a drink, but on swallowing it vomited immediately. Despite this, he continued; he was now able to see the other members of the Italian team, and two Swiss from Herrligkoffer's International Expedition, heading for the summit. But the sight of them was far from encouraging: 'An immense plateau, one kilometre across … It is a total surprise. I had not realized there was so much left to climb. I knew the mountain was big, but not this big.' Chamoux dumped everything he could, leaving behind his rucksack and carrying only a few small sweets in his pocket. Despite this he was forced to rest, occasionally sitting down in the snow, every twenty or thirty steps. At the top of the Bottleneck he became concerned about the size of the overhanging séracs. Trying to move more quickly made him vomit again and he had to rest despite the danger. He passed the Italians and Swiss returning from the summit, then passed into the mountain's shadow and was instantly cold. At 5pm, after a climb of 23 hours, he reached the summit. After descending, he slept at the top camp at 7600m (24,930ft), descending to Base Camp the next day. The mere mortals at Base Camp could, perhaps, take some heart from Chamoux's suggestion that he was, technically, not a very good climber and could not do hard routes: he was just quick on easier ground.

Kukuczka and Piotrowski on the South Face
Two Swiss climbers, Beda Furster and Rolf Zemp, also summitted on 5 July. They were members of Herrligkoffer's International team and had originally been with Jerzy Kukuczka and Tadeusz Piotrowski on their South Face climb, but had decided to take the easier route to the summit.

Kukuczka and Piotrowski were attempting to complete the route on the South-East Face which Kukuczka and Kurtyka had tried in 1982. Kukuczka had by this time climbed eleven 8000m peaks and it was clearly only a matter of time before he completed the set. Piotrowski was much less well-known outside his native Poland, but at home had a formidable reputation, particularly for a string of hard winter climbs in the Tatras. He had also made the first winter ascent of Noshaq (7492m/24,580ft) with Andrzej Zawada in 1973, the first-ever ascent of a 7000m peak in winter.

Kukuczka's account of the climb starts with his joining the Herrligkoffer expedition, at Piotrowski's suggestion, and being amazed by the leader's attitude to money. On his previous expeditions he had been forced to spend hours if not days negotiating and arguing in order to save a few dollars here and there, but now he was told to stop quibbling with people who wanted an extra few rupees and to spend whatever was necessary to get things moving. Rather than cooking his own cheap meals in the rooms of the cheapest hotels, he found himself going to restaurants and ordering whatever he wanted. He watched, astonished, as the expedition's three hundred porters were given new trainers and Swiss wool socks (which they promptly sold before trekking in their old sandals); Kukuczka himself had always wanted a pair of Swiss wool socks, but had never been able to afford them. Even more astonishing was the fact that there was hot water for washing at Base Camp. On Polish expeditions fuel was so precious that no one would ever contemplate squandering it to heat water just for washing.[10]

At Base Camp three Swiss and a German agreed to go with the two Poles, but two Swiss (Furster and Zemp) retreated after one night at Camp I, claiming the route was too dangerous. As noted above, they subsequently summitted along the Abruzzi. The two Poles, now with two companions, continued upwards. A cornice on the ridge broke beneath Kukuczka, proving the last straw for the remaining Swiss, who immediately set down his load and quickly retreated. The three remaining climbers fixed ropes on the ridge, then went back to Base Camp, where Herrligkoffer announced that the expedition had one aim, the South Face, and that anyone who would not aid the Poles on it could go home. Fortunately for the Austrian, German and Swiss climbers faced with this ultimatum, Herrligkoffer then had to take a helicopter back to civilisation as he was ill, possibly with pulmonary oedema. With him gone, the team felt able to ignore his ruling, only the German Toni Freudig being willing to help the Poles.

Back on the route Freudig soon became unwell with a stomach upset and was forced to descend, so Kukuczka and Piotrowski started out from Camp I alone. They had found a safer route past the '20 minutes of fear' sérac (though it still took 15 minutes to cross beneath it), fixed ropes to about 7000m and cut a tent platform at 7200m (23,625ft) before bad weather forced them to descend to Base Camp. When good weather returned they climbed back to Camp I and next day continued to the 7200m camp. They then continued up to 7800m and bivouaced, and the following day pushed the route out to 8200m (26,900ft). Above this, the gully they had been following (christened Hockey Stick Gully because of its shape) led to a rock barrier that could not be turned. Leaving their sleeping bags and tent behind, they set off towards it carrying only their climbing equipment. Kukuczka led and

> in the first few metres I saw that it was going to be damned hard, and that we would never manage it in one day. No chance ... The barrier was about a hundred metres high and almost vertical. The hardest section was about thirty metres long and about Grade V+ in difficulty ... I gained height one centimetre after another. We did not have too much equipment, altogether three pitons, one ice screw and two thirty-metre ropes, one thin, one thick. That had to suffice for the fight with the rock which was murderously hard at this altitude. I fought for every step.

It took all day to climb the 30m wall, and for much of the time Kukuczka was watching bad weather approaching, knowing that they had to get to the summit in order to descend the easier Abruzzi.

After fixing a rope on the 30m wall the two returned to their bivouac. Kukuczka then knocked their last gas cylinder down the face so cooking was impossible, as was making drinks. In the morning they used a candle stub to melt one cup of water each, then set off towards the rock barrier. They climbed the fixed rope and by 3pm had reached the top of the barrier and the summit ridge. It was misty and snowing lightly, but they continued after abandoning everything that wasn't essential, following footprints at first, but then forging a route through the deepening snow. Kukuczka found some soup wrappers and feared he was at the Barrard team's last bivouac, not realising soup had been made just below the summit. Yet despite this fear he continued, and soon after reached his twelfth 8000m summit. For Piotrowski it was the first.

They returned to their equipment dump, dug a snow cave and spent a miserable night, hungry, thirsty and shaking with cold. In the morning visibility was poor and the two men had to work their way down extremely carefully as they had no knowledge of the Abruzzi. An old rope gave them the line, but the descent was so slow they were forced to bivouac again, their fourth night in the open above 8000m. They had now been almost 48 hours without eating or drinking. But the weather had cleared by morning and Kukuczka could now see they were on the upper slopes of the Shoulder. With luck they would soon be at the top camp of another expedition. Soon they could see tents, but the slope steepened. Kukuczka wanted to rope up, but Piotrowski had left their rope at the last bivouac. Facing in, Kukuczka descended carefully. Halfway down he

> looked up again exactly in time to see a crampon fall off Tadek's foot! I shouted something, but what happened in the next second I just could not have foreseen.

The other crampon was falling down as well! Tadeusz was left clinging on to his ice axe. I shouted 'Look out!' But it was too late, no warning would be of any use. Tadeusz only seemed to struggle to hold on for a second, but was in the position of someone who has just had a ladder removed from under him. He tried desperately to improve his grip on the ice axe, which was firmly planted into the ice, but he failed. The ice axe stayed in place. Tadek fell.

Piotrowski slid into, then over Kukuczka, then down the slope and out of sight. Now alone, Kukuczka descended to the tents he had seen. He tried to radio to the mountain's base, then ate his first meal in a very long time and fell asleep. Next day he descended fixed ropes as far as a South Korean camp, where he was looked after. Kukuczka had frostbite to both hands and feet, but with medical treatment at Base Camp and an early exit to Skardu, recovered completely. Pietrowski's body was not found.

Casarotto on the Magic Line
Meanwhile Renato Casarotto had made two attempts on the Magic Line, each time reaching a height of about 8200m (26,900ft). As Kukuczka was preparing to leave Base Camp, he notes that the Italian stopped at his tent to share a cup of tea. He confided in the Pole that his third attempt would be his last. He also wanted to visit Poland to give some lectures. They agreed to meet there. Casarotto 'clasped my hand for a long time before going on his way'.

As noted in Chapter 5, Reinhold Messner had been scathing about Casarotto's abilities after their combined attempt on K2. Jim Curran speculates on whether Casarotto was driven on by the need to redeem himself in his own eyes, especially as Messner, on hearing of his intended solo of the Magic Line, had said dismissively, 'He'll never make it!'. The Italian had apparently told another climber at Base Camp that if he reached K2's summit along the Magic Line it would be his last solo climb.

On his third attempt Casarotto did not improve on his previous high spot before he was again forced back by bad weather. He descended the entire route safely, reaching the moraine at the base of the mountain, less than an hour's walk from Base Camp. He had covered that walk safely many times, but on this occasion, apparently taking a short cut, he fell into a crevasse. The climber to whom Casarotto had confided his view that K2 would be his last solo climb wondered if the trauma of failing for the third time had psychologically shaken him so that he had dropped his normally acute guard. Kurt Diemberger had been watching his descent from Base Camp and saw Casarotto suddenly disappear. Fearing, correctly, that he had fallen into a crevasse, he went to Casarotto's tent and asked his wife Goretta if she had heard from him. Soon after Renato came on to the radio, telling his wife that he had fallen, was dying and needed help quickly. Diemberger, Julie Tullis, the Italian climber Gianni Calcagno and Wanda Rutkiewicz immediately went to the crevasse.

Casarotto had fallen 40m (130ft) into the crevasse but had no broken bones and no obvious signs of injury. However, he told his rescuers he had lost feeling in his lower body and was cold. A pulley system was arranged, and those at the surface were encouraged to see Casarotto helping in the job of getting him out of the crevasse. But before he reached the surface he had lost consciousness and collapsed on to the rescue rope. He was laid out on the surface and covered in a sleeping bag. Other rescuers, including a doctor, had by now arrived, but it was too late. Casarotto had died. With his wife's permission, his body was lowered back into the crevasse.

The Final Act: Opening Scene
On the North-West Ridge the British expedition, having lost two members who were forced to return home because of business commitments, and finding the climbing slow and, with the need to fix ropes, tedious and unsatisfying, had abandoned the route and were intending to try the Abruzzi instead. They did not have permission for the route but their own liaison officer, who would definitely stop them if he found out, had become estranged from them, had had little contact for several weeks and had finally left on his own for Skardu. They therefore reasoned that as long as they were discreet, so that other liaison officers or climbers did not complain, they would be fine. But with bad weather and diminishing enthusiasm, the British team gradually shrank in size. Then Al Rouse decided that he would attempt the Abruzzi with a Polish climber, Dobrosława Miodowicz–Wolf, from Janusz Majer's Polish team attempting the Magic Line. The Pole, nicknamed Mrówka (pronounced Mrufka and meaning 'ant', because she was constantly busy), had found the climb too hard. She struck up a friendship with Rouse, who suggested that when the Magic Line climb was over, if she had not summitted, the two of them could attempt the Abruzzi together. Mrówka had accepted immediately, much to the annoyance of Dave Wilkinson, a member of the British team, who was also keen to try the Abruzzi and had assumed he would climb with Rouse. So Rouse suggested the three try as a team, but Wilkinson pointed out, correctly, that in such a situation everyone was usually worse off, and he prepared to leave the expedition.[11]

On the evening of 29 July Rouse and Mrówka left for the Abruzzi, while the remaining members of Janusz Majer's team went back to the Magic Line. Starting out a day ahead of Rouse and Mrówka on the Abruzzi were the remnants of the Austrian team, as well as Kurt Diemberger and Julie Tullis. The latter pair had already tried for the summit once before, but now, with good weather having arrived and looking as though it would continue for a while, they were trying again. Also on the Abruzzi were the South Koreans, whose siege tactics had established a line of camps and fixed ropes up the Spur which had already proved useful in aiding the descent of desperate climbers.

On the Magic Line the Poles Przemsław Piasecki and Wojciech Wróż, with the Czech Peter Božík, had made good progress, reaching Camp II on their first day and continuing up to bivouac at 8000m (26,250ft) on 2 August.[12] Ahead now they had only reasonably straightforward climbing – the Japanese West Ridge route joined the Magic Line high on the mountain and so they had information from Nazir Sabir about the upper section of the climb. One day behind them were Janusz Majer and the remaining two Polish female climbers, Anna Czerwińska and Krystyna Palmowska. The three were supporting the trio ahead of them, who were intending to take the 'easy' route down the Abruzzi after they had summitted, but also wanted to summit if the weather held. On the Abruzzi three Koreans (the only team using supplementary oxygen), three Austrians, Diemberger and Tullis, and Rouse and Mrówka were all in a camp at the Shoulder.

At 4.15pm on 3 August the three Koreans, Chang Bong-Wan, Kim Chang-Son and Chang Byong-Ho reached the summit. A little later the two Poles and the Czech completed the Magic Line and started to descend along the Abruzzi. The Koreans were the first of their nation to climb K2, the Poles and Czech the first to make a full ascent of the Magic Line, a marvellous achievement even though almost all the route had been explored previously. But on the descent to Camp IV, the top camp on the Abruzzi, it seems that Wojciech Wróż, who had been so close to the summit twice, and had now achieved his ambition of standing on top of K2, fell and was killed. The most likely explanation for his death lies with the inadvertent actions of one of the descending Koreans. On the traverse above the Bottleneck there was a line of fixed ropes, but it was not continuous. One of the Koreans, concerned about a missing section of rope on an awkward section, cut a piece of rope from above the gap, and fixed it in position. But he did not fix the end of the rope he had shortened, perhaps because he did not have the equipment, perhaps because it was on an easy section and he did not realise how it might be used. He informed one of his Korean colleagues, who was above him, what he had done. Above that Korean was Wróż, exhausted and climbing slowly. Above Wróż was the third Korean, so exhausted that he had belayed himself to a fixed rope and was planning to bivouac. The second Korean climbed past Wróż and urged the third to descend, but failed to convince him. He therefore started descending again, again passing Wróż in the process. Whether he passed on the message about the unsecured rope is not known, but even if he tried, the language barrier and Wróż's exhausted state may have meant the message was not understood. It is likely that Wróż, taking every opportunity to save energy, abseiled down the rope – and off the unsecured end. He fell to his death. The next day, 4 August, the sirdar of the Koreans' high-altitude Hunza porters, Mohammed Ali, was hit and killed instantly by a falling stone at one of their lower camps.

The Final Act: Closing Sequence
On that same day, 4 August, seven climbers were attempting to reach the summit from Camp IV on the Abruzzi Shoulder. The account of events during the period

2–10 August below is derived largely from the accounts of Willi Bauer[13] and Kurt Diemberger,[14] with some details from the books by Jim Curran (see Note 8) and the Korean team leader.[15]

When the Austrians reached their Camp III they discovered it had been destroyed by an avalanche. They therefore apparently made an arrangement with the Koreans to borrow a tent which they would carry up and erect at the Shoulder camp (Camp IV) to use before their summit bid, in exchange for fixing ropes above the Bottleneck. The Korean expedition leader confirms this arrangement. The Austrians – Willi Bauer, Alfred Imitzer and Hannes Wieser – continued to the Shoulder, arriving in the evening. They set off for the summit early on 2 August. As they climbed up, the Koreans, Tullis and Diemberger, Rouse and Mrówka were climbing up to the Shoulder. When they arrived, the Koreans occupied the tent erected for them, while the other two pairs set up their own tents. At 4pm the Austrians, delayed by fixing ropes, as agreed, were at 8400m (27,560ft). Bauer says it was too late to continue and they climbed down, but Diemberger says that Imitzer told him they retreated because the snow was in a dangerous condition. The Austrians arrived at Camp IV at 7pm and begged those at the camp to be allowed to stay the night so they could make another attempt next day. According to Chang Byong-ho and Diemberger, an argument broke out, the Koreans pointing out that the Austrians had agreed to descend to Camp III after their summit attempt. Bauer says that there was a discussion, not an argument, and that he had never agreed to descend to Camp III in earlier negotiations. He was therefore surprised that the Koreans had not brought another tent to Camp IV. Bauer says he expected the Koreans to bring another tent from Camp III. However, as the Koreans had been accompanied to Camp IV by several high-altitude porters, their decision not to bring another tent certainly implies that they believed the Austrians would not only erect their tent for them, but would not spend a second night in it at Camp IV. Given the language barrier between the Austrians and Koreans, it is very likely that neither side really understood the original arrangement clearly and that each was now taking a stand based on ambitions for the following day.

Eventually an agreement was reached. The Koreans, in a three-man tent, allowed Bauer and Wieser to join them, Imitzer joining Rouse and Mrówka after Diemberger had refused him permission. Diemberger's view was that if the Austrians wanted to stay at Camp IV they should bivouac in a snowhole. However, it is also the case that he and Tullis were using a French tent, given to them by Michel Parmentier, which was small even for two people, so they had no spare capacity. Diemberger also says that Julie Tullis was very angry that Imitzer imposed himself on Rouse and Mrówka, particularly after apparently agreeing initially that some, at least, of the Austrians should descend to Camp III. Diemberger shared her outrage, the two of them believing that the Austrians were selfishly compromising other people's summit climbs. But Diemberger's case is undermined by his own position. He and Tullis had expected to find a cache of food and equipment at the Camp IV site which they had left on their previous attempt, but were unable to do so: either it had been buried by new snow, or it had been looted. Implicit in Diemberger's account of his stay at Camp IV is the suggestion that he and Tullis had arrived with sufficient food for themselves, but Bauer maintains they arrived with none, and when the cache could not be found they were forced to beg food and drink from the others there. Whatever the truth of the various accusations and counter-accusations, it seems clear that everybody at Camp IV was infected with summit fever.

Next morning the Koreans set off for the summit. Diemberger claims they set off at about 8am, certainly no earlier than 7.30am, overcrowding in the tents being the cause of this late start. The Koreans deny this, claiming they set off at 6am, using supplementary oxygen immediately. Bauer says the Koreans left some time between 6am and 7am. As evidence in support of the later start time, Diemberger quotes an interview he gave to *Climber* magazine in December 1986,[16] but, of course, quoting yourself as a reference to a claim you have made is of little value.

The Koreans expected the rest of the climbers at Camp IV to follow them, using their tracks, but no one did, the other seven deciding to have a rest day. It was an extraordinary decision, considering that by 1986 the effect of prolonged stays at altitude was well known. Wiessner had made the same mistake in 1939, but he had no such information. Now, a party of experienced climbers was breaking the known rule of going high: go fast and come down soon. Though Rouse and Mrówka had had little sleep (Diemberger says a conversation between Rouse and Tullis confirmed this), and the Austrians were doubtless tired from their summit attempt on 2 August, for the seven to take a rest day at 8000m was as foolish as it was baffling. Diemberger does not give a satisfactory reason for his and Tullis's failure to follow the Koreans. He gives the pros and cons of choosing 3 August, which, he says, he considered on the evening of 2 August. He also says that Tullis really wanted to climb the mountain with fellow Briton Rouse, and later says that the lack of movement from the Rouse tent when the Koreans departed was the deciding factor in his and Tullis's decision not to climb. But he also says that the Korean's late start was another factor. The time taken to reach the summit by the Koreans does not help establish the departure time, as the oxygen flow rate they were using is not absolutely definite, and one, at least, of the climbers had leakage problems with his set. But with his tremendous experience at high altitude Diemberger must have realised that not going on 3 August was a mistake, particularly as he makes the point that without supplementary oxygen he and Tullis needed someone to help break trail – and who better than a team of Koreans using bottled gas? Was he, perhaps, thinking that seven climbers on 4 August offered better trail-breaking options than the three Koreans might?

After summitting, two of the three Koreans arrived back at Camp IV together with Piasecki and Božík (the third Korean, who bivouaced near the Bottleneck, climbed down safely the following morning). There was now one more person at the camp – eleven people squeezing into three tents made for seven. This time Imitzer joined his colleagues with the Koreans, while Piasecki and Božík went in with Rouse and Mrówka. It seems that to make room, Rouse slept outside, or partially outside, in a makeshift snowhole. At about 6am on 4 August Rouse led off towards the summit. He had had little sleep for two nights, what rest he had been able to have on 3 August being offset by the debilitating effect of altitude. But he was out in front for almost the entire day. The weather was excellent.[17] Behind him came Mrówka, then the Austrians, with Diemberger and Tullis behind again, taking longer as they were climbing roped and taking belays. Very soon Hannes Wieser stopped, complaining that he did not feel well.

At the end of the fixed ropes on the ice traverse above the Bottleneck Diemberger and Tullis left a rucksack with their emergency bivouac equipment hanging from a piton. As they started up again, Diemberger noticed that the other Karakoram 8000m peaks had disappeared below a sea of cloud.

Just below the summit Bauer and Imitzer finally caught up with Rouse. The Austrians had also passed Mrówka, urging her to go down as she was obviously exhausted, but she refused. When Diemberger and Tullis reached her she had apparently fallen asleep in the snow. They also urged her to go down, but she again refused.

Bauer says he and Imitzer reached the summit some time between 1pm and 2pm. Rouse reached it as they were leaving, probably 30 minutes later. On the way down the Austrians met Mrówka, Diemberger and Tullis at the end of the ice traverse after 1½ hours or so. Diemberger writes that Bauer asked him if he was still continuing to the summit, and that he (Diemberger) told him that he was, as it was only another hour to the top. To this, Diemberger says, Bauer replied that it had taken him and Imitzer 4 hours, and when Diemberger expressed astonishment, Bauer pointed to the mountain below and said '4 hours from down there'. This exchange has long been debated, since the idea of telling someone how long a summit climb will take from a point other than the one where the conversation is taking place is considered so remote from normal mountain behaviour as to be incredible. What makes the exchange even more remarkable is that Bauer denies giving Diemberger any information on time to the summit, claiming only to have told him that he would not reach the summit and get back to Camp IV before night fell but that there were crevasses above that could be used to bivouac. If there was no mention of time, why would Diemberger put such a strange story in his book? The incredulity his reported exchange generated seems to be one reason for the suggestion that Diemberger and Tullis did not, in fact, reach the summit.

On his descent, Rouse spoke with Diemberger and Tullis, the latter asking him to take care of Mrówka. Rouse managed to persuade the Pole to descend with him and they, and the two Austrians, reached Camp IV safely. There they found Hannes Wieser, who had declined an offer by Piasecki and Božík to accompany them down so he could help his colleagues when they reached camp. The Austrians had a conversation on the merits of descending that evening, but with Diemberger and Tullis still above, and concerns about climbing down in darkness, they decided to stay. Too many bad things had already happened this summer, they told themselves – it is better to go down tomorrow after a night's sleep.

In his book Diemberger says that he and Tullis reached the summit at 5.30pm with the weather worsening. This is at odds with Bauer's recollection: he says the weather was perfect right through until midnight, when the wind picked up. The time at which Diemberger and Tullis reached the summit is also disputed. Jim Curran states that Diemberger told him he reached the summit at 7pm when they spoke at Base Camp (which would accord more with '4 hours from here' than '4 hours from there'), and 7pm is also the time Diemberger told the Australian doctor who treated him at Base Camp. The time is important because it is relevant to Diemberger's decision regarding a bivouac – which both he and Bauer say the two spoke about when they met below the summit, Diemberger asking if there were crevasses that might be used; Diemberger also says he asked Rouse the same question when they met.[18]

A later summit arrival further fuels the question of whether the two actually did summit. I asked Willi Bauer for his view. It was, he said, of no more concern to him whether they summitted than if a Chinese man were to lose his bicycle. I pressed the point: he declined to give a yes/no answer, but the look on his face suggested he was doubtful. In part that doubt derived from Diemberger's description of the summit, in which he says that the large Austrian flag that had flown at Base Camp was there. Bauer denies taking it, showing me the pendants which were all he and Imitzer took on their climb. They left no flags behind, he says. It is a small point, and oxygen-starved climbers are known to make mistakes. But when I asked if Julie Tullis, during her time in his tent, had given any indication of whether they had summitted, Bauer says he asked her and that she nodded, but did not say yes.

Diemberger and Tullis left the summit in gathering gloom (something which itself suggests a later summit arrival time as night falls about 8pm). Not far below the summit Tullis fell, pulling Diemberger off as he was unable to plant his axe in time. The pair tumbled and slid 100m down the summit snowfield, coming to rest in soft snow close to the edge of the ice wall below the summit. A few more metres and they would undoubtedly have fallen to their deaths. However, Bauer says that Diemberger told him the fall had been arrested when their climbing rope became entangled in the fixed rope on the traverse below the summit. Whichever is correct, exhausted as well as severely shaken, they bivouaced (at about 8400m/27,560ft), but from where they were they were unable to retrieve the rucksack left on the ascent, with all its equipment. It was dark by now (which also confirms a late summit arrival time) and, unable to find a suitable crevasse or to excavate a snowhole, the two bivouaced in the open, enduring a long, cold night.

Next morning the weather had not worsened at first, but by the time the two were close to Camp IV it had become a near white-out. The Austrians, Rouse and Mrówka were still in Camp IV, unable to climb down in near-zero visibility; at about noon Bauer heard shouts from above. He went out to give answering calls and climbed up, meeting Diemberger and Tullis about 200m from the camp. Diemberger and Bauer now disagree completely on the state of Julie Tullis. Bauer maintains she was lying in the snow, facing downhill, her nose and cheeks blackened by frostbite, flesh hanging from an ungloved hand which was not bleeding, implying frostbite had already set in. She was also complaining of having difficulty seeing. Diemberger claims she walked into camp, though he does admit he had to pull her towards the tent, sliding her through the snow until they were just a few metres away and she could stand. He agrees Tullis lost a glove, but says this was just before the camp. Bauer says he assisted Tullis into his tent, carrying her part of the way. To explain the discrepancy Diemberger suggests Bauer was suffering a high-altitude hallucination. Such hallucinations do occur, but may, of course, happen to anyone.[19]

What is clear is that Tullis's condition was such that the Austrians took her into their tent, gave her drinks and made her warm, while Diemberger went back to his own tent. Diemberger's explanation for this is that the Korean tent was not big enough for five people (though it had accommodated six, uncomfortably, two nights before) and that he was too exhausted to look after Tullis properly himself. Bauer says that when the other Austrians saw Tullis they considered the possibility of lowering her to a point on the mountain where a helicopter could take her off. Diemberger is offhand about this idea, saying that Tullis herself dismissed the idea of a rescue, but he does agree the discussion took place, and it certainly suggests the Austrians thought her condition was serious. However, she clearly revived sufficiently to rejoin Diemberger the following day.

All day (5 August) the storm which had now broken grew worse. The following day the weather did not relent, the snowfall becoming so heavy that it eventually collapsed the Diemberger/Tullis tent. Hearing cries for help, Rouse and Bauer dug out the tent entrance. With the tent unusable, Tullis went with the Austrians, while Diemberger made his way to the Rouse/Mrówka tent. As Tullis was the smaller of the two, and Rouse was English, while Diemberger was Austrian, it seems a strange decision: Diemberger says Tullis made it – an equally strange decision given Tullis's enthusiasm for Rouse. More likely is Bauer's explanation that Imitzer had recalled his treatment on the night of 2 August and declined to allow Diemberger in.

Some time during the night of 6/7 or 7/8 August Julie Tullis died, probably of cerebral oedema, her failing eyesight being an indication of the condition. When Diemberger was told the news next day he was shattered. Diemberger says that Tullis walked across to Rouse's tent on 7 August and spoke to him, telling her she felt strange. He says she leaned forward at the tent entrance and he could see her hair. He says he was told of her death on the morning of 8 August. Bauer says she died during the night of 6/7 August and Diemberger was told of the death on the morning of the 7th.

Fuel for cooking ran out on either 8 or 9 August. It had been useful for melting snow, though by then almost all the food they had was also gone. While gas remained, Diemberger says, he and Rouse gave the hot water they prepared to Mrówka, settling for cold water and slush themselves. This account of masculine chivalry differs from the one Bauer had from Mrówka, the tiny Pole saying that Diemberger took up too much room in the tent and constantly attempted to take more than his share of food and drink.[20]

The situation was now desperate. The climbers had been in the Death Zone long enough for bodily deterioration to become critical, and they were now further weakened by dehydration. During 9 August Rouse's condition deteriorated markedly. He became delirious and constantly asked for water. Had 10 August seen no let up in the storm all six would likely have died. But the snow and wind eased a little and visibility improved. Willi Bauer, the strongest of the Austrians, therefore roused his colleagues and prepared to descend. He shouted to the Rouse tent, and Mrówka and Diemberger prepared to move. Alan Rouse was now muttering something about melting water in his sleeping bag and was clearly no longer able to help himself. With their limited reserves of strength, those who could move made the terrible decision to leave him. Diemberger says that when he asked Mrówka what they should do about Rouse, she answered 'Life is down there.' While there is no question that the statement was a clear-sighted statement of the truth of the climber's position, it does seem that the blame for the unpleasant, but understandable and necessary, decision is being shifted on to someone who can no longer offer a defence.

During the preparations to descend, Diemberger attributes his slowness in getting ready to the fact that he could not move until Mrówka had gone to his collapsed tent and retrieved his boots (p. 256), although he earlier states (p. 251) that she had retrieved them for him on 8 August. Bauer says that he had to fix the crampons on his colleagues' boots as both were very lethargic. About 200m from the camp, Imitzer and Wieser collapsed in the snow. Bauer says he went to Imitzer, who was mumbling that a friend (who was not on the expedition) was coming with water and after a drink he would start down. Seeing that Imitzer's goggles were not on correctly, he took them off and was horrified to see Imitzer's eyeballs fall from their sockets.[21] Not knowing what to do, he returned to Wieser, but he was now dead. He therefore went back to Imitzer, who made movements with his arms and then died. Bauer says he sat in the snow beside the two bodies and would have stayed there had not Mrówka arrived and asked him to help her down. That got him moving again. As he and Mrówka started to move, he saw Diemberger leaving his tent. When he hesitated, Bauer says, Mrówka saw he was waiting for Diemberger and told him they should 'leave that pig where he is'.

Diemberger says that when he reached the two Austrians, Imitzer was dead, but Wieser was still alive; he sat up and made rowing motions with his arms, but did not respond to his shouts. It is such a vivid picture that it is hard to imagine it is not correct, and that Bauer had been mistaken in believing Wieser had died.

On the descent Bauer made the track, followed by Mrówka. It was slow going and, as a result, the two of them were soon joined by Diemberger. In his book, Diemberger recounts a conversation with Mrówka in which, on the descent to Camp III, he asked if anyone had anything to eat and Mrufka said she had a single sweet. Diemberger suggested the three of them share it, but the Pole declined. Bauer has a very different version, saying he heard Mrówka shouting '*Lass mich du Schwein*' ('Leave me alone, you pig') when Diemberger attempted to get the sweet from the top pocket of her rucksack. Soon after, Bauer says, Diemberger began to fall behind and he called out to him that he must go faster or Bauer and Mrówka would be forced to leave him. Diemberger shouted back 'Please don't leave me.' At Camp III the camp had been almost destroyed: there was no gas and just a few biscuits to eat, and the three were forced to continue down towards Camp II. But now they had the advantage of fixed ropes. Neither Bauer nor Diemberger had figure-of-eight descendeurs at first (they found them at a lower camp), instead clipping in with a karabiner and going down the ropes using their hands. Mrówka also did not have a figure-of-eight, but was using a Sticht plate instead to which, to aid movement, she had attached to her harness with a short length of cord.[22] Bauer went ahead, freeing the ropes from the snow, then came Mrówka, with Diemberger third in line. Mrówka was moving very slowly because of the difficulty of threading cold ropes though the Sticht plate with her frostbitten fingers. Eventually, Diemberger says, at a 'comfortable spot', he asked if he could go past her and she did not object.

Bauer eventually arrived at Camp II as it was getting dark. He found gas and food, but with his hands frozen by extracting the fixed ropes he had problems lighting the stove. Holding the lighter between his teeth he switched on the gas, then struck the lighter with his hand. The gas exploded into life, scorching his face. Eventually Diemberger arrived. He said that Mrówka was behind him and would soon arrive. But she did not. The following day Bauer gave Diemberger his sleeping bag as he knew he would not reach Base Camp in one day, and set off. Bauer made it to Base Camp as the light was fading. His arrival at Base Camp, where by now everyone had assumed that all seven missing climbers were dead, is vividly described by Jim Curran in his book *K2, Triumph and Tragedy*:

There in the twilight, coming along the Strip [the name the climbers gave to Base Camp, which was strung out along the glacial moraine], was a small figure, staggering, stumbling and swaying from side to side. We gazed in awe and horror, stunned by the sight, as we realised that approaching us through the dusk was a survivor of the holocaust ... Poles, Koreans, the two Liaison Officers, porters, we

Celebrating the Italian success in 1954: (*above*) Italian stamps; (*below left*) a poster for the expedition film (with a suitable sharp summit and desperate flag planting); (*below right*) the triumphant front page of *La tribuna illustrata*. Exactly who the two foreground climbers with oxygen masks and the lone summit climber are is not stated.

The North-West Ridge from the top of the first pinnacle. Beyond, and still over 1800m above, is the summit. (*Jim Wickwire*)

During the second ascent in 1977 Japanese climbers had to wade through chest-deep snow during the last 200m to the summit.

Ashraf Aman, the first Pakistani to stand on K2's summit, during the Japanese expedition of 1977.

The knife-edge ridge between Camps III and IV photographed on the 1978 American North-East Ridge expedition. Jim Whittaker is just visible at the bottom right of the shot. (*Jim Wickwire*)

Lou Reichardt on the sickle-shaped ridge about 150m below the summit, during the 1978 American North-East Ridge expedition. (*Jim Wickwire*)

Lou Reichardt on the summit during the 1978 American North-East Ridge expedition. He was the first man to reach the summit without supplementary oxygen. (*Jim Wickwire*)

Broad Peak from Camp III on the West Ridge at 6600m during the 1981 Japanese West Ridge expedition.

Looking down on Angel Peak during the 1981 Japanese West Ridge expedition.

In 1982 the Japanese became the first team to attempt K2 from the north. Camels were used to transport equipment to the glacier base.

Climbers pushing the route out above Camp I during the 1982 Japanese North Ridge expedition.

High above the Chogori glacier on the 1982 Japanese North Ridge expedition.

Camp IV on the 1982 Italian North Ridge expedition.

Willi Bauer. (*Willi Bauer*)

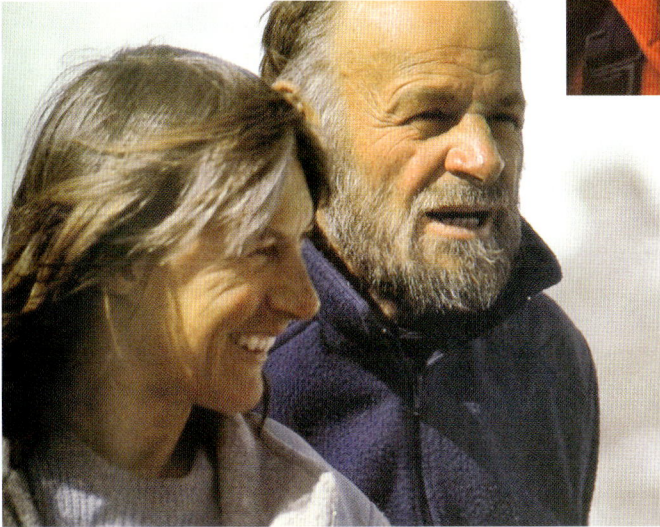

Julie Tullis and Kurt
Diemberger. (*Willi Bauer*)

Wanda Rutkiewicz and
Dobroslawa Miodowicz-Wolf
(Mrufka). (*Willi Bauer*)

House's Chimney. (*Willi Bauer*)

Imitzer and Mrufka at about 8300m. (*Willi Bauer*)

Al Rouse approaching the summit. (*Willi Bauer*)

Alfred Imitzer on the summit. (*Willi Bauer*)

Tadeusz Piotrowski photographed by Jerzy Kukuczka during their successful completion of the route on the south face originally attempted by Kukuczka and Kurtyka in 1982.

Christophe Profit on the summit in 1991. The flashes from the cameras of Profit and Pierre Béghin alerted a trekking party to the fact that there were climbers on the summit.

Camp II at 6750m during the Russian 2007 expedition which established a new route on the West Face.

Vadim Popovich and Ilyas Tukhvatullin at about 7200m on steep ground during the Russian 2007 West Face climb.

Approaching the Bottleneck on the summit climb in 2008. Above it looms the ice wall, the collapse of which would precipitate disaster. (*Lars Nessa*)

The last few feet to the summit. (*Lars Nessa*)

This photograph was taken at about 8am on 2 August 2008. In the foreground are the wands set up to guide climbers back to Camp IV on their return from the summit. Above them are Pasang Bhote and Tshering Bhote, setting off on their rescue mission for the men of the Korean expedition. Above them another figure can be seen at the bottom of the Bottleneck. This can only be Wilco van Rooijen. It appears as though he has taken off his rucksack, which lies on the snow in front of him. In his description of his descent with snowblindness, van Rooijen recalls seeing two shadowy figures, presumably the approaching Sherpas. They must have passed close to him and assumed he was safely making his way down to Camp IV. In fact he lost the trail and headed to his right, away from the camp. (*Lars Nessa*)

This photograph was taken by Pemba Gyalje at 9am on 2 August 2008. The two rescue Sherpas have progressed towards the base of the Bottleneck. Above them Marco Confortola can be seen in the Bottleneck couloir. On top of the ice wall immediately above the Bottleneck can be seen a figure. This is believed to be Karim Meherban, who was seen pacing backwards and forwards desperately seeking a way down. When this shot is blown up, four figures can be seen. One, believed to be Ger McDonnell, is standing above the others. He must have been attempting, and, of course, succeeding, in freeing them. (*Courtesy of Wilco van Rooijen*)

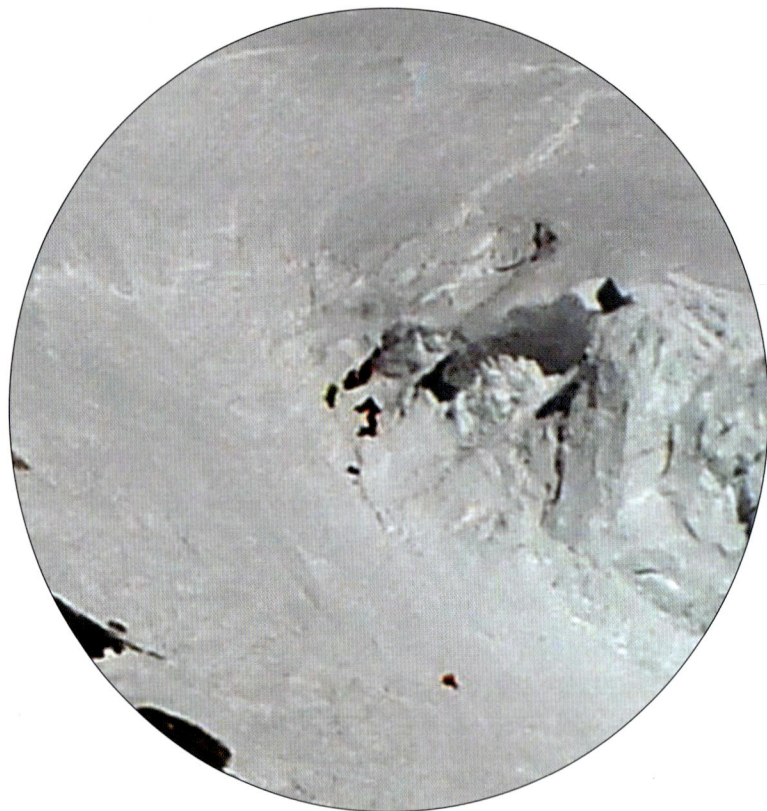

Enlargement of the Lars Nessa shot from overleaf. Several figures are also visible in this, one clearly standing. It is thought that the standing figure is Ger McDonnell. (*Lars Nessa*)

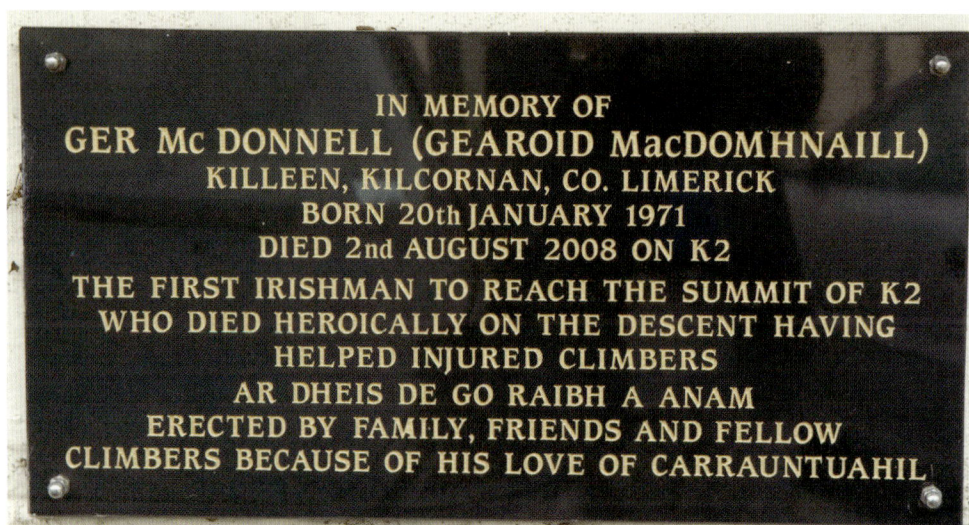

IN MEMORY OF
GER Mc DONNELL (GEAROID MacDOMHNAILL)
KILLEEN, KILCORNAN, CO. LIMERICK
BORN 20th JANUARY 1971
DIED 2nd AUGUST 2008 ON K2
THE FIRST IRISHMAN TO REACH THE SUMMIT OF K2
WHO DIED HEROICALLY ON THE DESCENT HAVING
HELPED INJURED CLIMBERS
AR DHEIS DE GO RAIBH A ANAM
ERECTED BY FAMILY, FRIENDS AND FELLOW
CLIMBERS BECAUSE OF HIS LOVE OF CARRAUNTUAHIL

The memorial plaque to Irish climber Ger McDonnell at the Cronin's Yard car park at the base of Carrauntoohill, Ireland's highest mountain. (*Author*) gathered as if by magic and ran towards the apparition. With a sharp pang of disappointment I realised quickly that it wasn't Al Rouse [one of Curran's best friends]. But who? Michael Messner [a member of the Austrian expedition], wide-eyed with incredulity, whispered, 'It is Willi'. Supported by porters, Willi Bauer half fell into his arms. He presented a ghastly sight, face cracked and caked in dried blood, clothing tattered and soiled. He pointed feebly to his mouth gesturing both for drink and to try to explain that he couldn't speak. He was, quite literally, on his last legs.

From Bauer the Base Camp climbers heard that Diemberger was following him, and so several, including Curran, went up into the night to try to find him. They made it to Advanced Base Camp where, in the dark, Curran was sure he heard a noise and climbed up towards the start of the fixed ropes:

Suddenly I became aware of a dark shape moving above. As with Willi, my first feeling was of horror, fear even. The shape got nearer and, almost colliding with him, I met Kurt. He was spreadeagled, facing into the slope, feebly kicking in his crampons, his right hand placing his axe in the snow. His head was actually resting against the snow. 'Kurt, Kurt. It's me, Jim, you're nearly safe now.' We met in a clumsy embrace. Kurt slowly registered my presence. In his heavy accent he murmured, 'I have seen the lights and heard the voices, but I think I am imagining things.' Then, distraught, he whispered, 'I have lost Julie.'

With the resources available only a limited rescue attempt for Mrówka could be organised. It reached Camp II, but could not go above. The following year her body was found, still attached to the fixed rope not far above Camp II. Willi Bauer thinks that the long sling Mrówka was using to attach the Sticht plate to her harness may have meant that when she slipped she couldn't reach the rope again. Bauer is haunted by her death, believing that her boost to his morale at the bodies of his friends near Camp IV was the factor that enabled him to survive. He remains unimpressed by Diemberger and disdainful of the story the latter now tells of the descent. But, during the interview with him, it became clear that Bauer is especially still disturbed by what happened to Mrówka and is sceptical of the existence of a convenient, comfortable spot where she and Diemberger could easily change places on the steep ground between the camps. At this point in the interview, upset, and with cold vehemence, Bauer said, '*Wenn ich je erfahren sollte, dass er* [i.e. Diemberger] *Mrufka nicht geholfen hat, dann werde ich ihm die Ohren nach vorne drehen.*'[23]

When she was found, Mrówka's body was taken down and buried at the base of the mountain. Diemberger lost a finger joint to frostbite, while Bauer lost the nails and small amounts of flesh from the tips of several fingers, though not to amputation, the tips being shed naturally as his hands healed.

Chapter 7

The Next Twenty Years

'I wander in circles around the summit, stunned to have arrived at a place I'd dreamed of for half a lifetime.'

Greg Child

Before 1986 thirty-nine climbers had stood on the summit of K2 and twelve climbers and porters had died in various attempts. That statistic, a little over 3 (3.25 to be precise) summit climbers for every death, made K2 a dangerous mountain. After the disastrous 1986 season sixty-six climbers had reached the summit, while twenty-five had died, the ratio of successes to fatalities falling to 2.6, overwhelmingly confirming the mountain's reputation as hazardous. During 1987, 1988 and 1989 sixteen expeditions attempted K2. Not one of them was successful, but the death toll increased by one, the Japanese climber Akira Suzuki dying in a fall high on the Abruzzi. This lack of success further increased the peak's already established reputation for difficulty, especially as most of the failed attempts were along the Abruzzi Spur, the 'easiest' way to the summit.

But new routes were also attempted in that period. In 1987 Briton Doug Scott led an international team on the East Face, that face also being attempted by an Austrian team under Eduard Koblmüller in 1989. Wojciech Kurtyka and Frenchman Jean Troillet attempted the West Face in 1987, the pair returning in 1989 with Swiss Erhard Loretan to attempt the North-West Face. All these attempts failed in the face of persistent bad weather. But the most significant expedition during this three-year period was a winter attempt of the Abruzzi by an international team, mostly of Polish climbers, under the leadership of Andrezj Zawada.[1] The first difficulty faced by the expedition was how to get the equipment necessary for the attempt along the Baltoro Glacier, local porters not surprisingly refusing even to contemplate carrying during the winter. The problem was solved by carrying all the supplies in during the autumn, guards then being posted to ensure that no looting occurred at the Base Camp before winter, and the climbing team, arrived. The climbers made a brave attempt, but at 7350m (24,100ft) they finally gave up the unequal struggle with vicious winds and frightening cold.

The North Side, 1990 and 1991

The year 1990 brought further failures on the Abruzzi, though the objective of the Free K2 expedition was the stripping of fixed ropes and other detritus from the Spur and the removal of much more rubbish from Base Camp, rather than an ascent of the mountain. As the removal of the rubbish required some four hundred porters trekking along the Baltoro, largely fed and watered by wood-fuelled fires, it seems reasonable to ask whether the whole thing was as eco-friendly as it was billed. But if there were no successes on the south side of K2, there were two impressive, and successful, climbs on the north. A Japanese team of twelve climbers and fifteen Sherpas, led by Tomaji Ueki, forged a new route up the western side of the North Face. From a Base Camp at 5000m (16,400ft), the team climbed a spur between the North and North-West Ridges, reaching the line followed from the Savoia Saddle close to Pt 6718 by the Poles in 1982. The Japanese then followed the Polish line, deviating along a lower line for a while, to reach the North Ridge. They then followed the original Japanese 1982 route up the ridge, then left across the high snow basin. On 9 August Hirotaka Imamura and Hideji Nazuka reached the summit using supplementary oxygen.[2]

Excellent though the Japanese climb was, and new routes are always impressive, particularly on a mountain where there are no easy lines, the ascent of the original Japanese 1982 North Ridge route by a six-man team at much the same time was more in keeping with the spirit of the age – a climb by a small team without supplementary oxygen. The team comprised Americans Phil Ershler and Steve Swenson and Australians Greg Child (then a resident of Seattle, and so effectively part of the US contingent), Lyle Closs, Greg Mortimer and Peter Keustler. Mortimer's partner Margaret Werner also went along. The Americans were highly experienced, Ershler having already climbed Everest and Kangchenjunga, while Swenson had twice failed to reach K2's summit. Child and Mortimer were also highly experienced, Mortimer in particular having been part of a small team of Australians that had climbed a direct route on Everest's enormous North Face (the 'White Limbo' climb), Mortimer and Tim Macartney-Snape reaching the summit without supplementary oxygen. By contrast Closs and Keustler were inexperienced, though the latter, a qualified doctor, was potentially vital in other ways. The presence of these two inexperienced climbers caused tensions between the Americans (and Child) and Mortimer, but these were resolved when, having reached 7300m (23,950ft), Closs and Keustler decided they had reached their limit. From there on it was a four-man team.

The larger team had placed fixed ropes and two camps to reach 7300m. A third camp was established at 7600m (24,390ft) and from it the four remaining team members made a first summit bid, rapidly retreating in the face of extreme cold and, they considered, inadequate acclimatisation. Bad weather allowed them to acclimatise at Base Camp, from where they set out on 17 August for a second attempt. At 8000m they reached a tent left by Imamura and Nazuka after their summit climb. The tent had apparently been left there deliberately:[3] in his article on the climb (see Note 4) Swenson says that the Japanese had asked permission to cross the US–Australian route high on the North Ridge, and so the donation of the tent was a gesture of mutual climbing goodwill. Rather than carve out another base for a second tent, the four down-clad Westerners used the tent, fitting poorly into fabric designed for two Japanese. As a result, sleep was minimal. Above the tent the four men moved into the snow basin which all previous climbers of the route had taken. But the slope looked set for windslab avalanche. A fixed rope left by the Japanese gave a measure of security, but having to retrieve it from the snow disturbed the windslab, posing the question of whether the freeing of the rope offered more danger than its presence offered safety. Swenson led across the slope, the others following gingerly in his footsteps.

Beyond the windslab slope the snow was less dangerous, but altitude now took its toll. The men, each climbing solo, moved on slowly. Child, seeing a discarded oxygen cylinder, wondered: 'How long can I keep up this pace without oxygen before my lungs give out? Will I be able to solo down?'[4] At about 8350m (27,400ft) Ershler succumbed to a vicious headache and retreated. The other three continued, reaching the summit ridge at about 8450m (27,720ft). It was now late afternoon, but they kept going. Swenson moved ahead of the others, reaching the summit at 8pm Beijing time. (The whole of China operates on that time, which is 3 hours ahead of Pakistan time: it was therefore 5pm Pakistan time.) Standing on the summit, Swenson writes, 'was not the euphoric experience that I had dreamed it would be. I felt a dull sense of achievement that was mostly overshadowed by the relief of not having to go any further. Hypoxia took the edge off everything as if a translucent screen had been pulled over my senses.' Swenson met Child just below the summit: 'My first impulse was to go back with him to verify that I had really been to the summit. I was afraid he would tell me later the true summit was just beyond where I had been.' But the need for self-preservation forced Swenson to continue down (and subsequent conversations with Child and Mortimer proved he really had been to the true summit).

At the summit, Child writes, 'I wander in circles around the summit, stunned to have arrived at a place I'd dreamed of for half a lifetime, a place I never really thought I'd reach.' About 25 minutes later Greg Mortimer arrived, becoming a member of the very small band of men who have summitted both Everest and K2 without supplementary oxygen.[5] When Mortimer arrived the two men hugged each other. Child writes, 'Until his arrival I'd been so outside myself I'd begun to doubt if I was really on the summit. I'd even begun to doubt my own existence. These seem ludicrous thoughts at sea level, but up here in la-la land, where brain cells are shorting by the bucketload, anything is possible.'

The two started to descend at 9pm (Beijing time), Child having been on the summit for almost an hour, in sharp contrast to Steve Swenson, who had stayed only 3 minutes. On the way down darkness overtook Child and Mortimer, the latter having to wait at one point because Child had the only head torch. At half-past midnight Child, his hands losing all feeling, stopped and declared he could go no further. In fact he was only about 100m from the tent and, ordered to continue by Mortimer, he made it by crawling. At the tent Swenson says he feared that he would never see the two of them again; as a storm was breaking, he thought that they might bivouac and would never make it down.

The storm broke, the descending climbers having to contend with snowfall that diminished visibility and increased the avalanche risk, but all reached Base Camp successfully.

The following year (1991) two French climbers, Pierre Béghin[6] and Christophe Profit, completed the line on the north side of the peak pioneered by the Poles in 1982. Although usually called the North-West Ridge, the route actually does very little climbing on the ridge itself, ascending to it from the Savoia Glacier rather than following it from the Savoia Saddle, and soon leaving it in favour of the North-West Face. The Poles had crossed the face as far as the Japanese North Ridge route, but failed to reach the summit. The French followed the Japanese line, thus completing the route, though probably covering little, if any, new ground. But the climb was extremely bold and deserves recognition as one of the major ascents of the 1990s.

Béghin and Profit travelled to K2 with two doctor friends who took no part in the climb itself. They spent six weeks on the lower part of the climb, six times reaching to about 7000m (23,000ft) either for acclimatisation or before being forced down by bad weather.[7] Finally they set themselves a deadline: the summit by the end of August or final retreat; as Profit put it, they were not going to spend the winter on the mountain. Finally on 14 August a weather window appeared to open. Climbing solo, and often side by side, the two reached 7800m (about 25,600ft), moving across terrain which Béghin describes as 'rock so fractured it looks like vertical scree' before the North Ridge and steeper, more exposed mountain was reached. They bivouaced at 7900m and the following morning set out, with minimal equipment, along the traverse that had frightened the American/Australian team the previous year. The French were equally daunted by the slope, but as Béghin writes: 'We haven't got any choice: either we cross, or we say goodbye to K2. I take the lead. Each step makes a big impression in the snow and adds another dot to my tracks. It's mentally exhausting; I'm terrified that I'll see the snow tearing apart along the "dotted line". Christophe follows on, using my steps so he doesn't dislodge the fragile layer.'

Above the slope the snow was thigh-deep and exhausting. Moving into the shade, the French found easier climbing, but the brutal cold forced Béghin to consider whether the summit was worth the risk of frostbite. He continued, but the difficulties increased: 'At 8500 metres the slope gets steeper and Christophe practically digs a trench in the loose snow. Underneath is very hard, blue ice. Our crampons only just bite. Out of breath, completely groggy from lack of oxygen, I'm now climbing instinctively.' As they neared the summit Béghin wondered whether they would actually reach it:

> In the fading light, our final reserves of energy get eaten up by the wind and the cold. One rest, then another, then more, on our knees or crouching. A few more steps. Slowly we nibble away at the mountain. We have now reached the final summit slope. It means we'll get to the top, whatever. Everything is suddenly very simple: only the summit at 8611 metres, us and the immense, painful tiredness lie between. It's a never-ending climb. To keep my spirits up, I don't look further than 2 metres ahead. Suddenly, instead of snow, the void. The other side of K2!

It was 6.50pm. At the exact moment the two took photographs of each other, a group of fifteen French trekkers far below were enjoying a view of K2 as the sun set; they were astonished to see bursts of light at the summit, the flashes of Béghin and Profit's cameras.

The descent was epic: 'a plunge into the bottomless black hole. Hours upon hours. No stopping, no hitches, no sudden obstacles: I move forward, insensitive to cold and my tiredness, with no concept of time and space.' At midnight, 16 hours after setting out, and having not eaten anything and drunk little, they arrived back at their tent. They had survived. As Béghin put it: 'the gates of high altitude didn't have a chance to close on us'.

K2, 1992–1997
In 1992 the Pole Wojciech Kurtyka and the Swiss Erhard Loretan (who had already climbed K2 in 1985) attempted an audacious new route on the West Face alpine-style, but retreated in the face of severe avalanche danger. But there were, after six years, successful ascents from the south, six climbers from an international team led by the Russian Vladimir Balyberdin, together with Frenchwoman Chantal Mauduit, who was actually from a separate team, reaching the summit along the Abruzzi Spur. Mauduit, the fourth woman to climb K2, was found by later summitters, having been forced to bivouac as she did not have a head torch. They helped her down. The Mexican climber Adrián Benítez, from a different international team, died when an abseil anchor failed.

The following year sixteen climbers reached the summit from the south. The most significant climb was the ascent of American Dan Mazur and Briton Jonathan Pratt, who made the second ascent of the West Ridge.[8] The two had been co-leaders of a twelve-man team, but bad weather and a number of deaths on the Abruzzi meant the team had dwindled to just the two after a seemingly final attempt had stopped at 8200m. Mazur and Pratt decided on one last attempt and were determined to climb day and night if necessary. On 30 August they reached the expedition's Camp IV, where they were held up by bad weather for three days. At 6.30am   on 2 September they set out for the summit. Occasionally passing debris from the Japanese 1981 climb, they reached the junction with the Magic Line at 8350m (27,400ft). Night overtook them at about 8550m (28,050ft), and they paused for a rest at an overhanging boulder. They finally reached the summit at 11.30pm. Descending to the boulder, they brewed tea and rested again. During the rest Pratt was lucky to survive a slip, stopping before sliding off the mountain. Continuing the descent, the pair reached Camp IV at 2pm, almost 32 hours after starting out. The descent from there passed without further incident, but they discovered their Base Camp had been destroyed by a falling sérac. Pratt was the first Briton to have reached K2's summit and descended the mountain alive. But the climb was greeted in some quarters, both in the UK and USA, with scepticism, in part fuelled by the announcement that the lack of summit photographs was because Pratt had forgotten his camera, but in larger part because the two men were comparatively unknown and the climb had demanded levels of technique and commitment normally seen in experienced, dedicated, high-altitude climbers. Later both Mazur and Pratt were to show that they had both in abundance and had just 'started big'. Their climb is now acknowledged as a major achievement.

But there was tragedy as well as success in 1993, five climbers dying, the second highest annual toll to date. Of the five, four – Dan Culver, Peter Metzger, Reinmar Joswig and Daniel Bidner – died during descents following successful summit climbs, three falling and one disappearing (and probably also falling to his death). The fifth man, Slovenian Boštjan Kekec, died low on the Abruzzi Ridge. The dangers of high-altitude climbing without supplementary oxygen could hardly have been more clearly written. Culver, who had already climbed Everest, was a member of the first Canadian team to climb K2, along with Jim Haberl. Haberl wrote an excellent book on the expedition,[9] in which he describes reaching a point 5m below the summit at about 3.50pm on 7 July, then waiting 45 minutes for Culver to arrive so the two could reach the top together. On the descent, Haberl was ahead of Culver as the two reached the top of the Bottleneck:

Camp 4 was just below and, as in the morning, my crampons dug confidently into the hard surface. I began the traverse towards Camp 4 and glanced up to see that Dan was entering the Bottleneck. Summit day was almost over. Finally. I wanted to relax and enjoy our success. Seconds later my brain was brutally invaded by a loud, crashing noise, a noise which in an instant shattered the silence and harmony of the day. I spun around to see Dan cartwheeling violently through the snow, rolling by me at high speed. I stared in horror. All I could see was Dan tumbling faster and faster, his blond hair in the tangle of the fall. As he hit the hard snow below me his limp body began gaining momentum. Only a miracle would stop him. There was no miracle.

To further bring home the reality of the dangers of K2, at Base Camp the remains of Art Gilkey and Pasang Kitar were set free from glacial ice near Base Camp.

In 1994 there were further successes on the Abruzzi Spur and four climbers also repeated the Japanese North Ridge route. On the south side a Basque expedition made the first ascent of the South–South-East Spur (occasionally called the Česen Route). As the route had been explored as far as the Shoulder, where it joined the Abruzzi route, the climb involved no unexplored terrain but it did complete the line from base to summit. The expedition was led by Juan Oiarzabal, who five years later would become the sixth man to complete the set of fourteen 8000m peaks. Also on the expedition were the brothers Alberto and Felix Iñurrategi, who were attempting to complete the set while climbing the peaks together. All three climbers reached the summit. The Iñurrategi brothers went on to complete twelve of the fourteen peaks together, but on their descent from the twelfth, Gasherbrum II, in 2000, an old fixed rope snapped and Felix, the younger brother, fell to his death. Despite the tragedy, Alberto safely reached the base of the mountain, and decided to continue in his quest. In 2002 he succeeded, becoming the tenth man to complete the set.

Five climbers also died on K2 in 1994. The exact nature of the fate of three of them, the Ukrainians Aleksei Khazaldin, Alexsandr Pazkhomenko and Dmitri Iszagin-Zade, is unknown. They set off from the Shoulder on 11 July together with Alexsandr Serpak, the latter returning from 8100m. The other three continued. Two weeks later the bodies of Khazaldin and Pazkhomenko were found at a bivouac at 8400m, while the remains of Iszagin-Zade were found lower down. Since the three men were unlikely to have bivouaced on their way up, it must be assumed they died during an enforced bivouac on descent. As the team had forgotten to take their radio, it will never be known whether that descent was after a successful summit climb, or after a retreat from close to the summit. Of the other fatalities, one, the Basque Atxo Apellániz, died during a descent from the summit on the north side of the peak. He and fellow Basque Juanito San Sebastián had reached the summit on 4 August, but were forced to bivouac on the descent. Next day San Sebastián was carried 400m (1300ft) down the mountain by an avalanche and was fortunate to stop on the edge of a huge vertical drop. Both San Sebastián and Apellániz were then forced to make a second bivouac, but the latter was already showing signs of cerebral oedema. He was still able to move, however, and the two reached Camp III, where they met rescuers. They were assisted down to Camp II but there Apellániz's condition worsened and he died. San Sebastián was successfully evacuated from the mountain but subsequently lost seven fingers to frostbite. After the evacuation, the Chinese were accused of displaying a 'scandalous attitude' towards the injured climber,[10] the claim being that the Chinese authorities had declined to arrange a helicopter rescue for trivial reasons; given the high prices and complex regulations imposed on climbers, this was deemed unacceptable.

In 1995 eight climbers died, six during their descent from the summit. They were part of a group of ten which left Camp IV on the Shoulder very early on the morning of 13 August. Four – Javier Escartín, José ('Pepe') Garcés, Javier Olivar and Lorenzo Ortiz – were from a Spanish team, a fifth member of that team (Lorenzo Ortas) staying at Camp IV as he was unwell. Four – Bruce Grant, Peter Hillary (son of Sir Edmund Hillary), Jeff Lakes and Kim Logan – were from a New Zealand expedition, a fifth member of that team (Matt Comesky) likewise staying at Camp IV as he had been ill on the ascent the previous day. The remaining two, American Rob Slater and British woman Alison Hargreaves,[11] were the last members of an Anglo-American expedition. Alan Hinkes, another Briton on this team, had already summitted almost a month before.

Early on Garcés, Hillary, Logan and Lakes returned to Camp IV, either because the cold of the early start overcame them or because they realised that a storm was heading towards the mountain. Above them, the six remaining climbers continued in weather which was near-perfect, despite the advancing storm. At Camp IV Comesky, Logan and Hillary decided to descend the mountain; Garcés, Ortas and Lakes decided to stay.

Curiously, the storm struck the lower mountain before the upper regions, those at Base Camp and Camp II being subjected to fierce winds by 5pm. Close to the summit, conditions were still excellent. At 6pm Lorenzo Ortiz reported by radio that he and Bruce Grant had reached the top. A further radio call confirmed that Hargreaves and Olivar summitted at 6.30pm, that call also indicating that Escartín and Slater were nearing the summit and would surely reach it. No further radio calls were made.

At Camp IV Garcés, Ortas and Lakes were hit by the storm some time between 8pm and 9pm. The wind was so strong that the tent the two Spaniards were in began to blow off the mountain, Ortas having to get out quickly and hang on to it to prevent both the tent and Garcés disappearing. The two men moved into the second tent and spent an anxious night wondering if it would survive. Lakes' tent was also flattened, forcing him to spend the night outside. He was chilled and exhausted to such an extent that despite managing to descend to Camp II the following day, after the storm had blown itself out, he died there.

Garcés and Ortas, both frostbitten (they were later to lose sections of fingers and toes), also descended. Before departing they looked up: the upper mountain was empty. On the way down the two men discovered a bloodstained boot, a jacket and harness. The boot had a built-in heating device. Only Alison Hargreaves was known to have been using such a boot: the jacket was also recognised as having belonged to her. The Spaniards also saw, at a distance, a body, which, to judge from its remaining clothing, was hers, and they made out three tracks in the snow above it, each streaked with blood. From the position and direction of the tracks they judged that the bodies which made them must have fallen from about 8500m. No other signs of the six summit climbers were discovered.

In 1996 there were successful ascents on both the north and south sides of the peak, along previously climbed lines, while in 1997 a Japanese expedition climbed a variant of the original Waseda West Ridge route.[12] The expedition started tragically, the leader Kazuo Tokushima being killed in an avalanche on Japan's Mount Hotaka just ten days before the team left for Pakistan. The new leader, Osamu Tanabe, was forced to use a different Base Camp due to problems with the porters, adding distance and height to the proposed route. More problems followed, the team being called to the aid of another Japanese expedition, to Broad Peak, which had been hit by an avalanche. Two bodies were recovered from the avalanche debris. Back on K2 the Japanese were rewarded for their patience by a sustained period of good weather – claimed to have been the best for twenty years – which allowed rapid progress. Following the Waseda line at first, then deviating towards the North-West Ridge rather than taking the 1981 face line, the Japanese finally reached the summit, three Japanese arriving there on 19 July. At the summit they left the ashes of Kazuo Tokushima and another member of their club. Nine days later four Japanese and four Sherpas reached the summit along the same route.

1998–2007

There were no successes in 1998 or 1999, though in 2000 twenty-five climbers reached the top, and in 2001 a further nine summitted. After the summit climbs of 2001 a section of the hanging glacier above the Bottleneck collapsed, making the lower section of the gully much more difficult, the time needed for the climb preventing anyone from summitting in 2002 and 2003. In 2002 film-makers Jeff Rhoades and Jennifer Jordan from an international team led by Spaniard Araceli Segarra found the remains of Dudley Wolfe on the glacier near Base Camp.

The year 2002 also saw another attempt to climb K2 in winter, as a Polish team sponsored by Netia, the largest television company in Poland, which transmitted daily, prime-time reports, headed for the north side of the mountain just before Christmas. Led by Krzystof Wielicki, and including not only some excellent Polish climbers but also experienced climbers from Georgia, Uzbekistan and Kazakhstan, the team reached the foot of the mountain in late December. Christmas Day was spent on the Aghil Pass, the team celebrating the day with the seventy camels that were transporting 6 tons of equipment and food. On New Year's Day 2003 the first ropes were fixed on the Japanese 1982 route. At first good progress was made, but then bad weather, with vicious winds, forced the team back to Base Camp. The non-Poles, apart from the Kazakh Dennis Urubko, then decided to leave the expedition, which reduced the number of lead climbers. When the weather improved, the route was pushed further up the peak, Camp IV being established at 7650m (25,100ft) on 12 February, but then atrocious weather, reputedly the worst for several years, forced another retreat to Base Camp. The intense cold now meant that several climbers dared not continue for fear of aggravating already frostbitten extremities (one man was to lose a toe), reducing still further those who could climb and those who could carry loads. The latter meant that the oxygen intended for a summit bid could not be taken above Camp I. The Poles decided on one last push, but the lead climbers, Dennis Urubko and the Pole Marcin Kaczkan, found, on reaching Camp IV, that it had been destroyed by the wind. Determined to make a summit attempt, the two men spent the night in a small bivouac tent. With just one sleeping bag between them, and using coiled ropes as they had no insulating mats, they endured a terrible night. By morning Kaczkan was ill, probably with cerebral oedema, and Urubko called for help. Kaczkan's condition improved slightly, and aided by Urubko he was able to descend to meet the rescue party which was climbing up with oxygen bottles. Everyone then descended safely, and Wielicki wisely decided to call off any further attempts.

The year 2004 was the 50th anniversary of the first ascent and a number of teams (eleven in total) headed for the peak. Not surprisingly, one of the teams was Italian, another being Swiss/Italian. Accompanying these teams, against his doctor's orders, was Lino Lacedelli, now approaching his 79th birthday, who returned to the Base Camp site from where he had climbed to the summit in 1954, in part to pay his respects at the grave of Mario Puchoz. Fittingly the expeditions included both a Compagnoni (Michele, Achille Compagnoni's grandson) and a Lacedelli (Mario, Lino's nephew). Both men were among the forty-one climbers who summitted in the three-day period from 26 to 28 July. On the summit, Mario Lacedelli persuaded a bemused companion to stand beside him while Mario threw an arm around his shoulder. Back in Italy, the shot was manipulated to remove the companion and insert the famous summit shot of Lino Lacedelli so that uncle and nephew appeared to be embracing across a distance of fifty years. As Mario was by then running Cortina's *K2 Sports* shop, the shot was excellent advertising material. As well as the forty-one summitters in late July, ten more climbers reached the summit in early August, one of these, the Catalan climber Jordi Corominas, making the second ascent of the Magic Line. Starting out with two companions, Oscar Cadich and Manuel de la Matta, Corominas continued alone when the others retreated due to cold and exhaustion. He summitted at midnight, then downclimbed the Abruzzi Spur, reaching a welcome tent and refreshments after 30 hours of continuous effort. Sadly, despite successfully downclimbing to Camp I on the Magic Line, de la Matta then died. He had been complaining of severe abdominal pains and probably died of peritonitis.

There were no successful ascents in 2005. In 2006 four climbers reached the summit, these including the Japanese Yuka Komatsu, the youngest female to date at 23 years and 10 months, and another Japanese, Tatsuya Aoki, who at 21 years 10 months is the youngest person to date. But these records were combined with tragedy when a team of four Russians was avalanched on the slopes just below the summit, all of them being killed. The following year another Russian team made the first new route on the mountain for ten years and, as the 1997 Japanese climb had been a variation on an existing route, the first truly independent new line for almost twenty years. Over a ten-week period the Russians[13] forced a route up the West Face, to the north of the West Ridge. Rotating groups of four climbers, each group having a leader who chose the other three members, the Russians took a deliberately direct and very difficult line, which could have been avoided by following a couloir to the left. The extraordinary ethics and team solidarity of the Russians on their climb are to be admired, even if other teams might find them hard to emulate. The life of one member who had thrombosis at Camp III was saved by another, who climbed up from Camp II through the night in bad weather to take up an oxygen bottle that saved his life. That defines friendship, but because of the Russian definition of ethics, the man who had used the bottled gas (taken along only for such a medical emergency) was then forbidden to take any further part in the climb as that would have destroyed the 'no supplementary oxygen, no Sherpas' rule the Russians had set.

The Russians had to contend with both bad weather and very steep rock before establishing Camp V at about 7850m (25,750ft). From there Alexei Bolotov, Gennadi Kirievski and Nikolai Totmjanin climbed through chest-deep snow to establish Camp VI at about 8150m (26,740ft). From there on 10 August they set out for the summit. Poor snow conditions slowed progress, and forced the men on to the West Ridge, where a vertical rock step, 50–70m high, at 8500m (27,900ft) stopped them, forcing them to abandon the climb. Not until 21 August was the weather good enough for another attempt. This time another camp was established, at 8400m (27,560ft), from where Andrei Mariev and Vadim Popovich set out. In improved snow conditions, and then finding a way around the vertical rock step, they successfully summitted. The following day nine more of the Russian team also summitted. Eleven climbers of the sixteen-man team reaching the summit was a magnificent achievement, and perhaps equally noteworthy is the fact that one of them, Pavel Shabalin, became a grandfather during the course of the expedition. Another member, Gleb Sokolov, was already a grandfather. When asked if the route could be undertaken alpine-style, the Russians demurred; they felt that the risks would likely be too high, as the difficulties involved demanded time, and time on K2 inevitably means bad weather at some stage which might overwhelm a small alpine-style team.

As the Russian team was summitting and then descending their route, on the north side of the mountain two Kazakhs, Serguey Samoilov and Dennis Urubko (who had been on the unsuccessful winter attempt in 2002/3), attempted an alpine-style ascent of a new route on the northern side of the peak. Arriving in September – very late in the summer climbing season – the two Kazakhs chose to acclimatise by following the Japanese North Ridge line (the usual ascent route from the north, seeing almost all of the infrequent northern ascents) to a height of about 8300m (27,200ft). The pair then rested in Base Camp but as they did so bad weather, with continuous snowfall, set in, making their projected route to the left of the Japanese line untenable owing to the avalanche risk. When a weather window finally appeared they therefore reclimbed the original route. Setting out from their top camp on 2 October, the two men made the latest-ever successful summit climb.

The Russian climb, completed without the use of supplementary oxygen, is now regarded as the hardest route to the world's second highest summit. Its completion, together with the two-man team on the North Ridge, made 2007 a memorable year on the mountain. The following year would be equally memorable, but for very different reasons.

Chapter 8

2008

'My life has been reduced to counting steps.'

Wilco van Rooijen

On 31 July seven expeditions (American, Dutch, French, Italian, Korean, Norwegian and Serbian), with a total of thirty-three climbers, had gathered at Camp IV at the foot of the shallow sloping Shoulder below the Bottleneck Couloir.[1] The climbers had endured a frustrating time, the season having, yet again, been plagued by a succession of extended periods of bad weather. Ropes had been fixed up both the Abruzzi and South-South-East Spurs during the short periods of climbable weather, but with no settled weather apparently in sight, many of the seventy-plus climbers at Base Camp had become disillusioned and were contemplating returning home. One in particular, Hugues d'Aubarède, a 61-year-old Frenchman who was climbing alone, but had hired two Pakistani high-altitude porters to help him reach the summit, had decided to go home. But then good weather arrived, giving the demoralised climbers a chance to attempt the summit and d'Aubarède was persuaded by climbers from other teams to wait just a few more days in order to fulfil his dream of standing on K2's summit.

With the arrival of better weather, those teams able to muster sufficient resources started up the hill, the Dutch – their team sponsored by Norit, a water purification company, and including the Irishman Gerard McDonnell – following their line up the South-South-East Spur, all the other teams taking the Abruzzi. Camp IV, a collection of tents from the seven teams, was placed low on the Shoulder, at 7800m (about 26,000ft), a practice that seems to have become more popular with later expeditions though, crucially, it adds a good hour to an ascent, and further time at the end of the descent, each of which may be critical on a long summit day.

First away on 1 August was the Basque Alberto Zerain, who actually left Camp III at 10pm on 31 July. Climbing with minimal equipment and without supplementary oxygen, he reached Camp IV in the amazing time of 2 hours (for about 750m/2460ft) of climbing. He says he attempted to rouse the climbers at Camp IV as he passed, but then climbed on alone.

It had been agreed between the various expeditions that a lead group of climbers would fix ropes in the Bottleneck Couloir and along the leftward traverse above it. The leader of the Korean team, Kim Jae-Su, felt that his team should take the lead in this as they were the best equipped and the most experienced. The latter was certainly true on K2 itself as Kim's team had already fixed the Abruzzi to Camp III. Kim agreed that two of his team and two Sherpas would aid in the rope fixing. The Serbian team agreed to allow Jahan Baig, their highly experienced Pakistani sirdar, who had summitted K2 in 2004, to join the rope fixing team. The Italians offered their two Pakistani high-altitude porters, while Karim Meherban, one of the Pakistanis with Hugues d'Aubarède, would also join. Pemba Gyalje from the Norit team would complete the group despite the fact that he, alone of the group, would be climbing without supplementary oxygen. Jahan Baig suggested the use of 600m of rope, together with a number of bamboo wands to be 'planted' from the camp to the base of the ropes as the Shoulder is a featureless, gently rising plateau on which it is easy to become disorientated in bad weather. The Koreans also took a further 200m of rope as a back-up.

But Jahan Baig, the nominal leader of the group, was sick and did not make it to the Shoulder. Others due to be in the rope fixing team also failed to appear by the agreed 10pm deadline, so it was early on 1 August before a reduced team set out to follow Alberto Zerain. Though the team was smaller than planned, it included the Pakistani Mohammad Hussain, who was also with the Serbian team and had summitted in 2004, and Tshering Dorje, pressed into service by Pemba Gyalje. Tshering was also climbing without supplementary oxygen. The exact plan regarding the rope fixing was later debated, but the Korean team Sherpas believed the intention was to fix rope from close to Camp IV all the way to the end of the traverse below the summit, and they began to fix ropes accordingly. But on the way from Camp III to Camp IV the Koreans had discovered that less rope than they believed had been fixed, and they used the 200m of back-up rope to complete the job. Consequently, rope began to run short before the traverse was reached, and a traffic jam formed as lengths were detached from low on the mountain and passed up to the lead climbers. To this delay was added the fact that with all the climbers clipping into the ropes for security, any individual was inevitably limited in terms of rate of progress by the speed of the man ahead of him. And so a genuine bottleneck occurred.

At 11am the Serb Dren Mandic unclipped from the fixed rope. Exactly why is not clear. The most likely explanation is that he had been held up because the climbers ahead had stopped, and had then decided to change his oxygen bottle, though unclipping from the rope to do that seems unnecessarily hazardous. Whatever the reason, the unsecured Mandic then fell. He collided with the Norwegian Cecilie Skog, who was climbing with two other Norwegians, her husband Rolf Bae and Lars Nessa. Skog was knocked off her feet, but was still attached to the fixed rope and survived. Desperately grabbing for the ropes, Mandic knocked off two more climbers, but then cartwheeled down the Bottleneck. When he finally came to rest, some say he stood up, but then fell again and slid further down the slope. When he finally came to a stop those above, and those at Camp IV, could see he was moving. The two Serbians climbing with him, Iso Planic and Predrag Zagorac, together with Muhammed Hussain, immediately climbed down towards him. At Camp IV the American Eric Meyer, who was actually the only doctor on the mountain, and Frederick Sträng, a Swede climbing with the Americans, had also seen that Mandic was moving and climbed up to him. These two men had also started for the summit that morning, but had given up when they realised the climbers were moving too slowly to ensure a safe return before nightfall. By the time the five reached Mandic he was dead. The five would-be rescuers were then joined by another Pakistani high-altitude porter, Jehain Baig, one of the high-altitude porters with Hugues d'Aubarède. Baig had accompanied d'Aubarède, carrying an extra oxygen bottle. Once he had passed it to the Frenchman, after his first bottle was exhausted, Baig had descended.

The Serbians with the body decided to move it to Camp IV. This was a strange decision, the recovery of bodies from above 8000m being rarely undertaken, despite frequent press articles registering horror (or, at the very least, disquiet) about them being left high on mountains. In reality, as previously noted, human beings above 8000m are dying, attempting to bring down a living casualty often being beyond their resources. Such rescues are also dangerous as mistakes among exhausted men are easily made. The retrieval of bodies is therefore seen as both futile and unwarranted. The decision to move Mandic was therefore surprising, and the reason why it was made is disputed. The Serbians claim they were told to by the team leader, Milivoj Erdeljan, who was at Base Camp; Erdeljan denies this. Whatever the truth, before any realistic effort could be made, Jehain Baig, who appeared not to be in full control of himself (earlier in the day he had showed some signs of altitude sickness, but had climbed up despite this), stumbled and became entangled in one of the ropes attached to the body. He fell, landing on Sträng and knocking him over. Sträng shouted at Baig to get off him,[3] fearful they would both tumble down the hill. Baig did nothing. Sträng shouted again. Finally, without apparently attempting to use either his ice axe or crampons to anchor himself, Baig let go of the rope he was holding and started to slide down the hill on his backside. He made no attempt to use his axe to self-arrest, gathered speed, flipped over so that he was sliding head first, then disappeared over the edge of the Shoulder.

As well as Meyer and Sträng, their team mate Chris Klinke had also climbed down, as had Jelle Staleman of the Norit team, the American Nick Rice and the Italian Roberto Manni, all concerned that the slow pace of movement in the Bottleneck would not allow Camp IV to be safely reached after a summit climb. The Norwegian Oystein Stangeland turned back from the start of the traverse having come to the same conclusion. At 12.08pm Klinke took a photograph from Camp IV which shows a line of climbers on the fixed ropes of the traverse. Despite the deaths, and the lateness of the hour, those on the traverse were still going up, though none of those in the Bottleneck knew Jehain Baig had died, and some were unaware of Mandic's fall. After taking his shot, Klinke descended towards Camp III. At 3pm he looked up and reckoned that in the nearly 3 hours since he had left Camp IV the line of climbers had climbed only 50m or so, but they were still moving upwards.

As Klinke was looking up again at 3pm, Alberto Zerain was just reaching the summit. On his way down he says he attempted to persuade those still climbing up to retreat, but summit fever and group mentality meant he was ignored. Of those on the traverse, all but two summitted. An exhausted Rolf Bae stopped about 100m below the top. There he waited for his wife. Cecilie Skog and Lars Nessa reached the top just after Pasang, a high-altitude porter with the Korean team. Pasang is referred to in the books by Bowley and Wilkinson as Pasang Lama, but as a Bhutia (rather than a Sherpa) he should more correctly be called Pasang Bhote – but there was already a Pasang Bhote on the Korean expedition, who was to become inextricably linked to the events of 2008. Recognising the problem, Bowley refers to 'Big' Pasang Bhote and 'Little' Pasang Lama, the two nicknames having been used on the expedition because the men had the same name. In the text here, the name Pasang Bhote (Lama) is used for 'Little' Pasang. Behind them another fourteen climbers reached the summit at times between about 5pm and 7pm, many of them using satellite phones to tell loved ones of their success. Jumik Bhote, a Sherpa with the Korean team, was told that he had become a father three days before. K2's summit and a baby son in just a few minutes: he was ecstatic.

On the descent, Zerain was the first across the traverse and into the Bottleneck. He used the fixed ropes to descend to Camp IV, then continued down to Camp III, anxious to get as low as possible. The next across the traverse were the Norwegian trio. At the head of them was Bae, who insisted on leading, and had placed his wife between himself and Lars Nessa. Bae was moving towards the top of the Bottleneck Couloir when a section of the hanging glacier that broods over it collapsed. The glacier front, appearing as a more or less continuous vertical or overhanging ice wall about 170m (550ft) high rather than as a series of gigantic séracs, has threatened climbers attempting to reach the summit slopes since the first attempts on the peak, the danger it represented having persuaded Wiessner to attempt the more difficult rock route to the upper slopes in 1939, and intimidated Compagnoni and Lacedelli during the first successful ascent in 1954. During the years of ascents and attempts on the peak there have been few sightings of a wall collapse, though, of course, given the number of days of bad weather and the relative paucity of observers that is not entirely surprising. (Comparisons with the frequent collapses – 'calving' – of the fronts of tidewater glaciers are irrelevant as they are largely the result of undermining of the ice by the sea.) In photographs of the wall from across the years it looks remarkably similar, though that, too, is not a great surprise. But the glacier must move, and as it does tensions within the ice cause vertical cracks which separate the apparently uniform ice wall into a series of séracs, horizontal cracks meaning the séracs sometimes appear as a pile of ice blocks. Because it moves, collapses must occur, photographs revealing a layer of ice rubble at the base of the clean-cut wall which indicates a succession of collapses. The collapse of 2008 implies that the wall remains stable for relatively long periods, but when it becomes unstable it collapses as a series of falls over many hours. This is not surprising: on any glacial front the collapse of one section of ice creates instabilities around the collapse centre and further falls are likely, these either becoming smaller as a new (relatively) stable front is formed, or leading to further large collapses as instability grows.

Now, as night fell on 1 August, and Bae was leading across the last section of the traverse, a major collapse occurred. Cecilie Skog and Lars Nessa behind her heard the collapse and resulting avalanche, Skog being pulled off the hill as the rope to which she was clipped was hauled away, then snapped, by the ice debris. Regaining her balance, Skog shouted to her husband. There was no reply and the light of his head torch was no longer visible. Despite the shock of her husband's sudden death, Skog maintained her composure. The Norwegians were carrying 50m of light rope which Skog and Nessa attached to the remaining fixed rope, and then abseiled into the Bottleneck. There the pair found that the collapsing ice had destroyed the fixed ropes, forcing them to downclimb. They successfully accomplished this, Skog taking one fall, and they regained Camp IV in the early hours of 2 August. Behind them Cas van de Gevel and Sherpa Pemba Gyalje also safely reached Camp IV, as did two of the Koreans, Ms Go Mi-Young and Kim Jae-Su, and the Sherpas Tshering Dorje and Pasang Bhote (Lama).

As he was descending, Cas van de Gevel caught and passed Hugues d'Aubarède about halfway across the traverse. As he was downclimbing the Bottleneck Couloir, he heard a noise and saw a dark form cartwheeling past. Van de Gevel is certain he recognised d'Aubarède's rucksack. As the bottom end of the rope left by the Norwegians was not fixed, it is likely the Frenchman had abseiled off its end or fell from the steep ice after detaching from the rope: his body was never found.

On their descent, Tshering Dorje, Pasang Bhote (Lama) and Pemba Gyalje found the rope left by Cecilie Skog and abseiled down it, but when they discovered the fixed ropes were missing their position became critical as Pasang Lama had left his ice axe anchoring the bottom of a fixed rope at the far end of the traverse. He did not need it for descending fixed ropes, but to downclimb without one was impossible. In an amazing act of courage and skill, Tshering Dorje tied Pasang Lama to himself by a short piece of rope, then downclimbed with the other Sherpa immediately below him. Though Pasang Lama had his crampons, he had nothing for his hands other than using them to balance, placing them against the ice. He was, more or less, hanging from Tshering Dorje's harness. One false move by either of them would have resulted in the deaths of both and possibly also that of Pemba Gyalje, who climbed below the pair, seeking out the best line and occasionally shining his head torch upwards to give a little more light to Tshering Dorje.

Above the Bottleneck Karim Meherban, Ger McDonnell, Wilco van Rooijen, Marco Confortola, Hwang Dong-Jin, Park Keyong-Hyo, Kim Hyo-Gyung and Jumik Bhote were all still descending when night fell and they were forced to bivouac. In the aftermath of the tragedy, most newspaper articles claimed that these climbers had been stranded by the collapse of the ice wall and the destruction of the fixed ropes in the Bottleneck Couloir, but that is not the case. From the evidence of the survivors, none of those who chose to bivouac was aware of the wall collapse or had reached the couloir. For everyone, the bivouac was terrible: without bivouac equipment, food, water or cooking stoves, it was a long, cold night.

Marco Confortola and Ger McDonnell bivouaced together, the Italian making a seat for the Irishman who, he says, was having a difficult time. Later the two were joined by Wilco van Rooijen, who saw their lights. The three men had been climbing without supplementary oxygen, had reached the summit late and were among the last to leave it. Their bivouac was probably 300m from the top of the Bottleneck. When dawn at last brought an end to the miserable night, van Rooijen set off immediately as his eyesight was failing (due to snow-blindness) and getting down quickly was imperative. Though unsure of the route he finally found the end of the fixed ropes. As he descended he arrived at a horrifying scene. Ahead of him were three members of the Korean team. Van Rooijen says that one was hanging upside down, moaning from pain and cold. The second was staring into space. The third man, Jumik Bhote, asked for a pair of gloves, which van Rooijen gave him. All three were enmeshed in ropes, clearly the result of a fall. The Sherpa then told him that a rescue party was on its way. Van Rooijen was fearful that his failing eyesight would soon mean he was unable to get down alone. He therefore hurried on.

Confortola says[2] that he and McDonnell spent 3 hours with the Koreans. He says Jumik Bhote had lost a boot and his foot was covered only by a sock, and that when he and McDonnell reached them two were already unconscious. They attempted to untangle the three men from their ropes, but ultimately all three had died and so he and McDonnell continued down. Soon after, Confortola says, McDonnell turned and, without saying a word, headed back towards the summit. As the Italian continued to descend, an avalanche swept past him: within the tumbling mass of snow he saw body parts and recognised the yellow boots of Ger McDonnell. (In one account he says he picked up an eyeball, then placed it back on the snow.) It is difficult to know exactly where Confortola was when this happened, but as we shall see, from another witness to the accident, there are two possible explanations for what the Italian actually saw.

Wilco van Rooijen, his eyesight failing, lost the fixed ropes on his descent and was lucky to regain them when, climbing back up,

at times everything goes black before my eyes. I look up and it seems as if I am not making any progress. I look at the sun, which is beating down on me. I stare straight at the sun and ask: is this the end? The worldly has become the spiritual … I no longer have any sense of time. It is agony. My life has been reduced to counting steps. The sun's heat is causing me to dehydrate even faster. I do not know where I am, or which direction I need to go. It's been a long time since I had anything to eat or drink. I have no strength left, I am alone, no one can save me. Without realising I am regularly falling asleep, leaning on my axe.

But he did find the ropes, and abseiled into the Bottleneck Couloir; then, finding no more rope, he climbed down to the Shoulder. But to add to the problems of his failing eyesight, the Shoulder was now enveloped in mist.

Unable to read the numbers stored on his satellite phone, van Rooijen, who could still see the dial pad numbers, dialled the only one he could remember, his home in Holland. His wife answered. Soon after, Cas van de Gevel at Camp IV received a radio call from Base Camp telling him that van Rooijen had called his wife and told her that he was below the Bottleneck but, with failing vision, was unsure of his position and needed help. Van de Gevel and Pemba Gyalje immediately searched the local area. They also called van Rooijen via another satellite phone and agreed a plan: Van Rooijen must move left, as would van de Gevel and Pemba. That way they should intercept each other. But they did not, and on increasingly dangerous ground van Rooijen was forced to move to the right. Eventually darkness fell again and he had to make a second bivouac.

Having failed to find van Rooijen, van de Gevel and Pemba Gyalje were preparing to leave Camp IV as they needed to descend for their own safety. The camp was now almost deserted, most climbers having descended the Abruzzi, apart from Tshering Dorje and some members of the Korean expedition, two Sherpas from which (Pasang Bhote and Tshering Bhote) had been told to climb up to assist the remaining members of the team by leader Kim Jae-Su (Kim and Ms Go had then descended towards Camp III Abruzzi). Pemba Gyalje then received a radio message from Pasang Bhote telling him he had found a man asleep in the Bottleneck Couloir. It was the exhausted Marco Confortola. Pasang asked Pemba to climb up to rescue the man as he and Tshering Bhote had to continue up towards the remaining Koreans and Jumik Bhote. Reluctantly Pemba agreed. He climbed up with van de Gevel, but the latter was soon forced to stop, saying he would wait to help Pemba when he returned: he would also be a useful 'lighthouse' for the returning climbers as the weather was now closing in, making visibility poor.

When Pemba found Confortola the Italian had begun to undress, a sure sign of hypothermia as in its advanced stage the victim feels he is overheating and throws off his clothes, hastening lethal cooling. Pemba gave him oxygen, dressed him and the two started down. As they did, Pasang radioed Pemba again with the news that he had reached the Koreans and Jumik Bhote, that they were frostbitten but could walk, and they were all climbing down. Tshering Bhote was below him, still climbing up the couloir. Pasang also said that he had seen one person, at the back of the group, hit by another sérac collapse. The person had been wearing a red down suit with black patches. Pemba knew this was probably Ger McDonnell.

As Pemba and Confortola descended, there was another collapse on the ice wall and an avalanche streamed down the couloir. Pemba saw several human bodies in the ice mass. Confortola was hit on the head – Pemba says by ice, the Italian claims it was an oxygen bottle – and the Sherpa grabbed his neck to prevent him becoming yet another victim. As they climbed down, Pemba saw the bodies of two Koreans, Pasang Bhote and Jumik Bhote. Tshering Bhote later climbed down alone. In order to have landed where they did, at the base of the Bottleneck Couloir, the two Koreans and Jumik Bhote must have climbed 200m horizontally from where they were seen by Marco Confortola and Wilco van Rooijen.

The meeting of Confortola, McDonnell and van Rooijen with the three members of the Korean team and the subsequent events have been the subject of considerable speculation and argument, much of it unfortunate, in the time since. All those who consider the various statements will form their own view, but it seems the most likely sequence of events was as follows. Some time during the descent from the summit during the early darkness of 1 August the three Koreans and Sherpa Jumik Bhote had an accident, the end point of which saw three men caught up in ropes, unable to help themselves either because they were completely entangled or because they could not release the weight of partners attached to them. What happened to the fourth man is pure speculation. It is possible, perhaps likely, that the third Korean was also involved in the accident, became detached from the ropes and fell to his death, but one interesting account of the night of 1 August needs to be taken into consideration. That night, Pasang Bhote and Tshering Bhote set off from Camp IV in the direction of the Bottleneck Couloir. They had arrived with a second group of Koreans who were intending to attempt the summit next day. Now they were looking for members of the first team. They found Kim Jae-Su, who told them Go Mi-Young was behind him. Looking for her, they saw several headlamps above them: then two of those lamps fell, one down the couloir, the other off towards the East Face. The one in the couloir turned out to be Ms Go: she was alive and relatively unscathed, though the two Sherpas had to assist her back to Camp IV. Who was the climber who fell down the East Face? Given that everyone else was ultimately accounted for (or very likely accounted for in the case of Karim Meherban), it is possible that this was the missing third Korean. If it was, it is likely that the fittest of the three Koreans left on the mountain, unwilling to bivouac, had decided to climb down alone, only to fall to his death from the couloir. As the other two Koreans and Jumik Bhote also died, we will never be sure. It is also possible that the two Sherpas saw the Frenchman Hugues d'Aubarède falling, being mistaken on the exact timeline of what they had seen. But as they had already passed Cas van de Gevel, it seems more likely they had seen the third Korean.

From the statements of Pasang Bhote (Lama) it is known that the least experienced of the Koreans, Kim Hyo-Gyung, was having problems after his supplementary oxygen ran out and it is conjectured that he precipitated the accident which left the others entangled. When the three Westerners arrived the following morning, they found the three survivors in a poor state. Forced by failing eyesight to move on, and apparently unable to offer help, Wilco van Rooijen and Marco Confortola continued their descents. But Ger McDonnell appears to have decided that more could be done. He was experienced in mountain rescue, an important part of which is learning techniques to release the weight of fall victims from those attached to them. It seems he was able to do this. Once one man was freed, assuming he was still fit enough to help, the freeing of the others would have been easier. Clearly, eventually, all three men were freed from the ropes and were able to descend, with McDonnell taking up a position at the rear of the others, probably because he was in the best condition and therefore took charge of the descent. As the four men approached Pasang Bhote a fresh sérac fall hit McDonnell, sending him to his death. A few minutes later, probably no more than 5 minutes, Tshering Bhote, who had climbed more slowly than Pasang Bhote, watched in horror as the remaining four were swept away by another collapsing sérac.

There remains only the question of what exactly Marco Confortola saw. The Italian describes two separate avalanches passing him, the first with the remains of a man in yellow boots, the second in which he saw several falling climbers. Given the explicit radio conversation between Pasang Bhote and Pemba Gyalje regarding the death of one climber in a red, black-patched, down suit, and the fact that Pemba saw the avalanche which killed the Koreans and the two Sherpas after he had reached Confortola, one explanation is that the Italian's memory of events, particularly the timeline of them, was unclear and that his two events were separated only by minutes, not the lengthy time he suggests. Given his condition, this would not be surprising. But another explanation seems more likely. Early in the morning of 2 August Pemba Gyalje took a photograph of the summit area with Ger MacDonnell's camera, which he had been carrying since taking the summit shots of the Norit climbers. On it a group of four climbers can be seen at the far end of the traverse: these are McDonnell, the two Koreans and Jumik Bhote. Towards the bottom of the Bottleneck Couloir a single figure can be seen. This is

Marco Confortola. Approaching him from below are two men, Pasang Bhote and Tshering Bhote setting off on their rescue climb. But there is another figure, above the ice wall and almost directly above the Bottleneck. Pemba says the lone figure was moving backwards and forwards, searching for a way down. This must be Karim Meherban. After he summitted with Hugues d'Aubarède, none of the survivors has any reliable information on the whereabouts of the Pakistani. It seems likely that, in gathering darkness and moving alone, he mistakenly went too far to the east and, after bivouacing, found himself far off route above the ice wall. The appalling state of mind of this poor man as he paced back and forth in a dreadful, desperate, but ultimately futile, attempt to find a way down the sheer ice wall cannot be contemplated without an upwelling of compassion. In another photograph taken by Pemba 5 hours later, the man has gone. Presumably he fell from the top of the ice wall. His fall would have precipitated another avalanche. Karim was also wearing yellow boots and his fall was far enough for any impacts to have caused terrible injuries: the body parts and yellow boots Marco Confortola saw in the first avalanche he witnessed were those of Karim Meherban. The sérac fall which caused Ger McDonnell's death would have created a separate, third, avalanche, but because of its position it would have been unseen by the Italian.

However, while this suggested storyline fits the known facts, other experts have suggested that Confortola's version, that Ger McDonnell set off up the mountain away from the Koreans and Jumik Bhote, perhaps because oxygen deprivation had scrambled his mind, and that he died in a fall or avalanche soon after the Italian had left the three trapped men, is equally plausible. It must be pointed out, though, that this scenario requires the three men to have untangled themselves, something they had been unable to do in the hours before, and it leaves the question of who Pasang Bhote saw killed by a sérac fall.

After seeing the avalanche that took the lives of the last four men to die in the tragic events of 1–2 August, Pemba Gyalje brought Marco Confortola down from the couloir and left him with Pasang Lama, Tsering Bhote and the Koreans. Pemba and van de Gevel then descended in darkness towards Camp III on the South-South-East Spur, sweeping the snow to their right with their torches as they had now been told that van Rooijen was between the two camps, but off to the west. They failed to find him. Pemba, leading the way, reached Camp III, but the exhausted van de Gevel could not, and spent the night in the open, his hands becoming frostbitten when he took off his gloves to prepare his sleeping bag and fell asleep without replacing them.

Less than 300m away from van de Gevel, van Rooijen was also bivouacing. He had descended too far to his right, a nightmare descent during which he had almost lost hope of surviving. Still descending he came across two bodies, still roped together. Not far from them when darkness fell, he was forced to endure a second night out. Next morning van Rooijen could be seen from Base Camp. He was 300m west and 100m above the Dutch Camp III, and Pemba and van de Gevel, who had made it to the camp in the early morning, were directed to where he was and found him. Considering his traumatic descent and two bivouacs, van Rooijen was in reasonable condition and the two men were able to guide him down to Base Camp, Pemba Gyalje declining any help from below on the grounds that more people on the route would likely create further problems rather than help the situation. Perhaps surprised by this reaction, other team members climbed up from Base Camp and fixed an additional 400m of rope to aid the three who were descending. On the Abruzzi it took another day to get Confortola down as he was in a poorer state.

At Base Camp Eric Meyer warmed the frostbitten digits of van de Gevel and van Rooijen in water baths to thaw the tissue. He then administered alteplase.[4] Meyer had three doses of this, and gave them to the two Dutch climbers, as Marco Confortola was still descending. The drug needs to be administered within a couple of hours for its conventional patients, i.e. heart attack and stroke victims, and within 24 hours for frostbite injury. Van de Gevel had received his injuries during his descent from Camp IV and so fitted this profile. Van Rooijen had received his injuries earlier, but Meyer thought the drug worth trying. Both men were then evacuated by helicopter. Meyer's treatment saved Cas van de Gevel's hands (he had no frostbite to his feet) for which, as a carpenter, he was extremely grateful. Wilco van Rooijen was less fortunate: his fingers were saved, but he lost all the toes of his left foot and most toe joints of his right foot. Confortola's injuries were 72 hours old by time he reached Base Camp; the damage to his feet was severe, and all his toes were later amputated.

In the aftermath of the climb, with eleven men dead in shocking circumstances, there was a rash of newspaper reports, many of them critical of mountaineering in general[5] and the unwarranted risk that climbers take, together with the suffering they occasionally oblige their loved ones to endure. Reinhold Messner, the first man to climb all fourteen 8000m peaks, and arguably the greatest of all high-altitude mountaineers, told the German N24 television news channel that 'people are booking K2 package deals almost as if they were buying an all-inclusive trip to Bangkok. Something like that is not professional: it is pure stupidity.' From such an authority the point seemed a good one, but in fact there were no commercial climbers on K2, in the sense that there are each year on Everest, and many of the summit climbers were highly experienced high-altitude climbers.[6] But despite the experience of the climbers, the fact was that ropes were fixed and then used by everyone on 1 August. The fixing of ropes was questioned because that is exactly what happens on commercial climbs on Everest, the implication being that it proved the commercial nature of K2 in 2008. In general, K2 climbers do not resort to fixed ropes, being experienced and technically competent enough to summit and return without them. (It is worth pointing out here that all those who reached

Camp IV descended the Bottleneck without the aid of fixed ropes.) Fixing ropes is also time-consuming, but once the decision had been taken to fix the ropes it would have been a very confident climber who chose to ignore them in favour of making his own route. Fixed ropes offer added security and few would willingly turn that down on a peak as difficult as K2. The use of the fixed ropes clearly slowed the general speed of the climbers, particularly in the Bottleneck where there was only one line, the man ahead defining your speed. The decision of faster climbers not to detach from the fixed ropes on the traverse is less understandable, but it must be remembered that when climbing past another climber, one who is attached to the fixed rope, a very wide berth must be given in case he slips and knocks you off. The extra effort such a detour would require explains why few decided upon it.

Others questioned the actions of the Sherpas on summit day, implying that those who climbed down to Camp IV should have helped in bringing down those who bivouaced. The clear expectation of those in the western media was that if Sherpas were on the hill, then their job was to look after western climbers and, if necessary, to be loyal unto death, an opinion based in part on the altruistic behaviour of Pasang Kikuli, Pintso and Pasang Kitar on K2 in 1939, and the sacrifice of others in the high hills. The fact that there were fixed ropes reinforced the prejudice – on Everest these are now routinely fixed from Base Camp to summit on the Nepalese side, and for much of the way on the north side, the ropes being regularly maintained by Sherpas. The additional fact that on K2 in 2008 the ropes were fixed by a team of Koreans, Pakistanis and Sherpas, i.e. non-westerners, reinforced the prevailing view (and may also have influenced the western climbers themselves). But Pemba Gyalje and Tshering Dorje were climbing as equal members of their teams and were therefore in a completely different situation from the Sherpas on other expeditions. Just as other team members were free to make their own decisions as night fell and to choose whether or not to make their way down, so were they. And while it is true that Pasang Bhote (Lama) was a Sherpa with the Korean team and descended rather than staying with those still on the mountain, it should be recalled that he did not have an ice axe, and climbing up to retrieve it in the dark was dangerous and would leave a rope unanchored, and therefore he either had to descend with Tshering's help or, probably, die. It should also be remembered that the Korean expedition leader and one (perhaps two) other team members also left their team mates on the hill and descended.

Also questioned was the use of supplementary oxygen. There is an on-going debate regarding the advantages or otherwise of using bottled gas at high altitude. Briefly the advantages are the extra speed and extra warmth it gives the user, the disadvantage being that if the gas is exhausted before the user regains the top camp, it leaves him/her extremely vulnerable as the situation is much worse than if supplementary gas had not been used.[7] After Lou Reichardt had become the first person to summit K2 without supplementary oxygen, the trend was for it not to be used, but over recent years that tendency has been reversed, with more climbers using it than not. Of course it is also the case that in the early years of successful climbs almost all the summitters were world-class (and world-renowned) climbers, while lately less well-known names have been in the majority.

All who read about the events of 1–2 August 2008 will form their own opinion about the various issues raised. What is clear is that at least six of those who died (Rolf Bae, Gerard McDonnell, two Koreans, Jumik Bhote and Pasang Bhote) were killed by falling ice. They were unlucky: the ice wall which had allowed dozens to pass unharmed chose that time to collapse. What is equally clear is that despite the critical perception of selfish, egotistical climbers risking other people's lives to achieve their ambitions, there was selfless heroism on the mountain: Tshering Dorje attaching himself to Pasang Bhote (Lama) and ensuring both got down safely; Pemba Gyalje climbing up to rescue Marco Confortola, then looking for Wilco van Rooijen; Cas van de Gevel aiding in the search for van Rooijen; Pasang Bhote and Tshering Bhote climbing to the Bottleneck in an effort to bring down the last of their team; and Gerard McDonnell declining to leave the Koreans and Jumik Bhote and rescuing them. It is a terrible irony that the rescued men were then killed by a sérac fall, and an even more terrible irony that had an earlier sérac fall not killed him, McDonnell (if it is agreed that he was with the Koreans and Sherpas) would have died just 5 minutes later in the avalanche that killed the men he had rescued.

Chapter 9

The Next Step

'Everyone will be doing them when the sun comes out.'

Don Whillans

2009–2011

There were no successful ascents of K2 in 2009, but one climber, the Italian Michele Fait, was killed when skiing down the South-South-East Ridge. In 2010 there were, again, no successful ascents, but the death count on the mountain rose by two, the Bulgarian Petar Unzhiev dying of altitude sickness on the Abruzzi Spur, and the Swede Fredrik Ericsson dying in a fall close to the Bottleneck. Ericsson had been climbing with the Austrian Gerlinde Kaltenbrunner. Kaltenbrunner is married to the German Rolf Dujmovits, who in 2009 had become the sixteenth person to have climbed the full set of fourteen 8000m peaks, and she needed only K2 to complete the full set herself. Climbing solo, she and Ericsson set out for the summit from their top camp on the Shoulder. High in the Bottleneck Ericsson, who was ahead, fell. Exactly why is not clear, but it seems he may have been fixing a piton, perhaps to anchor a rope for an abseil on his return from the summit and when testing it, it gave way, causing him to overbalance. Ericsson fell to his death past the shocked Kaltenbrunner, who abandoned her own climb.

But though there were no summit climbs in 2010, there was one claimed ascent, on 12 August, by the Austrian speed climber Christian Stangl. Other climbers on the mountain doubted his ascent, having seen no evidence of a summit climb on that day and claiming that Stangl's condition at Base Camp did not indicate the expected exhaustion of a man who had rapidly ascended the world's second highest mountain without supplementary oxygen. Back in Austria Stangl told a press conference that the views of other climbers were embarrassing and he was unwilling to discuss or defend his claim. He did not, he said, climb for any reason other than personal satisfaction and had no wish to be on any summitter list.[1] The latter was certainly at odds with the fact that Stangl was claiming to be the first person to complete the set of seven second summits (the second-highest continental peaks) and his claims of other record ascents. Finally, in a television interview[2] Stangl admitted that he had only 'imagined' his summit climb. He put this imagination down to stress and fear of failure, but it immediately led to a reassessment of his earlier claims on 8000m peaks. As Eberhard Jurgalski notes, Stangl's claim of a solo of Shisha Pangma is at odds with the discovery that he was with a Basque expedition, sharing tents with other members; that his claim of a new route, solo, on Cho Oyu is at odds with the fact that much of his route was along the standard line and that, again, he had shared tents with others; and that his claimed speed ascent of the north side of Everest from ABC had, according to others on the mountain at the same time, started from the North Col. During an early press conference, when he was still claiming the K2 ascent, Stangl said that the requirement of others to have proof of everything put the free spirit of mountaineering in danger. But that freedom exists only if trust also exists: it is baseless claims that endanger climbing's free spirit.

In 2011 Gerlinde Kaltenbrunner returned to K2, this time on the north side, and together with Kazakhs Vassili Pivtsov and Maksut Zhumayev, and Pole Darek Załuski summitted on 23 August. In doing so Kaltenbrunner became the second undisputed woman to complete the set of 14 8000m peaks, and the first to climb all 14 without supplementary oxygen. Pivtsov and Zhumayev were also completing their own sets of all 14 8000m peaks.

The Future

Much has changed in the 150 or so years since Thomas Montgomerie caught sight of a very fine peak far away in the Karakoram. In the hundred years after Montgomerie's observation the base of K2 was reached by only nine expeditions, just four of which made any realistic attempt to climb it. The mountain's North Face was glimpsed only three times by non-native eyes, and its northern base was never reached. Today trekkers in their hundreds regularly reach the base, rather fewer on the northern side it is true, but that is largely due to logistical difficulties rather than any lack of desire.

After the first ascent in 1954 it was more than twenty years before another man stood on the summit (though some of this delay can undoubtedly be put down to the decision of the Pakistani government to make the Baltoro off-limits). To cast an eye down the list of those who reached the summit in the early years of climbing history on the mountain is to read through a history of mountaineering in the last quarter of the twentieth century, the great names of the sport choosing to measure their abilities against the mountain of mountains. But ease of travel, together with improvements in equipment which meant that vast weights of food and clothing, etc., no longer had to be transported to the mountain's base, meant that the huge sponsorship deals required for the early ascents, which took so much time, became less necessary. There was also a general improvement in the standard of climbing, as is inevitable in any sport. Don Whillans' famous comment correctly predicted that the routes he and Joe Brown were putting up, routes with reputations for hard, fierce climbing, would eventually be seen as run-of-the-mill by a new generation who would push the boundaries of the possible even further.

And so K2, once essentially the preserve of the high-altitude climbing elite, was no longer so restricted. But as the number of climbers on the peak increased, so did the dangers. While almost all expeditions to the peak had installed fixed ropes low down to assist in the setting up and supplying of camps, in general the early climbers dispensed with these on summit day, trading their climbing experience and technique against the extra time required to fix them – and time is critical on the long K2 summit day where technical difficulty is added to altitude. Later ascents tended to fix ropes on summit day, primarily to protect the descent when the summit climber is tired and the likelihood of mistakes consequently increases. Later ascents also brought more climbers to the hill so that summit days also involved greater numbers. If ropes are fixed to protect against a slip, it is a strong-minded climber who will ignore them. If they are fixed at points where there is essentially just a single route, it may not be possible to ignore them. But fixed ropes slow any individual to the speed of the climber ahead. They also create the group mentality that Alberto Zerain noted on his descent in 2008. Summit fever, the illusion of safety in numbers and the idea that upwards is the way to be going because everyone else is going that way mix to a dangerous cocktail. Add high-altitude, a propensity to storms and the objective dangers of the ice wall above the Bottleneck, and only the lucky may escape a lethal combination that will find the flaws in all but the most competent.

K2's statistics are not reassuring to the potential summitter, yet the final years of the first decade of the twenty-first century – the Russian climb in 2007 and the deaths of 2008 – have reinforced those qualities which have made K2 so alluring to the world's mountaineers. It demands the highest level of commitment. In the future, though most who come will follow the Abruzzi Spur or South-South-East Ridge to the summit, others will look for new lines, on the faces of the Pakistani side or the still largely unexplored north. At some stage K2 will be climbed in winter.

But whatever the future holds for this beautiful, magnificent mountain, those that do reach its summit will join a select band. To date, for every climber who has stood on K2's summit twenty have stood on top of Everest and there is no reason to believe that statistic is likely to change radically.

K2 Statistics

With thanks to Eberhard Jurgalski.

Up to the end of 2011 there had been 306 ascents of K2, 80 people having died on the mountain. Arranged in reasonable blocks, the figures show:

Date	Ascents	Deaths during descent from the summit	Total deaths
To 1989	66	9	27
1990–99	98	13	22
2000–2011	142	9	31
Totals	**306**	**31**	**80**

These numbers indicate that until 1989 a summit climber had a 1 in 8 chance of dying on descent, and that for every 2.5 climbers who reached the top 1 climber died on the mountain. In the subsequent decade the mountain became less lethal, summit climbers having a 1 in 10 chance of dying on descent, while 1 climber died on the mountain for every 4 who summitted. In the first decade of the new century, despite the appalling loss of life in 2008, K2 became still less lethal, summit climbers having a 1 in 15 chance of dying on descent and 4.5 reaching the summit for every climber dying on the hill. The improvement in the chances of summit climbers surviving the descent is likely to be due to the increased use of supplementary oxygen by many of those climbing the Abruzzi Spur. Those testing themselves against K2, both in terms of new routes, alpine-style ascents and bottled gas-free climbs (and often all of these combined), are very much more likely to be highly experienced high-altitude and technically able climbers, but the risks remain high.

The effect of the reducing death toll of later years means that if present statistics remain valid in the next decade, 1 in 10 summit climbers will die on descent and 1 climber will die for every 4 who reach the summit. Of all the 8000m peaks only Annapurna, a mountain renowned for its avalanche risk, with 157 ascents (the fewest of any 8000m peak) and 60 deaths, is more dangerous to the aspirant summitter (see Table below). Nanga Parbat, though less lethal, has comparable statistics to K2, but these are weighted by the dreadful death tolls of the early German expeditions.

	Ascents	Number of individual climbers	Deaths	Ratio of Deaths/ Ascents
Annapurna	157	154	60	38.0%
K2	306	302	80	26.0%
Nanga Parbat	326	322	68	21.0%
Manaslu	297	289	58	20.0%
Kangchenjunga	243	230	40	16.0%
Dhaulagiri	417	403	62	15.0%
Makalu	323	314	29	9.0%
Gasherbrum I	298	290	26	8.7%
Shisha Pangma	285	280	24	8.4%
Broad Peak	385	381	21	5.5%
Everest	4571	2890	216	4.7%
Lhotse	396	377	12	3.0%
Gasherbrum II	872	841	20	2.3%
Cho Oyu	2790	2363	43	1.5%

Notes:
1. Data is complete to 2010 for all peaks except K2, which is complete to 2011.
2. Everest data may not have complete ascent figures as the Chinese have become cautious about releasing figures since the furore over the Olympic Games climb (and other problems associated with the Games) and the bad publicity over the death of David Sharp in 2006.

For many, the important comparison is with Everest. On the world's highest mountain 1 climber dies for every 20 who summit, a vastly different figure to the 1 in 4 on K2. It is also notable that on Everest there are numerous climbers with multiple ascents (there are, for instance, more than a dozen Sherpas who have climbed the peak ten or more times), yet only four climbers have reached K2's summit more than once, and no one has climbed it three times. This lack of multiple ascents confirms K2's reputation as a dangerous mountain. It can be (successfully) argued that on Everest the chief contributory cause of death is the climber him/herself. On K2 climbers are killed by the mountain.

Notes

Introduction
1. J. Curran, *K2: The Story of the Savage Mountain* (Hodder & Stoughton, London, 1995). The paperback edition mentioned in the text was published by the same publisher (Coronet edition) in 1996.

Chapter 1
1. Alfred Wegener (1880–1930) was a member of the Danish 1906 Greenland expedition which explored the north-east of the island searching for the Peary Channel, which Robert Peary claimed to have observed. The channel did not, in fact, exist and three men died attempting to return to the expedition's base after an abortive search. It was on this expedition that Wegener observed the movement of ice floes and developed his theory of continental drift. Wegener returned to Greenland in 1912 on an expedition which made a 1,100km crossing of the Inland Ice (the ice sheet that covers almost all of Greenland). On another expedition in 1930 Wegener led a party taking food to a camp on the Inland Ice where it was intended two men should overwinter. The party was hit by appalling weather, with temperatures as low as –60°C, one man's toes becoming badly frostbitten and requiring amputation with a penknife, without anaesthetic. Many of the party returned to base, but Wegener and two others continued. Finding the camp too short of supplies for everyone to remain through the winter, Wegener and the Greenlander Rasmus Villumsen set off for the coastal base camp. Wegener died on the way; Villumsen, having buried him, continued alone. He was never seen again. Wegener's book on continental drift theory was translated into English as *The Origin of Continents and Oceans* in 1924. The most recent translation is by John Biram (Methuen, London, 1968). A book on Wegener's 1930 expedition, important both scientifically and for its record of human endurance, based on team member diaries and edited by his wife, is Else Wegener (ed.) *Greenland Journey* (Blackie & Son, London, 1939).
2. Harry Hammond Hess (1906–1969) was an American geologist. He served in the US Navy, rising to the rank of rear admiral, and as captain of a vessel during the Second World War used the ship's echo-sounder to map the floor of the Pacific Ocean. Captain George Nares of the British Navy had already identified the Mid-Atlantic Ridge, that and his Pacific data convincing Hess that mid-ocean ridges were the driving force for the movement of continents.
3. In Greek mythology Tethys was the sea-goddess daughter of Gaia, the Earth Mother, and Uranus, the Sky Father. Gaia is now better known as the name given to James Lovelock's hypothesis that the Earth's biosphere, as an environment for life, is dynamic and self-sustaining.
4. The geological pre- and post-collision history of the Himalaya and Karakoram is complex and still the subject of academic debate. A good overview of the topic as regards the

Karakoram is given in M.P. Searle, *Geology and Tectonics of the Karakoram* (John Wiley, 1991). Though now a little dated, and in the process of revision, the book is still extremely useful and contains an excellent 1:250,000 scale geological map of the central Karakoram, including the Hunza valley, Snow Lake, Biafo, Baltoro-Muztagh and the Hushe valley systems. For a later view of the collision history (specifically of the Karakoram), see M.P. Searle, R.R. Parrish, A.V. Thow, S.R. Noble, R.J. Phillips and D.J. Waters, 'Anatomy, age and evolution of a collisional mountain belt: the Baltoro granite batholith and Karakoram Complex, Pakistani Karakoram', *Journal of the Geological Society, London* (2010, vol. 167), pp. 183–202. For a collision history specifically for the western Himalaya, see O.R. Green, M.P. Searle, R.I. Corfield and R.M. Corfield, 'Cretaceous–Tertiary Carbonate Platform Evolution and the Age of the India–Asia Collision along the Ladakh Himalaya (Northwest India)', *Journal of Geology* (2008, vol. 116), pp. 331—53.

5. The first mapping of the geology of K2 and the surrounding area is found in A. Desio and B. Zanettin, *Geology of the Baltoro Basin*, vol. 2 (Brill, Leiden, 1970). For a later assessment of the area, see the map referred to in Note 4 above and the article by M.P. Searle et al, also mentioned in Note 4. The specific geology of K2 is to be found in M.P. Searle, R.R. Parish, R. Tirrul and D.C. Rex, 'Age of crystallization and cooling of the K2 gneiss in the Baltoro Karakoram', *Journal of the Geological Society, London* (1990, vol. 147), pp. 603–6.

6. William Lambton (1753–1823) was a farmer's son from north Yorkshire. He was a gifted mathematician which enabled him to obtain a commission in the British Army. He served during the American War of Independence, being captured at Yorktown. Later he served in India where his commander was his friend Arthur Wellesley, later the Duke of Wellington. After Lambton's proposal for a survey of India, he became the first superintendent of what was to become the Great Trigonometric Survey (GTS) of India.

7. For a more detailed examination of the origins and work of the GTS see R. Sale, *Mapping the Himalaya* (Carreg, Ross-on-Wye, 2009).

8. For a review of these designations and the final naming of the peak after Sir George Everest, a later superintendent of the GTS, see R. Sale and G. Rodway, *Everest and Conquest in the Himalaya* (Pen & Sword, Barnsley, 2011), pp. 12–13 and Sale, *Mapping the Himalaya*, pp. 43–4.

9. Thomas George Montgomerie (1830–1878) joined the GTS at the age of 22. By the time of his death he had been promoted to lieutenant-colonel. Though most famous for the discovery of K2, Montgomerie's principal contribution to history was the suggestion of the use of native surveyors to map Tibet and other areas to which the British could not gain official entry. Montgomerie noted that 'a European, even if disguised, attracts attention when travelling among Asiatics, and his presence, if detected, is now-a-days often apt to lead to outrage'. This was a masterful understatement, the summary execution of two Britons in what is now Uzbekistan having caused significant embarrassment for the British government. The use of native surveyors would lessen the likelihood of detection, could be denied if they were discovered, and would not lead to calls for retaliation if they were executed. The data they obtained would also be crucial in the political manoeuvring now known as the Great Game. For a detailed discussion of the background to the use of native surveyors (the Pundits) and of their journeys, see Sale, *Mapping the Himalaya*.

10. The name is now spelt Haramukh. It is about 40km (25 miles) north of Srinigar.

11. See R.H. Phillimore, *Historical Records of the Survey of India*, vol. 5, *1844–1861* (Survey of India, Dehra Dun, 1968), pp. 87–90. A shorter (and more easily accessible) account is given in R.H. Phillimore, 'Survey of Kashmir and Jammu, 1855 to 1865', *Himalayan Journal* (1959–60, 22), pp. 95–102.

12. Quoted in Sale, *Mapping the Himalaya*, p. 44.

13. *Ibid.*

14. The report on the Karakoram Conference is in *Geographical Journal* (1938, vol. 91), pp. 129–52. The same volume also has an article by Kenneth Mason (pp. 123–8), which lists the main findings.
15. F. Maraini, *Karakoram: The Ascent of Gasherbrum IV* (Hutchinson/Viking Press, 1961), p. 150.
16. *Ibid*, p. 154.
17. The word monsoon derives from the Arabic *mausim* (season) and to the meteorologist it refers to any wind which blows persistently during the course of a season. Thus the Asian monsoon is the wind which blows air from above the Indian Ocean towards the Himalaya, rather than the rain that results.
18. P. Béghin, 'K2: Pyramid of Storms', *Mountain* (January/February 1992, vol. 143).
19. G. Child, 'A Margin of Luck', *Climbing* (February/March 1991). The article is also reproduced in a collection of Child's writings published as *Mixed Emotions* (The Mountaineers, Seattle/Cordee, Leicester, 1993).

Chapter 2

1. Marco Polo (*c.* 1254–1324) was a Venetian trader who wrote an account of his journey through Asia, accompanied his father and uncle, which had taken over twenty years. The account is now generally agreed to be based on reality, but there are still those who doubt its authenticity. Rabbani Shawma, a Uygur Christian living in what is now Beijing, made a journey from there to Rome in the mid-thirteenth century, the text of the account he wrote only being discovered in 1887. Shawma's journey is the exact one claimed by Marco Polo (though in reverse). Not wishing to draw attention to a divided country, Shawma's text does not mention the Great Wall of China. Marco Polo doesn't mention it either, which is strange as it is at least as remarkable as much that he does mention. Many scholars have interpreted this omission as an indication that Polo's book was based more on Shawma's than on an actual journey.
2. For more details on the early travellers in high Asia, together with details of later journeys, including those of British members of the Survey of India and the Pundits (native surveyors employed by the British), see Sale, *Mapping the Himalaya*. Grüber's drawing of the original Potala Palace, mentioned in the text, is reproduced in that book.
3. The three Schlagintweit brothers, Adolph, Hermann and Robert (actually three of five sons of a Bavarian surgeon) spent the period from 1854 to 1857 travelling in India and high Asia, their journeys the result of a chance meeting in Berlin with Alexander von Humboldt; the great man recommended them to the East India Company, which took them on to carry out a magnetic survey of India, much to the disgust of many in Britain who were appalled by the loss of opportunity and fearful for the security of the continent. Travelling alone, Hermann visited Assam and Bhutan, while the other two brothers failed in a bid to reach Tibet. Reunited in 1856, Hermann and Robert crossed the Karakoram Pass, while Adolph crossed the New Mustagh Pass alone. The three met up again in Srinigar in October 1856. After further short journeys, Hermann and Robert returned to Berlin, but Adolph remained in India with a plan to cross central Asia to Russia. He crossed the Karakoram Pass and continued to Kashgar, but was then arrested as a possible Chinese spy and beheaded in August 1857. A book on their travels, *Results of a Scientific Mission to India and High Asia undertaken between the years MDCCCLIV and MDCCCLVIII*, with all three brothers noted as its authors, was published in London in 1861, with another, in German, published in Jena in 1880 (*Reisen in Indien und Hoch Asien*).
4. Prior to the Schlagintweit brothers' crossing of the Karakoram Pass, there may have been an earlier European journey over it by the enigmatic 'Colonel' Alexander Gardiner. American-

born to a Scottish doctor and a half-English/half-Spanish mother, Gardiner may have achieved some of the most remarkable journeys in high Asia in the early years of the nineteenth century. His writings suggest he probably did make some astounding journeys, but detail is so lacking that it is hard to establish where exactly he went, as a consequence of which many authorities dismiss him completely. For an excellent resumé of Gardiner's possible exploratory career see J. Keay, *Where Men and Mountains Meet* (John Murray, London, 1977).

5. Godfrey Thomas Vigne (1801–63) is often thought of as French, because of his surname. But he pronounced his name 'vine' and was thoroughly English. He played cricket for the MCC and, after giving up law to travel in India, spent all his spare time shooting the local wildlife, his list of kills amounting to a field guide of the mammals and game birds of northern India. When not hunting with a rifle, he hunted with a falcon, with hounds and even with cheetahs. He also fished, and once combined his loves of hunting and fishing by shooting mullet as they rose to the surface to feed. His book of his journeys, *Travels in Kashmir, Ladak and Iskardo ...* (Henry Colburn, London, 1842), was very well received at the time, and is now recognised as one of the classics of high Asia travel.

6. R. di Cortanze, Marquis Oswaldo, *Cashemir, Piccolo e Medio Thibet e Turkestan* (Turin, 1881).

7. Henry Haversham Godwin-Austen (1834–1923) was one of a large family of seventeen children. As the son of a distinguished geologist and grandson of a general, a career as a geologist/surveyor in the British Army was natural, and after education at Sandhurst he joined the GTS in India. His father adopted the surname Godwin-Austen (adding his wife's maiden name, Godwin, to his own) only in 1853, the son being known simply as Henry Austen for many years before the longer version became established. Following his expedition, Godwin-Austen spent two more years in Ladakh, then transferred to Darjeeling. There he fell ill and was sent back to Britain, where he recovered and lived a long and successful life as an artist and scientist. His work in science was recognised by election to the Royal Society. Though the suggestion that his name be given to K2 was thankfully rejected, it was given to the glacier that links Concordia to the base of the mountain. More recently, this ice stream has occasionally been marked as 'K2 Glacier' on maps.

8. H.H. Godwin-Austen, 'On the Glacier of the Mustakh Range', *Journal of the Royal Geographical Society* (1864, vol. 34), pp. 19–56.

9. Godwin-Austen refers to 'Peaks K3 and K3a (Gūsherbrūm) towering up ahead'. K3a is Gasherbrum IV, K3 is Gasherbrum III. The usual translation of Gasherbrum is 'shining wall' or 'beautiful wall', which reflects Gasherbrum IV's western face. However, Godwin-Austen claims the name means 'fine gold peak', and backs this up with a story that gold was washed out of the glacier by the Biaho river and that a change in the river's outflow four or five years previously had made sifting for gold unprofitable.

10. Francis Edward Younghusband (1863–1942) was born in India, the son of a major general in the British Army. He was educated in England at Clifton College and Sandhurst before being commissioned into the 1st King's Dragoons. In 1890, after completing his historic Karakoram journeys, Younghusband was seconded to the Indian Political Service at a time of continuing concerns over Russian ambitions in central Asia. The 'Great Game', as the manoeuvring of the two powers has become known, was coming to an end, but perceived threats in the early years of the twentieth century led, in 1903, to Younghusband, now promoted to colonel, leading an expedition to Tibet, in charge of its political aspects. The expedition was co-led by General Macdonald, who was sent to handle military matters, but he left Younghusband in no doubt as to who was the superior officer. The nominal reason for

the expedition was political – the settlement of the border between Tibet and Sikkim – but it was actually a de facto invasion. The advance was greeted initially by sullen acceptance, but at Guru, a village on the road to Gyantse, the men were met by 1500 Tibetan troops and monks, armed only with matchlocks and carrying charms that they believed would protect them from bullets. As Macdonald's men attempted to disarm the Tibetans, a shot was fired. Within moments, 628 Tibetans lay dead, with a further 222 wounded, mown down by overwhelming and disciplined firepower (almost 16,000 rounds were fired, together with 50 shrapnel shells). The British casualties were six badly wounded, six more lightly wounded. The invasion was the last act of the Great Game and, despite the death toll of Tibetans, it was, in general, viewed by officialdom as a job well done, though not everyone in Britain shared that view. Younghusband was knighted in 1904 (as was Macdonald). He became President of the Royal Geographical Society (having been the youngest-ever Fellow after his journey across the Muztagh Pass) and in 1921 was made Chairman of the Mount Everest Committee, which was formed to oversee the reconnaissance expedition of the mountain that year, and the first attempt to climb it in 1922. In later life Younghusband became a mystic and an advocate of free love after his marriage collapsed. He died in Dorset in the arms of his lover and is buried in Lychett Matravers churchyard. His headstone bears a relief carving of the Potala Palace. The quotations in the text are taken from Younghusband's book of his journeys in high Asia: *The Heart of a Continent* (John Murray, London, 1896). The 1887 journey is also covered by an article in the *Proceedings of the Royal Geographical Society* (1888, vol. 10 (8)), pp. 485–518, and another in the *Alpine Journal* (August 1888–November 1889, vol. 14), pp. 50–5.

An excellent biography of Younghusband is P. French, *Younghusband: The Last Great Imperial Adventurer* (HarperCollins, London, 1994). For more details on the Tibetan invasion and Younghusband's involvement in the Great Game, see P. Hopkirk, *The Great Game: On Secret Service in High Asia* (John Murray, London, 1990).

11. In Filippi's book of the Abruzzi expedition he states that the Muztagh Pass was crossed by a Jesuit named D'Espinaha in 1760, over a century before Younghusband's journey. Filippi's source for this story is Charles de Ujfalvy. This was the adopted name of the Hungarian ethnographer Károly Jenö Ujfalvy (1842–1904), who travelled in central Asia and Kashmir and produced two important books on the area, *Les Aryens au nord et au sud de l'Hindou-Kouch* (Paris, 1896) and *Aus dem westlichen Himalaya* (Leipzig, 1884), each of which is now available, in the original language, in paperback form. Though reference to D'Espinaha's journey dies with Ujfalvy, it is very likely that his original source was credible. It is known that the pass was in regular use before avalanche and/or glacial changes made it impassable and it is certainly possible that for an earlier traveller the pass might have been a far easier undertaking than it was in 1887. Whether D'Espinaha crossed the older or newer versions of the Muztagh Pass, he would have eventually descended to the Oprang valley along the same route, in reverse, used by Younghusband, and would very likely have seen K2's North Face.

12. *Alpinismo Italiano in Karakoram/Italian Mountaineering in the Karakoram* (Museo Nazionale della Montagna 'Duca degli Abruzzi', Club Alpino Italiano, Turin 1991). The book is in both Italian and English. Aldo Audisio, the Museum Director, is usually described in catalogues as the book's author.

13. Letters of Roberto Lerco to Hermann Burchardt, Archives of the National Library of Israel, Jerusalem.

14. Francesco Cavazzani, 'Roberto Lerco', *Revista del CAI* (December 1954, vol. 73), pp. 403–4.

15. William Martin Conway (1856–1937) was the son of an Anglican vicar (later Dean of Westminster). After being educated at Repton and Cambridge University (where he studied mathematics), Conway became interested in fine art, particularly wood-cuttings and their use in the illustrating of early books. Later he was a professor of fine art at Cambridge. His exploration of the Baltoro Karakoram was the first of several important expeditions: in 1896/7 he crossed the interior of Spitsbergen; in 1898 he went to South America, exploring the Bolivian Andes and Tierra del Fuego, and making an early ascent of Aconcagua. He was knighted in 1895 for his work in surveying the Baltoro and was later elevated to the peerage as Baron of Allington, a title which died with him. The quotes in the text are taken from Conway's book about the expedition, *Climbing and Exploration in the Karakoram-Himalayas* (T. Fisher Unwin, London, 1894).

16. Oscar Eckenstein (1859–1921) was a rock-climber and mountaineer of phenomenal strength, able to do one-arm pull-ups. He used bouldering as a way of improving strength and technique, and organised a bouldering tournament with Baltoro porters, the first example of a pure climbing competition. A mathematician-turned-railway engineer, Eckenstein is credited with the invention of the crampon and also used a short ice-axe almost a century before such tools became commonplace. He had a reputation for being opinionated and arrogant, though in part this seems to have been a consequence of a long-running feud he had with the Alpine Club, as a result of their refusal to admit him to membership. The exact reasons for this are still disputed – though Eckenstein's outspokenness did not help: he once informed an ex-President of the Club who had climbed the Matterhorn that he could get a cow up the peak as long as he was allowed to tie its legs – quoted by Aleister Crowley, in *The Confessions of Aleister Crowley: An Autohagiography* (Hill & Wang, New York, 1970) – but seem to have resulted, at least in part, from the snobbery of an 'establishment' club for someone from the 'lower orders'. Eckenstein allied outspokenness to socialism, a lethal combination at the time in British Alpinism circles, which were dominated by those with private money. That Eckenstein took his climbing seriously enough to practise, and produced more efficient climbing equipment, seems to have been too much for an organisation which, at that time, viewed such things as deeply suspicious – an echo of the British upper class view that, just a few years later, would be disdainful and patronising about Roald Amundsen reaching the South Pole using dogs, while the plucky team of Captain Scott man-hauled his sledges. That Scott came second and died in the process seemed merely to emphasise the correctness of the approach. It is also difficult to suppress the thought that Eckenstein's German Jewish origins were also an issue, particularly as the way he behaved was very similar to that of foreign climbers whose astonishing achievements were routinely ignored by the Club. Thankfully, things are very different now.

Eckenstein also wrote a book about the trip, *The Karakoram and Kashmir. An account of a journey* (Fisher Unwin, London, 1896), which has recently been reproduced in facsimile form as part of the British Library's Historical Collection (published 2010). Other versions have also been published in the last few years. The Eckenstein quotes in the text are taken from this book.

17. Arthur David McCormick (1860–1943) was a Coleraine-born artist famous primarily for his naval paintings, though he was highly proficient across a range of subjects. His drawings illustrate Conway's expedition book, and also formed the basis of his own book which has recently been re-issued: *An Artist in the Himalayas (1895)* (Kessinger Publishing, Montana, 2009).

18. Matthias Zurbriggen (1856–1917) was an alpine guide. With Oscar Eckenstein he made the first ascent of the Stecknadelhorn (4241m) in the Pennine Alps. He was on Fitzgerald's expedition to New Zealand and South America, where he made the second ascent of Mount Cook solo, and the first ascent of Aconcagua, also solo. He was the first guide to write a book, *From the Alps to the Andes: Being the Autobiography of a Mountain Guide* (London, 1899), which, with his achievements, made him famous. But the fame had dimmed by his later years and he descended into penury and vagrancy, finally committing suicide.

19. Charles Granville Bruce (1866–1939) was the youngest of the fourteen children of Lord Aberdare, a minor British nobleman. Although an officer in the British Army, Bruce had accumulated considerable climbing experience in the European Alps, where he spent ten seasons. After the Conway expedition, Bruce accompanied Younghusband on his 1893 journey, and was on the 1895 expedition to Nanga Parbat. This, led by Alfred Mummery, the foremost British climber of the day, was the first true expedition to an 8000m peak but it ended with the deaths of Mummery and two Gurkhas. In 1907 Bruce was on the Longstaff expedition which climbed Trisul, the highest summit reached at that time. In 1922 he led the British expedition to Everest. He also led the 1924 expedition, but left early after a bout of malaria.

20. In *Climbing and Exploration in the Karakoram-Himalayas* Conway noted: 'There was a fine breadth of mountain splendour displaying itself on the right of our view – a huge Breithorn, as it were, filling the space between K.2 and the hidden Gusherbrum [*sic*].' This mass Conway later named Broad Peak. It is the 12th highest mountain in the world. Despite attempts to create a local name by translating 'broad peak' into Balti (Falchan Kangri, itself an approximation to the true Balti translation P'alchan Kangri, *P'* being rendered wrongly as *Ph* which was then changed to *F*), Conway's name is still that used by the vast majority of mountaineers.

During his exploration of the Baltoro towards Golden Throne, Conway saw the highest of the Gasherbrum peaks which, because it was tucked away behind other peaks (if 'tucked away' is an appropriate phrase for an 8080m/26,502ft mountain, the 11th highest in the world), he named Hidden Peak. That name is still occasionally used, though Gasherbrum I is now the common name for the peak.

21. Curran, *K2: The Story of the Savage Mountain*.

22. Fanny Bullock-Workman (1859–1925) was an American explorer and mountaineer, and long-time champion of women's rights. A formidable lady, she claimed to have reached the highest altitude ever by a female and vigorously defended the claim when it was challenged by Annie Smith Peck after the latter's climbs in the Andes. She was married to William Hunter Workman (1847–1912), a physician from Massachusetts. The pair wrote eight books on their various explorations, including a couple which include journeys in the Karakoram and were very popular in the USA, though some of their opinions on Asians and their culture are likely to make the modern reader wince. While many experts believe some of their claims to have been exaggerated, there is no doubt that they were persistent and accomplished explorers, and that Fanny was a pioneering female mountaineer. Some geographical claims were later proved false, though it is almost certainly the case that in these the Workmans made errors rather than deliberately false claims. It is less obvious that some of the heights claimed are error rather than exaggeration.

23. Edward Alexander Crowley (1875–1947) was born to Plymouth Brethren parents who attempted to instil devotion to their faith in him. After his father's death, his mother's attempts became ever more insistent, any suggestion of disobedience or of the boy seeking to enjoy himself with ordinary behaviour being severely chastised. The young Crowley was

frequently declared sinful and routinely called 'The Beast'. Perhaps not surprisingly the boy rebelled against the harsh regime, changing his name to Aleister, turning initially to eastern religions, then to 'magick' and the occult, and applying the soubriquet 'Great Beast 666' to himself, almost certainly as that was mentioned in the Revelation to St John and his parents' faith believed in the literal truth of the Bible. Crowley was an intelligent man and an extremely good chess player, and some of his enthusiasms, for yoga for instance, are entirely rational. But he is now known almost exclusively for his wilder beliefs, in Satanism, in ancient Egyptian gods, in drug use and, for the time, outrageous sexual ideas, which during his lifetime led to his being called the 'wickedest man in the world', a soubriquet Crowley seems to have enjoyed and which his enthusiasm for self-publicity certainly did nothing to dispel. The inclusion of his image on the cover of the Beatles' *Sgt Pepper's Lonely Hearts Club Band* led to the suggestion that Crowley was the original hippie, but that is at odds with his stated life theory of 'Do what thou wilt shall be the whole of the Law', which puts anarchic self-interest above the hippie creed of love, peace and worldwide brotherhood. In addition to the abilities noted above, Crowley was a gifted mountaineer (though, like Eckenstein, he was never a member of the Alpine Club, not surprisingly in view of his opinion of some of its members: 'various old fogeys who could not have climbed the simplest rocks in Cumberland or led across an easy Alpine pass, had been personally conducted by peasants up a few mountains and written themselves into fame'), his abilities in that field being significantly greater than his ability to conjure up the devil at the Black Masses he held. The quotes in the text are taken from his book *The Confessions of Aleister Crowley*. The book varies from the delightfully discursive to the difficult, and occasionally is so dense as to be downright unreadable, but the mountaineering sections are interesting.

24. In his book Crowley stated that 'thanks to the Alpine Club, there were no Englishmen of mountaineering ability and experience available', as a result of which he and Eckenstein chose Guy Knowles, a 22-year-old Cambridge student. It was a curious choice, as Crowley readily admitted that Knowles was 'far too young for this kind of work ... [and] knew practically nothing of mountains'. The reason for the choice seems, apparently, to have been that Knowles was willing to finance the trip. Crowley commented that he and Knowles paid the expenses of everyone except Eckenstein, but that seems to have been overstating his own contribution. Heinrich Pfannl and Victor Wesseley were Austrian, and among the best European climbers of the time. Pfannl was a judge, Wesseley a lawyer. Pfannl in particular was a fine climber, who accomplished some of the hardest climbs in the eastern Alps, often with Wesseley. Pfannl wrote two accounts of the expedition, both published in 1904: Dr H. Pfannl, 'Von meiner Reise zum K2 in den Bergen Baltistans', Mitteilungen der Geographischen Gesellschaft in Wien (1904, vol. 47), pp. 247–60; and Dr H. Pfannl, 'Eine Belagerung des Tschogo-Ri (K2) in der Mustaghkette des Hindu-kusch (8720m)', Keitschrift des Deutschen und Österreichischen Alpenvereins (1904, vol. XXXV), pp. 88–104. Dr Jules Jacot-Guillarmod, a Swiss doctor, also wrote a book on the expedition: J. Jacot-Guillarmod, *Six mois dans L'Himalaya, Le Karakorum et L'Hindu-Kush* (W. Sandoz, Neuchatel, not dated, but probably 1904). Some quotes in the text are from the Pfannl articles and Jacot-Guillarmod's book.

    Guy Knowles wrote notes on the expedition which were later collected, though never formally published. A bound copy of these, erroneously termed 'Diary of the K2 expedition 1902 by G.F.J. Knowles', is kept at the Alpine Club Library, London.

25. L. Baume, *Sivalaya: The 8000-metre peaks of the Himalaya* (Gastons-West Col, Goring, 1978).

26. Curran, *K2: The Story of the Savage Mountain*.

27. The apparent understanding of high-altitude illness illustrated by the diagnosis is in contrast to the relatively poor understanding of acclimatisation shown by Crowley, who wrote: 'To talk of acclimatization is to adopt the psychology of the man who trained his horse gradually to live on a single straw a day, and would have revolutionized our system of nutrition, if the balky brute had not been aggravating enough to die on his hands. If you want to acclimatize yourself to mountain conditions, you can go and live a bit higher than the hillmen of Tibet. If you do this for fifteen generations or so, your descendants will acquire a thorax like a beer barrel and a heart capable of doing three times the work it can at present. If you then get incarnated in your clan, you can lay siege to Chogo Ri with a reasonable prospect of success ... This programme is, however, hardly acceptable to Western minds, so little penetrated with Einstein's ideas that everything has to be done in a hurry. We may therefore leave "acclimatization" to the mentally defective heroes of the Everest expedition of 1921 and 1922.' He then went on to note that 'any kind of prolonged hardship gradually wears one down ... it is pitiful to have to insist on such obvious truths', before ending with yet another dig at a familiar target: 'Anyone on earth except a member of the English Alpine Club would take it to heart.'

28. Prince Luigi Amedeo Giuseppe Maria Ferdinando Francesco di Savoia-Aosta (1873–1933) was the grandson of Vittorio Emmanuele II, King of Italy, son of King Amedeo of Spain (though his father abdicated shortly after Luigi's birth), and held the title Duke of the Abruzzi, a region of Italy lying east of Rome and occupying what is now, more or less, the region of Abruzzo. Having an interest in and aptitude for both mountaineering and exploration, the Duke used his family's wealth and influence to aid a number of worthwhile expeditions across the planet. In 1897 he led an expedition which made the first ascent of Mount St Elias, a peak on the border of Yukon Territory and Alaska; the second highest peak in both Canada and the USA, it was not climbed again until 1946. In 1899 he organised an attempt on the North Pole, taking an expedition to Franz Josef Land aboard the *Stella Polare* ('*Pole Star*'), from where a team using dog sledges went north to 86° 34', establishing a new 'furthest north' record. Then in 1906 he led an expedition to the Rwenzori Mountains of central Africa, which climbed most of the range's highest peaks. The 1909 Karakoram expedition was the last of the Duke's major trips.

29. Vittorio Sella (1859–1943) had a genius for both framing a scene and isolating the exact mix of sun and shadow for illuminating it, qualities that have ensured he is now regarded as one of the finest of all mountain photographers. While this accolade is due in large part to his technical and artistic abilities, it was aided by the use of very large photographic plates, so large that they required considerable organisation and perseverance to get into position on the hill. Sella's major expeditions included the European Alps, Caucasus and Kangchenjunga, and all three of the Duke of the Abruzzi's mountain trips (i.e. Mount St Elias, Rwenzori and Karakoram). A superb book of Sella's images from his mountain trips is *Summit: Vittorio Sella, Mountaineer and Photographer: The Years 1879–1909* (Aperture Foundation, New York, 1999).

30. Filippo De Filippi (1869–1938) studied medicine but was something of a polymath, contributing a broad range of scientific studies to the Duke's three mountain expeditions. He was also author of the definitive histories of the expeditions. His book on the Karakoram trip, *Karakoram and Western Himalaya 1909* (Constable, London, 1912), includes a much-prized second volume of maps and panoramic photos by Vittorio Sella.

31. The word 'coolie' is now considered (correctly) to be derogatory. Not entirely surprised to find the word in the English translation of Filippi's book, the author read the relevant section of the original Italian and was surprised to find the same word used. Presumably the

Italians had copied it from the English, who, it is believed, had taken the name for a Gujerati tribe, the *Kuli*, to describe all native load-carriers, servants, etc.

32. The Duke had reached a point about 150m (500ft) below the summit. In 1957 the same ascent route was attempted by the Austrians Hermann Buhl and Kurt Diemberger. Retreating in poor weather from a lower point on the final ridge, Buhl walked on to a cornice which collapsed. His body has never been found. The following year a Japanese team followed the same route, two men (Fujihira and Hirai) reaching the summit. Chogolisa has two summits separated by a high ridge. The summit reached by the Japanese (7654m) is the lower of the two. The higher one (7665m) was climbed in 1975 by the Austrians Pressl and Ammerer.

33. Tom George Longstaff (1875–1964) was an English doctor, explorer and mountaineer, most famous for being the first person to reach a summit of over 7,000m. He also made important explorations and climbs in Tibet, Nepal, the Karakoram, Spitsbergen, Greenland and Baffin Island. His autobiography, *This is my Voyage* (John Murray, London, 1950), is a classic work of Alpine literature. Further details of his eastern Karakoram explorations are to be found in T.G. Longstaff, 'Glacier exploration in the eastern Karakoram', *Geographical Journal* (1910, vol. 35), pp. 622–58 and T.G. Longstaff, 'The Saltoro Pass', *Alpine Journal* (1911, vol. 25), pp. 485–8.

34. This exploration was carried out by a team led by Kenneth Mason (1887–1976), a Royal Engineer officer on the staff of the Survey of India. After his service in India Mason became Professor of Geography at Oxford University. His book *Abode of Snow* (Rupert Hart-Davis, London, 1955; reprinted by Diadem Books Ltd, 1987), is a classic on exploration and climbing in the Himalaya and Karakoram until the mid-1950s. The book also includes an account of Mason's Shaksgam trip.

35. Giotto Dainelli (1878–1968) was a respected geologist/geographer who had made several important journeys in East Africa and Asia.

36. Umberto Nobile (1885–1978) was an aeronautical engineer who designed the airship N–1 (Nobile 1). The craft had given the Norwegian polar explorer Roald Amundsen the idea of a flight over the North Pole and he brought both it and Nobile to Spitsbergen for a projected flight financed, in part, by the American Lincoln Ellsworth. The flight was a major success, the airship, renamed *Norge*, and its crew of 16 (including Amundsen, Ellsworth and Nobile) reaching the pole on 12 May 1926. The aftermath of the flight was controversial. With Mussolini's backing (the dictator asked Nobile to lecture to the 'Italian colonies' in the US), Nobile received the lion's share of post-flight publicity, claiming he was the mastermind behind the expedition and had piloted the craft, neither of which was correct. At a reception in Seattle Nobile wore a military uniform and gave the fascist salute, which embarrassed Amundsen, Ellsworth and the USA. On his return to Italy Nobile was greeted as a hero and promoted to general. The controversy over these antics has tended to mask the brilliance of the trip, which almost certainly resulted in the first human sight of the North Pole. For a more complete account of the *Norge* expedition, and a justification for why it involved the first sight of the pole, see R. Sale, *The Arctic: The Complete Story* (Francis Lincoln, 2008).

37. Nobile claimed that the Swedish pilot of the rescue plane had insisted on taking him back on the first flight so that he could organise the rescue of the remaining men. While it was true that the pilot had made that suggestion, it was foolish of Nobile to have agreed, and his later claim that he had not realised the implications rings somewhat hollow. In 1931 Nobile moved to the USSR and from there moved to the USA. He returned to Italy only in 1942. In 1945 he was formally cleared on all charges relating to the *Italia* crash, his rank was restored and he was given back pay dating from 1928. For a fuller account of the *Italia* expedition see Sale, *The Arctic: The Complete Story*

38. Aimone Roberto Margherita Maria Giuseppe Torino (1900–1948) was an Italian prince of the House of Savoy, the same royal line as the Duke of the Abruzzi. He inherited the title Duke of Spoleto in 1904, the duchy of the name being a medieval territory east of the Papal States. An officer in the Italian Navy, he was nominated as King of Croatia in 1941, though he declined to be crowned or to set foot in his 'state'. After the Second World War he left Italy for South America, dying in Buenos Aires in 1948. With Ardito Desio, he co-authored the book of the 1929 expedition, *La Spedizione Geografica Italiana Al Karakoram (1929–VII E.F.): Storia Del Viaggio E Risultati Ge* (Arti Grafiche Bertarelli, Milan, 1936). A more succinct account of the expedition (and one in English) was produced by the Duke alone, HRH the Prince Aimone of Savoia-Aosta, Duke of Spoleto, 'The Italian Expedition to the Karakorum in 1929', *Geographical Journal* (May 1930, vol. 75), pp. 385–401.

39. The Vissers produced a massive work in two volumes on their explorations, *Expedition in den Karakorum und die angrenzenden Gebiete in den Jahren 1922, 1925, 1929/30 und 1935*, vol. 1 (Brockhaus, Leipzig, 1935) and vol. 2 (Brill, Leiden, 1938). Volume 1 covers geography, ethnography and zoology, volume 2 covers glaciology. A more amenable work on their early trips, and in English rather than German, is *Among the Kara-Korum Glaciers in 1925* (Arnold, London, 1926), though this is a very rare book. The early trips are also covered in P.C. Vissers, 'Explorations in the Karakoram', *Geographical Journal* (1926, vol. 69), pp. 457–73.

40. Eric Earle Shipton (1907–1977) was born in Ceylon (now Sri Lanka), the son of a tea planter. Working as a coffee grower in Kenya, he climbed Nelion Peak on Mount Kenya in 1929 with Tilman. In 1931 he made the first ascent of Kamet with Frank Smythe, R.L. Holdsworth and the Sherpas Nima Dorje and Lewa, the highest summit to have been reached at that time. (The photograph taken of Holdsworth sitting on the summit shows him with a pipe firmly clenched in his teeth – perhaps it had been there throughout the climb. The photograph, and the fact that in Smythe's book of the expedition he refers to his colleagues only by their surnames, rather beautifully illustrates the Britain of the period.) Following Kamet, Shipton took part in all four of the British Everest expeditions of the 1930s, and led the 1951 Reconnaissance and the 1952 Cho Oyu expeditions. It was expected that he would be offered the leadership of the 1953 Everest expedition, but doubts were expressed about his suitability. Did he have the streak of ruthlessness inevitably needed to ensure success? It was a doubt that Shipton himself shared, and ultimately he was replaced by John Hunt. Though almost everyone now agrees that the change was necessary to maximise the chances of success, the manner of Shipton's replacement has been consistently criticised. Even Hunt thought it was poorly handled. After 1953 Shipton made several exploratory journeys to South America and travelled extensively. On one such trip, to Bhutan, he became ill. Back in Britain he was diagnosed with the cancer from which he died. Shipton wrote an account of the 1937 expedition, *Blank on the Map* (Hodder & Stoughton, London, 1938) – from which the quotations in the text are taken.

41. Harold William ('Bill') Tilman (1898–1977) was the son of a sugar trader. Commissioned in the Royal Artillery, Tilman fought in the First World War, receiving the Military Cross and bar. He also fought in the Second World War. Tilman climbed with Shipton in Africa, and was on the 1935 and 1938 Everest expeditions, leading that in 1938. He explored the Nanda Devi region with Shipton in 1934, and in 1936 led the small team of American and British climbers who made the first ascent of the peak (7816m), the highest summit reached until the French climbed Annapurna in 1950. As well as being a climber, Tilman was an enthusiastic ocean sailor. In 1977, at the age of 79, he accepted an invitation to join a team sailing to Smith Island in Antarctica to climb. The ship arrived in Rio de Janeiro, but disappeared on the subsequent journey to the Falkland Islands.

42. F.S. Smythe, *Kamet Conquered* (Gollancz, 1932).
43. H.W. Tilman, *The Ascent of Nanda Devi* (Cambridge University Press, 1937), p. 196.
44. The Chogori Glacier on K2's northern side is also called the K2 Glacier, which can cause confusion with the Godwin-Austen Glacier on the southern side which is also occasionally given that name.

Chapter 3

1. C.S. Houston and R.H. Bates, *Five Miles High* (Dodd, Mead & Co., New York, 1939). Quotes in the text relating to the 1938 climb are taken from this book.
2. The original party had been eight strong, but in China they were met by a man who claimed to be able to lead them to a mountain higher than Everest. Intrigued, the Americans agreed to go with him, only to discover that he had soon disappeared with their cash. At this point four members decided to go home, but Dick Burdsall, Art Emmons, Terris Moore and Jack Young persevered, and Burdsall and Moore reached the summit. This intriguing tale appears in a footnote in A.J. Kauffman and W.L. Putnam, *K2: the 1939 Tragedy* (The Mountaineers, Seattle, 1992).
3. Charles Snead Houston (1913–2009) was a physician and high-altitude physiologist, his book on the latter, *Going High: The Story of Man and Altitude* (C.S. Houston/American Alpine Club, 1980), is a fine treatise on the topic. Houston's father Oscar, a lawyer, believed in the educational advantages of travel, and on one trip to Chamonix the 12-year-old Charles became hooked on mountains and climbing, as did his father, the two later going on climbing trips together. While studying at Harvard, Houston joined the Mountaineering Club, other members, including Bradford Washburn, Terris Moore and Robert Bates, becoming lifelong friends and further fuelling ambitions for great climbs. In 1934 Houston led an expedition, which included his father, to Mount Foraker, summitting with two others. The climb caused a sensation in depression-hit America, Foraker being the fourth highest mountain in the USA, and made Houston's reputation as a mountaineer of note. The 1936 Nanda Devi expedition followed, then, in 1938, the first US expedition to K2. In late 1950 Houston was a member of the team, which included Oscar Houston and Bill Tilman, that made the first exploration of Everest's southern side. Charles Houston and Tilman reached the Khumbu Icefall, but were discouraged by what they saw, thinking a southern route up the mountain was not feasible. K2 in 1953 was Houston's last expedition. Later he was Director of the Peace Corps in India and a Professor of Medicine at the University of Vermont. For his work on high-altitude physiology he received many honours: though pleased about these, he was also astonishingly self-deprecating, noting 'you get old enough, you can get anything'. Those interested in Houston's long and interesting life should read the marvellous biography by Bernadette McDonald, *Brotherhood of the Rope* (The Mountaineers, Seattle, 2007).
4. There were numerous reports, complete with photographs of the glacier, for example in the *Independent* newspaper of 22 January 2010, and on the websites of both *Scientific American* and *National Geographic*. In Ladakh the glaciers which had provided water had retreated 10km and the snowline had risen 150m. Walls were constructed to divert water into a shaded area where embankments slowed the flow as it ran into a walled reservoir. During the winter the water froze, creating an artificial glacier which fed the reservoir. The process was a complete success.
5. Fritz Wiessner's account of the 1939 expedition is in his book, *K2: Tragödien unde Sieg am zweithöchsten Berg der Erde* (Rudolf Rother, Munich, 1955). The book covers early explorations of/attempts on K2, as well as the 1953 American and 1954 Italian expeditions. The book has never been translated into English, but the bulk of the account of the 1939 expedition was translated and published in F.H. Wiessner, 'The K2 Expedition of 1939',

Appalachia (1956, vol. 122), pp. 60–73. Wiessner also co-wrote an article, C. Cranmer and F. Wiessner, 'The Second American Expedition to K2', *American Alpine Journal* (1940, vol. 4), pp. 9–19. There are two recent accounts of the expedition. One, using previously unpublished diary entries from Jack Durrance, as well as Wiessner's accounts and his expedition diary, and material from other sources is Kauffman and Putnam, *K2: the 1939 Tragedy*. Kauffman is a well-known American climber who in 1958 reached the summit of Gasherbrum I with Pete Schoening on the mountain's first ascent. Wiessner's report to the American Alpine Club is an Appendix to the Kauffman/Putnam book. The other source is J. Jordan, *The Last Man on the Mountain* (W.W. Norton & Co., New York, 2010). Nominally a biography of Dudley Wolfe, the book is mostly about the K2 expedition with only a couple of short chapters on Wolfe's early life. Jordan's book is based on extensive research, though it also uses the device of imagined thoughts/dialogue for dramatic effect. This, together with a smattering of factual errors on climbing history and techniques, will likely irritate the climbing-knowledgeable reader. Jordan writes that climbers 'rappelled each other back down the rock face', and claims at one point that falling when descending is worse than when ascending, as on the way up you 'merely fall into the slope at your face' rather than falling 'into the abyss at your feet'! A reading of the two books gives an immediate indication of where the sympathies of the authors lie. The account of climbers Kauffman and Putnam tends to the view that Wolfe was something of a liability and that unfortunate decisions by the real climbers on the mountain led to his demise, while reporter Jordan is a good deal more sympathetic towards Wolfe and implies that he was let down by his team mates, though she stops short of pointing a finger at anyone in particular. While Wiessner comes out worst, no one (apart from Dudley Wolfe) emerges from her book well, which is probably not so far from the truth. Jordan's book is particularly good on the aftermath of the climb and the later lives of the expedition members. Quotes and comments in the text are from these sources.

6. Fritz Wiessner (1900–1988) was born in Dresden but moved to the USA in 1929. The move was supposed to have been merely a visit – Wiessner had started a chain of pharmacies in Dresden, and then moved into import-export, making ski waxes and polishes which he sent to the US in exchange for resins coming the other way. But temporary became permanent and Wiessner took US citizenship in 1935. Short (1.68m/5ft 6ins) and stocky, Wiessner was an outstanding rock climber, climbing routes in the early 1920s that were significantly harder than most of his contemporaries attempted, both in the eastern Alps and in the Dolomites. His 1925 routes on the South-East Face of the Fleischbank in the Tyrol and of the North Face of the Furchetta in the Dolomites were considered to be among the hardest rock climbs in the world at the time. After arriving in the US he made an immediate impact on the standard of rock climbing with a long list of hard climbs which included the first free ascent of the Devil's Tower in Wyoming, and the ascent of Mount Waddington (with Bill House). In 1932 Wiessner was a member of the first German expedition to Nanga Parbat, his only Himalayan expedition before K2.

7. Dudley Francis Wolfe (1896–1939) was the son of a rich British coffee merchant of eastern European Jewish extraction and the daughter of a US precious metals baron. Academically poor, though good at sport, Wolfe left college in an attempt to fight in the First World War; turned down by the US Army because of poor eyesight, he spent some time as an ambulance driver, a job which took him close to the horrors of the front line, and which he carried out with distinction, before joining the French Foreign Legion, although he arrived at the front line too late to engage in fighting. Despite that, his war service was honoured by both the US and France, and he returned home highly decorated. Extremely wealthy, Wolfe's life in the US has frequently been described as mirroring that of the protagonist in F. Scott Fitzgerald's *The Great Gatsby*. Wolfe married late, to Alice Damrosch, and the pair were

going through the divorce process when Wiessner offered him the chance to go to K2. However, Wolfe and Alice remained very fond of each other and Jack Durrance claimed that Wolfe's decision to join the expedition was an attempt to impress her. However, Wolfe also had a streak of recklessness which saw him race large power-boats, so a taste for pure adventure cannot be ruled out as a motive. As well as the power-boats, Wolfe was also the owner of a number of fast sailing vessels which won several important races. He was a capable skier and a relatively experienced mountaineer. But he was heavy and clumsy, which, combined with his poor eyesight, meant that on the climbs he undertook he was always guided, the guides having to occasionally do more than the usual amount of work to get their client to the top. He did, though, have a good sense of humour and was usually cheerful, which made him an excellent companion. He was also very strong and determined, qualities which became apparent on K2. Jennifer Jordan's book, *The Last Man on the Mountain*, though mostly concerned with the 1939 K2 expedition, does have early biographical chapters. In 2002 Jordan, with fellow American Jeff Rhoades, discovered the remains of Dudley Wolfe on the glacier near Base Camp.

8. Neither HAPE nor celiac sprue is associated with fever as neither is infectious in origin. As Cranmer was feverish, it is highly probable that he was suffering from a combination of a locally contracted infectious gastroenteritis as well as a problem that had the potential to be lethal. Given the symptoms, HAPE is much more likely to have been the latter as Cranmer showed none of the more normal precursor symptoms of celiac sprue prior to his illness. Although celiac sprue is associated with diarrhoea, the latter is usually mild and/or intermittent, which does not fit well with the frequent and explosive diarrhoea exhibited by Cranmer, that being much more indicative of severe gastroenteritis. The author is indebted to Dr George Rodway for assistance with this Note. For a fuller analysis of the development of an understanding of high-altitude physiology and the various forms and symptoms of mountain sickness – high-altitude pulmonary oedema (HAPE) and high-altitude cerebral oedema (HACE) – and other problems faced by climbers at altitude, see Sale and Rodway, *Everest and Conquest in the Himalaya*.

9. While received opinion has it that Wolfe was willing to be the expedition's cash cow in exchange for his position on the trip (as well as footing far more than a fair share of expedition expenses, Wolfe also upgraded the entire team to first class on the ship to India, which he chose to do willingly), in her book Jennifer Jordan sets down compelling evidence that by the time he had reached the mountain Wolfe was fed up with his role as expedition cashbox, for instance taking care to ensure that none of the photographs he was taking on his very expensive cameras were to be available to other members of the team post-expedition. But, of course, once the Baltoro was reached Wolfe's largesse was much less required – Wiessner had his expedition in place. But to be fair, Wolfe could also afford to be parsimonious – he was on his mountain and there was nothing to spend money on.

10. Jennifer Jordan claims this statement was also made by Wiessner during the first evening after he had arrived at Base Camp, her source being a letter that Trench wrote to Dudley Wolfe's brother. If that is true, then the implication is that Wiessner knew that abandoning Wolfe would likely lead to his death and may have been the source of Cromwell's accusation of murder. However, the letter was written in May 1940, many months after Wiessner's use of the phrase in New York. Given Trench's antipathy to Wiessner, it is not beyond the bounds of possibility that Trench's recall of an earlier, identical, comment was a convenient, rather than clear, memory.

11. After the expedition had returned to the US there was a rumour that the team had been selected by Houston's golden retriever Honey. Bernadette McDonald's biography of Houston suggests that there was a nugget of truth, albeit a very small nugget, in the story.

Candidates for membership were invited to the leader's house. The story ran that if Honey didn't like them, they were rejected, but Houston notes that Honey didn't like the people he didn't like and so too much should not be read into it. Houston notes that he was much more reliant on his wife's view than his dog's. Those rejected included Barry Bishop and Willi Unsoeld, both of whom were to summit Everest when the US sent its first team to the mountain in 1963, Unsoeld partnering Tom Hornbein on the first ascent of the West Ridge, still regarded as one of the finest climbs on the peak. Fritz Wiessner was apparently not even considered as a member, but, of course, by then he would have been 53 years old.

12. Peter Schoening (1927–2004), a chemical engineer, was one of the foremost American climbers of the latter half of the twentieth century. As well as being a member of the 1953 K2 expedition, Schoening was a member of the successful American Gasherbrum I expedition in 1958, reaching the summit with Andy Kauffman. In 1966 he was a member of the team which made the first ascent of Vinson, the highest mountain on Antarctica (and therefore one of the 'Seven Summits'). In 1996, at the age of 68, he went to Everest with his nephew Klev. Health problems prevented him from going high and he therefore avoided the fatal storm which killed a total of eight people.

13. The expedition was self-financing but sought, and was given, financial support as well as food and equipment, by a number of companies, all of whom were acknowledged in the expedition book. The National Broadcasting Company (NBC) offered a contract which gave money in exchange for a film. When Houston arrived in the company president's office to sign the contract he noted that it was for $50,000, which exceeded the total budget of the expedition. The contract was already signed by the president. Houston thanked him for his generosity, noting the huge amount. The president, taken aback, commented that it should actually have said $5,000, not $50,000. In any Hollywood movie, the president would have allowed the incorrect amount to stand, Houston's team would therefore have been able to complete the climb, the summit would have been reached and the right person would have got the girl. In this case, the president made a phone call to his lawyer and the amount was changed. (To be fair to NBC, they did agree they would pay the higher amount if Houston insisted, but to be equally fair that did place Houston in an unenviable position, which almost guaranteed he would not. And he didn't.)

14. C.S. Houston and R.H. Bates, *K2: The Savage Mountain* (McGraw-Hill, New York, 1954). The book title was the first use of the epithet for the mountain. Too good to avoid, it has featured in the title of many books published on the mountain since (including this one!), occasionally chosen by publishers to the despair of authors.

15. On Everest the non-stop questioning over whether Hillary or Tenzing had been first to the summit eventually overcame the expedition's endeavours to maintain that two men connected by a rope create one team not two individuals, that idea not in any way satisfying an insistent press. Perhaps a more relevant example was the 1957 Broad Peak expedition when four Austrians, Marcus Schmuck, Fritz Wintersteller, Hermann Buhl and Kurt Diemberger, made an important advance in the climbing of 8000m peaks by making the first ascent without either porters on the hill or supplementary oxygen. The summit was reached by all four on the same day, but the first two named arrived first, followed an hour or so later by Diemberger, and some time after by Buhl. The four agreed that this order would not be broadcast, an announcement noting only that the four had reached the summit on the same day. The decision failed to outlast the first days at Base Camp after the climb, though exactly who broke the agreement is still argued – see R. Sale, *Broad Peak* (Carreg, Ross-on-Wye, 2004).

16. During their descent of the mountain the Americans looked for signs of Gilkey and at one point saw a broken ice axe jammed in rocks and a tangle of ropes. After the expedition there

was speculation that Gilkey may have realised what had happened and, fearing for his companions' safety and realising they might all die if the attempt to rescue him continued, had removed the anchoring ice axes and allowed himself to slide off the mountain. Houston never took this story seriously, claiming that he had administered a morphine injection just before the accident so Gilkey was only semi-conscious and would not have been able to carry out such a manoeuvre. However, in describing the aftermath of the accident Bates notes that when Molenaar reached him, Gilkey gave him his ice axe to aid the arranging of his belay. There were also the shouts from Gilkey when the men were at Camp VII. These events certainly imply that Gilkey was rather more than semi-conscious, though whether he was capable of untangling himself from the rope cradle strung around the tent that encased him and heaving two axes out of the ice is another matter. The memorial raised to Art Gilkey has, over the years, acquired many more memorial plates as the death toll on the mountain has increased.

In 1985 the head of an ice axe was found close to the mountain base, probably that from the broken shaft seen by the descending climbers in 1953. Then, in 1993 Gilkey's remains were found near Base Camp. The bones were gathered and sent back to the USA for burial in the family plot.

17. It is interesting to speculate what would have happened had the Americans not been delayed in Camp VIII by the prolonged storm (and then Gilkey's condition forced a retreat). In 1953 Everest had been climbed by a large team using supplementary oxygen. Because the Americans failed to reach the summit, the Italians in 1954 replicated the British method and, by succeeding, gave it a seal of approval, which meant that Kangchenjunga (1955), Lhotse (1956), Makalu (1955), Manaslu (1956) and Gasherbrum I (1958) used the same blueprint. Though Cho Oyu was climbed by a small team with a limited number of porters and no supplementary oxygen in 1954 it was seen as a one-off, achieved because the peak, though high, was technically unchallenging. Had the Americans succeeded in 1953 on K2, perhaps the history of the first ascents on the remaining 8000m peaks might have been very different.

Chapter 4

1. Ardito Desio (1897–2001) is one of a small band of people who have lived in three centuries. He was 104 years and 8 months old when he died in December 2001. A geologist by training, Desio held the prestigious professorial chair of geology at Milan University (in part as Emeritus Professor) until 1972. During his long and distinguished career as a geologist he was involved in many expeditions to Africa and Asia, as well as making important advances in the understanding of the Alps and Apennines. During his life he received many honours, both academic and civil. These included the Patron's Medal of the Royal Geographical Society and the Knight Grand Cross of the Italian Republic, the country's highest honour. Prior to the 1954 K2 expedition, Desio had co-led the 1929 Spoleto expedition during which he had attempted, and very nearly succeeded, in circumnavigating the mountain. Facially, Desio resembled the busts of Roman emperors, and he behaved accordingly, certainly as far as the climbers of 1954 were concerned. They called him *il Ducetto*, the little Duce (little Mussolini), which was hardly a flattering nickname. At the time of the 1954 expedition Desio was 57, but then, and later, he defied his age in remarkable fashion. In 1961 he was the first Italian to reach the South Pole, though he flew in rather than trekking, and he was still active at a scientific station near Everest's southern base camp in his 90s. He wrote the official book on the 1954 expedition, *Ascent of K2* (Elek Books, London, 1955). Two things about this English translation of the Italian original are interesting. First, the title was not a direct translation of the Italian *La Conquista del K2*, the publisher having presumably taken

heed of John Hunt's refusal to use the word conquest in the title of his book of the 1953 Everest expedition, pointing out (correctly) that man cannot conquer mountains, merely ascend them; and secondly the authorship is given as *Prof Ardito Desio* rather than the plain *Ardito Desio* of the Italian, presumably as an act of deference by the English publisher. Quotations in the text attributed to Desio or those he quotes are taken from this book.

2. Riccardo Cassin (1909–2009) was the leading Italian climber of the inter-war years, and arguably the foremost from any nation during that period. He led several thousand first ascents, including the Walker Spur on the Grandes Jorasses and the North-East Face of the Piz Badile, two of the 'six great north faces' of the Alps. Cassin had also been intent on adding another of the six, the north wall of the Eiger, but arrived to discover it had just been climbed. After 1954 Cassin led several expeditions to the greater ranges, including that which made the first ascent of Gasherbrum IV in 1958. In 1961 he led the team which made the first ascent of the 'Cassin Ridge' on Mount McKinley (Denali). In 1975 he led an unsuccessful attempt on the formidable South Face of Lhotse. His autobiography, *50 Years of Alpinism* (Diadem Books, London/The Mountaineers, Seattle, 1981), is one of the great mountain books. The quotes in the text are taken from it.

3. Walter Bonatti (1930–). Though only 24 at the time of the K2 expedition, Bonatti was already considered one of the finest climbers of the time, with a string of audacious ascents to his name, including the fourth ascent of the Walker Spur on the Grandes Jorasses and the third ascent of the North-East Face of the Piz Badile, each with limited equipment and in poor conditions, winter ascents of the Tre Cime di Laveredo, and the first ascent of the East Face of the Grand Capucin. After K2 he surpassed these climbs with a solo ascent of the South-West (Bonatti) Pillar of the Dru and a solo winter ascent of a new route on the North Face of the Matterhorn. He was also in the summit team which made the first ascent of Gasherbrum IV. There were other great alpine climbs as well, but also some which ended in tragedy, for which he received unwarranted bad publicity. Following the Matterhorn solo in 1965 he gave up climbing, in part because of the bitterness the aftermath of the 1954 K2 climb had provoked. He then became a photojournalist, carrying out a fine series of wilderness trips around the world. His account of the K2 summit climb was published in the first part of his climbing autobiography, *On the Heights* (Rupert Hart-Davis, London, 1964), and reprised in a comprehensive full climbing biography, *The Mountains of My Life* (The Modern Library, New York, 2001). It is these books which were used for the quotations in the text. Bonatti also wrote *K2: La Verità 1954–2004* (Baldini Castoldi Dalai, Milan, 2005), which dealt with the climb and its aftermath. This has not been translated into English, but the same ground, and new material bringing the story up to date, is covered in R. Marshall, *K2: Lies and Treachery* (Carreg, Ross-on-Wye, 2009).

4. Achille Compagnoni (1914–2009). Compared to the standard set by Bonatti, Compagnoni was a climber of modest ability with few first ascents. He was, though, a very competent mountain guide. Based at Cervinia, he had climbed both the Matterhorn and Monte Rosa over a hundred times. He was also a ski instructor and had been on many mountain rescues. After the K2 expedition, Compagnoni clearly revelled in the fame the summit had brought him. He received many honours including the Knight Grand Cross of the Italian Republic. The honours are proudly displayed in a book, *Conquista Italiana: Tra Storia e Memoria* (Bolis Edizione, Azzano San Paolo, 2004). Neither that nor two earlier books, *Uomini sul K2* (Veronelli Editore, Milan, 1958) and *Il Tricolore sul K2* (Mondadori, 1965), have been published in English. None adds greatly to the account of the summit climb that Compagnoni wrote for Desio's expedition book.

5. Lino Lacedelli (1925–2009) was a native of Cortina d'Ampezzo (he lived all his life in the same house), where he opened the *K2 Sports* shop after the 1954 expedition. He was

renowned in his pre-K2 career for fast ascents of difficult routes and for several important first ascents. He had achieved wider fame with a repeat of Bonatti's ascent on the Grand Capucin (see Note 6 below). After the return of the K2 expedition to Italy Lacedelli mostly remained silent until, in 2004, he published his own account in a book co-written with author/mountaineer Giovanni Cenacchi (1963–2006). The book was subsequently published in English as *K2: The Price of Conquest* (Carreg, Ross-on-Wye, 2006). The quotes in the text are from this book.

6. Lacedelli had achieved wide fame after a claimed repeat of Bonatti's route on the East Face of the Grand Capucin in eighteen hours (with Bibi Ghedina); Bonatti and Luciano Ghigo had taken four days on the first ascent. The French pair of Paragot and Bérardini made the third ascent in three days. Paragot, a very strong climber, wrote an account of that climb many years later in which he echoed what he had considered at the time, that the Lacedelli/Ghedina claim was false. Not only was their description of the upper part of the route wildly inaccurate, but the Italians had claimed to have abseiled down the ascent route and the French found no evidence of the abseil pitons or loops that such a descent would have required. Paragot ended his account by stating 'these guys [Lacedelli and Ghedina] are sellers of smoke – they never reached the top. They started up the Capucin, no doubt, but they sure didn't finish it' – see R. Paragot and L. Bérardini, *Vingt Ans de Cordée* (Flammarion, Paris, 1974).

7. Desio's account of the final days of the climb necessarily draws on those of the climbers, in particular that of Compagnoni. Of the climb by Abram, Bonatti, Gallotti and Rey from Camp VII to Camp VIII, Desio says they were carrying 'a tent and other camping equipment as well as two oxygen-masks complete with cylinders'. Later he notes that 'the two oxygen masks had been left half-way between Camps VII and VIII'. It was these 'oxygen masks' that Desio says Bonatti and Gallotti retrieved on 30 July. To be fair to Desio, the translator of the Italian original into English renders 'due respiratori ad ossigno completi' as 'two oxygen masks complete with oxygen cylinders' and 'due respiratori ad ossigno' as 'two oxygen masks'. However, the Italian original certainly does imply that the oxygen masks as well as the oxygen cylinders (the complete system) were left between Camps VII and VIII. It also needs to be pointed out that there is more information on the Bonatti/Mahdi climb in the English translation than there is in the Italian original, so extra information must have been sought and obtained.

8. After the publication of Lacedelli's book at the behest of Robert Marshall (see Note 13 below), Bonatti marked a copy where his own memory of events differed from Lacedelli's. Those marked comments have been translated into English in a copy in the author's possession and have been used to add Bonatti's comments in parenthesis.

9. This was the Colle di Bottiglia – Bottleneck – which had been seen as the most probable route to the upper reaches of the mountain, but which had been found to be too treacherous to climb in the morning.

10. The English translation in Bonatti's book *On the Heights* has the conversation as – 'Have you the oxygen?' 'Yes.' 'Good! Then leave it there and come up at once!' 'I can't! Mahdi can't make it.' But the translation is incorrect. As pointed out in both *The Mountains of My Life* and in Marshall, *K2: Lies and Treachery*, *scendete* ('go down') was translated as though it were *ascendete* ('come up'). Thus, instead of Bonatti appearing to ignore a request to reach the safety of Camp IX, Lacedelli was actually telling him to go back to Camp VIII.

11. A good idea of the effect of the successful expedition on the Italian populace and of the range of companies that associated themselves and their products with K2 can be obtained from *K2: millenovecentoconquantaquattro*, published by the CAI's Museo Nazionale della Montagna 'Ducca degli Abruzzi', Turin, in 1994 to coincide with the 40th anniversary of the ascent.

12. *Life* magazine, 11 October 1954. The magazine, first published in 1936, was the market leader for several decades selling, at its peak, over 10 million copies weekly.
13. The conclusions of the inquiry are set down in Marshall, *K2: Lies and Treachery*. Robert Marshall, who sadly died in early 2011, was an Australian surgeon who, though not a mountaineer, became interested in Bonatti's continuing quest to have the full facts of the K2 summit climb brought to light. Marshall therefore taught himself Italian so as to be able to read all the relevant material in the original language. He also corresponded with Bonatti. As a consequence of the latter relationship, Marshall translated *The Mountains of My Life* into English, as well as adding a commentary of his own. After the production of the final report into the CAI's inquiry into the K2 affair, he wrote his own book which drew together all aspects of the story.
14. When the present author asked Cenacchi why Lacedelli had made this comment, given the free-flow nature of the system, the response was simply a restatement of the erroneous idea that increased breathing rate depleted the oxygen more quickly. Before the matter could be pursued, Cenacchi sadly died. An attempt to ask Lacedelli the same question during an interview in Cortina failed when the translator helping with the interview (the author's spoken Italian being poor, Lacedelli's English non-existent) declined to put the question to the climber.
15. In Compagnoni's account in Desio's book he says the two men began the climb to the oxygen sets at 5am and that after reaching them, the climb proper started at 6.15am. However, in a television interview which he and Lacedelli gave in July 1984 to celebrate the 30th anniversary of their climb, in answer to a question about the time the two started, Compagnoni produced a watch and said that it was the watch he used on the day and that they had started at 4am, perhaps earlier. The interviewer says 'So then you left the tent at about four in the morning?' Compagnoni replies 'Well, four, half past four,' and Lacedelli adds 'About four, half past four'. In his book, Lacedelli says he made a mistake when agreeing with Compagnoni over the time (see transcript of the interview in Marshall, *K2: Lies and Treachery*).
16. N. Giglio, 'After Ten Years the Truth about K2: How Bonatti tried to precede Compagnoni and Lacedelli', *People's New Sunday Gazette*, Turin, 26 July 1964, and 'Ten Years of K2 celebrated at the home of Compagnoni', *People's New Sunday Gazette*, Turin, 1 August 1964.
17. Bonatti's case against Giglio was actually one of four court cases resulting from the expedition. Compagnoni sued the CAI and the company which made the film of the expedition for compensation for the loss of finger joints which, he claimed, resulted from taking photographs at the summit – he lost; Desio sued the expedition photographer Mario Fantin, claiming he had taken some film, but was forced to withdraw his action when one of the expedition scientists admitted taking it; and the CAI sued Desio over money apparently missing from the expedition's coffers – an understanding was reached out of court.
18. *The Mountain World* was an annual publication in Switzerland. Begun in the early 1950s, it lasted only until the 1960s.
19. *La Repubblica*, Italy's second biggest-selling newspaper, published an article on 27 June 2001 in which it accused *La Grande Italia* of hypocrisy over the Bonatti affair. In August of the same year two articles supporting Bonatti and his version of events were published in the French newspaper *Le Monde* and simultaneously in *La Stampa*, another highly influential Italian newspaper. In these, author Charles Buffet actually maintained that the events leading to the enforced bivouac of Bonatti and Mahdi amounted to 'attempted homicide'. However, such articles were an exception.
20. Exactly why Lacedelli decided to wait fifty years before publishing his account is a difficult question to answer. When asked by co-author Cenacchi, Lacedelli implies that he waited as

long as possible to avoid any suggestion that he was acting out of self-interest and merely settling old scores. That seems a wholly inadequate reason for such a long silence. In his book Lacedelli claims it was Bonatti who massaged his fingers in Camp VIII and may therefore have been instrumental in saving them. That being the case, fifty years is a long time to wait to say thank you when you are aware of, and can correct in an instant, a grave injustice. During a meeting with Lacedelli in Cortina, the present author was struck by what a simple (in the sense of unsophisticated, innocent, rather than intellectually lacking), somewhat unworldly, man he was. It seemed possible that while he had understood that Bonatti had been wronged, he did not quite understand by just how much and what it had done to him. But it is also possible that Lacedelli understood very well what had happened to Bonatti and was very much afraid that Desio would do exactly the same to him if he spoke out against the official line. It is clear from his book that while Lacedelli disliked Desio, he was also afraid of him. Desio died in December 2001. Lacedelli's book was published in July 2004. The time between the two events, more than two years, seems long, but to those familiar with the publishing world it is not, particularly if the book was ready but was held back for a few months awaiting the 50th anniversary. It is even credible that Lacedelli took up his pen (or, as the book was based on interviews, picked up the phone), on hearing the news of Desio's death.

21. Club Alpino Italiano, *K2: Una Storia Finita* (Priuli & Verlucca, Turin, 2007). The main findings of this book, including the *tre saggi* report, are also reproduced in Marshall, *K2: Lies and Treachery.*
22. Interview by John Crace, *Guardian* newspaper, 30 July 2010.
23. Private conversation, Marshall–Sale, London, 2009.

Chapter 5
1. See M. Isserman and S. Weaver, *Fallen Giants* (Yale University Press, New Haven, 2008). The reference to Houston's 1958 idea is in Note 71 on p. 318.
2. For details of the discovery, exploration and ascent history of the fourteen 8000m peaks, see R. Sale and J. Cleare, *On Top of the World* (HarperCollins, London, 2000).
3. J. Hackett and R. Conrad, *Climb to Glory: the Adventures of Bill Hackett* (Beaverton, 2003). See also L. Greissl, 'K2 – Der König des Karakorum', *Keitschrift des Deutschen und Österreichischen Alpenvereins* (1961, vol. 86), pp. 127–34, and D. Bohn, 'K2: Giant of the Karakoram', *AAJ* (1961, vol. 12, no. 1), pp. 263–7.
4. When the Baltoro was opened again, albeit in a limited way, two elder statesmen of American climbing, Bob Bates, who had been on the 1938 and 1953 Houston expeditions, and Adams Carter, who had been on the 1936 Nanda Devi expedition, both now in their sixties, trekked to K2 with their wives in 1974 and carried out a photographic reconnaissance, hampered by bad weather, of the projected North-West Ridge route. Louis Baume, in his book *Sivalaya: The 8000-metre peaks of the Himalaya*, also states that the Pakistani government gave permission for a Polish team to make an attempt on K2 in 1974, but the Poles had been unable to organise an expedition in time. That is not surprising as the decision to allow teams into the Baltoro was taken late, and few climbing expeditions took place that year.
5. In his autobiography, co-written with Dorothy Bullitt, *Addicted to Danger* (Pocket Books, New York, 1998), Jim Wickwire says that it was Jim Whittaker's inclusion that allowed the Americans to obtain permission for K2. Whittaker was a personal friend of Ted and Robert Kennedy, having climbed with the latter and been a pall-bearer at his funeral. Whittaker approached Ted Kennedy, who approached the Pakistani government. In his 'Prelude' to Rick Ridgeway's book on the 1978 expedition, *The Last Step: The American Ascent of K2* (The Mountaineers, Seattle, 1980), Whittaker says he asked Kennedy to help with

permission in 1978 after a formal application had been rejected because the British had already received permission.

6. Galen Rowell (1940–2002) was a climber and wilderness photographer. His superb photography won several awards, including the Ansel Adams, and appeared in numerous magazines including *National Geographic*. His book on the 1975 expedition, *In the Throne Room of the Mountain Gods* (Sierra Club Books, San Francisco, 1977), set new standards in expedition books. Those on early expeditions (including the first ascents of the 8000m peaks) almost exclusively noted the general bonhomie of the team, and emphasised the collective spirit which had resulted in success. British climber Chris Bonington, in his books on the Annapurna South Face and Everest South-West Face expeditions, included episodes such as what it was like to suffer chronic diarrhoea while on a fixed rope, which had never been written about before. Bonington also occasionally mentioned team friction, but not in the detail that Rowell gave in his book. The book can therefore be seen as a ground-breaking work of expedition realism. Rowell was killed, together with his wife and two pilots, when a light aircraft crashed during a return flight from an Alaskan photographic trip. Quotes in the book are taken from Rowell's book, and also from the Wickwire/Bullitt book, *Addicted to Danger*.

7. In *Addicted to Danger* Wickwire says that he and Lou Whittaker were told at Base Camp by Jim Whittaker that they would be the first team to attempt the summit, giving some credence to the suggestion, even if Base Camp was far from Seattle. Certainly, such a comment from the expedition leader would have affected the way the pair saw the climb.

8. The team included Leszek Cichy (see Note 18); Andrzej Czok, who, with Jerzy Kukuczka made the first ascent of Everest's North Pillar in 1980, and the first winter ascent of Dhaulagiri in 1985, before being killed on Kangchenjunga in 1986; and Wojciech Kurtyka, whose ascent of the West Face of Gasherbrum IV with Robert Schauer in 1985 is considered one of the greatest climbs of the twentieth century. Janusz Kurczab wrote an article on the climb, 'Polska wyprawa na K2' for the Polish magazine *Taternik* (1977, no. 2), pp. 54–63. Eugeniusz Chrobak wrote an article on the summit climb, '15 sierpinia' ('15 August') in the same magazine. Later Kurczab also wrote a book on the expedition, *K02 8611m: Ostana Bariera* (Wydawnictwo 'Sport i Turystyka', Warsaw, 1980), in Polish, not translated into English. However, the chief source of information for the expedition is an article by Janusz Onyszkiewicz and Eugeniusz Chrobak, 'The Polish K2 expedition', *Mountain* (July/August 1977, vol. 56), pp. 16–21. As a young man, Onyszkiewicz was a gifted mathematician as well as a climber. He was a leading spokesman for Solidarity in the years of anti-communism, being imprisoned before the strength of the movement led to the fall of the pro-Soviet government in 1989 and the election of Lech Walesa. In later Polish governments he was twice defence minister. Later he was elected as a Member of the European Parliament, becoming its vice-president in 2004. He married the English climber Alison Chadwick. The two of them, together with Wanda Rutkiewicz and Krzysztof Zdzitowiecki, made the first ascent of Gasherbrum III, the highest non-8000m peak in the world (and therefore, at 7952m, the world's fifteenth highest mountain). Chadwick was killed on Annapurna I in 1978. Chrobak was one of five Poles who died on Everest in 1989 when an avalanche swept them away. Another victim was Zygmunt Andrzej Heinrich, who was also on K2 in 1976. Chrobak, who had summitted Everest three days before, survived the avalanche, but died of his injuries.

9. The official account of the Japanese expedition is in a book published by the Japanese Mountaineering Association, *K2, 8611m: At the end of the White Glacier* (Kôdan-sha, Tokyo, 1978). It is in Japanese, but with a (very concise) English account of the climb. The excellent

colour photographs have captions in both Japanese and English. There are also accounts by members of the expedition, the best of which is by deputy leader Isao Shinkai, *K2: The Mountain of my Heart* (Soshisha-shuppan, Tokyo, 1978), which has some exquisite black and white photographs. Shinkai's book is in Japanese only. Brief details of the expedition are given in a note by Ichiro Yoshizawa of the AAC and Japanese Alpine Club in *AAJ* (1978, vol. 21), pp. 614–16.

10. Sir Christian Bonington (1934–), a graduate of Sandhurst Military College and a commissioned officer in the British Army, initially came to prominence in the climbing world as a forceful rock climber. In 1958 he was part of the team which made the first British ascent of the South-West (Bonatti) Pillar on the Dru. In 1960 he was a member of a Joint British-Indian-Nepalese Services Expedition to Annapurna II (7937m), reaching the summit with Dick Grant. In 1961 he was part of the team which made the first ascent of the Central Pillar of Freney. The following year he made the first British ascent of the Eiger's North Face with Ian Clough and reached the summit of Nuptse (7,861m) as part of the British expedition. Bonington's fame, particularly among the general public, rests largely on his ability to raise finance for, and to organise, expeditions, his skills as a communicator, and his understanding of what fired PR companies and the media, allowing him to raise the financial backing for a series of impressive expeditions. He was also shrewd in picking expedition members, which, together with his climbing ability – often overlooked by those reviewing his achievements: at his peak Bonington was a superb climber, which enabled him to command respect from the members of his teams – meant his expeditions usually went without a hitch, though his occasional bouts of vacillation made for some rather more traumatic episodes. After a series of largely successful expeditions, Bonington was knighted in 1996. The quotes in the text are taken from his account of the K2 climb in his book *The Everest Years: A Climber's Life* (Hodder & Stoughton, London, 1986). Other quotes are taken from accounts by others on the expedition: Doug Scott, *Himalayan Climber* (Diadem, London, 1992) and Joe Tasker, *Savage Arena* (Methuen, London, 1982).

11. In *Himalayan Climber*, Scott says that some years after the accident Jim Duff told him that on the trek-in to K2 Nick Estcourt had told Duff that he had had a dream in which he saw Scott looking among ice blocks for his body.

12. Ridgeway wrote a book about the expedition, *The Last Step: The American Ascent of K2*. Quotes in the text are taken from this. Quotes are also taken from Jim Wickwire's biography, written with Dorothy Bullitt, *Addicted to Danger*.

13. Reinhold Messner (1944–) was born in Bressanone, Italy. He is an Italian national, but derives from the ethnically German South Tyrol. His early climbs included a new route on the North Wall of the Eiger with his younger brother Günther, Toni Hiebeler and Fritz Maschke. The climb was one reason why the two brothers were chosen for the 1970 German Nanga Parbat expedition. The Germans climbed the huge Rupal Face, the two brothers successfully making the summit (as did two other team mates the next day). But the climb was marred by tragedy and controversy, Günther Messner being killed during an unplanned descent of the Diamir Face. Messner lost toes to frostbite on the descent and feared his climbing career might be over, but he was invited to Manaslu in 1972. Again there was tragedy and controversy, Messner continuing to the summit after his companion, Franz Jäger, had turned back. On returning to the top camp in a white-out, Messner found Jäger was not there. Two other team mates, Horst Fankhauser and Andi Schlick, were there; assuming Jäger was looking for Messner, they went out to search for him. Unable to regain the camp, Fankhauser and Schlick dug a snow hole. During the night Schlick left the hole for reasons unknown: he and Jäger were never seen again. Following his ascent of K2,

Messner went on to become the first man to climb all fourteen 8000m peaks, all ascents being made without supplementary oxygen. He also soloed both Everest and Nanga Parbat, and climbed two other 8000m peaks twice for a total of eighteen ascents on the fourteen peaks. Messner also crossed Antarctica by ski. Later he became a Member of the European Parliament (representing the Italian Green Party). The quotes in the text are taken from the book Gogna and Messner wrote (with contributions from other team members) about the expedition, *K2: Mountain of Mountains* (Kaye & Ward, London/OUP, New York, 1981), and from Messner's later book on his 8000m climbs, *All 14 Eight-Thousanders* (Crowood Press, Ramsbury, 1988; revised edition, 1999).

14. B. Mellet, *K2: La Victoire Suspendue* (Aventures Extraordinaires, Grenoble, 1980).
15. *Waseda University K2 Expedition* (Tokyo, 1983). The book is in Japanese, but has Japanese and English captions to the colour photographs and an English summary translated from a summary of the climb by the leader Teruo Matsuura. Matsuura and Naomi Uemura were the first Japanese to climb Everest in 1970. The text is taken from Matsuura's account, together with an account he wrote for the AAJ ('K2's West Face', *AAJ* (1982, vol. 24), pp. 83–7), supplemented by an interview which Nazir Sabir gave to Greg Child for an article: 'Profile: Nazir Sabir, Pakistan's World-Class Mountaineer', *Climbing* (October 1987).
16. The official account of the climb is the Japan Mountaineering Association's *The Ascent of Chogori* (Nippon-hoso-shuppan-kyokai, Tokyo 1982). A book on the expedition illustrated with very much better photographs is Asahi Newspaper's *The Road to Chogori* (1982). Both are in Japanese only, with no English summary or photograph captions. Some information on the climb is presented in *Mountain* magazine (March/April 1983, vol. 90), this including Konishi's dramatic summit statement, though it states 'If you miscalculate, naturally you should die' – which is a good deal more blunt than the translation offered in the text.
17. Brief details are given in Janusz Kurczab, 'K2: Northwest Ridge Attempt', *AAJ* (1983, vol. 25), p. 274.
18. Leszek Cichy (1951–) made the first winter ascent of Everest (and the first winter ascent of any 8000m peak), together with Krysztof Wielicki, on 17 February 1980. Wojciech Wróż (1942–1986) had been to 8400m on K2 during the Polish attempt on the North-East Ridge in 1976. In 1986 he was one of the victims of the appalling summer of 1986 on K2, having finally reached the top along the Magic Line.
19. Wanda Rutkiewicz (1943–1992) was, at the time of her death, the world's leading high-altitude female climber. At the time of the 1982 expedition she was still recovering from a broken leg sustained in a fall on Elbrus and was on crutches (and therefore unable to go above Base Camp). The quote in the text is taken from G. Reinisch, *Wanda Rutkiewicz: A Caravan of Dreams* (Carreg, Ross-on-Wye, 2000). For further details on Rutkiewicz, see Chapter 6, Note 2.
20. Details of the Kukuczka/Kurtyka Broad Peak and K2 climbs are to be found in Jerzy Kukuczka's book, *My Vertical World* (Hodder & Stoughton, London, 1992).
21. Together with Agostino Da Polenza, Santon wrote a book on the expedition, *K2: Lo Spigolo Nord, L'Altra Riva* (Venice, 1983). It has not been translated into English.
22. For Fausto De Stefani (1952–) and Sergio Martini (1949–) summitting K2 in 1983 was the first step on the ladder to the completion of all fourteen 8000m peaks. In 1998 De Stefani claimed to have completed the set, the sixth person to do so, but his claim to have climbed Lhotse in 1997 with Sergio Martini was considered dubious as other climbers who followed them a few days later said their footprints stopped short of the top. The Italians complained that in the poor visibility at the time of their ascent they were sure they had reached the summit, or as close to it as dangerous conditions would allow. Despite these protestations,

their claim was rejected. Martini reclimbed Lhotse in 2000 and therefore became a member (the seventh) of the 'all fourteen' club. De Stefani still requires Lhotse to complete his set.

23. Julie Tullis wrote about the 1983 K2 expedition in her book *Clouds from Both Sides* (Grafton, London, 1986), while Kurt Diemberger described it in *The Endless Knot: K2, Mountain of Dreams and Destiny* (Grafton Books, London/The Mountaineers, Seattle, 1990). Quotes in the text are from these books.

24. Scott's description of the route can be found in his book, *Himalayan Climber*, and in more detail in his contribution to D. Scott and A. Rouse, 'Karakoram Alpine Style', *Mountain* (September/October 1983, vol. 93). The quote in the text comes from this article.

Chapter 6

1. Maurice Barrard (1941–1986) and Liliane Barrard (1948–1986) had successfully climbed Gasherbrum II in 1982 and Nanga Parbat in 1984, Liliane becoming the first woman to have climbed the latter. The pair described themselves as the 'world's highest couple'.

2. Wanda Rutkiewicz (1943–1992) was, at the time, the world's leading female high-altitude climber. At the time of her death she had climbed eight 8000m peaks and attempted three others. Her climbs included a solo ascent of Annapurna's South Face, and a solo ascent of Cho Oyu. She disappeared during a third attempt to climb Kangchenjunga. The quotes in the text are taken from Reinisch, *Wanda Rutkiewicz: A Caravan of Dreams*.

3. Kurt Diemberger (1932–) is one of only two climbers to have been in the summit parties on the first ascent of two 8000m peaks (Broad Peak and Dhaulagiri), the other being Hermann Buhl (Nanga Parbat and Broad Peak). The Sherpa Gyalzen Norbu was in the first team to climb Manaslu, having been in the second team to climb Makalu, the day after the first ascent. By 1986 Diemberger had climbed five 8000m peaks, and a few years earlier had been regarded as a potential rival to Reinhold Messner as the first climber to complete all fourteen. Diemberger is an excellent photographer and in later life became an equally proficient film-maker. He is also a prolific author. The quotes in the text are from his book on the K2 expedition, *The Endless Knot: K2, Mountain of Dreams and Destiny*.

4. Benoît Chamoux (1961–1995). At the time of his death Chamoux had climbed twelve 8000m peaks and had also reached the central summit of Shisha Pangma, which he was claiming as his thirteenth peak. This claim was rightly disputed. His claim of climbing Cho Oyu was also disputed as he had only reached the edge of the summit plateau, not the actual summit. In 1995 both Chamoux and the Swiss climber Erhard Loretan, who had thirteen undisputed 8000m peak ascents, were at the base of Kangchenjunga. So too was a scrum of French media intent on covering the 'race' to be third person to complete the set of fourteen 8000m peaks, with Loretan needing Kangchenjunga to complete his set, Chamoux needing it to complete his disputed set. The Swiss and his companions climbed faster than Chamoux and his climbing partner Pierre Royer (who was also filming the climb). At a rest stop one of Chamoux's Sherpas fell to his death. The other Sherpas descended to assist their colleague, but the two Frenchmen declined to help. They continued upwards, meeting Loretan as he descended from the summit. Though Chamoux had lost the 'race', as he had radio communication to the media at the mountain's base he was still intent on winning the media race. In a world where news moves quickly and the public's interest moves equally rapidly, the first with the news is often credited as first, irrespective of the truth. At 4.30pm on 6 October 1995 Royer radioed down that he was tired and descending. At 8pm Chamoux radioed that he was nearing the summit and continuing. Neither was ever heard from or seen again. In an unpleasant aftermath to their disappearance, the Sherpas declined to search for either climber as they had refused to go to the aid of their colleague. The quotes in the book

are taken from Chamoux's book on his climbs, *Le Vertige de L'Infini* (Albin Michel, 1988). It has not been translated into English.

5. Karl-Maria Herrligkoffer (1916–1991) was a German physician. He was a half-brother of Willy Merkl, who had led, and died on, the 1934 Nanga Parbat expedition. Herrligkoffer idolised his older sibling and was determined to climb the mountain in his honour. Though of only limited climbing ability, Herrligkoffer organised the successful 1953 expedition. Under his erratic leadership, however, the expedition would have failed had it not been for an extraordinary solo climb by Hermann Buhl. Herrligkoffer's treatment of Buhl after his climb, from both a medical and a human point of view, left much to be desired. After the 1953 Nanga Parbat expedition Herrligkoffer organised many other expeditions, several of which ended in controversy.

6. Jerzy Kukuczka (1948–1989) was born in Katowice, Poland. He was the second man to complete the set of fourteen 8000m peaks and climbed each of them in fine style, making new routes on Broad Peak (during his own second ascent of the mountain: he had previously climbed it on the 'standard' route), Everest, Gasherbrum I, Gasherbrum II, K2, Makalu, Nanga Parbat and Shisha Pangma, first winter ascents of Annapurna, Dhaulagiri and Kangchenjunga, and a new route during the second winter ascent of Cho Oyu. He climbed all the peaks apart from Everest without supplementary oxygen. He was killed during an alpine-style attempt on the unclimbed South Face of Lhotse. Having overcome all the major difficulties of the face, and nearing the summit ridge at 8200m, he slipped. The 6mm rope, bought cheaply in Kathmandu, which linked him to his second snapped and he fell to his death. The quotes in the text are taken from the book he wrote on his fourteen 8000m climbs, *My Vertical World*. Further details are taken from Kukuczka's brief article, 'K2's South Face', *AAJ* (1987, vol. 29), pp. 14–16.

7. Norman Dyrhenfurth was the son of Günther Dyrhenfurth, a famous mountaineer/ explorer of the early twentieth century. Norman led the successful 1963 American Everest expedition and the ill-fated 1971 International Everest expedition. The latter, organised to prove that climbers of many nations could unite to a common purpose and climb a new, hard route, proved just the opposite, personal ambition and national stereotypes overriding altruism, just as the critics had said it would.

8. This, and some other details, of the events of 1986 are taken from various sources, including Jim Curran's two books, *K2, Triumph and Tragedy* (Hodder & Stoughton, London, 1987) and *K2: The Story of the Savage Mountain*, and *Mountain* magazine (September/October 1986, vol. 111). However, the majority of the data is given in the books mentioned in the notes below.

9. Chamoux's feat in climbing Broad Peak in 24 hours is amazing, but it has to be pointed out that those who were on the mountain on the same day claim he did not, in fact, reach the main summit, only the Forepeak. The main summit of Broad Peak is only a few feet higher than the Forepeak but is at some distance from it, and many of those claiming an ascent actually get no further than the first top. Soro Dorotei, Martino Moretti and Josef Rakoncaj of the Italian Quota 8000 team also reached the top of both Broad Peak and K2, all doing the double. The Swiss climbers Beda Furster and Rolf Zemp also completed the double of Broad Peak and K2.

10. In his book Kukuczka goes on to complain abut the attitude of some of the young Swiss guides on the expedition who were interested only in reaching the summit anyhow because the inclusion of K2 on their CV would impress potential clients. They wanted to climb the peak quickly, then go home. He writes that they must not risk too much: 'an adventure, yes. Risk, no.' He then goes on to deliver his famous analogy of western and Polish attitudes to

climbing with western and Polish cars: 'To be able to compare western and Polish mountaineers it is necessary to have a look at a western car. It is excellent on perfect roads. A Polish car is poor, heavy, uneconomical, but it survives much better on rough tracks where it could sometimes replace a tank. The westerners are also first-class performers in perfect weather, when they can see the route, when they are relaxed and there is no risk. Then they out-perform others. But they have to have the conditions just right, they have to have a beautifully finished motorway with no pot-holes. If the road is not too good they rapidly pack up.' The paragraph has been quoted often, usually with the comment that the disparaging remarks were ill judged. But at the time it was the case that most of the cutting-edge routes on the highest peaks were being made by Polish and other eastern European climbers.

11. See John Barry's idiosyncratic but entertaining, warts and all, account of the British 1986 K2 expedition, *K2: Savage Mountain, Savage Summer* (Oxford Illustrated Press, 1987).

12. Brief details of the Polish 'Magic Line' expedition are given in Janusz Majer, 'K2's Magic Line', *AAJ* (1987, vol. 29), pp. 10–13. Anna Czerwińska also wrote a book on the expedition, which also included some details of the climbs of the other Poles (i.e. Rutkiewicz, Kukuczka and Piotrowski) on the mountain at the same time: *Groza Wokół K2* (Wydawnictwo 'Sport i Turystyka', Warsaw, 1990).

13. Willi Bauer wrote a book on the 1986 expedition with the Austrian journalist Gertrude Reinisch, *Licht und Schatten am K2* (Pinguin-Verlag, Innsbruck, 1988). It has not been translated into English. The book is a difficult read, its third-person style occasionally making it hard to work out who is saying what to whom. However, the quotes in the text are not from this book, but from a taped interview by the author with Bauer (aided by an interpreter). The story told on that December day in 2009 is substantially similar to that set down in the book.

14. Diemberger, *The Endless Knot: K2, Mountain of Dreams and Destiny*. In 2000 John Cleare and I produced a book which dealt with the history of the fourteen 8000m peaks: Sale and Cleare, *On Top of the World*. The publisher wished to use Kurt Diemberger's iconic photograph of Hermann Buhl at the summit of Broad Peak at sunset and contacted him for permission. In response he provided them with a contract (Diemberger later termed it an 'agreement', but the publisher called it a contract) which stipulated, among other things, that for any of the climbs in which he had been involved 'because even the best writers continue to make factual errors and mix-ups on what happened on Broad Peak, Chogolisa, Dhaulagiri, K2, I will grant the use of my pictures only if the author does send me the few actual pages of his text, which shall be illustrated with my pictures, in time to tell him such factual errors … it remains his free will to correct or not'. When the book was finally published, I discovered, to my dismay, that my text on Broad Peak had been rewritten. The publisher told me that at a very late stage in production, some time after sending Diemberger the pages that included his climbs, as requested, they had received a letter informing them that permission for the use of his photographs was withdrawn unless changes to the text were made. Otherwise Diemberger would sue the publisher. Knowing I would refuse permission for changes, knowing too that I was aware of the contract/agreement which did not require them, but not wishing to risk litigation, the publisher allowed Diemberger to rewrite the text, choosing not to tell me. Not surprisingly I was irate, but not as irate as Marcus Schmuck and Fritz Wintersteller, who had been on the Broad Peak expedition and had given me their version of it. I visited them in Salzburg to apologise, and decided that I would write a history of the Broad Peak climb, using their climbing diaries, which they loaned me, and the diary and reports of Hermann Buhl. I also

visited Diemberger in Bologna. He must have been apprehensive that I wanted to talk about the 8000m book, but by then I was much more interested in whether he had a climbing diary from Broad Peak. He hadn't kept one, all his writings on that climb being from memory, backed by Buhl's diary which he had seen.

When the book was published (Sale, *Broad Peak*), it told a story in which Diemberger and Buhl were not the lead characters, that role being taken by Schmuck and Wintersteller, who did most of the trail-breaking and reached the summit some time before the other two. It also noted that the three diary accounts suggested that Diemberger's claim of great friendship with Buhl was not the case, and that the claim that Chogolisa represented a great step forward in the history of climbing as the first alpine-style attempt on a 7000m peak was flawed, both because on Chogolisa Buhl and Diemberger set up a supply dump on the hill before their climb and, most significantly, because before Chogolisa Schmuck and Wintersteller had made an astonishingly fast (52½ hours Base Camp–summit–Base Camp) true alpine-style ascent of the 7360m (24,147ft) Skil Brum. Not surprisingly, given the number of times he had told another story, Diemberger was not pleased with the book, writing of me at one stage, in *Seiltanz: Die Geschichten meines Lebens* (Malik, 2007), not translated into English, *seitdem mast er mich* ('since then [the *On Top of the World* incident] he hates me'), and suggesting that this was the reason I had published *Broad Peak*.

Any writing about K2 in 1986 that suggests a story other than that told in *The Endless Knot* will allow him to use the same argument for why I am again suggesting his account is flawed. But as with Broad Peak, I am only setting down the versions of the story told by Bauer and Diemberger, the only survivors, so that the reader can compare and contrast and reach an informed opinion. While I was with him in Bologna Diemberger showed me around his house, pointing out wonderful mementos from his climbing career. On his writing desk was a copy of one of Jim Curran's books (I don't recall which) opened at a page describing some events of 1986. Seeing me looking at the book, which had copious writing in red ink in the margins, he picked it up and flicked through other pages which were similarly marked. This is all wrong, he declared. He (Curran) knows nothing of what went on. You know, he said, that of those present only Bauer disagrees with what I said took place. As a guest in his house, I felt I could not point out that of those present only Bauer and he had survived.

15. Kim Byung-Joon, *The Mountain that Summons Death* (Yea Moon-sa, Seoul, 1987). The book is available in two versions, soft- and hard-back, but only in Korean. For confirmation of the Korean climber Chang Byong-ho's comments regarding the Korean-Austrian agreement in English, see an article written by Peter Gillman, initially for *The Times*, but included in a book of his climbing articles: P. Gillman, *In Balance: Twenty Years of Mountaineering Journalism* (Hodder & Stoughton, London, 1989).

16. 'K2: The Facts. Dennis Kemp interviews Kurt Diemberger', *Climber* (December 1986, vol. XXV, no. 12), pp. 16–20.

17. The weather was excellent from the Shoulder to the summit, but others could see that it was changing. Diemberger notes that Yugoslav climbers at the summit of Broad Peak could see veils of thin cloud forming away from K2. On K2 itself the lower slopes were also shrouded in cloud. One of the teams on Broad Peak was led by Slovenian Viktor (Viki) Grošelj, who has now climbed ten of the fourteen 8000m peaks. One team member was fellow Slovenian Tomo Česen, who on 3 August made an illegal solo ascent of the South-South-East Spur. Though most of the Spur had been climbed before (by Doug Scott and his party in 1983 – see Chapter 5), Česen followed the Spur all the way to the edge of the Shoulder. There, at about 7800m, he retreated down the Abruzzi on 4 August in the face of poor visibility and

snowfall. The Polish support team on the Magic Line also retreated in poor weather. Doubts were raised after Česen's claimed ascent as no one saw him on the mountain (though, in fairness, there was actually no one on the Abruzzi at the time of his descent, the Koreans and Poles being above him, and as he was very unlikely to have known that, then claiming that line – usually the most populated on the peak – for his retreat if he had not taken it would have been very foolish.) The doubts have continued, not helped by a claimed solo of Lhotse's South Face, which is viewed as dubious by many. Ironically, in view of Česen's illegal ascent and the fact that no more than 200m, perhaps less, of new climbing were accomplished, the Spur is now often referred to as the Česen Route.

18. The point has been made before, but is worth making again, that after his meeting with Hermann Buhl below the summit of Broad Peak, and his return to the summit with him, Diemberger has seemed romantically attached to the idea of pushing summit days to the limit, with late or sunset summit arrivals and darkness descents or bivouacs. Buhl had already done this, solo, on Nanga Parbat and had done it again on Broad Peak, and Diemberger, as he makes clear many times, hero-worshipped Buhl.

19. Diemberger repeated the claim that Willi Bauer had suffered memory problems as a consequence of altitude in a letter he wrote to the *Alpine Journal* in an effort to correct perceived mistakes in accounts of the events of 1986: see his letter to the editor of 1 March 1988, *Alpine Journal* (1988/89, vol. 93), pp. 216–18. There seems to be an implicit view in Diemberger's statements that as Bauer was climbing above 8000m for the first time, he was more likely to be prone to its effects than an old hand such as Diemberger himself. However, science does not support this contention, and it is worth noting that although he had indeed climbed several 8000m peaks, K2 was Diemberger's first time above 8200m without the use of supplementary oxygen.

20. During the Broad Peak expedition Diemberger had, according to the other team members, often eaten more than his share of the available food, to their aggravation, to such an extent that the Pakistani liaison officer Qader Saeed nicknamed him 'Hungry Wolf', a name which he still uses. This information is set down in Sale, *Broad Peak*, which is based on the climbing diaries of the other three team members, and was confirmed in numerous interviews with Marcus Schmuck, Fritz Wintersteller and Qader Saeed both during production of the book and subsequently.

21. During the taped interview Bauer says that he was told by the doctor with the Korean expedition that this was due to extreme blood thickening and that when Imitzer began to move this would have forced the eyeballs from the sockets. In conversation with Dr George Rodway, the author was told that this was a puzzling suggestion as the mechanism was highly unlikely. Cerebral oedema was also unlikely as a cause, as pressure of the magnitude required to detach eyeballs would be so large that Imitzer would not have been able to leave the tent, and would likely have already died. Had Imitzer's eyeballs frozen to his goggles, or had a grief-stricken, horrified Bauer been so shocked by his friend's appearance he saw rather more than was real?

22. A figure-of-eight is shaped just as the name suggests, with one large circle of metal, through which the rope is passed, joined to another, smaller circle which is clipped to the climber's harness. The device is used for fast, efficient abseiling and has the added advantage of being quick and easy to attach to the rope. The Sticht plate, named for its designer, the Austrian climber Franz Sticht, is a belay device. It is a circle of metal into which two slots have been cut. When climbing with two ropes one is passed through each slot (only one slot being used for single rope climbing) and fastened to the climber's harness with a karabiner. The tight turn of the rope through the slot aids friction and so assists a climber holding a falling

companion. The plate can be used to abseil, but has several disadvantages: the friction that is so useful when holding a falling climber is now unhelpful as it slows the abseiler; the plate is prone to jamming; and the tight turn required in the rope makes it difficult to thread through the slot and so wastes time in multiple abseils.

23. The phrase translates as 'If I ever find out that he did not help Mrówka, then I will turn his ears forward.' *Werde ich ihm die Ohren nach vorne drehen* is a standard German expression, perhaps best translated into English as 'tear his head off'. In the interview Bauer actually used a west Austrian dialect version of the expression, *werd I eahm die Ohrwaschln viri drahn,* which is a good deal more dramatic and earthy, and implies that more than just the ears will be turned around. There is, of course, no hope of Bauer, or anyone else, finding out.

Chapter 7

1. Andrezj Zawada (1928–2000) was one of the leaders of the Polish generation of climbers who brought winter climbing to the high hills. With Tadeusz Piotrowski he made the first winter ascent of a 7000m peak (Noshaq, 7492m/24,580ft) in 1973 and led the expeditions which made the first winter ascents of Everest (1980) and Cho Oyu (1985).

2. Further details (in Japanese) on the climb are given in the Japanese climbing magazine *Iwa To Yuki* (1991, vol. 143), pp. 34–5.

3. See L. Hall, *First Ascent: The Life and Climbs of Greg Mortimer* (Simon & Schuster, Australia, 1996).

4. The quotes in the text are from Child, 'A Margin of Luck'. The article is also reproduced in a collection of Child's writings, *Mixed Emotions*. Further information is from S.J. Swenson, 'K2: The North Ridge', *AAJ* (1991, vol. 33), pp. 19–32.

5. Reinhold Messner and Erhard Loretan had preceded him. So had Hiroshi Yoshino, but he had died on the descent from Everest's summit. Some authorities believe this invalidates his claim, which seems unfair.

6. Pierre Béghin (1951–1992) had a doctorate in fluid mechanics and was an expert on avalanches. He was also an outstanding climber with a list of bold and important climbs, including the first ascent of Manaslu's West Face and Dhaulagiri's Japanese Buttress on the South Face, the first solo ascent of Kangchenjunga and a solo ascent of a new route on Makalu's South Face. In 1992 he attempted a new line on Annapurna's South Face with Jean-Christophe Lafaille. Retreating from 7500m, Béghin fixed a *Friend* (a camming device) for an abseil to save a precious piton for lower on the face. The Friend pulled and Béghin fell to his death. Lafaille was then forced to downclimb until he reached a camp at 7000m. There he found a 20m rope. Using that and tent pegs as pitons, he continued down. At 6500m stonefall broke his right arm. As he was right-handed this was a major problem, forcing him, after constructing a makeshift splint, to fix abseils with his 'wrong' hand and to abseil using, in part, his teeth. He survived the descent.

7. P. Béghin, 'K2: Pyramid of Storms', *Mountain*, 143, January/February 1992.

8. Daniel Mazur, 'K2 via the West Ridge', *AAJ* (1994, vol. 36), pp. 244–5.

9. J. Haberl, *K2: Dreams and Reality* (Tantalus Publishing, Vancouver, 1994). Haberl was killed in an avalanche in Alaska in 1999.

10. S. Alvaro, 'K2 North Buttress via the Japanese Route, Ascent and Tragedy', *AAJ* (1995, vol. 37), pp. 314–15.

11. Alison Hargreaves (1962–1995) had climbed several of the great climbs of the Alps, including completing the first ascent by a British female of the Eiger's North Face, before she became known to the wider public for her ascent of Everest from the north in May 1995. The ascent was unsupported and she did not use supplementary oxygen. At the time,

because doubts had been raised over a claimed ascent of Everest by Lydia Bradey from the Nepalese side (Bradey, who did not have permission for the climb, was seen at the South Summit by other climbers, who insisted there had been insufficient time for her to have summitted before they saw her again on arrival at the South Col), Hargreaves' ascent was heralded as the first female, bottled gas-free climb. Today Bradey's climb has been recognised by the Nepalese, though sceptics still remain. The intense publicity generated by the Everest climb spurred Hargreaves on to attempt K2 in the same year. Climbing the two highest peaks without supplementary oxygen in the space of three months was a remarkable achievement, and had she survived would surely have established her position in the climbing world and, probably, secured her financial future, something which clearly was one of several driving forces behind her climbs. But Hargreaves had two young children, and as much, probably more, newspaper ink was used in condemning her taking such risks as a mother, as was used in lauding her Everest climb and K2 ambitions. In general, the view was that while it was reasonable for men with families to take part in high-risk endeavours, for women to do so was outrageous. Interestingly, some notable feminists took this view. A useful biography of Hargreaves, revealing a complex, far less dogmatic, two-dimensional character than the one who formed the basis of much of the publicity which surrounded her climbs and death, is D. Rose and E. Douglas, *Regions of the Heart* (Michael Joseph, London, 1999).
12. Osamu Tanabe, 'K2: West Face Variation', *AAJ* (1998, vol. 40), pp. 325–7.
13. The team of sixteen climbers included several who had already established very hard new routes on Lhotse's middle summit, Jannu, and Everest's North Face. Brief details of the climb are to be found in an article and an interview (a translated extract from an interview with team leader Viktor Kozlov in the Russian magazine *Verticalniy Mir*, no. 68) in *AAJ* (2008, vol. 50), pp. 339–42. There is also an article by Pavel Shabalin in *Alpinist* (Spring 2008, 23), pp. 44–51. The article has more to do with the philosophy of the climb than details of it, but is fascinating (and arguably more interesting) for that reason.

Chapter 8
1. In the wake of the tragedy there were many articles in newspapers and magazines, as well as on websites, on the events of 1 and 2 August. The articles were followed by several books. The account given here derives from these numerous sources. The books are:

    G. Bowley, *No Way Down: Life and Death on K2* (Viking/Penguin Group, 2010). This book performed the remarkable feat of reaching number ten in the bestsellers list. It has its faults – a few trivial factual errors and the thoughts of Jumik Bhote after the accident to the Korean party presented as fact when there is no supporting evidence – but it is highly readable. The book's Epilogue casts doubt on the role of Ger McDonnell in freeing the Koreans, but the evidence he sets down, from Chris Klinke, is completely at odds with the position of the bodies seen at the base of the Bottleneck Couloir after the final incident of the tragic sequence of events.

    F. Wilkinson, *One Mountain Thousand Summits: The Untold Story of Tragedy and True Heroism on K2* (New American Library, New York, 2010). This book is particularly good at covering in detail the way in which the news of the story was broken, both to the world and to the relatives of the dead. The news was largely conveyed by blog and internet, the immediacy of both being both a blessing (as written words can no longer be unwritten or rewritten) and a curse (as rumour can be stated as truth, to the anguish of those awaiting news of loved ones). Those readers less interested in the intricacy of blogs, etc., the intimacy of responses to bad news, and the technicalities of meetings with the Sherpa survivors of the climb may find the early part of the book difficult, particularly as the author favours a somewhat disjointed style. But his timeline of the unfolding tragedy, once it starts, is excellent, while his decision to trace and interview the surviving Sherpas is exemplary.

Two survivors of the 1–2 August bivouac have also written books:

M. Confortola, *Giorni Di Ghiaccio: Agosto 2008, La Tragedia del K2* (Baldini Castoldi Dalai, 2009). It is available in Italian only.

W. van Rooijen, *Surviving K2* (G+J Publishing CV, Diemen, Holland, 2010). This book is in English. A table in the book states that Pasang Bhote reached the summit and died on the descent. As the text notes, it was Pasang Bhote (Lama) who reached the summit (and descended successfully with the amazing help of Tshering Dorje), while Pasang Bhote was killed attempting a rescue. Van Rooijen's table has eighteen climbers reaching the summit (correct) with eight dying on the descent (incorrect); in fact seven died on the descent, while another four men who did not summit also died.

Cecilie Skog has also written a book. Entitled *Til Rolf: Tusen fine turer og en trist* (*For Rolf: A thousand beautiful journeys and a sad one*), it is about their lives together, with a single chapter on K2 in 2008. It was published by Gyldendal, Oslo, in 2009.

2. Marco Confortola gave several versions of what happened when he and Ger McDonnell reached the Korean team. The most detailed was one he later posted on his website (http://www.marcoconfortola.it). Most significantly he says here that there were two Koreans and the Sherpa Jumik Bhote, having originally given the impression that all three were Koreans. That clears up one aspect of the attempted rescue, Pasang Bhote clearly telling Pemba Gyalje that Jumik Bhote was present. It did, though, create another problem – what happened to the third Korean? An explanation is offered in the text.

3. Frederick Sträng, the Swede on the American team, was filming the summit attempt on 1 August. After abandoning his climb and descending to Camp IV, he joined the team climbing up to aid Dren Mandic, reaching him after Mandic's Serbian teammates had reached him and found him dead. To help take Mandic's body down, Sträng put his camera into his pocket, but had failed to turn it off. His increasingly desperate shouts as he attempted to get Jehain Baig off him and then his agonising realisation that the Pakistani was sliding to his death were therefore recorded. They were included in the DVD made of the climb: *K2: A Cry from the Top of the World*, West Cannon Media Ltd.

4. Alteplase is a tissue plasminogen activator (tPA), a protein essential to the body's ability to break down blood clots. Because it works on the clotting system, tPA is most typically used in clinical settings to treat blood clots (treatment known as 'thrombolytic therapy') that cause serious health problems such as myocardial infarction (heart attack) and stroke. The goal of thrombolytic therapy in frostbite injury is to address the microvascular clotting that accompanies cold-induced soft tissue injury. Use of intravenous and intra-arterial tPA within 24 hours of injury is recommended by current clinical guidelines. Ideally the treatment should occur in a facility with intensive care monitoring capabilities. As these are usually lacking in mountain situations, the use of tPA in the field is not recommended because it may not be possible to detect and treat bleeding complications and, by its very nature, tPA hinders the body's ability to clot naturally. Meyer also administered heparin, an injectable blood anticoagulant. Whereas tPA is an actual 'clot-buster', heparin only prevent blood clots from forming (i.e. it cannot break up a clot once it has formed). For the initial management of frostbite, giving heparin by itself is not standard practice and is not supported in the literature. However, published medical protocols include the use of heparin in conjunction with thrombolytic therapy (i.e. tPA) to prevent local clotting.

Meyer also gave Tshering Dorje and Pemba Gyalje (who both summitted without oxygen) dexamethasone and provigil. Dexamethasone is a glucocorticoid (steroid) drug known to be an effective prophylaxis and treatment for altitude illness, particularly acute mountain sickness and the similar (pathogenesis-wise) but neurologically more serious disease known as high-altitude cerebral oedema (HACE). Provigil (generically known as modafinil) promotes wakefulness. Although still debated, it is considered most likely that the drug alters the neurotransmitters in the brain that control the sleep/wake cycle. It also enhances attention capacity and vigilance, but its pharmacological profile is notably different from that of amphetamines and traditional stimulants. Importantly, it is less likely to cause jitteriness and anxiety when compared to traditional stimulants. According to the Bowley and Wilkinson books Meyer also administered Dexedrine (a dextroamphetamine), a psychostimulant amphetamine known to produce increased wakefulness and focus in association with decreased fatigue and decreased appetite. It is a potent central nervous system stimulant and consequently side effects such as anorexia, hyperactivity, restlessness, heart rhythm disturbances, blood pressure changes, tremors and dizziness (to name but a few) are possible. Military pilots are known to take dextroamphetamine as one of the stimulant pills dispensed to them on long missions to help them remain focused and alert. As is the case with any amphetamine, dextroamphetamine has a high potential for misuse (and abuse), though in the hands of a medical specialist in the mountaineering arena, such possibilities are extremely limited. The author is indebted to Dr George Rodway for assistance with this note.

5. Many of the articles emphasised the pointless nature of climbing. It was as though, and not for the first time, commentators felt the need to admonish climbers for what, they assumed, climbers had not realised – the essential uselessness of climbing achievements. But all of us who climb are perfectly well aware of this. Fifty years ago the autobiography of the great French climber Lionel Terray was titled *Conquistadors of the Useless* (Gollancz, London, 1963). It would be foolish to deny that competition and egotism do not exist in, and between, climbers over individual achievements. But accepting that these things exist does not explain why people climb, and pointing them out will not make them desist.

6. Alberto Zerain had previously climbed Everest, Gasherbrum I, Gasherbrum II, Lhotse and Makalu, and would later climb Kangchenjunga. As he was climbing solo, and was ahead of the team fixing ropes, it is fair to assume he was immune from Messner's criticism. Gerard McDonnell had climbed Broad Peak and Everest, and had tried K2 before, in 2006, together with Wilco van Rooijen; he was injured by falling rocks and had been helped down by Wilco. Wilco himself had also climbed Everest, without supplementary oxygen. The third Norit summit climber, Cas van de Gevel, was new to 8000m mountaineering, but was an accomplished and highly experienced ice climber with ascents in Peru and lower Himalayan peaks. On the Korean team Kim Jae-Su, the team leader, had summitted Everest, Broad Peak, Shisha Pangma and Lhotse in a little over 12 months with Go Mi-yeong, while she had previously also climbed Makalu, Dhaulagiri and Kangchenjunga in six weeks. Ms Go (her name was occasionally written Go Mi-sun) was on her way to completing the fourteen 8000m peaks; she died descending from the summit of Nanga Parbat in 2009. Two of the three Koreans who died also had several 8000m peaks to their credit. Rolf Bae and Cecilie Skog, the Norwegian husband and wife team, were highly experienced polar explorers and mountaineers. Skog was the first woman to have skied to the North and South Poles and to have climbed the Seven Summits. In 2000/01 Bae and a colleague had made what was then the longest-ever unsupported ski journey when they crossed Antarctica. Bae was also a superb rock climber who had climbed a route on Great Trango before moving to K2. Lars Nessa was, by comparison, inexperienced. Frenchman Hugues d'Aubarède had begun climbing late in life, but he had climbed Everest aged 57 and Nanga Parbat the following year. He was on his third attempt at K2. The Sherpas who reached the summit were among

212   The Challenge of K2

the most experienced of all the climbers. All had climbed Everest, several having climbed it numerous times. Chhiring Dorje had summitted Everest ten times, and had reached 8000m summits seventeen times in all, while Pemba Gyalje had climbed past 8000m more than fifty times. The Pakistani climbers were less experienced, but of these only one, Karim Meherban, went to the summit.

Yet despite all this high-altitude experience, there were still many who claimed that the combination of high altitude and technical difficulty on even the 'standard' route on K2 calls for a level of skill and experience much greater than that required for the mere 'peak-bagging' of 8000m peaks, particularly those peaks favoured by the 'baggers' – Everest and Cho Oyu especially – which require only limited climbing ability. In support of that, it is notable that the most technically competent of the Norit team's western members (who were also climbing without supplementary oxygen) was Cas van de Gevel, who was actually the least experienced on 8000m peaks. It was van de Gevel who regained Camp IV on 1 August.

7. For a more detailed consideration of the arguments for and against supplementary oxygen, and an understanding of human physiology relating to the high-altitude environment, see Sale and Rodway, *Everest and Conquest in the Himalaya*.

Chapter 9
1. See 'News' on Eberhard Jurgalski's website, www.8000ers.com/cms/history-of-chronicles-mainmenu-183.html.
2. Interview on ORF, the Austrian television channel, on 7 September 2010.

Appendix 1

K2 Ascent Data

Key: x = ascent without supplementary oxygen
f = female climber

Note: climbers ascending the peak for the second time are listed but not numbered in this table.

1	Achille COMPAGNONI		It	31. 07. 1954	Abruzzi Spur
2	Lino LACEDELLI		It	31. 07. 1954	Abruzzi Spur
3	Shoji NAKAMURA		Jp	08. 08. 1977	Abruzzi Spur
4	Tsuneo SHIGEHIRO		Jp	08. 08. 1977	Abruzzi Spur
5	Takayoshi TAKATSUKA		Jp	08. 08. 1977	Abruzzi Spur
6	Ashraf AMAN		Pak	09. 08. 1977	Abruzzi Spur
7	Mitsuo HIROSHIMA		Jp	09. 08. 1977	Abruzzi Spur
8	Masahide ONODERA		Jp	09. 08. 1977	Abruzzi Spur
9	Hideo YAMAMOTO		Jp	09. 08. 1977	Abruzzi Spur
10	Louis F. REICHARDT	x	USA	06. 09. 1978	NE Ridge – Abruzzi Spur
11	James WICKWIRE		USA	06. 09. 1978	NE Ridge – Abruzzi Spur
12	Richard RIDGEWAY		USA	07. 09. 1978	NE Ridge – Abruzzi Spur
13	John ROSKELLEY	x	USA	07. 09. 1978	NE Ridge – Abruzzi Spur
14	Michael DACHER	x	Ger	12. 07. 1979	Abruzzi Spur
15	Reinhold MESSNER	x	It	12. 07. 1979	Abruzzi Spur
16	Eiho OHTANI		Jp	07. 08. 1981	West Ridge/SW side
17	Nazir Ahmad SABIR		Pak	07. 08. 1981	West Ridge/SW side
18	Naoé SAKASHITA	x	Jp	14. 08. 1982	North Ridge
19	Yukihiro YANAGISAWA	x	Jp	14. 08. 1982	North Ridge
20	Hiroshi YOSHINO	x	Jp	14. 08. 1982	North Ridge
21	Hironobu KAMURO	x	Jp	15. 08. 1982	North Ridge
22	Haruichi KAWAMURA	x	Jp	15. 08. 1982	North Ridge
23	Tatsuji SHIGENO	x	Jp	15. 08. 1982	North Ridge
24	Kazushige TAKAMI	x	Jp	15. 08. 1982	North Ridge
25	Agostino DA POLENZA	x	It	31. 07. 1983	North Ridge
26	Josef RAKONCAJ	x	Cz	31. 07. 1983	North Ridge
27	Sergio MARTINI	x	It	04. 08. 1983	North Ridge
28	Fausto DE STEFANI	x	It	04. 08. 1983	North Ridge
29	Norbert JOOS	x	CH	19. 06. 1985	Abruzzi Spur
30	Marcel RUEDI	x	CH	19. 06. 1985	Abruzzi Spur
31	Erhard LORETAN	x	CH	06. 07. 1985	Abruzzi Spur

32	Pierre MORAND		x CH	06. 07. 1985	Abruzzi Spur
33	Jean TROILLET		x CH	06. 07. 1985	Abruzzi Spur
34	Eric ESCOFFIER		x F	06. 07. 1985	Abruzzi Spur
35	Daniel LACROIX		x F	07. 07. 1985	Abruzzi Spur
36	Stephane SCHAFFTER		x CH	07. 07. 1985	Abruzzi Spur
37	Kazunari MURAKAMI		Jp	24. 07. 1985	Abruzzi Spur
38	Noboru YAMADA		x Jp	24. 07. 1985	Abruzzi Spur
39	Kenji YOSHIDA		Jp	24. 07. 1985	Abruzzi Spur
40	Wanda RUTKIEWICZ	f	x Pol	23. 06. 1986	Abruzzi Spur
41	Liliane BARRARD	f	x F	23. 06. 1986	Abruzzi Spur
42	Maurice BARRARD		x F	23. 06. 1986	Abruzzi Spur
43	Michel PARMENTIER		x F	23. 06. 1986	Abruzzi Spur
44	Mari ABREGO		x E	23. 06. 1986	Abruzzi Spur
45	Josema CASIMIRO		x E	23. 06. 1986	Abruzzi Spur
46	Giovanni CALCAGNO		x It	05. 07. 1986	Abruzzi Spur
47	Benoît CHAMOUX		x F	05. 07. 1986	Abruzzi Spur
48	Soro DOROTEI		x It	05. 07. 1986	Abruzzi Spur
49	Martino MORETTI		x It	05. 07. 1986	Abruzzi Spur
	Josef RAKONCAJ		x Cz	05. 07. 1986	Abruzzi Spur
50	Tullio VIDONI		x It	05. 07. 1986	Abruzzi Spur
51	Beda FUSTER		x CH	05. 07. 1986	Abruzzi Spur
52	Rolf ZEMP		x CH	05. 07. 1986	Abruzzi Spur
53	Jerzy KUKUCZKA		x Pol	08 .07. 1986	South Face (Central Rib)
54	Tadeusz PIOTROWSKI		x Pol	08 .07. 1986	South Face (Central Rib)
55	Bong-Wan JANG		SK	03. 08. 1986	Abruzzi Spur
56	Byong-Ho CHANG		SK	03. 08. 1986	Abruzzi Spur
57	Chang-Sun KIM		SK	03. 08. 1986	Abruzzi Spur
58	Peter BOŽÍK		x Slk	03. 08. 1986	SSW Pillar ('Magic Line')
59	Przemysław PIASECKI		x Pol	03. 08. 1986	SSW Pillar ('Magic Line')
60	Wojciech WRÓŻ		x Pol	03. 08. 1986	SSW Pillar ('Magic Line')
61	Wilhelm BAUER		x A	04. 08. 1986	Abruzzi Spur
62	Alfred IMITZER		x A	04. 08. 1986	Abruzzi Spur
63	Alan ROUSE		x UK	04. 08. 1986	Abruzzi Spur
64	Kurt DIEMBERGER		x A	04. 08. 1986	Abruzzi Spur
65	Julie TULLIS	f	x UK	04. 08. 1986	Abruzzi Spur
66	Hirotaka IMAMURA		Jp	09. 08. 1990	NW Face – North Ridge/ Face
67	Hideji NAZUKA		Jp	09. 08. 1990	NW Face – North Ridge/ Face
68	Gregory CHILD		x Aus	20. 08. 1990	North Ridge
69	Gregory MORTIMER		x Aus	20. 08. 1990	North Ridge
70	Steve SWENSON		x USA	20. 08. 1990	North Ridge
71	Pierre BÉGHIN		x F	15. 08. 1991	NW Ridge – North Ridge
72	Christophe PROFIT		x F	15. 08. 1991	NW Ridge – North Ridge
73	Vladimir BALYBERDIN		x Rus	01. 08. 1992	Abruzzi Spur
74	Gennadi KOPIEKA		x Ukr	01. 08. 1992	Abruzzi Spur
75	Chantal MAUDUIT	f	x F	03. 08. 1992	Abruzzi Spur
76	Aleksei NIKIFOROV		x Rus	03. 08. 1992	Abruzzi Spur

77	Scott FISCHER	x	USA	16. 08. 1992	Abruzzi Spur
78	Charles MACE	x	USA	16. 08. 1992	Abruzzi Spur
79	Ed VIESTURS	x	USA	16. 08. 1992	Abruzzi Spur
80	Stripe BOŽIĆ	x	Cro	13. 06. 1993	Abruzzi Spur
81	Carlos CARSOLIO	x	Mex	13. 06. 1993	Abruzzi Spur
82	Viktor GROŠELJ	x	Slo	13. 06. 1993	Abruzzi Spur
83	Zvonko POŽGAJ	x	Slo	13. 06. 1993	Abruzzi Spur
84	Göran KROPP	x	S	23. 06. 1993	Abruzzi Spur
85	Philip POWERS	x	USA	07. 07. 1993	Abruzzi Spur
86	Dan CULVER	x	Can	07. 07. 1993	Abruzzi Spur
87	James HABERL	x	Can	07. 07. 1993	Abruzzi Spur
88	Anatoli BUKREEV	x	Kaz	30. 07. 1993	Abruzzi Spur
89	Peter MEZGER	x	Ger	30. 07. 1993	Abruzzi Spur
90	Andrew LOCK	x	Aus	30. 07. 1993	Abruzzi Spur
91	Rafael JENSEN	x	DK	30. 07. 1993	Abruzzi Spur
92	Reinmar JOSWIG	x	Ger	30. 07. 1993	Abruzzi Spur
93	Daniel BIDNER	x	S	30. 07. 1993	Abruzzi Spur
94	Daniel MAZUR	x	USA	02. 09. 1993	West Ridge/SW side
95	Jonathan PRATT	x	UK	02. 09. 1993	West Ridge/SW side
96	Juan TOMÁS	x	E	24. 06. 1994	SSE Ridge - Abruzzi Spur
97	Alberto IÑURRATEGI	x	E	24. 06. 1994	SSE Ridge - Abruzzi Spur
98	Félix IÑURRATEGI	x	E	24. 06. 1994	SSE Ridge - Abruzzi Spur
99	Juan Eusebio OIARZABAL	x	E	24. 06. 1994	SSE Ridge - Abruzzi Spur
100	Enríque (Kike) DE PABLO	x	E	24. 06. 1994	SSE Ridge - Abruzzi Spur
101	Robert HALL		NZ	09. 07. 1994	Abruzzi Spur
102	Ralf DUJMOVITS	x	Ger	23. 07. 1994	Abruzzi Spur
103	Veikka GUSTAFSSON	x	Fin	23. 07. 1994	Abruzzi Spur
104	Axel SCHLÖNVOGT	x	Ger	23. 07. 1994	Abruzzi Spur
105	Michael WÄRTHL	x	Ger	23. 07. 1994	Abruzzi Spur
106	Michael GROOM	x	Aus	23. 07. 1994	Abruzzi Spur
107	Mstislav GORBENKO	x	Ukr	23. 07. 1994	Abruzzi Spur
108	Vladislav TERZYUL	x	Ukr	23. 07. 1994	Abruzzi Spur
109	Sebastian DE LA CRUZ	x	Arg	30. 07. 1994	North Ridge
110	José-Carlos TAMAYO	x	E	30. 07. 1994	North Ridge
111	Juan Ignacio APELLANIZ	x	E	04. 08. 1984	North Ridge
112	Juan José SAN SEBASTIAN	x	E	04. 08. 1984	North Ridge
113	Rajab SHAH	x	Pak	17. 07. 1995	Abruzzi Spur
114	Mehrban SHAH	x	Pak	17. 07. 1995	Abruzzi Spur
115	Hans VAN DER MEULEN	x	NL	17. 07. 1995	Abruzzi Spur
116	Alan HINKES	x	UK	17. 07. 1995	Abruzzi Spur
117	Ronald NAAR		NL	17. 07. 1995	Abruzzi Spur
118	Bruce GRANT	x	NZ	13. 08. 1995	Abruzzi Spur
119	Lorenzo ORTIZ	x	E	13. 08. 1995	SSE Ridge - Abruzzi Spur
120	Javier OLIVAR	x	E	13. 08. 1995	SSE Ridge - Abruzzi Spur
121	Alison HARGREAVES f	x	UK	13. 08. 1995	Abruzzi Spur
122	Rob SLATER	x	USA	13. 08. 1995	Abruzzi Spur
123	Javier ESCARTÍN	x	E	13. 08. 1995	SSE Ridge - Abruzzi Spur
124	Masafumi TODAKA	x	Jp	29. 07. 1996	Abruzzi Spur

125	Salvatore PANZERI	x	It	29. 07. 1996	Abruzzi Spur
126	Giulio MAGGIONI	x	It	29. 07. 1996	Abruzzi Spur
127	Mario PANZERI	x	It	29. 07. 1996	Abruzzi Spur
128	Lorenzo MAZZOLENI	x	It	29. 07. 1996	Abruzzi Spur
129	Marco BIANCHI		It	10. 08. 1996	North Ridge
130	Christian KUNTNER	x	It	10. 08. 1996	North Ridge
131	Krzysztof WIELICKI	x	Pol	10. 08. 1996	North Ridge
132	Masayuki MATSUBARA		Jp	12. 08. 1996	SSE Ridge – Abruzzi Spur
133	Kenzo AKASAKA		Jp	12. 08. 1996	SSE Ridge – Abruzzi Spur
134	Bunsho MURATA		Jp	12. 08. 1996	SSE Ridge – Abruzzi Spur
135	Yuichi YOSHIDA		Jp	12. 08. 1996	SSE Ridge – Abruzzi Spur
136	Taro TANIGAWA		Jp	12. 08. 1996	SSE Ridge – Abruzzi Spur
137	Atsushi SHIINA		Jp	12. 08. 1996	SSE Ridge – Abruzzi Spur
138	Cristián GARCÍA-HUIDOBRO		Chl	13. 08. 1996	SSE Ridge – Abruzzi Spur
139	Michael PURCELL		Chl	13. 08. 1996	SSE Ridge – Abruzzi Spur
140	Misael ALVIAL		Chl	13. 08. 1996	SSE Ridge – Abruzzi Spur
141	Waldo FARIAS		Chl	13. 08. 1996	SSE Ridge – Abruzzi Spur
142	Atsushi YAMAMOTO		Jp	14. 08. 1996	SSE Ridge – Abruzzi Spur
143	Hideki INABA		Jp	14. 08. 1996	SSE Ridge – Abruzzi Spur
144	Koji NAGAKUBO		Jp	14. 08. 1996	SSE Ridge – Abruzzi Spur
145	Hirotaka TAKEUCHI		Jp	14. 08. 1996	SSE Ridge – Abruzzi Spur
146	Kazuhiro TAKAHASHI		Jp	14. 08. 1996	SSE Ridge – Abruzzi Spur
147	Takashi SANO		Jp	14. 08. 1996	SSE Ridge – Abruzzi Spur
148	Piotr PUSTELNIK		Pol	14. 08. 1996	North Ridge
149	Ryszard PAWLOWSKI	x	Pol	14. 08. 1996	North Ridge
150	Carlos P. BUHLER	x	USA	14. 08. 1996	North Ridge
151	Igor BENKIN	x	Rus	14. 08. 1996	North Ridge
152	Sergei PENZOV	x	Rus	14. 08. 1996	North Ridge
153	Osamu TANABE		Jp	19. 07. 1997	West Ridge/Face variation
154	Mikio SUZUKI		Jp	19. 07. 1997	West Ridge/Face variation
155	Kunihito NAKAGAWA		Jp	19. 07. 1997	West Ridge/Face variation
156	Masamiki TAKINE		Jp	28. 07. 1997	West Ridge/Face variation
157	Akira NAKAJIMA		Jp	28. 07. 1997	West Ridge/Face variation
158	Ryoji YAMADA		Jp	28. 07. 1997	West Ridge/Face variation
159	Masami KOBAYASHI		Jp	28. 07. 1997	West Ridge/Face variation
160	DAWA TASJO		Np	28. 07. 1997	West Ridge/Face variation
161	GYALBU		Np	28. 07. 1997	West Ridge/Face variation
162	MINGMA TSHERING		Np	28. 07. 1997	West Ridge/Face variation
163	NAWANG THILE		Np	28. 07. 1997	West Ridge/Face variation
164	Jung-Hun PARK	x	SK	26. 06. 2000	SSE Ridge – Abruzzi Spur
165	Yeon-Ryong KANG		SK	26. 06. 2000	SSE Ridge – Abruzzi Spur
166	Jung-Hyun YUN		SK	26. 06. 2000	SSE Ridge – Abruzzi Spur
167	Woo-Pyoung JOO		SK	26. 06. 2000	SSE Ridge – Abruzzi Spur
168	Chi-Won YUN		SK	29. 06. 2000	SSE Ridge – Abruzzi Spur
169	Jeong-Hyun LEE		SK	29. 06. 2000	SSE Ridge – Abruzzi Spur
170	Joo-Hyung KIM		SK	29. 06. 2000	SSE Ridge – Abruzzi Spur
171	Soon-Ook YOO		SK	29. 06. 2000	SSE Ridge – Abruzzi Spur
172	Abele BLANC	x	It	29. 07. 2000	Abruzzi Spur
173	Marco CAMANDONA	x	It	29. 07. 2000	Abruzzi Spur

174	Nasuh MAHRUKI	x	Tur	29. 07. 2000	Abruzzi Spur
175	Waldemar NICHLEVICZ	x	Bra	29. 07. 2000	Abruzzi Spur
176	Ki-Young HWANG		SK	30. 07. 2000	Abruzzi Spur
177	Yasushi YAMANOI		Jp	30. 07. 2000	SSE Ridge - Abruzzi Spur
178	Christopher SHAW	x	USA	30. 07. 2000	Abruzzi Spur
179	Andrew EVANS	x	Can	30. 07. 2000	Abruzzi Spur
180	Andrew COLLINS	x	UK	30. 07. 2000	Abruzzi Spur
181	William PIERSON	x	USA	30. 07. 2000	Abruzzi Spur
182	SHERAP JAMGBU		Np	31. 07. 2000	SSE Ridge - Abruzzi Spur
183	Hong-Gil UM		SK	31. 07. 2000	SSE Ridge - Abruzzi Spur
184	Sang-Hyun MO		SK	31. 07. 2000	SSE Ridge - Abruzzi Spur
185	Mu-Taek PARK		SK	31. 07. 2000	SSE Ridge - Abruzzi Spur
186	Han-Kyu YOO		SK	31. 07. 2000	SSE Ridge - Abruzzi Spur
187	Wang-Yong HAN	x	SK	31. 07. 2000	SSE Ridge - Abruzzi Spur
188	Iván VALLEJO	x	Ecu	31. 07. 2000	Abruzzi Spur
189	Carlos PAUNER		E	22. 07. 2001	Abruzzi Spur
	SHERAP JANGBU		Np	22. 07. 2001	Abruzzi Spur
190	PASANG TSHERING III		Np	22. 07. 2001	Abruzzi Spur
191	Jean-Christophe LAFAILLE	x	F	22. 07. 2001	SSE Ridge - Abruzzi Spur
192	Hans KAMMERLANDER	x	It	22. 07. 2001	SSE Ridge - Abruzzi Spur
193	Young-Seok PARK		SK	22. 07. 2001	Abruzzi Spur
194	Seong-Gya KANG		SK	22. 07. 2001	Abruzzi Spur
195	Hee-Joon OH		SK	22. 07. 2001	Abruzzi Spur
196	José-Antonio GARCÉS	x	E	22. 07. 2001	Abruzzi Spur
197	Karl UNTERKIRCHER	x	It	26. 07. 2004	Abruzzi Spur
198	Silvio MONDINELLI	x	It	26. 07. 2004	Abruzzi Spur
199	Juan VALLEJO	x	E	26. 07. 2004	Abruzzi Spur
200	Mikel VALLEJO	x	E	26. 07. 2004	Abruzzi Spur
201	Walter NONES	x	It	26. 07. 2004	Abruzzi Spur
202	Michele COMPAGNONI	x	It	26. 07. 2004	Abruzzi Spur
203	Ugo GIACOMELLI	x	It	26. 07. 2004	Abruzzi Spur
	Juan Eusebio OIARZABAL		E	26. 07. 2004	Abruzzi Spur
204	Edurne PASABAN	f x	E	26. 07. 2004	Abruzzi Spur
205	MINGMA		Np	27. 07. 2004	Abruzzi Spur
206	THILEN	x	Np	27. 07. 2004	Abruzzi Spur
207	Hasan ASAD KHAN	x	Pak	27. 07. 2004	Abruzzi Spur
208	Jonannes (Hannes) BLASER		CH	27. 07. 2004	Abruzzi Spur
209	Mario DIBONA		It	27. 07. 2004	Abruzzi Spur
210	Renzo BENEDETTI		It	27. 07. 2004	Abruzzi Spur
211	Renato SOTTSASS		It	27. 07. 2004	Abruzzi Spur
212	Marco DA POZZA		It	27. 07. 2004	Abruzzi Spur
213	BIANBA ZAXI (PEMBA TASHI)		Chn	27. 07. 2004	Abruzzi Spur
214	CERING DOJE (TSHERING DORJE)		Chn	27. 07. 2004	Abruzzi Spur
215	RENA (REN NA)		Chn	27. 07. 2004	Abruzzi Spur
216	LUOZE (LODUE)		Chn	27. 07. 2004	Abruzzi Spur
217	ZAXI CEDRING (TASHI TSHERING)		Chn	27. 07. 2004	Abruzzi Spur
218	PHUBU THUNDRUP		Chn	27. 07. 2004	Abruzzi Spur

219	BIANBA THUNDRUP		Chn	27. 07. 2004	Abruzzi Spur
220	Nisar HUSSAIN		Pak	27. 07. 2004	Abruzzi Spur
221	Mohammad HUSSAIN		Pak	27. 07. 2004	Abruzzi Spur
222	Vicente (Tente) LAGUNILLA	x	E	27. 07. 2004	Abruzzi Spur
223	Fernando GONZÁLEZ-RUBIO	x	Col	27. 07. 2004	Abruzzi Spur
224	Carlos SORIA		E	28. 07. 2004	Abruzzi Spur
225	MUKTU LHAKPA		Np	28. 07. 2004	Abruzzi Spur
226	Michel André (Mischu)		CH	28. 07. 2004	Abruzzi Spur
227	Iñaki OCHOA DE OLZA	x	E	28. 07. 2004	Abruzzi Spur
228	Jahan BAIG	x	Pak	28. 07. 2004	Abruzzi Spur
229	Mohammad III ALI		Pak	28. 07. 2004	Abruzzi Spur
230	Horia COLIBASANU	x	Rom	28. 07. 2004	Abruzzi Spur
231	Mario LACEDELLI		It	28. 07. 2004	Abruzzi Spur
232	Luciano ZARDINI		It	28. 07. 2004	Abruzzi Spur
233	Cedric HÄHLEN		CH	28. 07. 2004	Abruzzi Spur
234	Daniel SURCHAT		CH	28. 07. 2004	Abruzzi Spur
235	Vladimir SURCHAT	x	Kaz	28. 07. 2004	Abruzzi Spur
236	Aleksandr GUBAEV	x	Kyr	28. 07. 2004	Abruzzi Spur
237	Toshiaki YANO		Jp	07. 08.2004	Abruzzi Spur
238	Yoshiki SEINO		Jp	07. 08.2004	Abruzzi Spur
239	Yasyguji MOCHIZUKI	x	Jp	07. 08.2004	Abruzzi Spur
240	Takashi KAWASHIMA		Jp	07. 08.2004	Abruzzi Spur
241	PHURBA CHHIRI		Np	07. 08.2004	Abruzzi Spur
242	TIKA RAM GURUNG		Np	07. 08.2004	Abruzzi Spur
243	Masahide MATSUMOTO		Jp	16. 08. 2004	SSE Ridge – Abruzzi Spur
244	Aska INUI		Jp	16. 08. 2004	SSE Ridge – Abruzzi Spur
245	Tomoya TAKESAKO		Jp	16. 08. 2004	SSE Ridge – Abruzzi Spur
246	Jordi COROMINAS	x	E	17. 08. 2004	SSW Pillar ('Magic Line')
247	Romano BENET	x	It	26. 07. 2006	Abruzzi Spur
248	Nives MEROI	f x	It	26. 07. 2006	Abruzzi Spur
249	Tatsuya AOKI		Jp	01. 08. 2006	SSE Ridge – Abruzzi Spur
250	Yuka KOMATSU	f	Jp	01. 08. 2006	SSE Ridge – Abruzzi Spur
251	Nikolai KADOSHNIKOV		Rus	20. 07. 2007	Abruzzi Spur
252	Victor AGANASJEV		Rus	20. 07. 2007	Abruzzi Spur
253	Aleksandr ELISEEV		Rus	20. 07. 2007	Abruzzi Spur
254	Ramano GUBANOV		Rus	20. 07. 2007	Abruzzi Spur
255	Christopher (Chris) WARNER	x	USA	20. 07. 2007	Abruzzi Spur
256	Bruce NORMAND	x	UK	20. 07. 2007	Abruzzi Spur
257	João GARCIA	x	Por	20. 07. 2007	Abruzzi Spur
258	Donald (Don) BOWIE	x	Can	20. 07. 2007	Abruzzi Spur
259	Libor UHER	x	Cz	20. 07. 2007	SSE Ridge – Abruzzi Spur
260	Chang-Ho KIM	x	SK	20. 07. 2007	Abruzzi Spur
261	Jin-Tae KIM		SK	20. 07. 2007	Abruzzi Spur
262	Eun-Sun OH	f	SK	20. 07. 2007	Abruzzi Spur
	THILEN		Np	20. 07. 2007	Abruzzi Spur
263	MINGMA THINKUK		Np	20. 07. 2007	Abruzzi Spur
264	Kazem FARIDYAN	x	Irn	20. 07. 2007	Abruzzi Spur
265	Daniele NARDI	x	It	20. 07. 2007	Abruzzi Spur

266	Mario VIELMO		x	It	20. 07. 2007	Abruzzi Spur
267	Stefano ZAVKA		x	It	20. 07. 2007	Abruzzi Spur
268	Andrei MARIEV		x	Rus	21. 08. 2007	West Face
269	Vadim POPOVICH		x	Rus	21. 08. 2007	West Face
270	Nikolai TOTMYANIN		x	Rus	22. 08. 2007	West Face
271	Aleksei BOLOTOV		x	Rus	22. 08. 2007	West Face
272	Gleb SOKOLOV		x	Rus	22. 08. 2007	West Face
273	Yevgeni VINOGRADSKI		x	Rus	22. 08. 2007	West Face
274	Victor VOLODIN		x	Rus	22. 08. 2007	West Face
275	Gennadi KIRIEVSKI		x	Rus	22. 08. 2007	West Face
276	Vitali GORELIK		x	Rus	22. 08. 2007	West Face
277	Pavel SHABALIN		x	Rus	22. 08. 2007	West Face
278	Ilyas TUKHVATULLIN		x	Uzb	22. 08. 2007	West Face
279	Denis URUBKO		x	Kaz	02. 10. 2007	North Ridge
280	Sergei SAMOILOV		x	Kaz	02. 10. 2007	North Ridge
281	Alberto (Zeras) ZERAIN		x	E	01. 08. 2008	Abruzzi Spur
282	Cecile SKOG	f		Nor	01. 08. 2008	Abruzzi Spur
283	Lars Flatø NESSA			Nor	01. 08. 2008	Abruzzi Spur
284	TSHERING DORJE II		x	Np	01. 08. 2008	Abruzzi Spur
285	PASANG BHOTE I			Np	01. 08. 2008	Abruzzi Spur
286	JUMIK BHOTE			Np	01. 08. 2008	Abruzzi Spur
287	Dong-Jin HWANG			SK	01. 08. 2008	Abruzzi Spur
288	Hyo-Gyung KIM			SK	01. 08. 2008	Abruzzi Spur
289	Jae-Soo KIM			SK	01. 08. 2008	Abruzzi Spur
290	Mi-Sun (Mi-Young) GO	f		SK	01. 08. 2008	Abruzzi Spur
291	Kyeong-Hyo PARK			SK	01. 08. 2008	Abruzzi Spur
292	Gerard McDONNELL		x	Ire	01. 08. 2008	SSE Ridge - Abruzzi Spur
293	Marco CONFORTOLA			It	01. 08. 2008	Abruzzi Spur
294	Hugues D'AUBAREDE			F	01. 08. 2008	SSE Ridge - Abruzzi Spur
295	Mehrban KARIM		x	Pak	01. 08. 2008	SSE Ridge - Abruzzi Spur
296	Cas VAN DER GEVEL		x	NL	01. 08. 2008	SSE Ridge - Abruzzi Spur
297	Wilco VAN ROOIJEN		x	NL	01. 08. 2008	SSE Ridge - Abruzzi Spur
298	PEMBA GYALZEN I		x	Np	01. 08. 2008	SSE Ridge - Abruzzi Spur
299	Gerlinde KALTENBRUNNER	f	x	A	23. 08. 2011	North Ridge
300	Vassili PIVTSOV		x	Kaz	23. 08. 2011	North Ridge
301	Maksut ZHUMAYEV		x	Kaz	23. 08. 2011	North Ridge
302	Daniusz (Darek) ZAŁUSKI		x	Pol	23. 08. 2011	North Ridge

Appendix 2

Fatalities on K2

Key: x = death on descent from summit
     f = female climber

#	Name		Nat	Date	Location
1	Dudley WOLFE		USA	30. 07. 1939	Abruzzi Camp VII
2	PASANG KIKULI		Np	31. 07. 1939	Abruzzi between Camp VI and VII
3	PASANG KITAR		Np	31. 07. 1939	Abruzzi between Camp VI and VII
4	PINTSO		Np	31. 07. 1939	Abruzzi between Camp VI and VII
5	Arthur GILKEY		USA	10. 08. 1953	Abruzzi between Camp VI and VII
6	Mario PUCHOZ		It	21. 06. 1954	Abruzzi near Camp VII
7	Nicholas J. (Nick) ESTCOURT		UK	12. 06. 1978	W Ridge near Camp II
8	Ali KAZIM		Pak	09. 06. 1979	Savoia Glacier
9	Laskhar KHAN		Pak	19. 08. 1979	SSE Ridge between Camp III and IV
10	Halina KRÜGER-SYROKOMSKA	f	Pol	30. 07. 1982	Abruzzi Camp II
11	Yukihiro YANAGISAWA	x	Jpn	15. 08. 1982	N Ridge during Descent
12	Daniel LACROIX	x	F	07. 07. 1985	Abruzzi during Descent
13	Alan PENNINGTON		USA	21. 06. 1986	SSW Ridge
14	John SMOLICH		USA	21. 06. 1986	SSW Ridge
15	Liliane BARRARD	f x	F	24. 06. 1986	Abruzzi during Descent
16	Maurice BARRARD	x	F	24. 06. 1986	Abruzzi during Descent
17	Tadeusz PIOTROWSKI	x	Pol	10. 07. 1986	S Face during Descent
18	Renato CASAROTTO		It	16. 07. 1986	SSW Ridge
19	Wojciech WRÓŻ	x	Pol	03. 08. 1986	SSW Ridge during Descent
20	Mohammad ALI		Pak	04. 08. 1986	Abruzzi near Camp I
21	Julie TULLIS	f x	UK	07. 08. 1986	Abruzzi Camp IV
22	Alan ROUSE	x	UK	10. 08. 1986	Abruzzi Camp IV
23	Alfred IMITZER	x	A	10. 08. 1986	Abruzzi below Camp IV
24	Hannes WIESER		A	10. 08. 1986	Abruzzi below Camp IV
25	Dobrosława MIODOWICZ-WOLF	f	Pol	10. 08. 1986	Abruzzi between Camp II and III
26	Akura SUZUKI		Jp	24. 08. 1987	Abruzzi
27	Hans BÄRNTHALER		A	28. 07. 1989	E Face
28	Adrián BENÍTEZ		Mex	14. 08. 1992	Abruzzi
29	Boštjan KEKEC		Slo	15. 06. 1993	Abruzzi below Camp IV

30	Dan CULVER		x	Can	07. 07. 1933	Abruzzi during Descent
31	Daniel BIDNER		x	S	30. 07. 1993	Abruzzi above Camp IV
32	Reinmar JOSWIG		x	Ger	30. 07. 1993	Abruzzi during Descent
33	Peter MEZGER		x	Ger	30. 07. 1993	Abruzzi during Descent
34	Dmitri IBRAJIM-ZADE			Ukr	10. 07. 1994	Abruzzi
35	Aleksei KHARALDIN			Ukr	10. 07. 1994	Abruzzi
36	Aleksandr PARKHOMENKO			Ukr	10. 07. 1994	Abruzzi
37	Steve UNTCH			USA	24. 07. 1994	SSE Ridge above Camp I
38	Juan Ignacio (Atxo) APELLANIZ		x	E	11. 08. 1994	N Ridge Camp II
39	Jordi ANGLÉS			E	06. 07. 1995	Abruzzi near Base Camp
40	Javier ESCARTÍN		x	E	13. 08. 1995	Abruzzi during Descent
41	Bruce GRANT		x	NZ	13. 08. 1995	Abruzzi during Descent
42	Alison HARGREAVES	f	x	UK	13. 08. 1995	Abruzzi during Descent
43	Javier OLIVAR		x	E	13. 08. 1995	SSE Ridge during Descent
44	Lorenzo ORTIZ		x	E	13. 08. 1995	SSE Ridge during Descent
45	Rob SLATER		x	USA	13. 08. 1995	Abruzzi during Descent
46	Jeff LAKES			Can	15. 08. 1995	Abruzzi Camp II
47	Lorenzo MAZZOLENI		x	It	29. 07. 1996	Abruzzi
48	Igor BENKIN		x	Rus	14. 08. 1986	N Ridge
49	Mihai CIOROIANU			Rom	10. 07.1999	Abruzzi below Camp I
50	Young-Do PARK			SK	22. 07. 2001	SSE Ridge near Camp IV
51	Sher AJMAN			Pak	13. 07. 2002	SSE Ridge below Camp I
52	Muhammad IQBAL			Pak	22. 07. 2002	Abruzzi near Camp III
53	Klaus-Dieter GROHS			Ger	21. 07. 2003	Abruzzi
54	Hwa-Hyeung LEE			SK	08. 06.2004	N Ridge
55	Kae-Young LEE			SK	08. 06.2004	N Ridge
56	Kyong-Kyu PAE			SK	08. 06.2004	N Ridge
57	Aleksandr GUBAEV		x	Kyr	29. 07. 2004	Abruzzi during Descent
58	Sergei SOKOLOV			Rus	02. 08. 2004	Abruzzi between C4 and C3
59	Davoud KHADEM			Irn	02. 08. 2004	Abruzzi between C4 and C3
60	Manel DE LA MATTA			E	19. 08. 2004	SSW Ridge in Camp I
61	Yuri UTESHEV			Rus	13. 08. 2006	Abruzzi on Summit Ridge
62	Piotr KUZNETSOV			Rus	13. 08. 2006	Abruzzi on Summit Ridge
63	Aleksandr FOIGT			Rus	13. 08. 2006	Abruzzi on Summit Ridge
64	Arkadi KUVAKIN			Rus	13. 08. 2006	Abruzzi on Summit Ridge
65	NIMA NURBU			Np	20. 07. 2007	Abruzzi
66	Stefano ZAVKA		x	It	20. 07. 2007	Abruzzi
67	Dren MANDIĆ			Ser	01. 08. 2008	Abruzzi below Bottleneck
68	Jehain BAIG			Pak	01. 08. 2008	Abruzzi below Bottleneck
69	Rolf BAE			Nor	01. 08. 2008	Abruzzi at Bottleneck
70	JUMIK BHOTE		x	Np	01. 08. 2008	Abruzzi at Bottleneck
71	PASANG BHOTE			Np	01. 08. 2008	Abruzzi at Bottleneck
72	Gerard McDONNELL		x	Ire	02. 08. 2008	Abruzzi at Bottleneck
73	Hugues D'AUBAREDE		x	F	02. 08. 2008	Abruzzi at Bottleneck
74	Mehrban KARIM		x	Pak	02. 08. 2008	Abruzzi above Bottleneck
75	Hyo-Gyung KIM		x	SK	02. 08. 2008	Abruzzi at Bottleneck
76	Kyeong-Hyo PARK		x	SK	02. 08. 2008	Abruzzi at Bottleneck
77	Dong-Jin HWANG		x	SK	02. 08. 2008	Abruzzi at Bottleneck
78	Michele FIAT			It	23. 06. 2009	SSE Ridge Skiing
79	Petar Georgiev UNZHIEV			Bul	17. 07. 2010	Abruzzi
80	Fredrik ERICSSON			S	06. 08. 2010	Abruzzi at Bottleneck

Index

Abram, Enrico 79, 82, 83, 84, 86,
87, 94, 197
Abrego, Mari 130, 134
Abruzzi, Duke of the 8, 14, 35–40,
41, 42, 46, 48, 51, 52, 102, 184,
188, 189, 190
acclimatisation 62–3, 128, 151, 153,
188
Afanassieff, Jean 121, 129
airships 41–2, 189
Akbar the Great 13
Ali, Mohammed 141
Alpine Club 185, 187
alteplase 172, 210
altitude and oxygen 62–3, 92
Aman, Ashraf 107, 123
American Alpine Club (AAC) 49,
56, 57, 62, 67
American expeditions 49–50, 90,
97
1938 K2 50–6
1939 K2 56–68
1953 K2 68–75, 77, 80
1960 Abruzzi Ridge 98
1975 North-West Ridge 98–103,
126, 132
1978 North-East Ridge 33,
109–15, 117, 124
1990 North Side 151–3
2008 Abruzzi Spur 162
Amundsen, Roald 42, 185, 189
Anderson, Craig 109, 111
Andrade, Antonio de 13
Ang Tharkay 45
Angelino, Ugo 79
Annapurna 76, 92, 97, 98, 178, 179,
190, 200, 201, 203, 204, 208
Aoki, Tatsuya 160
Apellániz, Atxo 156
Asiatic Society of Bengal 6
Ata Ullah, Colonel 68, 70, 77, 80,
81, 90

d'Aubarède, Hugues 162, 163, 164,
166, 170, 171
Auden, John 44, 45
Australian expeditions 151
Austrian expeditions
1957 Broad Peak 194
1982 Abruzzi Spur 127
1986 Abruzzi Spur 141–9
1987 East Face 150
avalanches 21, 37, 53, 108–9
1981 Japanese expedition 122
1982 British expedition 120
2006 Russian expedition 160
2008 expeditions 166, 167, 169,
170, 171

Bachler, George 127
Bae, Rolf 163, 165, 166
Baig, Jahain 163, 164, 165
Balestreri, Umberto 43
Baltis 9, 18, 36, 43, 51, 100
Baltoro Glacier 3, 4, 7, 9
exploration 16–17, 20, 21, 22, 23,
27–8
Balyberdin, Vladimir 154
Bareux, Ernest 35
Barrard, Liliane Michel 131, 133,
134, 135, 136, 203
Barrard, Maurice 117, 131, 133, 134,
135, 136, 203
Barry, John 131, 205
Basque expeditions 131, 134, 135,
162, 176
1994 South-South-East Spur 156
Bates, Robert 47, 50–1, 52, 53, 54,
55, 56, 68, 71, 72, 73, 74, 191,
194, 195, 199
Bauer, Willi 142, 143–9, 205, 206,
207, 208
Baume, Louis 32, 187, 199
Baxter-Jones, Roger 129–30
Bech, Cherie 109, 110, 111, 115

Bech, Terry 109, 110–11, 112–13,
115
Béghin, Pierre 10, 117, 118, 153–4,
182, 208
Bell, George 68, 70, 72, 73, 74
Bell, Mark 18
Benítez, Adrián 154
Bidner, Daniel 155
Boardman, Peter 107–8, 109, 118,
119, 120
bodies, retrieval 164
Boivin, Jean-Marc 117–18
Bolotov, Alexei 160
Bonatti, Walter 79–80, 82–3, 84,
90–1, 93–4, 95, 96, 97, 196, 197,
198, 199
account of the climb 86–8, 88–9
Bong-Wan, Chang 141
Bonington, Chris 107, 108, 109, 118,
200, 201
Bowley, G. *No Way Down* 165, 211
Bozik, Peter 140–1, 143, 144
Bradey, Lydia 209
Braithwaite, Paul 'Tut' 107
Bremer-Kamp, Cherie 115
British expeditions,
1861 Karakoram 14–17
1887 and 1889 Karakoram 17–22
1892 Karakoram 23–9
1902 K2 29–35
1922 Everest 40, 43, 49, 50
1937 Karakoram 43–6
1953 Everest 92, 93
1970 Annapurna 98
1975 Everest 107–8
1978 West Ridge 107–9
1979 Kangchenjunga 118
1980 West Ridge and Abruzzi
Spur 118–21
1987 East Face 150
Broad Peak 2, 4, 8, 23, 28, 41, 52,
53, 85, 127–8, 129, 135, 158, 179,

186, 194, 202, 203, 204, 205–6, 207, 211
Brocherel, Alexis 30, 35
Brocherel, Emil 35, 40
Brocherel, Henri 30, 35, 39, 40
Brown, Joe 176
Brown, T. Graham 49
Bruce, Charles Granville 24, 25, 26, 28, 186
Bruce, General 43
Buhl, Hermann 189, 194, 203, 204, 205, 206, 207
Bullock-Workman, Fanny 29, 186
Burchardt, Hermann 22–3
Burdsall, Dick 50, 52, 53, 68, 191

Cadich, Oscar 159
Calcagno, Gianni 135
Cambiaso, Federico Negrotto 35
Canadian expedition (1993) 155–6
Carter, Adams 49, 199
Casarotto, Goretta 131, 139
Casarotto, Renato 115–16, 116–17, 131, 132, 134, 139–40
Casimiro, Josema 134
Cassin, Riccardo 77–9, 196
Cenacchi, Giovanni 88, 91, 197, 198
Chamoux, Benoît 131, 135–6, 203–4, 204
Chandler, Chris 109, 110–11, 112, 115
Chang Byong-Ho 141
Changabang 108
Chhiring Dorje 210, 211
Child, Greg 12, 151, 152–3, 182
China 13, 15, 17, 103, 124, 126, 132, 152
  border disputes 98
  climbing permits 98, 127, 157
  Tibet 97
Chinese expeditions 124
  1964 Shisha Pangma 97
Chinese Mountaineering Association 124
Cho Oyu 47, 58, 176, 179, 190, 195, 203, 204, 208, 212
Chogolisa 28, 39–40, 189, 205, 206
Chomolungma 6, 7
Chrobak, Eugeniusz 104, 105–6, 200
Cichy, Leszek 104, 127, 200, 202
Closs, Lyle 151
Comesky, Matt 157
commercial climbing 99, 172
Compagnoni, Achille 79, 83, 87, 88–9, 90, 91–3, 94, 95, 96, 159, 165, 196, 197, 198

friendship with Desio 80, 81, 82
summit climb 84–6
Compagnoni, Michele 159
Confortola, Marco 167, 168–9, 170–1, 172, 174, 210
continental drift 1–2, 181
Conway, William Martin 23–9, 31, 32, 36, 37, 185, 186
Cook, Frederick 49
Corominas, Jordi 159
Cortanze, Oswaldo Roero, Marquis di 14, 183
Craig, Bob 68, 69, 70, 71, 72, 73
Cranmer, Chappell 57, 58–9, 192, 193
Cromwell, Tony 57, 59, 61, 65, 67, 193
Crowley, Aleister 28, 29–35, 37, 38, 39, 47–8, 185, 186–7, 188
Culver, Dan 155–6
Curran, Jim 29, 32, 139, 142, 145, 148–9, 180, 186, 187, 204, 206
Curzon, Lord 32
Czechs 128, 135, 140, 141
Czerwińska, Anna 141, 205

Da Polenza, Agostino 128, 131, 202
Dacher, Michl 115, 116, 117
Dainelli, Giotto 41, 42, 44, 189
de la Matta, Manuel 159
De Marchi, Giuliano 128, 129
De Stefani, Fausto 128, 202, 203
Death Zone 63, 134, 147
dehydration 71, 92, 114, 147
Desideri, Ippolito 13–14
Desio, Ardito 3, 42–3, 45, 181, 190, 195–6, 197, 198, 199
  1954 expedition 76–83,
  aftermath of 1954 expedition 90, 91, 94, 95–6
  summit climb 84–6
dexamethasone 210
Dhaulagiri 97, 109–10, 179, 200, 203, 204, 205, 208, 211
Diemberger, Kurt 128, 129, 131, 139, 140–9, 194, 203, 205–7, 214
Dorotei, Soro 135
drugs 210–11
Duff, Jim 108, 201
Dujmovits, Rolf 175
Dunagiri 118, 119
Dunham, Fred 98, 101–2
Durrance, Jack 57, 58–9, 60–1, 65–6, 67, 192, 193
Dutch expeditions 43–4, 162, 172

2008 South-South-East Spur 162, 163, 164
Dyrhenfurth, Günther and Norman 48, 204

Eckenstein, Oscar 23–5, 26–7, 29–35, 37, 38, 39, 185, 186, 187
Edmonds, Skip 109, 111
Eiger 196, 201, 208
Eisenhower, Dwight D. 68
Elizabeth II 68
Emmons, Arthur 49, 191
equipment 50, 68, 83
  supplementary oxygen 84–5, 86–7, 91–5, 173–4, 195, 212
Erdeljan, Milivoj 164
Ericsson, Fredrik 175
Ershler, Phil 151, 152
Escartín, Javier 157
Estcourt, Nick 107, 108, 109, 118, 201
Everest 6, 7, 8, 9, 11–12, 18, 32, 43, 44, 47, 48, 49, 50, 69, 92, 107–8
  North Face 151
  supplementary oxygen-free climbs 111, 115, 152, 202, 208, 211
Everest, George 6, 181

Fait, Michele 175
Fankhauser, Horst 201
Filippi, Filippo De 35–6, 38, 39, 41, 184, 188
fixed ropes 172–3, 176–7
Floreanini, Cirillo 79
Free K2 expedition (1990) 151
French expeditions,
  1950 Annapurna 97
  1979 Magic Line 117–18
  1981 South Face 121
  1991 North Side 153–4
  1991 North-West Ridge 153–4
  2008 Abruzzi Spur 162
Freudig, Toni 137
Freyre, Emmanuel 13–14
frostbite 74, 83, 89, 115, 118, 146, 126, 149, 157, 172
Furster, Beda 137, 138, 204

Gallotti, Pino 79, 82–3, 86, 87, 88, 94, 197
Garcés, José 'Pepe' 157
Gardiner, Alexander 183
Gasherbrum I (Hidden Peak) 2, 3, 4, 7, 48, 74, 103, 115, 179, 186, 192, 194, 195, 204, 211

Gasherbrum II 2, 4, 127, 156, 179, 203, 204, 211
Gasherbrum III 183, 200
Gasherbrum IV 4, 7, 9, 17, 29, 36, 95, 115, 182, 183, 196, 200
Geological Survey of India 44
geology 2–4, 12, 181
German expeditions,
  1929, 1934 and 1937 K2 48
  1938 and 1939 Nanga Parbat 48
  1960 Abruzzi ridge 98
  1970 Nanga Parbat 98
Ghirardini, Ivan 117, 118, 119
Giglio, Nino 94, 198
Gilkey, Art 10, 68, 69, 70–2, 73, 74, 75, 80, 133, 156, 194–5
glaciers 3–4, 16–17, 42–3
  artificial glaciers 51, 191
  glacier collapse 165–6, 169
Glazek, Kazimierz 106
gliding 117–18
Go Mi-Young 166, 168, 169
Godwin-Austen, Henry Haversham 7, 14–17, 183
Goetz, Hans Martin 121
Gogna, Alessandro 115, 202
Gongga, China 49
Grant, Bruce 167
Grombtchevsky, Bronislav 21–2
Grüber, Johannes 13, 182
GTS (Great Trigonometric Survey) 6, 9, 14, 181, 183
Gurkhas 22, 24, 25, 28, 186

Habeler, Peter 103, 111, 115, 130
Haberl, Jim 155–6, 208
HACE (high-altitude cerebral oedema) *see* oedema
Hackett, William D. 98, 199
HAPE (high-altitude pulmonary oedema) *see* oedema
Hargreaves, Alison 157–8, 208–9
Harrer, Heinrich 48
headaches 28, 40, 50, 60, 152
helicopters 76, 103, 115, 137, 146, 157, 172
Herrligkoffer, Karl-Maria 131, 135, 136, 137, 204
Herzog, Maurice 92
Hess, Harry 1, 180
Hiebeler, Toni 201
high-altitude physiology 23, 34, 35, 62–3, 92, 191, 193, 212
Hillary, Edmund 69, 90, 157, 194
Hillary, Peter 157

Hinkes, Alan 157
Hiroshima, Mitsuo 107
Hodgson, Brian 6
Holnicki, Janek 104
House, Bill 50–6, 57, 68, 192
Houston, Charles 47, 49, 91–2, 97, 117, 191, 193–4, 195, 199
  1938 expedition 50–6, 57
  1953 expedition 68–75
Houston, Oscar 191
Hunt, John 79, 190, 196
Hunzas 68, 74, 81, 110
Hussain, Mohammad 163, 164
Hwang Dong-Jin 167
hypothermia 169
hypoxia 114, 152

Imaida, Kenjiro 124
Imamura, Hirotaka 151, 152
Imitzer, Alfred 131, 142, 144, 145, 146, 147, 148, 207
India 2
  border disputes 3, 68, 98
international expeditions 130
  1930, 1932 and 1934 K2 48
  1983 West Ridge 129–30
  1992 Abruzzi Spur 154
Iñurrategi, Alberto 156
Iñurrategi, Felix 156
Irvine, Sandy 44
Iszagin-Zade, Dmitri 156
Italian Alpine Club (CAI) 76, 77, 78, 95
Italian expeditions 41–2
  1890 Karakoram 22–3
  1909 K2 35–40
  1929 Karakoram 40–3
  1954 K2 76–83
    Bonatti's account 86–8
    Lacedelli's account 88–9
    summit climb 84–6
    supplementary oxygen 84–5, 86–7, 91–5
  1983 North Ridge 128–9
  2004 K2 159
  2008 Abruzzi Spur 162, 163, 164, 167
Italian Olympic Company 77
Iwata, Osamu 122

Jacot-Guillarmod, Jules 31, 33, 34–5, 48, 104, 187
Jäger, Franz 201
Japanese Alpine Club 124
Japanese expeditions 121

1977 Abruzzi Spur 107
1981 West Ridge 121–4, 200–1
1982 North Side 124–6, 151
1990 North Side 151
1996 Broad Peak 158
1997 West Ridge 158, 160
2006 K2 160
Jordan, Jennifer 57, 58, 60, 158, 192, 193
Joswig, Reinmar 155
Jumik Bhote 165, 167, 168, 169, 170, 171, 174, 209
Jurgalski, Eberhard 176, 178

K2 2, 47–50, 97–8, 131–2, 150, 176–7
  1902 Eckenstein and Crowley expedition 29–35
  1909 Abruzzi expedition 35–40
  1938 Houston expedition 50–6
  1939 Wiessner expedition 56–68, 191–2
  1953 Houston expedition 68–75
  1975 North-West Ridge 98–103
  1976 North-East Ridge 103–6
  1977 Abruzzi Spur 107
  1978 North-East Ridge 109–15
  1978 West Ridge 107–9
  1979 Magic Line 115–18
  1980 West Ridge and Abruzzi Spur 118–21
  1981 West Ridge 121–4
  1982 Abruzzi Spur 127
  1982 North Side 124–7
  1982 South-East Face 127–8
  1983 North Ridge 128–9
  1983 West Ridge 129–30
  1986 Abruzzi Spur 132–6
  1986 Magic Line 139–40, 140–1
  1986 South Face 136–9
  1986 summit attempts 141–9
  1990 Free K2 expedition 151
  1990 and 1991 North Side 151–4
  1992–1997 international expeditions 154–8
  1993 Mazur and Pratt expedition 154–5
  1994 South-South-East Spur 156
  1998–2007 international expeditions 158–61
  2008 international expeditions 162–74
  2010 summit attempts 175–6
  British survey 4–6
  challenge 12

Dramatis Locus 11–12
gliding 117–18
height 8
naming the mountain 6–9
statistics 178–9
supplementary oxygen-free climbs 84, 113, 114, 126, 151, 152, 161, 173, 178, 202, 204, 210, 212
weather 9–10
Kaczkan, Marcin 159
Kaltenbrunner, Gerlinde 175–6
Kamet 44, 190, 191
Kamuro, Hironobu 126
Kangchenjunga 31, 47–8, 49, 74, 115, 118, 151, 179, 188, 195, 200, 203, 204, 208, 211
Karakoram 2–4, 8, 13–14
1861 Godwin-Austen expedition 14–17
1887 and 1889 Younghusband expeditions 17–22
1892 Conway expedition 23–9
1929 Spoleto expedition 40–3
1937 Shipton expedition 43–6
Kashmir 2, 3, 5, 7, 14, 24, 27, 31, 98, 184
Kauffman, A.J. 57, 58, 191, 192
Kawamura, Haruichi 126
Kekec, Bostjan 155
Kennedy, Robert 199
Kennedy, Ted 199
Keustler, Peter 151
Khan, Lasker 117
Khan, Saleem 110
Khazaldin, Aleksei 156
Kim Byung-Joon 131, 206
Kim Chang-Son 141
Kim Hyo-Gyung 167, 170
Kim Jae-Su 163, 166, 168, 169
Kintopf, Piotr 106
Kirievski, Gennadi 160
Klinke, Chris 164, 165
Knowles, Guy 31, 34, 187
Koblmüller, Eduard 150
Komatsu, Yuka 160
Konishi, Masatsugu 125, 126, 202
Korean expeditions,
1986 Abruzzi Spur 131, 139, 140, 141, 142, 143–4, 206, 207
2008 Abruzzi Spur 162, 163, 165, 166–74, 209, 210, 211
Krüger-Syrokomska, Halima 127
Kukuczka, Jerzy 127, 128, 131, 136–9, 200, 202, 204–5

Kurczab, Janusz 103, 104, 126, 200, 202
Kurtyka, Wojwiech 115, 127, 128, 137, 150, 154, 200, 202

Lacedelli, Lino 79–80, 81, 82, 83, 87, 90, 91–2, 93–4, 95, 96, 128, 159, 165, 196–7, 198–9
account of the climb 88–9
summit climb 84–6
Lacedelli, Mario 128, 159
Lacroix, Daniel 130
Lakes, Jeff 157
Lambton, William 5, 181
Laukajtys 105
Lerco, Roberto 22–3, 29, 184–5
Leroy, Thierry 118
Lhotse 103, 179, 195, 196, 202, 203, 204, 207, 209, 211
Lloyd-Dickin, Lieutenant-Colonel 24
Lloyd, Peter 49
Logan, Kim 157
Longstaff, Tom 30, 35, 40–1, 43, 186, 189
Loomis, Farnie 49
Loretan, Erhard 130, 150, 154, 203, 208

Macartney-Snape, Tim 151
McCormick, Arthur David 24, 25, 26, 28, 29, 185
McDonald, Bernadette 56, 74, 191, 193
McDonnell, Ger 162, 167, 170, 171, 174, 209, 210, 211
Mahdi 83, 86–8, 89, 90–1, 94, 96, 197, 198
Majer, Janusz 131, 140, 141, 205
Makalu 179, 195, 203, 204, 208, 211
Mallory, George Leigh 44
Manaslu 115, 179, 195, 201, 203, 208
Mandric, Dren 163–4, 165
Manni, Roberto 164
Maraini, Fosco 7–9, 95, 182
Mariev, Andrei 160
Marques, Manuel 13
Marshall, Robert, *K2: Lies and Treachery* 90–1, 94, 96, 196, 197, 198, 199
Martini, Sergio 128, 202, 203
Marts, Steve 98, 100
Maschke, Fritz 201
Masherbrum (K1) 4, 6, 9, 15, 17, 29, 36

Mason, Kenneth, *Abode of Snow* 189
Matsuura, Teruo 121, 122, 123, 124, 160, 202
Matterhorn 185, 196
Mauduit, Chantal 154
Mazur, Dan 154–5, 208
medications 210–11
Megumi, Hideki 122
Meherban, Karim 163, 167, 170, 171
Mellet, Bernard 117, 118, 202
Merkl, Willy 204
Messner, Günther 201
Messner, Michael 149
Messner, Reinhold 103, 111, 128, 139, 172, 201–2, 203, 208, 211
1979 Magic Line 115–17
Metzger, Peter 155
Meyer, Eric 164, 172, 210, 211
Minya Konka, China 49
Miodowicz-Wolf, Dobroslawa *see* Mrówka
Molenaar, Dee 68, 69, 71, 72, 73, 195
Monaci, Daniel 118
monsoon 9, 15–16, 182
Montgomerie, Thomas 5–6, 8, 9, 14, 15, 176, 181
Monticone, Alberto 95
Moretti, Martino 135
Mortimer, Greg 151
Mosca, Jean-Claude 118
Mount Hotaka, Japan 158
Mount McKinley (Denali), USA 49, 196
Mount St Elias, Canada–USA 188
mountain sickness 129, 193, 210
Mrówka 130, 140, 141, 142, 143, 144–5, 146, 147, 148, 149, 208
Mummery, Alfred 48, 186
Museo Nazionale della Montagna 'Duca degli Abruzzi', Turin 22, 184, 197
Mussolini, Benito 41, 42, 76, 189
Mutschlechner, Friedl 115, 116

Nanda Devi 44, 49, 110, 190, 191, 199
Nanga Parbat 2, 4, 25, 47, 48, 59, 92, 115, 130, 178, 179, 186, 192, 202, 203, 204, 207, 211
Diamir Face 201
Rupal Face 98, 201
Nawang Samden 110
Nazuka, Hideji 151, 152
Nessa, Lars 163, 165, 166

Netia 158
New Zealand expedition (1995) 157
Nobile, Umberto 41–2, 189
Norit 162, 163, 164, 170
Norton, Edward 47
Norwegian expeditions,
    2008 Abruzzi Spur 162, 163–4,
    164–5, 166
Noshaq 137

Odell, Noel 44, 49
oedema 115, 127
    cerebral oedema 146, 156, 159,
    193, 207, 210
    pulmonary oedema 34, 48, 58–9,
    137, 193
Oiarzabal, Juan 156
Okopinska, Anna 127
Olivar, Javier 157
Onodera, Masahide 107
Onyszkiewicz, Janusz 103, 104, 105,
    200
Ortas, Lorenzo 157
Ortiz, Lorenzo 157
Otani, Eiho 122, 123, 124
Owens, Lance 132
oxygen,
    and altitude 62–3, 92
    supplementary 84–5, 86–7, 91–5,
    173–4, 195, 212
Ozaki, Takashi 125, 126

Pagani, Guido 90
Pakistan 2, 7, 9, 15, 90, 124, 152
    border disputes 3, 68, 98
    climbing permits 68, 77, 128–9,
    131, 132, 176, 199
    liaison officers 68, 77, 101, 110,
    116, 117, 119, 121, 123, 132,
    140, 148, 163, 207
Palmowska, Krystyna 141
Parbir Thapa 24, 28
Park Keyong-Hyo 167
Parkin, Andy 129
Parmentier, Michel 131, 133, 134,
    135, 136, 142
Pasang Bhote ('Big' Pasang) 165,
    210
Pasang Bhote (Lama) ('Little'
    Pasang) 165, 166–7, 168, 169,
    170, 171, 173, 174, 210
Pasang Dawa Lama 57–8, 61, 62, 63,
    64, 65, 67
Pasang Kikuli 50, 55, 57, 66, 130,
    173

Pasang Kitar 50, 66, 130, 156, 173
Patterson, Leif 98, 100
Pazkhomenko, Alexsandr 156
Peck, Annie Smith 186
Pemba Gyalje 163, 166, 167, 168–9,
    170, 171, 172
Pennington, Alan 132–3, 136
Petigax, Joe 35, 40
Petigax, Laurent 35
Petzoldt, Paul 50, 52, 53, 54, 55, 56,
    68
Pfannl, Heinrich 31, 32, 33, 34, 35,
    187
Piasecki, Przemlaw 140–1, 143, 144,
    145
Pintso 50, 66, 130, 173
Piotrowski, Tadeusz 136–9
Piz Badile 196
Planic, Iso 164
pneumonia 48, 58, 80, 102, 115
Polish expeditions,
    1976 North-East Ridge 103–6
    1982 Abruzzi Spur 127
    1982 North Side 126–7
    1982 South-East Face 127–8
    1989 Abruzzi Spur 150
    2002 K2 158–9
    Broad Peak 127–8, 202, 204
Polo, Marco 13, 182
Popovich, Vadim 160
Pratt, Jonathan 154–5
Profit, Christophe 10, 153–4
Puchoz, Mario 79, 89, 159
pulmonary embolism 71
Putnam, W.L. 57, 58, 191, 192

Qogir (K2) 7, 124
Quamajan 109

Rakaposhi 121
Rakoncaj, Josef 128, 131, 135, 204
Reichardt, Lou 109–10, 111–12,
    113–14, 173
Renshaw, Dick 118, 119, 120
retinal haemorrhages 117
Rey, Ubaldo 79, 80, 82, 83, 86, 197
Rhoades, Jeff 158
Rice, Nick 164
Ridgeway, Rick 109, 110, 111, 112,
    113, 114–15, 124, 199, 201
Riley, Tony 108, 109
Roberts, Dianne 98–9, 100–1, 109, 112
Robinson, Bestor 57
Rodway, George, *Everest and
    Conquest in the Himalaya* 193, 212

Roskelley, John 109–10, 111, 112,
    113, 114, 124
Roudebush, J.D. 24
Rouse, Alan 129, 131–2, 140, 141,
    142, 143, 144–5, 146–7, 149
Rowell, Galen 98, 99, 100, 101, 102,
    200
Royal Geographical Society (RGS)
    14, 18, 21, 41, 44, 184, 195
Russian expeditions 48
    2006 K2 160
    2007 West Face 160–1, 209
Rutkiewicz, Wanda 127, 128, 130,
    131, 133–5, 136, 139, 200, 202,
    203, 205

Sabir, Nazir Ahmad 121, 122–4, 141,
    202
Saeed, Qadar 207
Sakano, Toshitaka 126
Sakashita, Naoé 125, 126
Sale, Richard, *Broad Peak* 194, 206,
    207
    *Everest and Conquest in the
    Himalaya* 193, 212
    Mapping the Himalaya 181, 182
Samoilov, Serguey 161
Santon, Francesco 128, 202
Savoia, Albert 35
Schaller, Robert 98, 100, 109
Schauer, Robert 115, 200
Schlagintweit, Adolphe 182
Schlagintweit, Hermann and Robert
    14, 182, 183
Schlick, Andi 201
Schmuck, Marcus 194, 205, 206, 207
Schoening, Pete 68, 69, 70, 71, 72–3,
    74, 98, 192, 194
Scott, Doug 107, 108, 109, 118, 119,
    129, 150, 201, 203, 206
Sebastían, San 156–7
Segarra, Araceli 158
Seigneur, Yannick 117, 118, 121
Sella, Vittorio 35, 57, 188
séracs 2, 37, 104, 126, 128, 136, 137,
    155, 165–6, 169, 170, 171, 174
Serbian expeditions,
    2008 Abruzzi Spur 162, 163, 164
Shabalin, Pavel 160, 209
Sheldon, George 57, 59
Sherpas 12, 45, 50, 66–7, 68
    American expeditions 50, 53,
    57–8, 60, 61, 65, 66–7, 69
    Japanese expeditions 106, 151,
    158

Korean expeditions 163, 165, 166, 167, 168, 173
Shigehiro, Tsuneo 107
Shigeno, Tatsuji 126
Shinkai, Isaoh 125, 201
Shipton, Eric 43–6, 124, 190
Shisha Pangma 47, 97, 124, 176, 179, 203, 204, 211
Simpson, Joe 11
skiers 175
Skog, Cecilie 163–4, 165, 166
Slater, Rob 157
Slovenians 155, 206
Smolich, John 132, 133, 136
Smythe, Frank 44, 190, 191
snow-blindness 73, 167
Sokolov, Gleb 160
Soldà, Gino 79
Somervell, Howard 47
Soncini, Alberto 128, 129
Spanish expeditions 129
    1995 K2 157
    2004 K2 159
Spender, Michael 44
Spoleto, Duke of 40–3, 76, 190, 195
Staleman, Jelle 164
Stangeland, Oystein 164–5
Stangl, Christian 175–6
Stanley, Fred 98, 99, 102
Sticht plates 148, 149, 207–8
Sträng, Frederick 164
Streatfeild, Norman 50, 52, 53
Streather, Tony 67, 70, 71, 72, 73, 74
Sumner, Bill 109
supplementary oxygen *see* oxygen
Sustad, Steve 129
Suzuki, Akira 150
Swenson, Steve 151, 152–3
Swiss expeditions 47, 97

Tahir, Mohammed 116
Takami, Kazushige 126
Takatsuka, Takeyoshi 107
Tanabe, Osamu 158, 209
Tasker, Joe 107, 108, 109, 119, 120, 121–2, 201
Tenzing Norgay 69, 90, 194

Terray, Lionel 211
Thuiller, Henry 6
Tibet 2, 3, 4, 6, 9, 13, 31, 32, 47, 97, 181, 182, 183–4
Tilman, Bill 44, 45, 49, 50, 190, 191
Tokushima, Kazuo 158
Totmjanin, Nikolai 160
Trench, George 57, 67, 193
Trisul 30, 35, 186
Troillet, Jean 150
Tshering Bhote 168, 169, 170, 171, 173, 174
Tshering Dorje 163, 166–7, 168, 173, 174, 210
Tullis, Julie 128–9, 131, 139, 140, 141, 142–3, 144, 145–6, 146–7, 203

Ueki, Tomaji 151
Ukrainian expedition (1994) 156
Unsoeld, Willi 110, 194
Unzhief, Petar 175
Urubko, Dennis 159, 161

Van de Gevel, Cas 166, 168, 170, 171, 172, 174, 211
Van Rooijen, Wilco 167–8, 169, 171–2, 174, 210, 211
Vidoni, Tullio 135
Vigne, G.T. 14, 28, 183
Viotto, Sergio 79
Visser-Hooft, Jeanette 43–4, 190
Visser, Phillips Christian 43–4, 190

Wali 20, 21
Waseda University, Tokyo 121
weather 9-10
    1939 Wiessner expedition 59–60
    1953 Houston expedition 70–4
    1980 British expedition 119–21
    1981 Japanese expedition 122, 124
    1986 Austrian expedition 146, 147
Wegener, Alfred 1, 180
Werner, Margaret 151
Wesseley, Victor 31, 32, 33, 34, 35, 104, 187
Whillans, Don 176

Whittaker, Jim 98, 99, 100, 102, 109, 110, 111, 112, 199–200
Whittaker, Lou 98, 99, 101, 102, 200
Wickwire, Jim 98, 99, 100, 101, 102, 109, 111, 112, 113, 114, 115, 199, 200, 201
Wielicki, Krzysztof 158, 159, 202
Wieser, Hannes 142, 144, 145, 147, 148
Wiessner, Fritz 48, 49–50, 85, 143, 165, 192, 193, 194
    1939 expedition 56–68, 191–2
Wilkinson, Dave 140
Wilkinson, F., *One Mountain Thousand Summits* 165, 211
Wintersteller, Fritz 194, 205, 206, 207
Wolfe, Dudley 57, 59, 60–1, 63–7, 68, 69, 130, 158, 192–3
Workman, William Hunter 29, 186
Wróz, Wojciech 104, 105–6, 127, 140–1, 202

Yabuta, Harashige 122, 124
Yamamoto, Hideo 107
Yamashita, Matsui 122, 123, 124
Yanagisawa, Yukihiro 125, 126, 130
Yonemoto, Takao 122, 124
Yoshino, Hioshi 125, 126, 208
Yoshizawa, Ichiro 107, 201
Younghusband, Francis Edward 17–22, 183–4
Yugoslavian expeditions 206–7

Zagorac, Predrag 164
Zanzi, Luigi 95
Zawada, Andrzej 137, 150, 208
Zemp, Rolf 137, 138, 204
Zerain, Alberto 162, 163, 165, 177
Zurbriggen, Matthias 24, 25, 28, 33, 186